Fighting Bob La Follette

The University of North Carolina Press

*Chapel Hill & London*

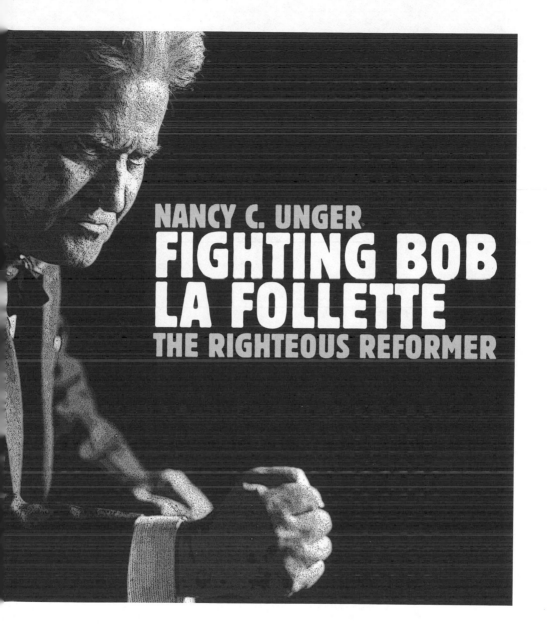

NANCY C. UNGER
# FIGHTING BOB LA FOLLETTE
## THE RIGHTEOUS REFORMER

© 2000 The University of North Carolina Press

All rights reserved

Manufactured in the United States of America

This book was set in New Baskerville

by G & S Typesetters

The paper in this book meets the guidelines for permanence
and durability of the Committee on Production Guidelines
for Book Longevity of the Council on Library Resources.

Library of Congress Cataloging-in-Publication Data

Unger, Nancy C.

Fighting Bob La Follette : the righteous reformer /
by Nancy C. Unger.

 p. cm.

Includes bibliographical references (p. ) and index.

ISBN 0-8078-2545-X (alk. paper)

1. La Follette, Robert M. (Robert Marion), 1855–1925.
2. United States — Politics and government — 1865–1933.
3. Progressivism (United States politics) 4. Wisconsin —
Politics and government — 1848–1950. 5. Legislators —
United States — Biography. 6. United States. Congress.
Senate — Biography. 7. Governors — Wisconsin — Biography.
I. Title.

E664.L16 U4 2000

977.5'04'092 — dc21  99-057829

04 03 02 01 00  5 4 3 2 1

*To Don, always*

# CONTENTS

# ILLUSTRATIONS

# ACKNOWLEDGMENTS

"It is hard to say the right thing about Bob La Follette," said Senator William Borah upon his colleague's death in 1925. "You know, he lived about 150 years." After researching La Follette's life, it seems longer than 150 years. Much longer. In 1993 I presented a paper on that research, entitled "Scaling the Mountain: The Challenges and Rewards of Researching a Twentieth-Century Family," at a conference at Stanford on "The Written Life." Clayborne Carson, director of the Martin Luther King Jr. Papers Project, and I tried but failed to sympathize with our copanelist Barbara Babcock as she lamented the dearth of materials on her subject, California's first woman lawyer Clara Foltz. Just the register of the La Follette Family Collection at the Library of Congress is 341 pages long, describing approximately 414,000 documents. I concluded that conference paper by resolving that my next biographical subject be someone who died young, single, and without children, and who either typed what little correspondence survives or wrote with a neat, clear hand. But I had to complete La Follette first, a labor of love that, due to the vast amount of available material, his longevity, and the complexity of both his politics and character, could never have come to fruition without the help of a great number of people.

The librarians and staff at California State University at Hayward, the Library of Congress, Stanford University's Special Collections, and the State Historical Society of Wisconsin (especially archivists Harold Miller, David Benjamin, and Andy Kraushaar) provided generous, courteous assistance. At Santa Clara University's Orradre Library, Cynthia Bradley of Bronco Express and George Carlson and Scott Blashek of Government Documents were especially helpful. Grants from Santa Clara University (SCU) financed the illustrations and the indexing. The SCU history department's generous funding to deliver a paper on Belle La Follette in the summer of 1997 in Madison, Wisconsin, allowed me to pursue research in collections related to La Follette at the State Historical Society. Elwood Mills of SCU is responsible for the excellent quality of the slides used in that presentation as well as for several reproductions presented in this book. Student researchers Ryan Heal and Michelle Pritchard tracked down a variety of sources.

Ed Perkins brought his expert editing skills to Chapter 12. Anonymous readers made additional valuable suggestions prior to the publication of versions of Chapters 10 and 12 in the *Psychohistory Review*. In preparation for the publication of a version of Chapter 4 in the *Wisconsin Magazine of History*, editor Margaret Dwyer provided valuable insight into the character of and the social and political context of Belle Case La Follette. Members of the Biographers' Seminar at Stanford University's Institute for Research on Women and Gender brought their usual rigorous critiquing skills to early versions of Chapters 4, 10, and 12; Barbara Babcock, Sue Bell, Bob Cherny, Anita Feferman, Mary Felstiner, Joe Frank, Estelle Freedman, Edith Gelles, Gerald Gunther, Pam Herr, Diane Middlebrook, Alexandra Nickliss, the late Peter Ostwald, Susan Sibbet, Neera Sohoni, Peter Stansky, Marilyn Yalom, and Helen Young provided particularly incisive commentary. The history department of Santa Clara University provided helpful feedback during a colloquium on Chapter 1, especially Bob Senkewicz (who edited additional chapters as well), Steven Gelber, Dorothea French, Jo Margadant, Istvan Moscy, Tom Turley, and Sita Raman. All of my colleagues, especially Barbara Molony, have been wonderful mentors and sources of support. John Wright made many valuable contributions to Chapter 14 and provided useful advice overall. While providing much appreciated moral support, Paul Finkelman and William McKinley (Mac) Runyan also offered helpful commentary on several chapters.

Several people were especially generous with their particular expertise. Harvard's Brett Flehinger took time from his own political study of the La Follette family to provide extensive and invaluable commentary. Editor Paul Hass put me in touch with author John Buenker, who sent me an electronic version of *The Progressive Era, 1893–1914* (Volume 4 of *The History of Wisconsin*) prior to its publication. Norman Greabner directed me to Gilbert Fite, who searched his files to provide a requested citation. Wisconsin's chief justice Shirley S. Abrahamson introduced me to Catherine Cleary, who supplied definitive information on Belle La Follette's status as the first woman to graduate from the University of Wisconsin Law School. Payson Parker volunteered the outtakes from the La Follette segment of his videotape *Great American Speeches: Eighty Years of Political Oratory*. Wisconsin's secretary of state Doug La Follette graciously shared his views on the family dynasty, and *Madison (Wisc.) Capital Times* editor John Nichols was generous with his time and expertise concerning both the La Follette family and the founding of that publication.

It has been a pleasure to work with the University of North Carolina Press. Executive editor Lewis Bateman garnered painstaking, extraordinarily helpful readers' reports from John Milton Cooper Jr. and Donald A. Ritchie and firmly yet kindly guided this first-time author through the entire publication process. Katherine Malin brought grace and wit as well as her expertise to the entire copyediting process. Pam Upton, Alison Waldenberg, Vicky Wells, Ron Maner, Kathleen Ketterman, and many others at the Press also provided prompt and courteous assistance.

As Bob Cherny and countless others have noted, one never thoroughly understands a subject until one teaches it. To my students—first at San Francisco State University and California State University, Hayward, and now at Santa Clara University—I offer my most sincere thanks for challenging me, for keeping the Progressive Era fresh and helping me to see that period in a number of different ways. Particular thanks go to the students in my Progressive Era and Historical Writing seminars.

Many people provided crucial support, encouragement, and/or advice, especially my mentors from Gonzaga University, Robert Carriker and Fran Polek, as well as friends Kate and Jim Coughlin, Sarah Curtis, John De Miguel, Chuck and Linda Green, Chris and Mike Maricich, Diane North, Sally Scully, Ann Warren, Karen Walker, and Mary Whisner. My dearest friend Sue Ruble, always my champion, brought her expert editing skills to the entire manuscript, correcting an embarrassingly large number of errors and making many valuable suggestions. My family has also been a constant source of encouragement and support. My cousin, Ellen Fehring, graciously shepherded me around Madison, Wisconsin. My mother, Eunice Unger, voluntarily carried out research, sent articles of interest, photocopied entire books, and even hunted down original La Follette campaign buttons in mint condition that are now among my most prized possessions. For her cheerful, selfless, and overwhelmingly generous contributions and support, my endless love and heartfelt gratitude are forever hers.

My husband, Don Whitebread, D.D.S., provided me not only with crucial financial (not to mention technical) support, but voluntarily and conscientiously photocopied voluminous articles and notes, proofread entire drafts, took our children on outings to give me time to work, and was perpetually cheerful, encouraging, patient, and very, very funny. My gratitude, like my love for him, is without measure. To my best friend Megan Lynch and my father Don Unger: I'm sorry I didn't get done in time for you to see this book. But I know you're both proud of me. To my children, Travis Whitebread and Megan Unger: All your lives (and long before) I've been working on this book. Thank you for your patience. We can go to the park now.

A single-volume biography of Robert La Follette is necessarily limited. I chose to keep my focus on the man and his family and tried to achieve what I thought was the appropriate balance between the personal and the political. Readers seeking more detail on his lifetime of programs and proposals or on relationships with other political figures will find a vast literature. Any significant omissions, like any errors, are my responsibility.

# INTRODUCTION
## DULL TOOLS

**W**hich has had the stronger hold upon the state and national legislation during the last twenty years," Governor Robert Marion La Follette asked the Wisconsin legislature in 1904, "the corporations or the people?" As congressman, governor, and senator, La Follette dedicated his life to returning power to the people. His efforts to establish his famed Wisconsin Idea nationwide brought about a truer democracy. Upon La Follette's death in 1925, U.S. representative James Sinclair (R-North Dakota) noted that "for half a century the fight has waged between the forces of special privilege and corrupt wealth on the one hand and the masses of the people on the other." Against the corrupt forces, he added, "Robert Marion La Follette waged unrelenting war." Counted among the victories in that war to which La Follette contributed are the direct election of senators; public disclosure of campaign contributions and expenditures; initiatives and referendums; and more equitable taxation. He worked to limit the power and wealth of big business and served American consumers by helping to create the Department of Labor, the Tariff Commission, and the Federal Trade Commission and by aiding in the enlargement of the powers of the Interstate Commerce Commission. He helped to legislate physical valuation of railroad property; rate classification; exemption of labor organizations from antitrust laws; regulation of telephone and telegraph rates and services; higher wages, lower hours, and better conditions for American laborers, most notably seamen and railroad workers; women's suffrage; the building and operation of the Alaskan railroad; and the investigation that revealed the Teapot Dome scandal. He also labored for civil rights of the racially and economically oppressed. Due to the intensity of his efforts, noted an astute observer, "he well deserved the affectionately bestowed, though not always affectionately used, title of 'Fighting Bob.'"[1]

In 1915, a political reporter compared La Follette with the "long despised agitators" who "hewed through a hardened public conscience" the trail for Abraham Lincoln's ascendancy: "Without the agitators we might never have had a Lincoln; and it is for men like La Follette to prepare the ground on which less fiery though not less patriotic followers can put the social order of the future upon a firm foundation." Upon La Follette's death, Senator William E. Borah (R-Idaho) noted, "agitation has its place and an indispensable place in the life of free government, and if a man is devoted to his country, as I believe La Follette always to have been, his service is often the highest type of statesmanship." Historian Kenneth C. MacKay concurs, crediting La Follette's final presidential campaign with keeping the embers of the reform spirit glowing during the prosperous and complacent 1920s, noting that much of La Follette's 1924 platform ultimately became law under President Franklin Roosevelt.[2]

However, even among those praising La Follette for his very real contributions to his country, many comment, as did La Follette himself, on things "left undone." In 1922, La Follette, still smarting over the vilification he endured during World War I, wrote, "I would be remembered as one who in the world's darkest hour, kept a clean conscience and stood in the end for the ideals of American democracy." Three years later, however, in the wake of the disintegration of much of his political power after the 1924 election and just shortly before he died, he confided wistfully to his oldest son, "I am at peace with all the world, but there is still a lot of work I still could do."[3]

La Follette's failures, most notably his inability to win the presidency or establish a permanent, powerful, and progressive Republican coalition, were frequently the result of a variety of political factors largely beyond his control. But he himself bears some share of the responsibility. "La Follette's fault," according to one contemporary critic, was "not toward being either a demagogue or a courier . . . [but] toward following his own opinions to a violent extreme of narrowness and of aloofness." Another concluded, "Mr. La Follette's weakness is not the weakness of the ordinary politician. It is not the weakness of ignorance or pretense. It is the weakness of temperament, his habits of thought, and his type of mind." The significance of La Follette's refusal to compromise on political issues and his "savage suspiciousness" of virtually all others was also noted: "His whole philosophy has just one root. He is an irreconcilable for the same reason that he is a radical and a radical for the same reason that he is an irreconcilable. . . . He is a man who was emotionally melted in the hottest furnaces of opposition ever lighted against any public man in our day and who now has run into a mold where he has hardened into a form that nothing can break, nothing can bend, nothing can any more even bruise. . . . He is perfectly antique in his view of the Republic. He has nothing in common with the radicals who sneer at the forefathers and who see no difference between the republic of George Washington and any other 'capitalistic' state. La Follette thinks there *was* a difference. He thinks there *is* such a thing as Americanism. He imagines himself to be trying to put it back into the American Government."[4]

"I can no more compromise," La Follette once said, "than I could by wishing it add twenty years to my life." Long on lofty goals, he was often short on realistic, acceptable means to achieve those goals, a debilitating fault exacerbated by his need to see himself, and himself alone, as the infallible judge of right and wrong and all opponents as insincere at best, corrupt at worst. Although other contemporaries contended that La Follette himself was a corrupt hypocrite, even most of his enemies were convinced of his sincerity. Clearly, however, in the world of politics, sincerity and devotion are usually abetted by realism and practicality. La Follette, dedicated and ambitious, possessed great vision hobbled by his frequent disdain for political expediency in favor of emotional satisfaction. His long, statistic-laden speeches mesmerized many but alienated others, while his perpetual unwillingness to delegate responsibility frequently led him to misdirect his energies. His need to defend his sense of moral superiority often had catastrophic results, as evidenced by his 1912 public loss of control in Philadelphia, his participation in campaigns doomed to failure, his nearly perpetual refusal to accept compromise, his insistence upon publishing *La Follette's Magazine* at great personal and financial cost, and his occasional symptoms of paranoia.[5]

La Follette's unquenchable thirst for approval had personal as well as political consequences. Frequent illness robbed him of valuable time and energy but gained him love and support. Moreover, through compensatory relationships, La Follette looked to those closest to him to assure him of his importance and significance. His perception of his wife, Belle, as a kind of emotional and moral thermostat placed severe burdens on their marriage. His desire that his sons serve as extensions of himself resulted in tremendous anguish and most likely contributed to his oldest son's suicide.

La Follette's emotional limitations are not always viewed as detrimental. "What are the facts about La Follette's sanity?" one journalist asked rhetorically. He invoked the poet Dryden, noting the fine line between greatness and madness, before concluding, "La Follette, who, from the standpoint of economic legislation, is the outstanding political genius of his time, often pushes his point with such desperation that his frenzy appears irrational — surely so to an opponent."[6]

La Follette is tragic because he is no longer recalled as a constructive statesman who strove for a more democratic social order but "merely" as a figure of undaunted courage, unlimited perseverance, and enormous dedication. La Follette's image as Fighting Bob survives to the present. He is praised for his devotion to integrity because his tenacity led to legislative triumphs unadulterated by compromise. Although one historian claims that "La Follette surely must rank as one of the greatest fragmenters of the [progressive] epoch," many hail his unwillingness to adhere to strict party lines as an inspiring show of independence and dedication to purpose. Many of his contemporaries admired him less for his legislative accomplishments than for his role as a "safety valve," a "commanding figure . . . scrupulous about law and order" who nonetheless pointed the "hopeful way to political revolution." Others stressed that it is not so much what he did as what his presence in public place prevented.[7]

La Follette's obviously genuine desire to do what he deemed right rather than merely popular brought him a fiercely devoted following convinced that he, perhaps more than any other politician of the time, had their best interests at heart and would fight for them despite all adversities. His following was defined "not so much as a body of friends who like him for his own sake as a body of disciples who have become persuaded of his doctrines." Even in view of his failures, they praised him for having kept the faith. In an effort to explain the Wisconsin voters' loyalty, despite La Follette's obvious shortcomings, one analyst concluded, "Why? Because he is honest and fearless and stands for something. Given these qualities it is amazing how much the electorate will overlook. It suddenly flashes into the minds of the electorate how inspiring is a man with a clear-cut mission, and how rare is the combination of honesty and courage in American public life — so rare when it comes to assailing the castle of privilege and custom, that even wisdom is not an indispensable handmaid."[8]

A cursory study of La Follette's politics reveals many apparent contradictions. While his greatest strengths and most debilitating weaknesses, politically and personally, can be traced back to his earliest beginnings in Primrose, Wisconsin, the path of his political development seems unclear. Was he, at various times, a follower, a leader, a conservative, a Republican, an independent, a progressive, a radical, an insurgent, a pragmatist — or merely always an opportunist? Closer study indicates La Follette always acted within the confines of his life as shaped by the emotional casualties of childhood. What appear to be political reversals and inconsistencies are actually quite consistent in view of La Follette's emotional needs. For example, he vilified political bosses even while his own powerful organization utilized some of the hallmarks of machine politics, especially the conferring of local patronage. However, because his machine was used to promote his political agenda rather than acquire personal wealth, La Follette remained confident that his actions were right, that the ends of such a morally superior man justified the means. Moreover, the very fears and longings that helped make him such a dedicated politician also frequently served to impair his effectiveness, although it is sometimes difficult to determine when they ceased to be a help and began to be a hindrance.[9]

"When the historian of the future comes to write of the first quarter of the twentieth century," *The Outlook* observed upon La Follette's death, "one of the figures which it will be necessary for him to paint, in however gloomy colors, will be that of Robert Marion La Follette." Relatively early in his political career La Follette confided to his brother, "I don't suppose anybody will like what I say except myself, but I hope to be fairly well pleased with it." A quarter of a century later he viewed things quite differently: "We shall find our greatest happiness day by day in giving happiness to others. At the finish we shall find that we have best served ourselves by serving humanity." He told his oldest son, "I don't know how the people feel toward me, but I shall take to my grave my love for them which has sustained me." In the end, he was not the perfect, selfless leader he publicly aspired to be, nor was he a selfish "gloomy colored," essentially unproductive zealot. He was merely a human being, struggling ceaselessly to combat competing feelings of emptiness and grandiosity. To call him what Alice Miller terms a "prisoner of childhood" is not meant as a way to ignore the effects of his political, social, and economic times, but is intended to help illuminate his reaction to that era. The personal and political life of Robert Marion La Follette is a compelling mixture of accomplishment and failure, triumph and tragedy. "When all is said and done," *Emporia Gazette* editor and La Follette intimate William Allen White concluded, "he and the insurgent group are the best element down here — the most sincere, the nearest to the people, the most truly representative of our national opinion. And it is too much to demand that they be immaculate white giants. Almighty God carves out his ends with dull tools — always."[10]

# 1: BEGINNINGS
## OH, MY IDOLIZED FATHER

**F**or a man who would be strongly associated with the dawning of modern, industrialized, urbanized America, Robert La Follette was born in 1855 into an astonishingly different time. Although La Follette would come to witness firsthand the rise of the Soviet Union, in the year of his birth Alexander II became czar of Russia. The glories of antebellum America were celebrated that same year in Walt Whitman's *Leaves of Grass*, an anonymously published new collection of poems including "Song of Myself." Precursors of the modern age, events that would more directly impact the life of Bob La Follette (and that he would impact in return) included the creation of America's first oil refinery, in Pittsburgh. The public's attention, however, was riveted on the brutal armed conflict over slavery in the newly formed Kansas territory, a series of incidents so violent they came to be known as "Bleeding Kansas." These dramatic incidents presaged the Civil War that would tear the nation apart and ultimately aid in the transformation of a predominantly rural, agricultural nation into an international industrial giant.

Robert La Follette lived out the ancient Chinese blessing (or is it a curse?), "May you live in interesting times," beginning with his birth, on 14 June 1855, in the township of Primrose, Wisconsin, a state which only seven years before had graduated from territorial status. No real understanding of La Follette or his life's work can come without an appreciation of his diverse and complex home state. Not yet "America's Dairyland," as proclaimed by its current license plates, Wisconsin could nevertheless already boast a long and unique history. Although much of its geography (and almost all of its 8,500 lakes) was the result of glacial movements during the last Ice Age, roughly a quarter of the state's 35 million acres was protected from glaciers. The result is a unique variety of landscapes that, prior to the coming of French explorers, were home to an estimated 20,000 Native Americans, most notably the Menominee and the Winnebago. Following encroachment by white trappers, traders, and farmers and the climactic defeat at the Battle of Wisconsin Heights in 1832, the relocation of the territory's tribes west of the Mississippi River proceeded with relatively few disturbances. Wisconsin, bereft of much of its native population, was awash with succeeding waves of new immigrants. By midcentury, the entire country was on the move (with one American in four moving across state lines), and a disproportionate number of its migrants were moving to Wisconsin. Migratory patterns were rarely simple, and instead involved a series of moves, as farms and homesteads were established only to be abandoned in a restless search for greener pastures.[1]

Robert La Follette took great pride in his pioneer beginnings. Living in an era filled with big business and big corruption in big cities, he stressed his humble birth — in a log cabin, no less — as proof of his inherent sturdiness, plainness, and integrity. His heritage was solidly American in the romantic tradition, the trail of his ancestors into Wisconsin long and complex. His maternal great-grandfather, a Scottish farmhand named John Fergeson, settled in North Carolina after crop failures and political oppression forced him to leave northern Ireland. Joseph Le Follet, La Follette's paternal great-grandfather, was a prosperous silk manufacturer who migrated to the Isle of Jersey after the massacre of St. Bartholomew in the sixteenth century. Le Follet's first wife, whose name remains unknown, was a Catholic who had escaped a convent school in France and was secreted out of the country in the traveling carriage of an English couple, customers of Jean Le Follet, Joseph's father. Despite her parents' opposition, she and Le Follet married around 1765. The couple emigrated to a French Huguenot colony near Newark, New Jersey, where in 1767 they produced one child, Isaac, before the young woman's death.[2]

Both Joseph Le Follet and John Fergeson fought against the British in the American Revolution. During the war the Le Follet family name underwent the transformation to its current spelling. (According to family legend, an ancestor named Usual was surnamed Le Follet, "the Reckless," near the end of the twelfth century because of personal bravery in the local provincial wars, and the name, as a family cognomen, was retained permanently.) "Le Follet" became "La Follette" following the arrival of Joseph's three brothers in America in 1776. The brothers were part of a French crew financed by the Marquis de La Fayette to bring supplies from his estate and help fight the British. All four brothers participated in the battles of Brandywine and Yorktown, and all but Joseph agreed to demonstrate their loyalty to La Fayette by changing the spelling of their name from the masculine to the feminine form. Joseph resisted this change, listing his first four children in the family Bible as "Le Follet," but eventually came to conform with his brothers, listing his five subsequent children as "La Follette." It is not known whether the brothers Americanized the pronunciation of their name when they altered the spelling, but their descendent, Robert La Follette, would "have none of the French pronunciation," insisting that the accent be placed on the penult [lah-FALL-it].[3]

John Fergeson returned to North Carolina after his Revolutionary War service. His son, also named John Fergeson, left in 1807 to farm in Indiana with his wife, Mary Green, a native of Maryland. There, on 22 November

1818, Robert La Follette's mother, Mary Fergeson, was born. Joseph La Follette moved from New Jersey to Virginia, but later he and his brothers traveled to Hardin County, Kentucky, where they settled permanently. Joseph's son Jesse, born in 1781, married there and fathered eleven children, including Josiah, Robert La Follette's father. Neighbors of the La Follettes included Thomas and Nancy Lincoln, parents of Abraham Lincoln. Thomas Lincoln and Joseph La Follette were appointed, among others, to appraise the estate of a deceased neighbor. In 1828, when Josiah was eleven, Jesse's family moved to a farm in Putnam County, Indiana, where Joseph's brother Usual had moved years before.[4]

In Putnam County, La Follette's parents, Josiah La Follette and Mary Fergeson, began their courtship and became engaged. They made a striking couple, for Josiah was a robust, swarthy man who stood about six feet tall, towering over his four-foot ten-inch fiancée, an attractive blue-eyed, light-haired woman with fair skin.[5] At some point Mary's brother married one of Josiah's older sisters. Mary nevertheless broke off her engagement to Josiah following a "lovers' quarrel," and he returned to his boyhood home in Kentucky where he engaged in agricultural work. In 1840 Mary, then twenty-three, wed Alexander Buchanan, a farmer. Their daughter Ellen had not yet been born when Buchanan was killed at a barn raising. Mother and daughter remained on the farm. According to family legend, someone coming from Indiana brought a paper with a notice of a party attended by the widow Buchanan. This social note was communicated to Josiah La Follette, a fine carpenter, as he was working on a roof: "He came down off the house, took off his apron, hung it on the ladder and said, 'I am going back to Indiana and marry the widow Buchanan.'" Return he did. Mary and Josiah married in 1845 and remained on the Buchanan farm until 1849, when Josiah's five unmarried brothers bought or preempted (gained right to purchase a public tract of land) 840 acres within an area three miles square in the township of Primrose, in southern Wisconsin, and sent favorable reports back to Indiana. Thus, Josiah and Mary, together with their two small sons William and Marion, and Mary's daughter Ellen Buchanan, came to settle, via two covered wagons and a covered buggy, in Wisconsin.[6]

The pioneer experience in Wisconsin has been popularized for modern audiences, especially children, by Laura Ingalls Wilder's *Little House in the Big Woods*. Set in the sparsely populated, central eastern portion of Wisconsin territory, the Ingalls family bravely endured the elements and eked out a living trapping, fishing, and hunting amidst the Big Woods (Wisconsin's woodlands then covered roughly three fifths of its northern area). Southern Wisconsin, new home of the La Follette family, offered a very different kind of pioneer experience. Although generally classed as rolling and fertile, the lands of southern Wisconsin offered a challenging range of soils, streams, thinly covered rocks, and elevations that made farming far less lucrative in some areas than in others. But natural lottery schemes such as these were nothing new to the La Follette clan, nor to most of their neighbors. More than two-thirds of Wisconsin's 1840 territorial population was under thirty, and these youthful seekers of a better life seemed resigned to early trials and setbacks.

Despite the leadership of an American-born minority, Wisconsin during its territorial period was a vast mosaic of loosely associated ethnic communities. Irish immigrants began arriving in the 1830s. They were joined by many of their fellow citizens as the toll of the potato famine accelerated, beginning in 1845. Protestant Scotch-Irish, some of them of Huguenot origin, also came to Wisconsin, as did Cornish miners (drawn by its rich lead fields), but the prevailing nationalities in territorial Wisconsin were British, German, Irish, Norwegian, and Swiss. By 1845, a reported quarter-million acres of farmland had been sold to the Germans alone. Following statehood in 1852, official efforts were successfully made to attract other immigrant groups, including Armenians, Belgians, Bohemians, Danes, Finns, Greeks, Hungarians, Icelanders, Italians, Latvians, Lithuanians, Poles, Russians, and Swedes. These additional nationalities made more intricate the existing multi-ethnic mosaic. One of the tiniest minority groups in Wisconsin was composed of African Americans, totaling only 1,171 by 1860, less than one-fifth of 1 percent of the state's population. While they were denied a number of rights and privileges, including the franchise, they were allowed to marry whites, own property, attend public schools, and serve on juries. This mosaic of ethnic and religious heritages produced a unique and complex political character, a character Robert La Follette would grow up with and understand perhaps better than any politician before or since.[7]

Due to his relatively late arrival in Dane County, a Norwegian stronghold since 1846, Josiah La Follette was forced to buy or preempt his 360 acres in three unadjoined lots. Josiah, like his brothers, was hardworking and quickly became a successful farmer. He owned and read a great number of books and, not content with mere financial success was also, like his brothers, politically active. The La Follettes were a well-educated clan as well. (The Indiana branch boasted seven lawyers, five physicians, and several ministers.) All were ardent abolitionists and members of the newly formed Republican party, an antislavery coalition of Northern Whigs, independent Democrats, and Free Soilers. Josiah added to his responsibilities in 1852 when, less than two years after his arrival in Primrose, he was elected town clerk, receiving all thirty-six votes cast. Tragedy struck Jo-

*If this image from a La Follette family photo album is indeed of Josiah La Follette (so identified "with some reasonable assuredness" by visual archivists of the State Historical Society of Wisconsin), it remained, tragically, undiscovered or unrecognized by his son Robert. However, in view of Belle La Follette's assertion that the fact that her husband "had no early memory, not even a picture of his father, was a source of much grief and heartache in his childhood, and of deep regret all his life," this may instead be a portrait of one of Josiah's five brothers. (State Historical Society of Wisconsin WHi[X3]111506)*

siah and Mary that same year with the death of their three-year-old son, Marion, an event not uncommon in these pioneer times of crude conditions and frequent epidemics. The following year marked Josiah's reelection to office and the birth of a daughter, Josephine. In 1854, Josiah was elected assessor and on 14 June 1855 was presented with a son, Robert Marion La Follette, called Bob.

At the time of Bob's birth, both parents were thirty-eight years old. Ellen

Buchanan was fourteen, William was eight, and Josephine was two. Josiah had for ten years been married to the woman who had been the sole object of his desire and who had for so long eluded him. Although Mary La Follette later told Bob that his father had been an agnostic, a neighbor remembered the entire La Follette family attending services at the Free Baptist Church in Postville. Whatever Josiah La Follette's religious beliefs, his neighbors respected him, and he had advanced rapidly up the political ladder, having been recently elected town chairman. Financially prudent, he was said to have been an intelligent, determined man of integrity and strong will.[8]

Josiah La Follette's death, despite the ministrations of family physician William Fox, came in February 1856, brought on by a complication of pneumonia and diabetes. His dying words: "I am not afraid to die, but I don't like to be forgotten." Bob was only eight months old. Josiah's widow wanted her husband buried with Marion, the toddler who had died three years before. Marion's coffin was removed from a hillside on the farm, brought into the house and opened. Family legend has it that the child's face was perfectly preserved, only to fall to ashes. Father and son were then buried in a single grave, the son under the father, in the nearby Postville cemetery on Green's prairie. This dramatic story was to be recounted to Robert La Follette, who would attempt to reenact it nearly forty years later.[9]

Mary and the children were bequeathed one of the best farms in the county, and the surviving La Follette brothers provided what aid they could. One brother, William, undertook the building of the frame house planned by Josiah. Another brother, Harvey, carried out the balance of Josiah's unfinished term as town chairman. During the first three years of her second widowhood, Mary La Follette was uncertain about staying in Primrose. In 1858, she and Bob visited relatives in Indiana, where she might have resettled her family had a neighbor, Dean Eastman, not provided a solution to her problems. Eastman married Ellen Buchanan, bought some of the La Follette land, and agreed to run the farm for half the profits. Diligent and ambitious, by 1860 Eastman had made the La Follette farm the second most valuable in all of Primrose. This new sense of security allowed Mary to remain in Wisconsin to raise her family.

Inaccurate accounts of Robert La Follette's early childhood abound. One sketch reports that at the death of his father, "the care of the whole family of several younger children fell upon Robert as the eldest son. For several years he supported the entire family." La Follette's own accounts are dramatic but vague. He begins his autobiography with his experiences in 1880, when he was already twenty-five years old, mentioning only that he had never known his father and that he had his mother and sister to support,

*After Josiah La Follette's death, his family remained sufficiently prosperous to commission a portrait in 1858. Three-year-old Bob nestles in his mother Mary's lap. His half sister Ellen stands behind sister Josephine, with brother William at right. (State Historical Society of Wisconsin WHi[X3]35771)*

contributing to the impression that he had taken sole responsibility for the family at an early age.[10] In truth, the farm under Josiah La Follette had been more prosperous than most, and Dean Eastman compounded the profits by producing butter for sale. The extended family lived under one roof, and Eastman, an energetic and popular man, treated his young brother-in-law with affection. Although Bob's half sister Ellen was a living reminder of his mother's rejection of his father in favor of another man, young Bob displayed no resentment toward her. Despite the large difference in their ages and the physical distances that later separated them, the two corresponded infrequently but regularly throughout their lives and freely expressed care and concern for one another, their spouses, and their families. Neighbors, too, paid enough attention to Bob to remain vividly in his memory.

Bob did not lack for male attention, but the people to whom he was closest throughout his childhood, indeed his lifetime, were women. "He was a tremendous favorite with ladies," a neighbor remembered of the youthful La Follette, "despite the fact that he was very mischievous. . . . They adored the handsome little bunch of energy that seemed all springs and fire." La Follette spoke openly of his dependence upon the women in his life: "My widowed mother was a woman of wise judgment, my sisters were my best friends and advisors, and in all the work of my public life my wife has been my constant companion." Bob doted on his sister Josephine, whom he called "Jo" or "Josie" and to whom he wrote in 1901: "From my very earliest recollections of childhood you were the other half. . . . Then as we grew older the companionship grew, if possible, closer. You knew all my hopes, ambitions, disappointments, and discouragements and shared them all. Without you and that dear spirit our sainted mother to encourage, to inspire with fortitude, to sacrifice and struggle for and with me I should have fallen far short and perhaps have failed all together in the work I am in some measure accomplishing as my part of life. Dear dear sister let us round out whatever there may be left to us in life in that close identification of feeling and interest and personality which makes all the past such a sweet and tender memory to us now."[11]

It was not always possible for the brother and sister to maintain such intimacy in adulthood, but they remained exceptionally close. Before his marriage to Belle Case, Bob expressed his joy that she and Jo had exchanged correspondence and resolved "they will love each other as sisters." In 1913, he wrote to Jo, "We shall always understand each other." Belle resembled Jo to the point that callers sometimes confused the two women. Jo's husband, Robert Siebecker, became Bob's law partner, and when the La Follettes' son Philip entered the University of Wisconsin, he lived his first year with "Uncle Robert" and "Aunt Josie." Bob wrote of his sister and brother-in-law, "No better man and woman ever lived in all this world. No one was better to their own parents, their own children, their own kin, their friends, their neighbors — and all whose lives they have touched in any way." Bob's lifelong dedication to Jo was reciprocated, for Robert Siebecker once confided in Phil that Jo's first love throughout her life was her own brother rather than himself. A letter from Jo to Bob reinforces that conviction: "Bob my dear brother I wonder if you know just how thoroughly my life and happiness is wrapped up in yours. We are more closely knit together I am sure than most brothers and sisters."[12]

Despite his attachment to Jo, Bob's strongest love during his childhood was for his mother. His memory of her was always "singularly fervent." He referred to his first seven years as "happy and normal" and told his wife that during those years "he worshiped his mother and never questioned the depth and warmth of her love. When she punished him he never resented it; his feeling was to throw his arms about her and beg forgiveness. She could not resist this sort of appeal. So long as she lived there was this perfect bond of mutual understanding between them."[13]

Bob remembered as a boy accompanying his mother on "all occasions," including church activities, neighborhood festivities, and visits. In 1903, a pair of mittens from a supporter evoked the memory "of a sainted mother as she wove the soft yarn of her spinning over her shining needles, for the protection and comfort of the loved ones at home. And there comes back again to me tonight the beautiful thoughts and precepts which she knitted into my life as good counsel ever kept pace with the work of her busy hands." Robert La Follette committed no mention of his mother's faults to print. They come instead through stories he would later tell his wife, Belle Case, and are augmented by Belle's own recollections of her mother-in-law. While her daughter-in-law called Mary a noble woman of great character and large soul to be emulated — industrious, capable, generous, prudent, fastidious, a fine seamstress, excellent cook, nurturing gardener, and capable nurse — she also commented on Mary's lack of schooling and poor grammar, her sarcasm, and the fact that she would "fret and scold" about little things. A neighbor recalled Mary La Follette as "an intelligent woman, not very demonstrative, particularly toward her children whom she ruled strongly by her quiet force of character." Some of Bob's earliest memories revolved around feelings of anxiety about his mother. He told his wife "he often pictured the sad journey his mother made on that cold, dreary day" of his father's funeral, for his mother "often recounted her suffering to her children."[14]

Like the great many of the children left bereft of a parent in the mid-nineteenth century, Bob was protective, possessive, and manipulative of his remaining parent. His mother, however, insisted that Bob worship his father's memory and emulate his life as much as possible. Above all, she stressed her late husband's integrity, his devotion to doing "right." At a very early age Bob was saddled with a great and unending responsibility: he must never do *anything* to dishonor his father's name. Family pride, said Bob, had been worked into his character by his mother. "It was the thing that she emphasized when she talked with me about my father."[15]

It was not unusual, then or now, for a parent, by stressing the deceased parent's most admirable characteristics, to encourage a child to create a positive vision of the absent parent. What is striking in the La Follettes' situation is the frequency and stridency of Mary's insistence. This was not the case of a mother simply wishing to ensure that a fatherless boy would harbor fond feelings toward an unknown father. Rather than supplying reassurance, Mary's urgings engendered anxiety. The impact of Mary La Follette's directive on her son cannot be overestimated. "The fact that he had no early memory, not even a picture of his father," wrote Belle La Follette after her husband's death, "was a source of much grief and heartache in his childhood, and of deep regret all his life." In order to emulate his father and to try to discover what behavior would have been pleasing to him, Bob went to extreme measures to satisfy his relentless desire for information about this idolized figure. Thoughts of his father, Bob later told his wife, were always part of his consciousness, even in his extreme youth, and his devotion to his memory was, in her words, "almost morbid." Bob spent his lifetime seeking the approval and acceptance of this phantom father, whom he had "thought of . . . by day and dreamed of . . . at night." At the age of twenty-four, Bob revealed in his diary the source of his impassioned search, both professionally and personally, for approval and his great desire to do and be "right": "[I]n my imagination I am standing beside my father's grave — Oh[,] my idolized father[,] lost to me before your image was stamped upon my child-mind — nothing left me but your name! What would I not give to have known the sound of your voice, to have received your approval when it was merited. How much pain & hardship & strife could have been spared to mother could you have kept at her side! How much unknown joy been added to our home had it been unbroken. How altered have been the whole course of my life had it not received this cruel stroke from the hard hand of fate!"[16]

In 1894, following his mother's death, Robert La Follette enacted this vision of standing at his father's grave. Bob and his brother William returned to the Green's Prairie cemetery at Postville to witness the disinterment of their father's remains in order to rebury them in Madison next to their mother's. When the grave digger discovered that the coffin had long since disintegrated, Bob, raised on the story of the perfect preservation of his dead brother's remains, carefully removed the remnants of his father's skeleton. In an interview twenty-six years later La Follette remembered, "Most of the principal bones of the skeleton were found and some of my father's hair." He carefully gathered the remains of both his father and his brother, wrapping them in paper before transporting them to Madison. According to family friend Dr. Cornelius Harper, who assisted at the reburial in Madison, Bob La Follette unwrapped the relics and laid them out on a piece of canvas on the ground. Although many bones were missing, the skull and teeth (in a "remarkable state of preservation"), thigh bones, and others were easily identifiable. "Bob studied the relics carefully," discussing them in great detail with Harper. "He asked me many questions," Harper recalled, "and looked at the remains from different angles and points of view. He seemed to be very intent on . . . reproducing in imagination the form of his father as he must have looked in life." La Follette noted his father's prominent forehead, and the hands and feet, small like his own. The tuft of hair received special notice: "It was long, of a slightly auburn hue and streaked a little with gray but it appeared to be of a very luxurious growth and to have still retained its waviness." Harper recalled that he "could . . . see where Bob received his luxurious and wavy hair." Only after "an hour or two" of intense study did La Follette place the relics in a new coffin lined with cotton batting and close the lid for reburial.[17]

A number of traits that would mark the character of Robert La Follette throughout his life emerged from his relationship — or, rather, his keenly felt lack of relationship — with his father. La Follette's image of his father as a totally righteous man was never tarnished by the words or actions of the real man, human and, therefore, flawed. Righteous perfection is a mighty daunting aspiration, no matter how urgently one is entreated to achieve it, but Robert La Follette would come to take up this challenge with a vengeance. Even as a youth, he began laying the groundwork. His mother's insistence that he constantly seek his father's approval was, of course, impossible, so La Follette sensibly did the next best thing. Although generally more trusting of women, he formed strong bonds with older men who resembled his father physically or morally and constantly looked to others for reassurance, approval, disapproval, punishment, and reward.

As a child, Bob La Follette was described as "irrepressible," "extroverted," "agile," "mischievous," and "social"; a short little boy with "a notable penchant for mischief." He was never handicapped by shyness and claimed to have made his first public speech between the ages of three and four at an entertainment at the local schoolhouse. So short he had to stand on the teacher's desk to be seen, he recited:

> You'd not expect one of my age
> To speak in public on the stage.

His proclivity for public speaking, fantasy, and drama lasted Bob a lifetime as he entertained friends, family, and public audiences with his oratory and acting abilities, skills especially appreciated in this pre-film, pre-television age.[18]

Bob's playmates were the children of various neighbors, most of whom had emigrated from Norway. Playing soldier was a popular pastime, for news of the impending Civil War had deeply impressed all of Primrose. However, the distance between neighbors often made it impossible for the children to get together, increasing the mutual dependency of Bob and Jo. Bob thrived on perpetual activity and yearned for appreciative audiences for his variety of antics. He started school at the age of four, probably the combined result of his own desire to be with Jo and with other children throughout the school day and of his mother's belief in the value of education. Although Mary La Follette declared in her petition to the court probating her late husband's estate that her income was "a very small remuneration indeed for the support and education of said three children," she nevertheless swore that whenever her finances forced her to sell some of the family land, she would use the income to finance the children's education.[19]

The excellent education Mary La Follette desired for her children was difficult to attain in antebellum Wisconsin, but not impossible. In 1859, the year Bob La Follette began his formal education, the minimum school year was only three months, to be expanded to five in 1866.[20] Whenever possible, Mary La Follette sent her children to private school, but even in an overcrowded country public school, young Bob La Follette stood out. Little record exists of Bob's scholastic performance at the Primrose district school, but in 1896 he received a letter from his former teacher, Carrie Baker Davenport. She remembered him well and was quite emotional about her longings for the "good old days" of Primrose. She ended her reminiscences with this plea: "Now Robbie please you just get down from the heights to which you have climbed and give me a few moments just as you used to when you combed and fixed my hair just to your fancy. Oh, Robbie, do you remember? I shall never forget."[21]

This is the earliest recorded instance of Bob's penchant for hairdressing. He enjoyed taking an active role in the appearance of others, for physical appearance was always important to him. While florid physical descriptions of major characters in the biographies of the day were common, even those individuals who play relatively insignificant roles in La Follette's 1912 autobiography merit a fairly detailed portrait. He found tall, massive, dark-haired, dark-eyed men to be "fine types" and seldom failed to make note of a beard — all characteristics, he had been told, of his unseen father. (As a young man, Bob himself sported, at various times, a mustache and a full beard, but was clean shaven during his last thirty years). As an adult, Bob had a tendency to equate aspects of his late father's physical appearance with character and integrity: "My first impression of [Grover] Cleveland was extremely unfavorable. The contrast with [Chester] Arthur, who was a fine handsome figure, was very striking. Cleveland's coarse face, his heavy, inert body, his great shapeless hands, confirmed in my mind the attacks made upon him during the campaign."[22]

Bob's fair complexion, blue eyes (he called them "dark blue or gray"), and small stature marked his resemblance to his mother rather than his father. Even as a child he affected a pompadour to give the illusion of greater height, the hair style that was later to become his trademark. Bob was quite vain about his hair and his later diaries reveal two recipes for hair tonic. His vanity did not cease at the hairline. Bob's personal letters and interviews are peppered with references to his fine or "manly" appearance. Although in 1911 he did allow that "I ain't quite as good lookin' as I was [in 1894], but I know a lot more," he paid great attention to his clothing and personal appearance throughout his life. Called "the most fastidious dresser in the Senate," he was said to have strutted rather than walked. He carried on lengthy correspondences detailing his displeasure and exact requirements for alteration if he judged a photo plate or engraving to be unflattering. A related absorbing interest that also lasted a lifetime was La Follette's preoccupation with physical strength, something his father was said to have possessed in great quantities. Many interviewers, particularly during his later years, mention the senator's urging them to feel the muscle in his arm. This preoccupation too can be traced to his childhood, for young Bob was a champion wrestler, a sport he greatly enjoyed from a very early age.[23]

Thus, by the time he was seven years old, certain key elements of Bob La Follette's personality were clearly in evidence. To ease some of his unique, potentially crippling childhood burdens, he had begun to establish certain relationships and behaviors, including special attention to physical appearance and, more significantly, a fledgling but fierce drive to live up to his mother's directive that he do "right" in order to merit approval. Despite the elements of tragedy in these years, they constituted a comparatively peaceful period in light of what was to immediately follow.

Eighteen sixty-two was the year the world of Bob La Follette fell apart. It was a tumultuous year for the state of Wisconsin and for the nation as well. While the war years strengthened the unity of the Republican party, Wisconsin Democrats found themselves divided, especially as emancipation became one of Lincoln's goals. And not all political divisions within the state fell cleanly along strict party lines. Although Wisconsin had voted solidly for Lincoln in the election of 1860, Irish and German Catholics and most German Lutherans (all vehemently opposed to the military conscription practices of the Old World) proved the exception. Rioting broke out in several Wisconsin cities in 1862 when drafting began. That same year, Sioux attacks in Minnesota brought some 40,000 refugees into Wisconsin. Although the violence did not cross state lines, fear and panic certainly did, leading Governor Edward Salomon to repeatedly (yet unsuccessfully) press Secretary of War Edwin Stanton for more arms and ammunition and for permission to utilize some of the newly recruited soldiers for local rather than national defense. Following a brief transition period, however, the state, like the others loyal to the union, enjoyed a new prosperity. Demand for grains, especially wheat, helped to stimulate the mechanization of Wisconsin farms and dramatically increased crop prices, setting off a chain of increased profits, wages, and spending.[1]

Despite her valuable farm, wealth managed to elude the widow La Follette as the cost of living also rose appreciably. Her youngest child, Bob, was seven years old in 1862. His mother's concern for the welfare of her growing children mounted as her assets dwindled. Mary La Follette developed an interest in John Z. Saxton, a fellow ardent Baptist, who served as a church deacon. On the surface, Saxton appeared to be a fine choice as stepfather to Mary's children, as he and his late wife had been generous to their adopted children. Recently widowed, he resided in Argyle, a small village twenty miles southeast of Primrose, where he was looked upon as a leading citizen. He had been town chairman, merchant, and postmaster and at one time also kept a hotel. Although a rival store had recently opened, he had a good country trade and was considered prosperous, even wealthy. In view of Mary's ambitious plans for her children's education, Saxton's fine home and Norwegian servant represented financial security. He was seventy in 1862, the year of their marriage; Mary was only forty-five, but unions were common between farm widows and older men.

After the wedding Mary Saxton, as was common practice in the case of remarriage, surrendered all authority, financial and familial, to her new husband. (Despite an 1850 statute establishing married women's property rights, wives in Wisconsin could not conduct business, make contracts, retain their own earnings or sue or be sued in their own names.) [2] With the move to Argyle came educational opportunities. In 1864, Bob attended a new private school. This was to be the only marked improvement in the family's situation, however. Mary Saxton's anticipation that her new husband would provide liberally for his stepchildren, guiding them and giving them advantages they might not otherwise enjoy, was unfulfilled. Remembered a neighbor, "In a way it seemed [the family] lived too high and they sold all the property and it seemed at last that they seemed hard up." That same neighbor's family was accustomed to driving across the La Follette property to get to the main road. Upon her remarriage, Mary Saxton asked 200–300 pounds of flour in exchange for that privilege. The total value of Saxton's real estate, appraised at $800 in 1859, had declined to $500 in the "golden year" of 1860, so-called because of an amazing wheat crop that placed Wisconsin second only to Illinois among wheat-producing states. Another big harvest the following year increased the state's general prosperity, soon further compounded by war profits, yet Saxton's finances continued to ebb as his new competitor took more and more of his business and the old man took no effective counteractive measures. It is not known exactly when Mary discovered that she would be supporting the man she had assumed would be providing for her family, but within the first week of their marriage the couple traveled to Madison to begin proceedings to appropriate $150, ostensibly on behalf of the children, from the La Follette estate. In less than three years, Saxton's personal estate dwindled to less than $100.[3]

Following the marriage of his beloved mother to an old and failing man, Bob saw much of the attention that he had enjoyed directed toward Mary's third husband. To a boy committed to revering his dead father, this was a bitter blow indeed, exacerbated by the humiliating realization that his mother may have deluded herself about Saxton's finances. Bob would have "gone to the stake" for his mother. Rather than finding fault with her for making such a poor choice in husbands, Bob preferred to see her as the victim of Saxton's misrepresentation of his wealth. Subsequently, Bob vehemently protested against any kind of clandestine dealings and clamored for rights to open discussion. He loathed secrecy, maintaining that "evil and corruption thrive best in the dark" and that most scandalous acts of dishonesty "could never have reached the first stage had they not been conceived and practically consummated in secret . . . and then carried through . . . with little or no discussion." To Bob, even an indulgent stepfather and provider would have been an insult to Josiah La Follette's memory, but the boy viewed the old man who kept itemized accounts of all the expenditures of his wife's money for the children, including their mending and washing, as parsimonious.[4]

Even worse for his stepson than Saxton's penny-pinching, with its implied resentment of each expenditure's recipient, was his religious fervor. Before her remarriage, Bob had enjoyed attending Baptist church sings with his mother. About the time of her marriage to Saxton, Mary and her daughter Josephine were baptized. A neighbor recalled that Bob's mother "was quite religious and used to give testimony of experiences at revival meetings." Bob, however, refrained from such religious enthusiasm, influenced by the knowledge of his father's agnosticism imparted by his mother as part of her insistence that her son "remember" Josiah La Follette. Saxton, however, unreservedly embraced a rigid and demanding set of beliefs and commanded that his new family conform to them. Mandatory Bible reading was carried out behind pulled shades for hours each Sunday. When asked in later years why he did not attend church as an adult, Bob answered, "I got fed up with that sort of a thing as a boy. My stepfather insisted on entertaining the Baptist minister every Sunday." Saxton's religious fervor was not reserved for the Sabbath only. He viewed it his Christian duty to discipline his stepchildren harshly for any deviance from his demanding code of behavior. He followed the era's prevailing theories of child rearing and believed that to spare the rod was to spoil the child. He considered poor manners, impoliteness, or discourtesy inexcusable. He responded with whippings so severe Mary occasionally intervened on the children's behalf.[5]

When denied reimbursement from the La Follette estate for the support of William La Follette once he turned fourteen, Saxton allowed William to remain with the family only if he worked for his board. Saxton continued to submit bills to the estate for the teenager's expenses, however. The animosity between Saxton and William grew so great that Mary sent her older son to live with his uncle in Indiana. Unsatisfied with conditions there as well, William returned to Wisconsin in 1865 and enlisted in the army, under age and without his mother's consent. Fortunately, by the time of William's enlistment the conflict was in its final months, and the only "action" he saw was guard duty.[6]

The Wisconsin legislature ratified the thirteenth amendment abolishing slavery in February 1865. Two months later Wisconsinites wildly celebrated the end of the war, only to mourn the death of their president with equal intensity a few days later. Bob heard the news of the assassination from a neighbor and ran home to tell his mother. They all cried. The glamour of the war captured his nine-year-old imagination and sealed his attraction to the Republican party. It was the party, in his view, not the Union army, that "had fought a desperate war for a great and righteous cause." The party's postwar actions only served to heighten the child's allegiance.[7]

The political, economic, racial, ethnic, and gender-based trends and transformations of the postwar era combined to shape the Wisconsin in which Robert La Follette came to manhood. At any given time, various elements of this swirl of events were discussed and debated in state and local papers; in churches, schools, and saloons; across fences, kitchen tables, and the counters of general stores. Growing up in this milieu, prior to the endless amusement and distraction provided by modern-day technologies, young La Follette, like most youths of his generation, was perpetually immersed in these endless debates and discussions.

Several Wisconsin politicians weighed in on Andrew Johnson's behalf during his program of presidential reconstruction. Former two-term Wisconsin governor Alexander W. Randall became head of the United States Post Office Department in 1866. Randall's friend, Elisha W. Keyes (future nemesis of Robert La Follette) was both postmaster as well as mayor of Madison, the state's capital. Keyes placed his influence within Wisconsin behind the new president's program to essentially restore white southerners to full rights and privileges, as did the state's senior senator, James R. Doolittle. Keyes's influence was considerable. Through Randall, Keyes controlled a large share of the jobs in more than one thousand Wisconsin post offices. Bosses like Keyes led highly organized political groups who expanded their power base by conferring patronage: making appointments to government jobs based on a variety of factors other than merit. Thus a local citizen might attain a job as a postal clerk not because he was better qualified than other applicants but because he was a loyal party member — or offered a kickback. Like the heads of most political machines, Keyes had a local "mouthpiece," the *Wisconsin State Journal*, a newspaper co-owned and coedited by Horace Rublee, chairman of the Republican state committee.[8]

Despite the combined support of Keyes and Doolittle, President Johnson's reluctance to alter the status quo, especially his veto of both the Freedman's Bureau Bill (to extend the life of that agency, designed to aid former slaves in their transition from enforced servitude to new lives as free wage earners and land owners) and the Civil Rights Bill (granting citizenship to native-born African Americans), alarmed the majority of Wisconsin Republicans. When Doolittle joined Johnson in his continued opposition to the Civil Rights Bill, now rewritten as the Fourteenth Amendment, his fellow Republicans in the state legislature, who ratified the amendment, viewed him as a traitor to the party. The battle over Reconstruction raged on and, in 1868, included the impeachment trial of Andrew Johnson. His party maintained the presidency by only one vote, and Johnson was soon replaced by the election of former Union general Ulysses S. Grant.

As Johnson's political stock plummeted, so did that of his Wisconsin supporters. Doolittle failed to be reelected in 1869. Elisha Keyes lay low, shifting his loyalties within the party so as to eventually reemerge as the state Republican boss. Despite concern about reconstruction issues, Wisconsin Republicans, who overwhelming controlled that state's congressional seats, continued to focus on needs within their own state, striving for funding for internal improvements, via land grants and river and harbor appropriation bills. The approval of such bills, however, did not necessarily result in such proposals coming to fruition. Congressman (and lumber magnate) Philetus Sawyer, for example, was highly successful in securing the passage of an 1870 river and harbor improvement bill as well as a bill to fund a canal that would convert his home city of Oshkosh into an inland seaport. However, notes Sawyer's biographer, "Much of the government money seemed simply to disappear in the shifting sands of the rivers to be 'improved,' and the dream of a great ship canal was never to be realized." The money served instead to strengthen Sawyer and his party within Wisconsin. To reinforce that strength by guaranteeing the loyalty of the large numbers of former soldiers, increased veterans' benefits would become a fixture in proposed legislation for years to come.[9]

Veterans streamed back into Wisconsin, as did a variety of new immigrants. Wisconsin actively recruited immigrants and, as in previous years, drew a variety of the foreign born, who continued to constitute roughly 35 percent of its population. By 1870, Wisconsin boasted a total population of slightly over one million, an increase of more than 186,000 since 1865. Ethnic divisions and enclaves continued to be well defined. Even long years of military service did little to ease the strictness of ethnic divisions in Wisconsin communities, because military companies had been created and perpetuated according to the ethnicity of its volunteers. As a result, wartime experiences in no way engendered ethnic harmony, especially as returning veterans were faced with fellow citizens who had resisted the draft based on their adherence to Old World attitudes. Tensions over issues such as Sunday laws (designed to enforce proper observance of the Sabbath, usually including the closure of shops and entertainments) and liquor control acts in the years following the war exacerbated animosities between members of various ethnic groups and religions.[10]

Veterans formed much of the power base for the Republican party that dominated Wisconsin politics until 1873. Louis Fairchild, who lost his left arm at Gettysburg, served as Wisconsin's first three-term governor (1866–

72). Fairchild helped to strengthen the public's association of Republicanism with loyalty and union and of Democratism with treason and rebellion, intoning, "Where the traitor's bullet failed[,] his ballot shall not conquer." Most loyal Republicans were, however, in agreement with Democrats when it came to denying former slaves the vote. Suffrage was ultimately granted to African Americans in Wisconsin not by popular vote (where it was soundly defeated) but by virtue of the state supreme court case *Gillespie v. Palmer et al.* in 1866.[11]

The majority of Wisconsinites, including returning veterans, continued to engage in agricultural enterprises. Among landholders, wartime shortages and crop failures in other parts of the country encouraged crop diversification. Postwar farmers experimented with various grains as well as hops, sugar beets, and the more exotic cranberry. Sheep still far outnumbered cattle throughout the 1860s, however. Dairying, with its high potential for spoilage, was considered too risky an enterprise for the average farmer, until standards and advice were made available through the creation of the Wisconsin Dairymen's Association in 1872, under the leadership of future governor William D. Hoard.

Second only to farming in the postwar economy was the lumber industry, accounting for 30 percent of industrial production and nearly 45 percent of industrial employment by 1870, the year Frederick Weyerhaeuser established the Mississippi River Logging Company, beginning a syndicate that would eventually stretch into the Pacific Northwest. Lumber giants of Wisconsin included Isaac Stephenson (who would bankroll many of Bob La Follette's early political efforts) and Philetus Sawyer. With very few exceptions, no thought was given to issues of forest preservation or even conservation. Instead the lumber and railroad corporate leaders combined to dominate the state legislature, guaranteeing themselves preferential treatment. The results were twofold: deforestation and an increase in politicians who increasingly served special interests rather than the state's general population.[12]

Despite the honorable war records of a number of Native American volunteers, the federal government was quick to grant sales of Native American pine lands to lumber companies. Wisconsin timber king Philetus Sawyer, like many a business leader of this time, enjoyed the virtual absence of the kind of conflict-of-interest laws in place today, and as a United States congressman in 1870, he obtained an act for the sale of part of the pine lands of Wisconsin's Menominee. While the Menominee retained sufficient pine lands to provide for themselves, other Native Americans, in Wisconsin and across the nation, were not so fortunate.[13]

Along with the growth of farming and lumber, the construction of new railroad track funded by federal land grants brought a corresponding growth in manufacturing. Even with federal aid, however, Wisconsin railroad promoters required additional capital, which they sought among the various local governments as well as Eastern financiers. The distribution of wealth in Wisconsin remained uneven. In 1866, when the land office made available to the public the last big federal land tract, over two-thirds went to capitalists outside the state. Potential homesteaders were often too poor to pay the $10 filing fee. The sum of all these various social, political, and economic changes ensured that the postwar period would by no means be serene and set the stage for a host of urban and industrial problems that Robert La Follette would later confront. There was, however, peace — real peace — at long last. The civil war within the Saxton–La Follette household, however, raged on.

With his brother William gone, Bob became the recipient of most of his stepfather's whippings. Nevertheless, the boy's involvement in mischief and pranks intensified. Bob's greatest animosity toward Saxton resulted not from the physical punishments but from the psychological ones. Saxton, faced with a stepson dedicated to revering the relatively youthful, successful man who had been married to his wife, made a daily ritual of preaching about the agonies of eternal hellfire and damnation for those who had died unbaptized and unrepentant. According to his wife's account, these indictments that his idealized father was burning in agony "created a passionate resentment and anguish which the young boy fought out alone in long, wakeful hours of the night." Bob's spirit "revolted at the thought. The desire was strong for a Hereafter where he might know his father." Saxton's badgering reveals an immensely significant aspect of Bob's personal beliefs that ruled a great many of his actions throughout his lifetime, affecting both personal and professional decisions. For, though his attitude toward organized religion always remained generally negative (not surprisingly, "he resented any religious teaching that closed the gates of Heaven to so just and upright a man as he knew his father to be"), Robert La Follette was indeed a religious man.[14] He believed fervently that the soul lived on after the body's death, that the good were rewarded and lived for eternity in heaven. He copied into a notebook, "There the wicked cease from troubling and there the weary be at rest" (Job 3:17) and many other Bible verses describing the briefness of life and the rewards of eternity. In short, denied the opportunity to know his father in life, La Follette's religious beliefs allowed for such a possibility in the afterlife. Accordingly, he believed that his own life must be led in such a way as to merit both entry into heaven and his father's long-sought approval.[15]

Whatever comfort his religious beliefs provided, his immediate concerns were far less soothing. Torn between his loyalty to his mother (in addition to the specter of being separated from her as William had been) and his resentment of his stepfather's abhorrent charges, Bob showed defiance toward Saxton's rigidity but never outright rebellion. Bob's determination to remain loyal to his idealized father, coupled with the resentment he harbored toward his stepfather, led him to reject Saxton within the limits of the situation. As a newcomer to Argyle, he was occasionally called "Saxton," to which his immediate response was a curt "My name is La Follette." As an adult, he told deprecating stories about his stepfather within the family and mimicked conversations between customers and the very deaf old man, making him appear impotent and foolish. But never, as a child or as an adult, did Bob openly express his wrathful indignation toward his stepfather, nor his hurt over his mother's actions. He did, however, omit completely any references even to Saxton's existence in his autobiography and in the authorized biography by Lincoln Steffens for *McClure's* magazine.[16]

During his college years, Bob, at the urging of Lawrence Barrett, the tragedian, made an in-depth examination of *Hamlet*. La Follette's analysis, "The World's Greatest Tragedy," was written after an initial year's study and was an oft-requested lecture throughout his entire career. Bob defended the character of Hamlet against those critics who conceived the prince as paralyzed into inertia by his propensity to think instead of act. Identifying strongly with Hamlet, Bob revealed much about himself and his feelings toward both his mother and his father: "When he first comes upon the scene, Prince Hamlet is suffering *anguish of mind*. . . . This noble, high souled youth, whose love for father and mother *passes almost into idolatry*, is at once overwhelmed with *grief* for the one and shame for the other . . . Hamlet, *proud, sensitive, refined, affectionate*, . . . is, *without warning, confronted* with this *wicked marriage*, and consumed with mortification because of his mother's conduct. He is shocked, benumbed, appalled. Every hour adds to his torture." "Alas!" La Follette exclaimed passionately, "Have the critics read these pages with closed eyes? Can anyone fail to see that, from the moment Hamlet knows the revolting truth respecting his mother, his relation to his whole environment, his attitude to everything and to every one around him, is changed? . . . Not only by the promptings of his own heart, his natural affection for his own mother, was Hamlet bound to guard and protect her good name, but he had ever before him, as a beautiful and holy memory, the love of his father for her." The ghost of Hamlet's father had commanded, "If thou didst ever thy dear father love,—Revenge his foul and most unnatural murder," but the spirit also urged Hamlet to "Taint not thy mind, nor let thy soul contrive, against thy mother aught." Like Hamlet, Bob was faced with a quandary as to how to resolve his conflicting feelings

concerning his parents. His "saintly" father deserted him early, leaving an impossible command as his legacy. His mother had twice rejected loyalty to his idealized father for other men and had been instrumental in burdening Bob with his father's directive that he be revered. Moreover, upon her marriage to Saxton, Mary withdrew much of the attention she had hitherto lavished on her youngest child.[17]

No longer the central focus of his mother's energies, Bob sought approval elsewhere. He entertained customers in Saxton's store by performing atop crates (he was a fine dancer) and giving recitations in local dialects at school picnics. Such activities did not keep him out of mischief, however. He confided to his mother that feigning unconsciousness was an effective means of cutting short his schoolmaster's violent beatings. The admiration of his classmates was worth more to him than good marks or praise from the teacher; worth even physical pain. Bob's antics earned him the approval of Charlie Pullen and Perry Wilder, both three years older than himself. The trio was involved in a variety of pranks. They once joined some other boys in prying loose a large cake of ice and were carried several miles down the Pecatonica River, missing Sunday School in the process. Bob said later that "his stepfather made it as hot for him when he got home as it had been cold on the ice raft."[18]

Bob had a propensity for missing Sunday School. He feigned illness often and used the time alone in the house to train his colt "Gipsy" to go up and down the stairs. On one occasion, he and his friends decided to raise money by putting on a show in the barn. Bob painted the entire body of one of his friends with indigo and was exhibiting him in a cage as a wild man when Saxton broke up this entertainment with his whip. Bob's various "crimes" do not appear to have been malicious, but they were certainly a major source of anger and outrage for an aged and rigid disciplinarian like Saxton. The old man was not blind to his stepson's finer qualities, however. He once remarked to his wife, "Mary, he will either turn out to be a very wonderful man or a very bad one. I haven't made up my mind which."[19]

Bob's childhood friendships were interrupted when the Saxton household moved in 1866. The family's assets had dwindled, despite the $800 obtained that same year from the sale of some of the La Follette farmland designated to provide for the children's maintenance and education. From the beginning of his marriage to Mary La Follette, John Saxton maintained that selling the La Follette property promoted the heirs' best interest. When denied permission to sell the land, he complained about property taxes and the cost of improvements. General George E. Bryant, who later became "political godfather" to Bob, allowed the sale which had been authorized by another judge two years before but had been delayed by the Civil War. Bryant made it clear, however, that he would allow no further sales, for the Primrose farm was capable of supporting the family.[20]

Unlike most of the northeastern states, Wisconsin suffered no appreciable business decline immediately following the war, yet Saxton continued to lose money in Argyle. Hoping a change of scene would change their luck, the family moved to Fayette, a small nearby town, where Saxton started a new store. There his personal financial difficulties were compounded, as Wisconsin and its neighboring states slid, in 1867, into a four-year slump. The region enjoyed a respite in 1871, brought to an abrupt end by the Panic (as depressions were called then) of 1873. Like all Wisconsin merchants, Saxton suffered from the effects of wide-scale shortages of both money and credit. Despite the downward spiral of the family's finances, however, the children continued to attend private school in Fayette, maintaining their position in the elite class among Wisconsin citizens. John Saxton's position within that class, however, was becoming increasingly precarious.

After spending a year trying to make a success of his Fayette store, Saxton moved the family back to Argyle in 1867. But living in town proved to be too expensive for the failing shopkeeper, so it was determined that the family would return to the farm in order to economize. Bob, then thirteen, was allowed to remain in Argyle, where education was superior to Primrose and where, although separated from his mother, he was free from the haunting taunts of his stepfather. For two years he lived with family friends and contributed to his own support by barbering in the local hotel, a logical occupation for one so attentive to physical appearance. This lifestyle continued until Bob was discovered drunk one Saturday night by his teacher and sent back to his mother. He found conditions at home dramatically changed, for Saxton had become quite feeble, and Bob's brother William had returned to Primrose with his new wife and son to assume direction of the farm.

As an invalid, Saxton no longer had the power to torment Bob with visions of his father's tortures in hell, so Bob remained on the farm, taking over as head after William moved his family west. Saxton's final decline was a lengthy one and he required Mary's almost constant attention. His eyes eventually failed and it was stepdaughter Jo's task to read to him from the Bible. He was very fond of Jo, who had caused him none of the trouble her brothers had. John Saxton died in November 1872 at the age of eighty. Bob La Follette was then seventeen and, like his state — indeed, his nation — about to embark on yet another journey of great transition.

# 3: THE UNIVERSITY YEARS
## TRAINING FOR THE DUTIES OF CITIZENSHIP

lthough La Follette's late teen years were spent working the family's Primrose farm, he frequently made the twenty-four-mile trip into Madison to market surplus produce. He and other farmers would spend the night at the Gorham House, better known as the Spring Hotel, a few miles out of town. There, and at the produce markets of Madison, La Follette listened to discussions and debates. Years later he told his wife that on those trips he felt the political issues of the day "swirling around him, the effect of which always stayed with him."[1]

Although Wisconsin remained Republican throughout the Reconstruction years, the party's unity was seriously undermined. The large numbers of Germans leaving the party (some to form the Liberal Republicans) were joined by farmers and businessmen of all ethnic backgrounds, angered by the decline of their individual power and wealth in the face of increasingly large corporations and monopolies. In Wisconsin, as in other states, much of the protest centered on the railroads. Railroad stock was increasingly "watered," meaning that it was distributed in excess of the real value of its assets. "All the market will bear" storage and transportation fees gouged farmers (primarily wheat growers) as well as wheat merchants. Rates varied enormously and were complicated by secret, privately negotiated rebates that further disadvantaged small, independent customers, especially farmers, and frequently resulted in ruthless rate wars. The Wisconsin legislature entertained a variety of proposed remedies between the end of the Civil War and 1873, but the only two to achieve passage did little to change the overall situation. (The 1867 law, for example, prevented the consolidation of two specific railroads but had no impact on the pooling arrangement subsequently established by those same two companies.) Protest against "politics as usual" mounted steadily.

In 1873, Wisconsin Grangers, members of the state branch of the national organization of farmers, demanded railroad regulation and an end to corruption in government. An organization known as the Reform Party — comprised of Grangers, Liberal Republicans, and Democrats — nominated its own slate of candidates, including Grange organizer William R. Taylor for governor. Railroad companies, cited by both parties as a major villain, were more fearful of Governor C. C. Washburn's reform agenda than Taylor's. Washburn denounced the unwritten "supreme law of railway managers" and advocated a nationalized telegraph, raising the fear of interference throughout the business community. Business and liquor interests joined in supporting the Reformers, who won not only the governor's chair but their entire state ticket. Young Bob La Follette applauded this "first powerful revolt in Wisconsin" and would later trace the genesis of the Progressive movement back to the Grangers.[2]

In early 1873, Wisconsin, like the rest of the nation, was at a crossroads. Its growth, from a relatively sleepy collection of farming communities into a dynamic and diverse state, was accelerating rapidly. The nearly universal approval of such growth as progress was somewhat tainted, however, by a certain uneasiness about the feasibility of an equitable distribution of power and wealth, no matter the affiliations of its political leadership. Could a nation, a state, a city, even a village, enjoy the benefits of the rise of big business and the wealth generated thereby and still retain the rights, freedoms, and elements of personal control enjoyed by its citizens in the past? At least one prominent Wisconsin politician, Edward G. Ryan, soon to become the state's chief justice, answered with a resounding "No!" Speaking in June 1873 in the state's capitol to the graduating class of the University of Wisconsin, Ryan prophesied, "There is looming up a new and dark power," consisting of "vast corporate combinations of unexampled capital." Money, Ryan warned, was "taking the field as an organized power" for the first time in politics, and as a political influence, it was "essentially corrupt . . . unscrupulous, arrogant, and overbearing." Ryan's ringing words would later be repeated in a great many speeches by one impressionable member of his audience, eighteen-year-old Bob La Follette, in town to ascertain the requirements to enter the state university. Ryan railed in particular against the big railroad companies of Wisconsin, charging that they were already threatening the prosperity of the state. He presented his youthful listeners with a portrait of conditions that raised not only political and economic issues but moral ones: "The question will arise and arise in your day . . . which shall rule — wealth or man; which shall lead — money or intellect; who shall fill public stations — educated and patriotic freemen, or the feudal serfs of corporate capital?"[3]

Ryan's emotion-laden speech appealed to young Bob La Follette's propensity toward righteousness. His immediate course of action does not, however, necessarily uphold his wife's later assertion that this stirring speech "did more than even Bob himself realized to shape his political future." Belle La Follette was sure that "his mind was made up that when the time came he would do his part to preserve the fundamental principle of justice and equality." At the time, however, Bob La Follette announced no particular goal beyond achieving his degree at the University of Wisconsin.[4]

The Constitution of 1848 made Wisconsin the eleventh state to found a public university, one dedicated to serving not just the intellectual elite but all citizens capable of benefiting from its offerings. Its curriculum served citizens' scholarly, professional, and practical needs. The university grew in size and prestige throughout the 1870s. Its student body was drawn primarily from nearby prosperous Dane County, making it La Follette's logical choice. The La Follettes' economic situation remained comparatively sound during the 1870s, despite the financial crisis that gripped the nation during that decade. Already rocked by scandals including the revelation in early 1873 of the Credit Mobilier (a construction company, organized to build the Union Pacific Railroad, that had bribed congressmen with stocks in return for land grant legislation), public confidence sank even lower that same year when the runaway escalation of railroad growth, unregulated by even the simple laws of supply and demand, came to a screeching halt, putting into motion the Panic of 1873. Dane County's farmlands, however, continued to be productive, and its proximity to the markets of Madison rendered its farmers, unlike their further flung counterparts, free from crippling railroad fees. The fact that a farming family would even consider sending its male head to school (for Bob had been in charge since his brother William's departure and Saxton's illness) despite awareness that the nation was entering a major depression reveals something of its relative wealth, as well as its dedication to education. Bowed but not broken by the financial losses accrued during her marriage to John Saxton, Mary Saxton once again rented the farm to her son-in-law Dean Eastman and moved to a house at 1224 Merry Street in Madison to advance her son Bob's education.[5]

In various accounts of his life, La Follette made much of the sacrifices he endured to procure his education at the University of Wisconsin at Madison. He claimed that he had to earn money enough to support himself, his sister, and his widowed mother. La Follette did, in fact, like many of his fellow students, work his way through college and law school. During his sophomore year, La Follette taught some classes at the George School in Madison. It was there that he met Robert G. Siebecker, his future law partner and his sister Jo's future husband. He also taught in the town of Burke, traveling the journey of five miles in each direction on his beloved horse, Gipsy. He also barbered, peddled books, and published the school newspaper. He was not, however, the sole means of support for his mother and sister. The Panic of 1873 lowered the already depressed farm prices, but the sale of an eighty-acre plot of the family farm to Dean Eastman for $760 substantially supplemented the rental income, particularly during their first years in Madison.

In addition, Mary and Jo cooked for a boys' club for a time and later took in boarders.[6]

This myth of a totally dependent family is an early example of La Follette's willingness to exaggerate, alter, or even fabricate circumstances that made him appear triumphant in the face of staggering adversity. Some of these flights from reality seem to have stemmed from wishful fantasies entertained for so long that La Follette "forgot" what was really true. Often he saw adversity, opposition, or persecution coming from quarters where little or none existed. Certainly La Follette worked hard to ensure his education, but it came as a result of family solidarity and sacrifice as well as individual effort.

Despite his attendance at a private school, La Follette, like many of his country neighbors, was still unable to qualify academically for immediate entrance into the University of Wisconsin. He spent the term of 1873–74 attending the Wisconsin Classical and Commercial Academy, a college preparatory school. This enabled him to enroll in the subfreshman preparatory class of the university in the fall of 1874, but he did not begin the actual four-year university program until 1875. The university's total enrollment that year was 345, its members part of the very elite group of the less than 27,000 students enrolled in four-year colleges in the United States.[7]

The University of Wisconsin gained national recognition and respect in the 1890s in large part due to two exceptional faculty members, economist Richard T. Ely and elocution instructor cum historian Frederick Jackson Turner, whose 1893 American Historical Association paper, "The Significance of the Frontier in American History," continues to spark controversy today. During La Follette's undergraduate years, however, the faculty was generally mediocre, as a low level of prestige and even lower salaries failed to attract top scholars. Due to the smallness of the faculty, professors were hired for their mastery of general knowledge of a subject rather than their development of a specialized subfield. They enjoyed little academic freedom: they were seldom consulted about new appointments; they could be reprimanded for venturing opinions, even privately, on controversial matters; and the regents had final approval of courses and texts.[8]

The university nevertheless had much to offer. La Follette was exposed to two exceptional influences as an undergraduate. One was William F. Allen, a historian whose work frequently appeared in the progressive periodical *The Nation*. The leading source of progressive ideas at the university, Allen was a favorite among students, including Belle Case, La Follette's future wife, who enjoyed the professor's easy, friendly manner and ability to present history in relation to the present. The other, who influenced La Follette far more profoundly, was the formal and dignified university president, John Bascom.[9]

Student reaction to Bascom varied dramatically. According to one, most students found the president cold and treated him more with deference than devotion, but another asserts that the students were more favorably impressed. Journalist French Strother concurred with the latter, hailing Bascom as having "the vision of an Isaiah and the persuasive tongue of a David." Bob La Follette found in Bascom an approving father figure. Bascom, said La Follette, was "the guiding spirit of my time." When they first met, Bascom was only a few years younger than La Follette's father would have been and shared many of Josiah La Follette's physical characteristics, including a rather imposing beard. As a philosopher, he dedicated much of his professional life to narrowing the conflict between science and religion. Bascom was, in La Follette's words, "the embodiment of moral force and moral enthusiasm," qualities La Follette had been assured his father had also possessed. Belle Case reacted somewhat differently: in her view, Bascom "stressed the spiritual side of life but was ever mindful of its inseparable relationship to the everyday world. Progressive in spirit, uncompromising with what he believed to be wrong, Dr. Bascom urged us to think and reason for ourselves and to translate our convictions into action. Especially did he emphasize the obligations of citizenship. Again and again he would tell us what we owed the State and impress upon us our duty to serve the State in return. [M]y understanding of what President Bascom was trying to implant seems to have been rather vague and general; while to Bob it was concrete truth, the living gospel, whose application was as plain as a pikestaff." Bascom promoted labor associations, economic cooperation, and the equitable distribution of wealth. A tireless prohibitionist, Bascom also championed women's rights, and social and economic justice, including public control of wealth in the public interest.[10]

Bascom's thirteen years as university president were marked by much controversy and countless quarrels with the Board of Regents over university policies concerning governance and finance, for he refused to respect the authority of the regents. He contended that the board was dominated by men with little understanding of university problems who were concerned primarily with promoting their own business and political interests. In short, Bascom's moral righteousness, in his mind anyway, superseded any merely legal rights when it came to university governance. His longstanding feud with political boss Elisha Keyes, whose 1877 appointment to the Board of Regents he bitterly opposed, culminated in Bascom's resignation from the university in 1886. Keyes, fumed Bascom, was "unscrupulous in small things, prodigal in large things, and negligent and dilatory in all things." This feud with Keyes would be resumed, albeit under different circumstances, by Bascom's protégé, Bob La Follette. The very first skirmish between Keyes and his future political foe came in 1885. Bascom had complained that some elms, purchased by the university from Keyes's nursery at a very high price, had been substandard in both quality and quantity. Confronted with the charges, Keyes quietly had the dead trees replaced and added some additional ones for good measure. Intent on exposing this cover-up, Bascom asked alumnus La Follette to examine the trees in question. La Follette's evaluation confirmed Bascom's suspicions, doing little to endear either of them to the "Boss."[11]

Throughout their long, acrimonious relationship, Bascom's moral idealism and certainty in his own righteousness made the president appear pompous to those who congratulated Keyes for his opposition to "the pretentious and egotistical supernumary of the University." But to Bob La Follette, the president's insistence upon viewing his opposition to the regents as "a necessary fight between good and evil" rendered Bascom's approval all the more desirable. John Bascom was one of the first university presidents to grasp many of the new social problems of the nation's nascent industrialization and urbanization. He was a leading pioneer in the development of the Social Gospel, whose proponents, primarily members of the middle class, concerned themselves with the betterment of the material as well as spiritual conditions of the poor. Social and economic issues were as central as religious ones to proponents of the Social Gospel. Bascom's weekly sermons on these and other topics impressed Bob La Follette enormously. Although they were to differ politically over the years, Bascom and La Follette always shared a great fondness and respected each other's willingness to think independently and act upon conviction. Bascom's teachings, personal interest, and much craved approval bolstered the young scholar and contributed to his resolve to "do right" and to serve the public.[12]

In his autobiography, a grateful La Follette recorded, "I owe what I am and what I have done largely to the inspiration I received while [at the university]." He took pride throughout his political career in the support he received from the university, and when it was not forthcoming, as was the case during his opposition to the entry of the United States into World War I, he was devastated. In a 1923 statement that was as much a tribute to Bascom as it was an indictment of Charles Van Hise, who presided over the University of Wisconsin during the war period, La Follette asserted that *"more than all else,* . . . [a university president] should be a *great moral and spiritual power,* strong enough to make that *the dominant influence in the university over which he presides.*" La Follette kept unusually extended personal acquaintance with students and alumni after his college days and received criticism for using patronage to keep a number of them supplied with jobs. While he was governor, La Follette's policies were so closely tied to the university that an article appeared in *World's Work* entitled, "A University That Runs a State." This close link was facilitated by the state's decision to place its university in the capital, rather than in an outlying town or city. La Follette's dedication to the university extended into the area of personal finance. Even when strapped for cash, a virtually perpetual state in their household, the La Follettes were loyal alumni who contributed privately to the university. Following his death, a resolution adopted unanimously by the alumni association proclaimed him the university's most able, devoted champion and loving, loyal son.[13]

The depth of La Follette's internalization of Bascom's views on the true goal of a university education were echoed in 1901 when La Follette remarked to the alumni: "I would not disparage scholarship, but venture to say, that before all things, the University owes it to the State to give it good citizens — men and women who will fight the battles of the state, against all combinations of evil. [T]he student . . . is primarily training for the duties of citizenship; and . . . when he goes out, whatever may be his occupation or profession, it should be as one who has enlisted for life in the service of the state." It is not surprising that La Follette emphasized the importance of citizenship over scholarship, not just because it reinforced Bascom's views, but also because it was one way of rationalizing his own very poor academic record. Except for the philosophy and psychology courses he took from Bascom in his senior year, La Follette appeared to have been a lazy and disinterested student. The rote recitations that were the order of the day, only occasionally augmented by lectures, were a particular trial to him and served to highlight his inability or unwillingness to learn. A fellow student recalled that La Follette would rise to recite but could only shake his head negatively in answer to the questions. Another wrote: "La Follette is a mystery to me. I don't know whether he has solid talent or not. If one only heard his recitations, he would conclude that he was a wooden head. He is at the tail of his class. Many and many a time I have explained the simplest principles of chemistry to him. It seemed as though he could not comprehend it." La Follette's poor classroom performance remained consistent throughout all four years at the university, and half of the faculty voted not to graduate him in 1879. John Bascom cast the tie-breaking vote in La Follette's favor, so enraging certain faculty members that this method of resolving questions of graduation qualification was immediately terminated.[14]

Faced with a choice between Ancient Classical, Modern Classical, or Scientific courses of study, La Follette selected Scientific, as had most of his fellow classmates, but he reserved his real enthusiasm for the more social aspects of university life. La Follette's speeches about the duties of citizenship might suggest he was too immersed in humanitarian matters to be bothered with mere academic exercises or leisure activities. In truth, he kept himself occupied with a whole host of activities, some more civic-minded than others. One of the leading pranksters on campus, La Follette engineered many escapades upon which he later looked back with much fondness. While he enjoyed tearing up sidewalks, playing cards in chapel (a flagrant show of disrespect for his stepfather's values), and stealing grapes from the experimental farm or croquet sets from the Ladies' Hall, his favorite memory was of the time he and his friends "borrowed" a domestic animal from a nearby farm and deposited it on the balcony of University Hall. Such exploits were publicized in the *University Press*. La Follette was remembered as the "chairman of the undergraduate greeters" and "quite a leader," and a "live wire." He also enjoyed sailing, dancing, wrestling, and acting, but he saved his greatest energies for oratory.[15]

La Follette without oratory is like Beethoven without music. La Follette's ability to vividly express ideas, to persuade and electrify audiences, is at the essence of not just his political success but his very being. In a time when there were no "sound bites" but rather entire speeches to be heard and evaluated, Bob La Follette excelled in reaching and holding audiences. Throughout his life his speeches provoked both adulation and controversy, but they were rarely met with indifference. He was an extraordinary speaker who could expertly gauge his audiences' desire to be entertained, educated, challenged, provoked, soothed, and/or inspired.[16]

La Follette's natural talents in public speaking, evident even in childhood, were appreciated and lovingly cultivated during his college years. Carl R. Burgchardt's "rhetorical biography" of La Follette notes, "La Follette attended college at a time when an education in oratory possessed a level of importance that it has lost today." Oratory was considered the domain of the best and brightest students and La Follette's prize-winning speeches in college more than compensated for his lackluster academic performance in other areas. His oratorical successes brought him much public acclaim, providing invaluable name recognition that supplied him with a springboard into political office.[17]

Although not much of a debater, La Follette was "the feature of every [rhetorical] program," at the Wisconsin Academy and, as "a brilliant elocutionist and declaimer," he was quickly welcomed into the prestigious Athena Literary Society while still a freshman at the University. That same

*The speaking style La Follette honed while an undergraduate served as the foundation for his lifelong legendary ability to captivate a crowd. (Image Hunters/Pieri & Spring Productions)*

year he mounted a successful protest against fraternity selection of candidates for intercollegiate speech competitions, resulting in more equitable representation of the student body. Elected each year as the society's spokesman at various functions, he also served on a large number of committees. La Follette devoted a great deal of his time to polishing his oratory skills, but he was absent at least as often as the average society member: about 30 percent of the time. He often found himself spread thin between schoolwork, social activities, oratory, and various income-producing occupations.[18]

La Follette tried his hand at a number of money-making activities before focusing on the unofficial school newspaper. According to the two-volume University history, "except for the literary societies and the joint debate, no extracurricular activity in the intellectual sphere was so important in undergraduate life as collegiate journalism." Unlike most university newspapers today, college papers at that time were frequently privately owned. At the end of his freshman year La Follette and another student paid $800 for the paper. La Follette's half was borrowed from a local lawyer and backed with a note signed by Mary Saxton. La Follette not only served as publisher and editor, he wrote copy, set the type, used his winning oratory to persuade local businesses to advertise in the pages of the *University Press*, and sold subscriptions. Many qualities La Follette exhibited in publishing the paper were to reappear throughout his life. He and his partner maintained a freshman at low wages to help with the workload, but La Follette's insistence on doing everything else himself proved both a blessing and a curse. Certainly his personal touch in attracting advertisers was desirable, but his insistence on typesetting netted many complaints.[19]

La Follette's articles and editorials not only celebrated local pranks and other challenges to authority but popularized the tradition of the self-made person. Despite his advantages, La Follette liked to consider himself a member of that revered group and frequently eulogized such people within his pages. The *University Press* condemned the indigents who populated the Wisconsin countryside after the Panic of 1873 had thrown them out of work, concluding, "Let these heartless wanderers whose oaths taint the purity of the country air, claiming that the world owes them a living, be placed at such work and in such confinement that they will soon learn to follow a regular employment." The American dream of equal opportunity and the notion that struggling to improve oneself lent integrity and honor very much appealed to La Follette.[20]

His venture into the newspaper business was a lucrative one, netting La Follette about $700 a year and eventually allowing him to repay his initial loan and buy out his partner. This self-made success may have inspired La Follette's investments in a variety of enterprises during his lifetime, including a horse ranch, an apartment house, a mining company, and a telephone company. Certainly it was a major motivating factor in the founding of *La Follette's Magazine* some thirty years later. Unfortunately, few of these business ventures were as successful as the original. The *University Press* contributed to the beginning of another lifelong trend: long periods of intense, uninterrupted work, followed by physical and/or emotional collapse. La Follette said of the years immediately subsequent to his university training: "Under the strain of all these [*University Press–*]related tasks, added to my regular college work, my health, naturally robust, gave way, and for four or five years I went down under the load at the end of every term of court."[21]

When not busy with the *University Press*, La Follette, working hard to develop his dramatic flair, discovered within himself a fine sense of timing and became increasingly aware of his ability to move audiences. Like many of his generation, he idolized Robert G. Ingersoll, a lawyer and exponent of agnosticism. La Follette especially admired Ingersoll's powerful, dramatic style. Ingersoll liberated his mind, La Follette claimed, because of the great speaker's dedication to freedom: "[Ingersoll] wanted the shackles off everywhere." Over the years La Follette and Ingersoll (and others as well) would share a great many themes within their speeches, including the superiority of the Republican party and, more importantly, "a spirit of reform and sense of moral earnestness."[22]

La Follette's speaking abilities were so well received on campus that he and four fellow Athenians performed in surrounding villages during the summer between their junior and senior years. After the quartet sang, La Follette gave dialect readings and finished the show with a hair raising rendition of *The Raven*. "He put more in it than Poe ever did," commented one of his fellow performers. According to a local editor, "Such powers of elocution and action . . . would do credit to a professional." It made for an enjoyable summer and even netted the group a small profit.[23]

La Follette's greatest collegiate triumph occurred in May 1879 at the Interstate Oratorical Contest in Iowa City, Iowa. His selection as the university's delegate to the preliminary competitions came as a surprise to virtually no one, except possibly La Follette himself. Despite unanimous assurances that he would be elected, La Follette went door to door on campus urging students to vote for him. This apparent unwillingness to recognize sure victory plagued La Follette throughout his political career. Although such extreme diligence was occasionally the difference between triumph and defeat, too often La Follette spent crucial time, money, and energy needlessly.

Once elected the University's delegate, La Follette devoted endless hours to his speech, a character analysis of *Othello*'s Iago. He consulted anyone and everyone he thought might be able to offer constructive criticism. Then, "having written and remodeled his oration until every sentence was an artistic period containing a complete thought, . . . La Follette's task was only partly done. He began . . . to put upon its rehearsal and delivery the same laborious work and extreme painstaking which had evolved the thought. Naturally a fine speaker, he cultivated his talent in that direction until he surprised his most ardent friends." The period of preparation for the contest was one of the very few times in his life La Follette had "enough" time to work on his speech, causing his wife to comment later that she often thought of "the joy it must have given him, for his disposition was to perfect and polish whatever he wrote, and he was always reluctant to let a manuscript leave his hands." La Follette won both semifinal competitions, and his performance in the finals merited him first place, attracting the approving attention of newspapers in several states.[24]

Of all Shakespeare's villains, *Othello*'s Iago is arguably the most complete and sadistic. His treacherous scheme to turn the love between the Moor of Venice and his beautiful wife into mistrust ultimately ends in death for all three. La Follette argued that Iago tried to compensate for his lack of emotional feeling with intellectual acuteness, resulting in character deformity. La Follette stressed the importance of emotion, deprecating pure intellect. On one level, given La Follette's low academic marks and his zest for social activities, this speech vindicates his university record as he denounced Iago, who "has no feeling, no sympathy, no affection, no fear. He is the cold passion of intellect whose icy touch chills the warm life in all its reaches. . . . He not only knows more than he feels; he knows everything, feels nothing. . . . Why do we follow his intricate windings with such intense interest? Why do we tolerate him? We find the answer in his great intellect. This is the core of his character — abstract intellectuality united to volitional force, devoid of all morality, divorced from all feeling. He is hardly human, yet he sounds humanity like a philosopher. He is wanting in ethical parts, yet he makes the nicest moral distinctions. . . . He does not care to justify himself except as an intellectual satisfaction. . . . [He is] thoroughly passionless, coldly intellectual."[25]

The tragedy of *Othello* was, in La Follette's view, not the human failings of Othello and Desdemona, but the evil of Iago, "a character without a conscience." This early speech contains several of La Follette's most deep-seated oratorical traits, most notably what has been termed the "melodramatic scenario," in which the villain gradually snares unsuspecting innocent victims. Such vivid representations of complex phenomena reduced to "good" and "evil" are hallmarks of later La Follette speeches on topics ranging from oleomargarine to political machines to railroads. The melodramatic scenario has been termed "an integral part of La Follette's total rhetorical personality — a personality that refused to compromise, that was concerned with loss of innocence and virtue, that was captivated with the contempt of the 'evil principle,' and that believed constant vigilance was required against unseen but menacing forces." La Follette used such colorful and easy-to-understand scenarios to influence audiences throughout his career. By alerting his previously unaware listeners to danger and convincing them of its magnitude, he established the need for his proposed immediate, morally unambiguous reform or action.[26]

La Follette's "Iago" was greeted with great enthusiasm by the press, who hailed it "a masterly dissection of the character of Iago," and "a remarkable analysis." More than one reviewer praised La Follette's thoroughness, and the *Madison Democrat* made note of the impressive length of the speech. Throughout his lifelong speaking career, La Follette's drive to be thorough was rarely supplemented with judicious editing. His speeches were often as long as four hours, and the amount of water he consumed while speaking earned him the reputation along the chautauqua circuit (a traveling program that usually included lectures, debates, and concerts) as a "four-pitcher man." He preferred to present all possible supporting evidence, make his point, and then hammer it home again and again, disliking to omit even the smallest shred of substantiating material, no matter how convincing his case might already be. His insistence on thoroughness would be the bane of many political reporters as he disdained virtually all interviews or questions from the press in favor of formal statements. La Follette wanted to be absolutely unimpeachable and as confident as possible that his audience would accept his views. He willingly sacrificed economy for activity, and often substituted superfluous detail for cohesive arguments. Moreover, he sometimes resorted even to distortion of the information he presented.[27]

La Follette's speech in Iowa City earned him more unequivocal approval than any other in his life. Feted as the best orator of the 10,000 university students of the six midwestern states, La Follette found his train home met by almost the entire Madison student body, who toted him around the city on their shoulders to the cries of "The Little Lion of the Northwest." They eventually deposited him at his home, where "the climax of the day of triumph awaited him — the happiness and pride of his spirited little mother." At a reception held in his honor in the Assembly chamber of the state capitol, a number of influential individuals helped to celebrate his victory, including Boss Keyes and General George B. Smith. The latter announced, "[La Follette] has honored his associates in the university, he has honored the institution to which he belongs; he has honored the State of Wisconsin; and above all, and many times more important than all else, he has honored his widowed mother."[28]

La Follette's oratorical triumph brought him more than even the adulation of others and the much desired approval of his mother. The political significance of his victory at Iowa City is also noteworthy. In those pre-radio, pre-television times, oratory vied with newspapers as the basic form of political communication, and La Follette's interstate victory merited him invaluable publicity. The triumph of "Iago" merited more press than the visit of President Rutherford B. Hayes to Madison at about the same time. Understandably, La Follette was reluctant to let the memory of his great success fade. For many years after his graduation he spent hours coaching university students for subsequent competitions, even when the pressure of his own work was intense. In writing letters of recommendation for a young

*The "Little Lion of the Northwest": Bob La Follette upon his contested graduation from the University of Wisconsin in 1879. (State Historical Society of Wisconsin WHi[X313]2497)*

University of Wisconsin Law School graduate, La Follette mentioned in one sentence the subject's "fine discriminating mind" and "sterling character" and spent the balance of the letter describing the young man's success at the interstate speech contest. Clearly, this alone was sufficient evidence that the new attorney in question was, in La Follette's estimation, highly desirable.

The overwhelming approval generated by La Follette's dramatic performance led him to seriously consider an acting career. Various accounts attribute his decision not to pursue a stage career to advice he received from an actor traveling through Madison shortly after La Follette's oratorical triumph. When a pamphlet reprinting the Iago speech reached John McCullough, the esteemed Shakespearean actor deemed La Follette's acting aspirations as "out of the question" because of his small size. However, a few months later, La Follette also met with famous tragedian Lawrence Barrett, who indignantly denounced McCullough's advice. A vindicated La Follette recalled, "He said that Mr. [Edwin] Booth was not more than half an inch taller than I; that as far as the physical side was concerned there was no bar to my entering on the stage career." According to an excerpt from La Follette's 1879 diary, discovered in 1934 in a volume of Shakespeare's plays, the actor continued: "You are young & your years are bright with promise. You have done a great service to the dramatic profession besides the addition in a literary way, your piece will greatly aid actors for all time."[29]

It is not surprising that La Follette was attracted to a career in drama. He retained, both as attorney and statesman, a heightened sense of drama that permeated his speeches and actions. He was known for his exaggerated gestures and movements and for his sweeping, impassioned statements. Such theatrics left him the object of much derision on the part of many who doubted his sincerity, but it also won him an intensely enthusiastic and faithful following. La Follette's true greatness as a speaker is questionable, considering his penchant for lengthy, unnecessarily detailed speeches, but his persuasive use of incontrovertible facts, enlivened by his dramatic flair and histrionic performances, mesmerized many, particularly entertainment hungry rural audiences. Under the headline, "La Follette Charms Crowds," the *Bloomington (Ind.) Daily Bulletin* concluded, "Much has been printed of this man La Follette, but to gather the full force of the passion with which he is fighting the battle of the people and the country one must touch shoulders with the man, must gaze into his fearless eye, must listen to his eloquence as it flows masterful and concise from the lips that have stirred the people from coast to coast."[30]

Although the stage may have been a temptation La Follette found hard to resist, he spent the years following his undergraduate education studying law in preparation for a career that more closely resembled that of his father's and was more likely to merit the praise of John Bascom. La Follette never detailed his reasons for rejecting acting as a profession. He may have thought it too unstable an occupation, both emotionally and financially, or his enthusiasm may have been dampened by the public's general disapproval of most actors as a "fast," rather immoral group. His speech delivered at the Junior Exhibition, "The Stage," was a historically based defense of the "great good which has been accomplished" by the theater. His audience that day may have been persuaded, but the bulk of the American public remained unconvinced. His decision was certainly influenced in part by Belle Case, the young woman who came to affect so many of the important decisions of La Follette's life.[31]

# 4: BELLE CASE LA FOLLETTE

One of the most intriguing and politically influential spouses in American history is Belle Case La Follette. Even when her husband's death brought an end to their forty-three years of married life, she remained a strong political influence. She rejected the opportunity to take her husband's virtually guaranteed senate seat in favor of their son, Robert M. La Follette Jr., and served as Bobbie's key adviser and confidant until her death in 1931. Thus the impact of her thinking and advice spanned two generations of national politics. Her obituary in the *New York Times* hailed her as "perhaps the least known, yet the most influential of all the American women who have had to do with public affairs in this country."[1]

Although the *Times* claimed that "her personality along with her work was merged in the fame of her menfolk," in fact Belle La Follette refused to support her husband unquestionably in all political efforts or to subvert her private interests to his. Instead, she played a vital role in setting rigorous standards and was quick to express concern when she disapproved of her husband's policies and actions. Bob La Follette depended enormously upon his wife's advice and counsel. Practical yet idealistic, the demanding Belle provided Bob with specific goals and ideals and, by her hard-earned approval, assured him of his significance and importance. The complex dynamics of their relationship reveal the enormous influence of this intelligent, demanding, yet at the same time retiring woman.[2]

Belle La Follette also symbolizes the great changes that affected American women as the gender prescriptions of the early to mid-nineteenth century gave way to the challenges and reforms of the twentieth. Belle's shyness and longings for the perceived security of a simple life as a housewife conflicted with her sense of duty to help others, especially her devotion to furthering women's rights. She seemed to have a foot in each century and struggled mightily with the strengths and limitations that each had to offer a woman of her position and class. Her mixed emotions over the conflicts between her personal and public aspirations may have complicated her dedication to progressivism, but rarely did they diminish her role among the myriad of women who labored tirelessly toward the betterment of society. She was, noted Senator Arthur Vandenberg (R-Michigan), "one of the rare characters in the history of motherhood and citizenship."[3]

Belle Case's forebears, predominantly Scottish and English, were among the early white settlers in Wisconsin, having migrated there from Ohio. Although most Americans still lived on farms in 1859, the year of Belle's birth, nearly a fifth were living in towns and cities. As the ranks of this more urban group swelled, their lifestyles, particularly their gender relationships, came to influence the way virtually all Americans defined woman's proper sphere, or "true womanhood." Although women were still denied the vote, a right granted to nearly all white men, they assumed a new, often more powerful and autonomous role within the home, as middle-class men were increasingly tied to the "outside" world of politics, power, business, professions, and money. This change for women was precarious and limited primarily to the urban middle class, yet its impact ultimately spread across geographic and class lines. Excluded from the male-dominated worlds of prestige and power, women enjoyed a new consciousness and value of themselves as unique contributors to society. A self-contained female world emerged as women found increasing solidarity with each other. In addition, advanced education was promoted to improve women's performance as mothers and housekeepers and to prepare them to follow their "natural" talents as teachers. A host of women's seminaries, academies, and colleges emerged in response. Middle-class women who had truly internalized the values of the "sphere" found themselves on the horns of a dilemma. Their prescribed world was wholly divorced from that of politics, business, and money. Yet to keep their domestic, feminine world safe from the evils of the masculine one, they often had no recourse but to immerse themselves into the latter — like someone who, despising the water, jumps from a boat to swim to the safety of the shore. The course from domestic to public life was a long and often convoluted one, but it was a journey a vast number of women felt they had no choice but to undertake.[4]

Although Belle Case would struggle mightily with the conflicting messages and pressures faced by women of her day, she viewed women as significant contributors to society, never as weak or ornamental. As a child in Baraboo, she idolized her grandmother Lucetta Moore Case and later admired the politically active women of previous generations. During Belle's formative years her parents devoted themselves to raising hops, while Wisconsin women seasoned in the trenches of the abolitionist movement pounced upon the growing evils of alcohol consumption. They honed their organizational skills and concentrated their forces in their temperance crusade. In 1869, leading suffrage advocates Susan B. Anthony and Elizabeth Cady Stanton came to Wisconsin for the first statewide suffrage convention and found a hotbed of temperance workers poised on the brink of adding suffrage to their agenda. The suffrage forces grew as alcohol consumption soared within Wisconsin by 30 percent following the Civil War. This increase was the result of bumper crops of hops and the establishment of hundreds of new breweries, which made beer Milwaukee's leading industry. Passage of a temperance law had little effect, and Wisconsin women mounted a widespread temperance crusade. Lavinia Goodell, who in 1874 would become the first woman in Wisconsin admitted to the bar, reported in a letter to the *Woman's Journal* entitled "Women Waking Up in Wisconsin" that those women who had held "strong prejudice" against "the principle that Woman's sphere may extend to the platform, and that she may labor for the State as well as for the family" soon found themselves "converted to . . . faith in the propriety of Woman's preaching." Moreover, several things, including the crusade against alcohol, "served to broaden and deepen thought on the subject of Woman's duties, and her relation to the community." Demands for the vote for women in Wisconsin would follow on the heels of one of the most active temperance crusades in the country. By the time Belle Case entered the University of Wisconsin in 1875, membership in the Wisconsin Women's Temperance Alliance was rising steadily, and the rhetoric of its members, whose press coverage was also growing, increasingly strayed from the narrow topic of temperance into broader issues of reform.[5]

Belle would come to admire Wisconsin's various activists and to add her own steady, calm voice to the call for a myriad of reforms to benefit women, but as she left for college, the bulk of her heroes could be found closer to home. In addition to her strong and self-sufficient grandmother, Belle Case greatly revered her own parents, Anson and Mary Nesbit Case. They were farmers who placed a high value on a university education and gladly sacrificed to ensure that their only daughter would reap the benefits of the University of Wisconsin's commitment to coeducation. Belle excelled in her studies: although she was more than four years younger than her future husband, the two were in the same class, and she finished near the top. Exceedingly conscientious, Belle never missed a class or was even tardy while attending the university. Not content with mere accurate memorization, she was original in her ideas and had a finely honed social conscience.

Despite the shyness that would plague her throughout her lifetime, Belle Case intelligently protested any measure or contrivance she felt stifled humanity's true nature. The dress, manners, morals, and prejudices of the day, frequently described as "natural," struck her as artificial and warping. Her faith in people in their unfettered state has been called almost Rousseauean. During her college years she spoke out in defense of humanity by attacking those institutions she judged to be interfering with people's genuinely natural modes of behavior. In her sophomore year, she railed against the artificiality of class badges in a speech reviewed favorably by the *Madison Democrat*: "With bitter sarcasm she portrayed the vanity of many of us in trying to make an empty display and neglecting for it true stability and depth of sentiment." The following year her speech "Children's Playthings," delivered at the Junior Exhibit, provided a thoughtful comparison between the effect caused by toys versus pets on children's expectations: "This love of dumb beasts, of pets, is one of the purest and healthiest means of developing the emotional nature. . . . If a girl spent the best part of her childhood in playing with her doll, she will spend the best part of her girlhood in dreaming dreams of impossible future happiness; she will spend the best part of her womanhood in learning how unreal were the dreams of her girlhood, and the disappointment makes her a dissatisfied, nervous, complaining woman." In her senior oration, Belle criticized adults for subverting children's natural curiosity by insisting that they conform to preconceived standards. The speech, "Learning to See," won the prestigious Lewis Prize and was delivered at commencement in the assembly chamber of the state capitol on 18 June 1879.[6]

Belle and Bob were initially attracted to each other by their mutual interests in speech and reform, in addition to their similar rural backgrounds. They began to see each other regularly, meeting frequently to work on various speeches. Although women were generally confined to the College of Letters and Sciences programs until after 1900, the University of Wisconsin was coeducational, and dating among students was commonplace. The young Belle was short and rather heavyset, with dark blonde hair and blue eyes. Reluctant to commit herself romantically (not unlike Mary Fergeson when she was first engaged to Bob's father, Josiah La Follette), Belle preferred to keep their relationship purely on the level of friendship, "free from sentiment, so lighthearted and joyous," at least until they had finished college. "Mamma laughed when I proposed to her," Bob would later tell their children. His persistence paid off at the end of their junior year, although the engagement was kept a secret for almost twelve months.[7]

La Follette's diary for 1879 includes entries for only a few days, but it reveals much about his feelings for women in general and Belle Case in particular during that painful year.[8] Within its pages he staunchly maintains the prescribed gender standards of the day in romantic, flowing language: all women are inherently weak, helpless, tender, virtuous, and consumed with yearning to be fulfilled by a home and family. By contrast, men are physically and intellectually stronger. Although frequently ruled by crude passion, they remain the "natural guardian and chivalrous protector" of women. Such notions, however romantic and chauvinistic, were contradicted by Belle's obvious reluctance, despite their engagement, to fully commit herself to him. Bob's idealistic certainty and eloquence on the true nature of woman disappeared completely when he wrote about Belle, rendering him an insecure, anxious man in the throes of a love he feared was unrequited. A brief entry in his diary suggests it was at Belle's insistence that their engagement be a secret and lengthy one, and several entries betray Bob's fears that she might one day end it altogether. He pleaded, "Oh hasten [the] time when I can see her the center of a home into which shall flow plenty from my own hands, over which shall hover happiness wooed hither by the loving content that glorifies the perfect home."[9]

Upon graduation, Belle both taught and served as assistant principal at Spring Green High School, thirty miles west of Madison, where she enjoyed immensely the sense of independence, pride, and accomplishment it brought her. Her contacts with her fiancé were not marked by the same enthusiasm. On at least two occasions when Bob failed to receive an expected letter from Belle he assured himself it would arrive the next day, but more often his confidence deserted him. His first weekend visit to Spring Green so disheartened him that his entry for the following Monday states only that he was "in no mood for writing," and the next day's entry reveals a most unhappy and insecure suitor: "Had the [first] evening mainly with Belle & was puzzled not a little to understand her. I hardly know why but she at times did not seem like herself nor could I shake this off nor dispel it all the time she was with me til Monday morning." On Saturday morning they took the train to Madison. Bob urged her to stay, "only to regret it very much. For though it seemed like the promise of our future to see her here in our house just as she would be in our own home; yet it seemed that I could read her thoughts that she half regretted having come." Belle's leave-taking was equally disappointing to Bob. Finding the train car full of "great coarse men & the air heavy with smoke," he recorded despondently, "I could have strangled myself for it all. Though almost blinded with unshed tears & looking the very picture [of] misery she would neither remain for another train nor permit me to accompany her (& miss a lecture) & so fearing to go [*sic*] lest I should add even more to her discomfort I left her as the train moved away. But oh how reluctantly & what a miserable day I passed. My dear Journal I tell you everything but I can't tell you that—I cannot frame misery in words—*it is a feeling.*"[10]

Bob's next note to Belle did not evoke the reassuring reply he desired, plunging him further into despair: "Oh how she has misunderstood and how much pain her words cost me. I know she did not mean to hurt me but it seemed like the black days of the past and brought me face to face with my old enemy [depression]. I had thought him well out of my way but he came, dark counselor that he is, with a power that I had nearly forgotten." It was typical of Bob to deny that Belle meant to hurt him. He so idolized her he praised her when she criticized him and even when she put him off by ridiculing him. His loyalty and belief in her nobility caused him to note,

*Belle Case La Follette in 1881, the year of her marriage.*
*(State Historical Society of Wisconsin WHi[X3]18015)*

after receiving a letter from her full of grumbling about being overworked, "She would not complain if it was not worse than it is." Her pleasure mattered more to him than his own, and he seemed to be almost completely at her mercy. Belle taught her second year of school in her hometown of Baraboo. In an incident that seems symbolic of their relationship, Bob decided "after much mental debate" to pay Belle a visit, but he did not arrive until after dark. Belle's window provided a guiding light until it unexpectedly went out, leaving her suitor totally "in the dark": "After knocking the bark off about all the trees in the front yard I succeeded in reaching the door & was 'taken in' literally and metaphysically [by Belle's parents] for Belle had retired."[11]

More than two years after these diary entries were recorded, Belle Case overcame her reluctance and married Bob. Perhaps his resentment of Belle's coolness during their long engagement contributed to Bob's having to make a note to "remind" himself to attend the ceremony, ostensibly because he was so immersed in his duties as the new district attorney. The ceremony was held New Year's Eve, 1881, in the Case home in Baraboo. It was attended only by the two families and a Unitarian minister, who honored the bride's request that the word "obey" be omitted from the marriage vows. Immediately following, Bob returned to his office to complete his day's work. The newlyweds spent their honeymoon in their new home, a dignified old mansion on West Wilson Street, where Bob's mother and Jo and Robert Siebecker, Bob's sister and brother-in-law, also resided. Any tensions, conflicts, or jealousies created by living with these family members were zealously repressed. Belle's mention of her mother-in-law's sarcasm and tendency to "fret and scold" is the harshest criticism preserved. In 1911, however, Belle wrote a story entitled, "I Married a Lawyer." This fictional work reveals many of Belle's unrealized desires and fantasies. In it, her fictitious husband's mother died during the summer following their senior year and only then did the couple become engaged. In reality, the beautifully appointed and very large house that they all shared had been purchased with the profits from the sale of the Primrose farm. Bob was so distraught over the sale that he consoled himself with the thought that he would some day buy it back. In order to rationalize their living in Madison when they had agreed that farm life was their mutual goal, Belle and Bob preferred to perceive the arrangement as only temporary, although it remained their primary residence for the next nineteen years.[12]

With her new husband vigorously pursuing a legal career, Belle was often left with her female in-laws. In September 1882, eight months and ten days after the wedding she gave birth to a daughter, Flora Dodge, called Fola, who remained an only child for the next thirteen years. When Bob spent evenings at home reading law books, Belle joined him. She enrolled in law school the same year Fola was born, a move that satisfied many of her needs: she excelled in an almost wholly male discipline far removed from her prescribed gendered sphere, demonstrating the intellectual equality of women; she was better able to understand, counsel, and influence her husband, and she was no longer left alone in the house with Mary and Jo and a new baby all day. In 1885, Belle Case La Follette became the first woman to graduate from the University of Wisconsin Law School. Although she never practiced law, she was an excellent student, and a brief she wrote for her husband broke new legal ground and won his case before the state's Supreme Court. Bob's obvious pride in correcting Justice W. P. Lyon, who later mistakenly complimented him as the author of Belle's brief, was unpatronizing, for he did not view Belle's intelligence, talents, or interests as a personal threat and never appeared to be jealous or competitive. He thus proved himself the exception to Crystal Eastman Benedict's caustic report to the National American Suffrage Association: "[T]he last thing a man becomes progressive about is the activities of his own wife."[13]

Belle's enthusiasm for sweeping, liberal, even radical, change never faltered. The seemingly endless temperance campaigns that had swept Wisconsin during her youth led women reformers to agendas expanded to combat the multitude of challenges faced by an urbanized, industrialized society. These included a variety of concerns generally perceived as women's issues, such as wages and working conditions for women and children, education, and impure food and drugs. In "Woman's Conscience and Social Amelioration," Hull House founder Jane Addams observed, "As society grows more complicated it is necessary that woman shall extend her sense of responsibility to many things outside of her home, if only in order to preserve the home in its entirety." But, like so many of her sister reformers, Belle did not confine her interests and activities to those based on gender. In 1919, for example, she wrote: "Just as I do not believe we can ever return to the old order of personal competition in the business world so I think we must accept some changed conditions in the political world. Communism seems to be the forward step in the solution of economic conditions at this state of society." (This initial interest in communism waned, however, after Belle witnessed firsthand the suppression of freedoms in the Soviet Union in 1923.)[14]

Belle Case La Follette spoke in support of world disarmament, civil rights, especially for African Americans, but always most avidly for women's rights. All three, she believed, were inextricably bound together, and she noted, "This business of being a woman is in many ways, like being a member of a despised race." It was her fervent belief that "if women had a larger voice in the counseling of nations, there would be no war slogans, no dreams of empire which could lead to the great sacrifice of life, which woman alone knows the real value." During World War I, she became one of the founders of the Women's Peace Party, later to become the Women's International League for Peace and Freedom, an organization still active today. She protested not only the draft but even the misleading nature of armed services' recruiting posters for their romanticization of war. Belle took on new challenges throughout her lifetime and championed causes ranging from the Montessori system of education to pure food and drug legislation and wage and prison reform. For ten years, until overwhelmed by her duties as governor's wife, Belle was president of the Emily Bishop League, a group devoted to exercise, pure fresh foods, and the more natural way of life she had so strongly advocated during her college years. She jogged regularly and further defied convention by abandoning stays and corsets for more comfortable, looser fitting garments.[15]

Belle's professors encouraged her to pursue a career in writing, advice she later regretted not heeding. She wrote hundreds of articles over a period of more than fifty years, primarily for *La Follette's Magazine*. According to the *Minneapolis Morning Tribune*, Belle La Follette was "a pioneer in the establishment of a new sort of women's page." As the editor of "one of the cleverest and most readable women's pages in the country," she provided "stronger intellectual food" than the usual fare of "vaseline and cold cream." Perhaps her most courageous columns were written in response to the plight of African Americans, especially in the wake of the racial segregation of the Treasury Department by President Wilson's secretary of the treasury, William McAdoo. Many African Americans were summarily discharged from their jobs, including those originally hired through the Civil Service's color-blind application process. These and a variety of other oppressive actions prompted Booker T. Washington's observation, "I have never seen the colored people so discouraged and bitter as they are at the present time." Within the pages of *La Follette's Magazine*, Belle openly criticized the administration's racial policies as well as the racist speeches of Senator James K. Vardaman (D-Mississippi) and Representative James T. Heflin (D-Alabama). In addition to pointing out the crucial role African Americans played in the nation's economy, she took up cudgels in the case of three African American women working in the Treasury Department who were suddenly forced to eat at a table separate from their white counterparts. One of the women, Rosebud Murraye, was fired immediately after granting Belle an interview, despite Murraye's faithful and efficient service of nine years. Belle appealed the case in letters to McAdoo and to President Wilson himself, reprinting in *La Follette's* the entire correspondence, including the replies upholding Murraye's dismissal as well as a variety of denials, excuses, justifications, and rationalizations concerning the segregation policy. Belle rather pointedly placed one letter from "a refined, intelligent colored woman" eloquently decrying American racism next to an article (on an unrelated matter) by President Wilson's daughter, Margaret.[16]

Belle received magazine subscription cancellations as well as hate mail, some of which she published in the pages of *La Follette's*. Undaunted, she spoke to black as well as white audiences against lynching, racial segregation, and the disfranchisement of women and African Americans. Her remarks on enforced segregation in government services were pointed: "To have the United States Government take a backward step, to have the color line drawn in places they have won on their merit, to be humiliated, repressed and degraded at the capital of the nation by their own government, which has no right to discriminate among its citizens, is a body blow to hope and pride and incentive." She reprinted retired brigadier general Richard H. Pratt's denunciation, in biting terms, of some of the more common justifications for segregation and discrimination. Despite the personal attacks it invited, Belle La Follette refused to let the subject die. When Wilson defended his segregationist policies in late 1914, Belle La Follette asked in *La Follette's*, "What becomes of the fundamental principles of our institutions if the color line or any other arbitrary line can be drawn by the government among its civil service employees?"[17]

When it came to civil rights and other subjects about which she felt passionately, Belle, like her husband, was an energetic speaker. Although her style was somewhat quieter, people often remarked that the two resembled each other both on and off the speaker's platform. Belle contrasted dramatically with her husband in other areas, however. Their son Phil noted, "People who knew [Belle] in her younger days reported her as being gay, high spirited, and having the most contagious laugh they ever heard." Belle's writings, both personal and public, reveal someone very different. Conscientious, highly principled, and self-disciplined, Belle appears earnest, sincere, and extremely serious. Although she spoke in favor of breaking free from confining habits and repressive customs, her writings reveal not a free-spirited, fun-loving woman, but an inflexible, rather stern one. On a lecture series promoting women's suffrage, she was accused of being "too argumentative — and not light enough for audiences." In a speech to university women she stated, "Discrimination and subordination of social life to more important duty should be a part of women's education." She found trifling gossip more annoying than serious misrepresentations, and she once rather prudishly reprimanded her daughter, then twenty-two, for wearing in a publicity picture a gown whose neckline was "too low to be pretty."[18] In contrast to her husband, Belle rarely displayed much facility for fantasy or levity even in private. In her speeches and in her letters to the family, jokes, teasing, or any general attempt at humor are conspicuous by their absence.[19]

Following his oft-quoted assertion in his autobiography that Belle was his "wisest and best counsellor," Bob added, "That this is not partial judgment, the Progressive leaders of Wisconsin who welcomed her to our conferences would bear witness. Her grasp of the great problems, sociological and economic, is unsurpassed by any of the strong men who have been associated with me in my work." In his later years, he spoke of the time "when we were governor." When not with Belle, Bob showered her with requests for her views on political matters. He so valued his wife's judgment that when he was urged to drop out of the 1912 presidential campaign and a statement of withdrawal was submitted for his signature, he read it and handed it back, saying he would sign no statement without consulting Belle: a committee resubmitted the paper to the couple in their home. Belle herself conceded, albeit via her fictionalized counterpart, "I had an easy way of grasping a subject and even a knotty law problem did not stagger me." Belle La Follette, maintained a family friend, "was the most thoroughly married woman I ever knew." According to son-in-law George Middleton, "Except John Adams with his Abigail, no man in public life was to have so equal a mate."[20]

"I know of no couple," stated a family friend, "more companionable, more helpful, sympathetic and complementary to one another than the La Follettes." The La Follettes agreed, claiming publicly to have a near-perfect marriage, and citing as evidence their lack of arguments. They liked to give the impression of complete and total unity, yet at the same time stressed their individuality and independence: "Mrs. La Follette has good health and unusual vital power. She leads a thoroughly normal and happy life. Although she is interested in her husband's work and appreciates his importance, she is not absorbed in it. She is his sincerest friend and most ardent admirer. They are good comrades. From the day of their engagement to the present time, they have not had a lovers' quarrel or domestic difference. . . . The family life is ideally happy." Belle shed some light on that vision of perfect harmony in her biography of Bob: "We seldom seriously differed, and I think I can honestly say we never quarreled. At times one or the other or both may have been deeply hurt, as happens in making life's adjustments; but we did not nurse the sense of wrong, nor did we discuss it. We treated it as we would physical pain — a cut or burn which it was useless to think much about and which would heal in time. We were ourselves good comrades and we were comrades with our children."[21]

The La Follettes liked to think of their marriage as one virtually untouched by disagreement, for they viewed an unspoken disagreement as a nonexistent one. This kind of reasoning kept them from pointless bickering, but it also prohibited them from speaking openly and constructively about the endless stream of differences and problems that afflict all couples. The La Follettes' dedication and love for each other was deep, and their correspondence contains many touching declarations of that love, although Bob seems to have been more effusive, at least on paper. Nonetheless, they lived with his relatives for many years, raised four children, endured endless political pressures, suffered financial strain and, at times, tremendous public disapproval, all conditions inevitably leading to tensions and differences. Regardless, in an interview in 1924 Belle said, "I have loved my life. I have been fortunate, marvelously lucky in having all these years a companion. True companionship is the greatest thing in the world. We have been through everything, my husband and I, bad times and good times, disappointments, illness, poverty, hard work, the struggle for principle, the climb to success. But when you have a companion to count upon through thick and thin, it's all easy. We two have kept together because — well, because our minds and our hearts matched."[22]

All these avowals of identical thoughts and desires do not alter the fact that the La Follettes did disagree over such issues as politics, personal goals, lifestyle, and money. At the time of her death, Belle had written several hundred pages of an ambitious biography of her husband. Their daughter Fola completed the study, adding a second volume. Belle's portion is well written and she emerges as a politically astute woman who does not allow sentiment or loyalty to prevent her from voicing opinions different from her husband's, while Fola is far more apt to rationalize or excuse her father's errors or failures.

Despite her outspokenness and her willingness to campaign in matters of importance, Belle La Follette was a very shy woman, uncomfortable with life in the public eye. At the age of fifty-eight she confided to her daughter Mary, "Even now after all my experience I suffer with anxiety and when I was your age, it was agony for me to even *recite* in class. I always hoped none of you children would take things like that as seriously as I did." Her competence as a speaker surprised her; in a letter to her husband she wondered, "if the nerve I have comes from long association with you or if it comes from within. Certainly I should not have believed I had it in myself alone to rise to the occasion as I have." Belle's early objections to her husband's political career were not based merely on her own discomfort with public speaking. When Bob proposed to run for Congress, Belle recalled, "instinctive love of home and the dread of change led me, in a mild way, to take the negative side of the argument." Her husband, she noted, "was on the road to success in his profession; Madison offered every advantage of a permanent home for ourselves and the children we wanted. Why sacrifice such a prospect for the uncertainty of a public career with its inevitable change in our mode of living? I was not insistent; I recognized his unusual gifts and wanted him to follow his bent. It was not long before I was happy and content in the thought of his going to Congress."[23]

This minimization of conflict is typical of Belle, but also typical was her very real desire to keep out of politics and remain in the safe, secure, familiar lifestyle they had already established and that was so heavily touted by the women's prescriptive literature of the day. Not surprisingly, in Belle's story "I Married a Lawyer," her fictional, ideal husband was very different: "While he has always taken an active interest in politics, where important issues were at stake, he has never yielded to the pressure that has often been brought to bear to make him a candidate for office. I sometimes think my love of home, dread of strife, and the demands of a large family of growing children have influenced him in this determination. However, when I suggest that he has sacrificed his personal ambitions to our comfort and happiness he tweaks my ear and makes me laugh." When Bob considered running for the governorship again after his first unsuccessful attempt, he believed he must fight for "the interests of better methods and better government for Wisconsin" or "quietly retire from the field and attend to 'private business.'" Claimed Bob, "The latter will be an alternative easy for me, as in so doing I will simply yield to the entreaties of Mrs. La Follette."[24]

Belle claimed in 1916 that the six years in the governor's residence had been "the most taxing from a woman's standpoint," citing personal threats against the family and "the continuous and merciless fire of newspaper criticism." During Bob's many years in federal service, she so disliked the constant shuttling between Washington, D.C., and Wisconsin that she and the children occasionally remained in Madison when Congress was in session. During one such separation Bob urged her to rest up in order to meet the demands of life in Washington in the coming year. She replied that it was not the social obligations she dreaded, but "the intense interest in you [which] seems too much for me at times."[25]

Despite her denial, Belle did indeed dread the many social obligations her husband's position forced upon her. Her article "What It Means to Be an Insurgent Senator's Wife" details her dislike of having to participate in the public officials' wives' fixed social program of making and receiving calls, often as many as twenty-five or thirty, and sometimes even more, in a day. Although she found some of these calls valuable, she abhorred many of them because of the snobbery of the hostess who received most of her guests with "a distant nod that made the magnificent house seem chilly and the outdoor sunshine welcome." To the query "What do Washington women talk about?" she answered, "Altogether too much about the weather. Women in official life come from all parts of the country, have widely varied experience as well as much in common. They are intelligent, and have insight. They might discuss current events, politics, religion, education, philosophy. But there is nothing of the French salon or English drawing-room in the social life of Washington. . . . An exceeding graciousness and desire to please pervades every function, like having all the meals only dessert. . . . Women in official circles are scarcely less interested in politics than men, the majority talk politics intelligently in the home, but it is characteristic of their social life to avoid discussion of public questions, where there is a difference of opinion, as they would a fire brand." Two years later she concluded more pointedly that such absence of purpose "reacts unfavorably on the country." "How," she queried, "can we continue to justify the expenditure of such an enormous amount of effort and money in formal visiting?" She pleaded for "an official social center" to serve as "a clearing house for official calls and receptions." "We are not supposed to belong to the butterfly and parasitic class," she reminded her sisters in Washington's official life, for "we should represent the earnest, intelligent womanhood of the nation." In her speech, "Our Story," Belle La Follette concluded: "Washington life is an unsettled existence. When we are there, we think about home. And when home, we think we must soon be going to Washington. . . . If she [the wife of a politician] sets her heart on some ambition,— his political success or her special supremacy, she is building on uncertainties. More than any other life, politics is full of the unexpected,— now success, now disappointment. It is a life of strain with few breathing places. One cannot tell and must always be prepared for what comes. And one must have an inner calm if she would be the mate of a political fighter and reformer."[26]

Belle's "inner calm" deserted her when she contemplated the family's finances. Throughout Bob's lifetime, his family never lacked the essentials and enjoyed many comforts, even extravagances (especially Maple Bluff Farm), but they never lived in a mortgage-free home or experienced life without debt. The family papers are rife with notes from various bill collectors dunning them for payments past due and pleas from Bob to various friends and supporters for money. Even though Bob's income was at times quite substantial, from official earnings supplemented by profits from writing and lecturing, according to Belle, "If funds were lacking when he thought it important to send out some political literature, he would pay for it out of his own pocket. If he hadn't the money, he borrowed, and debt accumulated." By remaining in a perpetual state of debt, Bob demonstrated to the world that he desired not material gain, but greater and more lasting rewards. To those who equated machine politics with personal financial gain, La Follette's relative poverty, in many ways voluntary, was proof of his uncorrupted state. Therefore, when Bob was criticized in the press for earning money on the speaker's platform to the neglect of official duties, his response was indignant: "We try to live economically but at that we have put by the chance to lay up anything for our children's future. We understand each other at home; we have talked it all out and are agreed. I wish to leave something to the state more lasting than bronze or marble and a better legacy to my children than mere wealth."[27]

"Mere wealth" was certainly not Belle's goal either, but the burden of their constant state of indebtedness usually weighed more heavily upon her than upon her husband. To his wife's letters detailing her frustration over their constant debt, Bob responded with perpetual optimism and encouraged her to view their indebtedness as a temporary condition, to not waste energy worrying but to save her "precious self" for him and the rest of the family. He chose to withhold from her his own frequent concerns about their financial status and left most of their personal bookkeeping up to her while making clear his own impatience with such matters.[28]

During roughly the first half of their forty-three years of marriage, depressed that the ideals she had espoused in her university days did not seem to be wholly successful on a practical level, Belle was more willing to berate herself for the family's predicament: "I think I must manage [the finances] badly for I seem to be so driven all the while that there is no time to think and consider. I keep looking forward to a time when I can systematize and regulate things but the time does not arrive and I am convinced I must have fallen into bad habits." Belle had been taught to abhor debt, and her concern over the grim state of the family's finances haunted her throughout her married life. Bob never understood, Belle confided to their son, that the uncertainty of the extent of their indebtedness was more of a strain on her than the actual knowledge. Even in her story, "I Married a Lawyer," her husband, as in real life, often tried to "protect" her from knowledge of the distressing state of their finances. The fictitious family is brought to financial ruin by the shady doings of an unscrupulous law partner, only to become successful again by dint of hard work and sacrifice. In reality, it was her husband who caused their financial woes, and Belle noted matter-of-factly in public: "We have always been under financial pressure, and I expect we always shall be." Privately, she was less calmly resigned to this eternal strife.[29]

The "temporary" condition of the La Follettes' finances remained constant throughout Bob's entire life. Son Phil painted a dark picture of the family's finances during his father's later years: "From September, 1919, to June, 1920, I ran the family checkbook. . . . Deficits were especially high at times, and it would show up in the family car's standing in the garage for want of a spare tire — or in Dad's wondering if the help might be pilfering a bit from the larder. I felt the painful frustration of stretching Dad's salary further than it would go. . . . This experience, on top of all that had gone before, gave me a horror of debt that stayed with me." As late as 1921, during hot weather that son Bobbie said "fries the juice right out of one even if he sits under a fan," Belle spent several discouraging weeks searching for a house to rent in Washington. For reasons both financial and political, the La Follettes had never purchased a home in the capital, and a rent increase had made their present dwelling unaffordable. It took Bob's death to put an end to the constant drain on the family's finances. Some of the land adjoining their house was sold and the mortgage on the La Follettes' Wisconsin home finally paid. Only then was Belle able to experience the financial freedom that had so long eluded her.[30]

At times during the first half of their marriage, Belle seems to have wholly internalized the prescribed sphere of "true womanhood": "Whenever I get discouraged I always think there is nothing I would rather be than your wife and the mother of your children and I have no ambition except to contribute to your happiness and theirs and to your success and theirs." Such internalization brought anxiety and feelings of inadequacy: "[S]ometimes I feel I am not well adapted to home making, and the constant efforts to hold myself and keep my balance in the midst of so many distractions wears me out." Belle's commitment to attaining an ideal had captured Bob's undivided attention during their university years, and that same quality kept it riveted to her throughout his life. Bob depended enormously on Belle's seriousness, her clear-sightedness, and most of all her idealism: "You give me such courage dear one for my work—Your letters are a great source of comfort and inspiration to me—You do not realize how deeply philosophical—how noble, lofty, and far seeing they are. I preserve them all as precious. They, like yourself, are a part of me." Belle's approval was vital to Bob. During their engagement, he wrote that "[truth] must be my rule in all my work & will give me the approval of my conscience & my little girl [Belle]."[31]

Belle's high standards made her approval all the more desirable during Bob's periods of relatively good health, but during his many illnesses, she responded maternally and generously. She wrote to a friend that it was "true Bob undertakes more work than he should," explaining, "He sees the end and not the difficulties and obstacles. But it is his faith and persistence that have sustained him through his long struggle. He has to live and act according to his light." Accordingly, Belle viewed herself as a guardian of her husband. Rather than insist he be responsible for his own habits and their negative effects, she claimed, "I had to be the ogre and insist on his getting sleep. His habit of talking too long grew out of his own desire to cover the ground thoroughly and the insistence of his audiences that he go on. When

I thought it was getting late, I would signal him to stop. He would sometimes give me away. 'There's my wife shaking her head and looking daggers at me. She thinks I'm talking too long.' The crowd would laugh and urge him to go ahead." Belle bought Bob a watch that chimed on the hour designated by her as a sensible stopping place. Greatly concerned about her husband's notorious habit for overwork, she often tried to persuade him not to push himself too hard. Bob once ended a rather long letter with: "Belle says to quit for tonight or she will claw me. I quit —." Belle utilized subtler means as well, such as pointing out that Bob could accomplish very little from a sickbed. Throughout their marriage Bob often took on the persona of an irresponsible, sometimes naughty child, with Belle playing the frustrated but loving mother. In keeping with this relationship, Bob often addressed Belle as "Mama" in his letters, and on at least one occasion closed with "I am always your boy."[32]

A tacit acceptance of constant debt, internalized feelings of anxiety and guilt over household finances, an acceptance of the role of monitor and ultimately the role of "Mama" for her husband are all reflections of attitudes and beliefs that existed as the norm for many nineteenth-century women. But a major shift in the way she perceived both herself and her husband occurred within Belle La Follette. It happened slowly and gradually yet was nonetheless profound. As Belle entered her middle years and the strict, gendered spheres that created nineteenth-century perceptions of the ideal woman began to expand and transform, she relieved herself of certain responsibilities. She no longer saw her husband's various frustrating behaviors as indicators of her own failures but viewed them instead as qualities of his personality that she was entirely unable to change, no matter how sincere and well-intentioned her efforts. Without this burden of guilt, she did not wholly abandon her personal ideals but was free to focus on creating coping mechanisms with which to best deal with her husband's more maddening behaviors. As Belle's love for Bob matured, being his wife involved increasing acceptance of his faults as well as his admirable qualities and an intensification of her own efforts to carry out desired social reforms in addition to supporting his.

The reasons for Belle's advocacy of women's suffrage are certainly in keeping with the strains she endured as Bob's wife. Her early arguments, which claimed the right to vote as merely the extension of woman's prescribed sphere, slowly evolved into a defense of woman's natural rights as an equal to man. Belle gradually ceased blaming herself for poor management and placed more responsibility on her husband for his willingness to incur debt. The woman who in 1905 claimed no ambition but to contribute to the happiness and success of her husband and children six years later was advocating women's full participation in society, urging them to free themselves from their parasitic dependence on their husbands, develop their talents, and be of service to humanity. A bright woman forced to lead a lifestyle different from that which she truly desired, her work on behalf of women may be seen as a way of protesting being so dominated by her husband's needs; of expressing her rebellion against the unfairness of being thrust against her will into public life, being continually in debt, and having to suffer with her husband the controversy and criticism only he had evoked. The expression of suffragist views allowed Belle a forum to protest her subserviency to her demanding husband without incurring his wrath but instead generating praise and approval. And yet, when she addressed the Senate Committee on Woman Suffrage on 26 April 1913, Belle's message was temperate. She insisted that equal suffrage "will make better homes," for "home, society [and] government are best when men and women keep together intellectually and spiritually." Woman suffrage was "a simple matter of common sense" which would not "bring about any great immediate changes," because, she explained, "it has always seemed to me natural that men and women of the same family should hold somewhat similar political views, much as fathers and sons and brothers do now."[33]

To Bob's great chagrin, Belle steadfastly refused to campaign for him directly. "She thinks she won't talk for me," Bob confided to a reporter during the 1912 campaign, "but I think she will. Why there isn't a man in the country whom I'd rather have making campaign speeches for me than my wife. There is no one in the world better fitted to be in politics than a brainy and conscientious woman and there isn't a brainier woman in the country than my wife, and she can make a fine speech." Belle's refusal remained firm, however, until 1924, when she campaigned actively for her husband's presidency.[34]

For all Belle's dislike of public life with its chaos and uncertainty, her frequent urgings that her husband not work so hard, and her criticisms of his strategies and policies, she labored tirelessly on his behalf. According to their daughter Fola, "[Belle] prepared briefs for his law firm and followed his legal and legislative work with professional understanding. While he was a Member of the House she attended the important debates and traveled with him on his speaking campaigns." Belle spent a great deal of time performing such routine, time-consuming chores as addressing and stuffing envelopes, personally responding to constituents' mail, and tracking down late shipments of campaign posters, pamphlets, and the like. Her work with the mailing lists made her familiar with names and addresses of constituents, enabling her, she said, "when I accompanied Mr. La Follette on his campaigns through his congressional district to sometimes jog even his ex-

*Belle La Follette on the stump for woman suffrage in Blue Mounds, Wisconsin, 1915. (State Historical Society of Wisconsin WHi[X3]3996)*

cellent memory with a hint as to 'who was who.'" During the congressional years and during his three terms as governor there were few important conferences in which she did not participate — probably none that he did not share with her. When he went to Washington as senator, she continued to participate in the more intimate conferences and shared every important aspect of his work, including the editing of a department in *La Follette's Magazine*. In 1907, Bob paid tribute to her continuing efficiency and capability when he reported, "When I met [muckraking journalist] Ida Tarbell the other day I told her I was not half so much in awe of her as I expected to be in meeting *next* to the ablest woman in America — due to the fact I believed that Mrs. La Follette [is] the ablest individual in the land [and she has] been my wife for a quarter of a century."[35]

Belle endured many conflicts between her desire for simplicity and security for herself and her family and her longing for positive political change. She wrote to their oldest son when Bob achieved an important political goal, "It makes this life seem worth all the strain if something like this goes through that is a real service to humanity." Whatever her personal suffering, Belle, a determined, intelligent woman, was a wife ideally suited for

Bob in many ways: she was, when they were in agreement, loving and supporting but also relentlessly challenging and demanding. Her uncompromising desires for "right" and "good" struck a very familiar chord within Bob. In many respects, during their early years she provided an even stronger incentive to attain "moral perfection" than had his mentor President Bascom, for Belle admitted openly, "I want you to be perfect in all things," and claimed, "No one can know as I know how truly great your character." In her "wifely anxiety that he should attain a standard of perfection," she conceded, "sometimes I was so eager to point out where he might do better that I forgot to express my appreciation of how well he had done." She maintained, "If he were doing one thing I thought wrong, and the world were praising him, I could not endure it; but so long as I believe he is right, and all the world is maligning him, I am proud." It was perhaps that quality more than any single other that drew Bob to Belle. During their many separations, despite the strength he drew from her letters, he often expressed his longings for her. Bob wrote, "She grows more wonderful to me as time passes. . . . She knows *what's* best and just about *when* it's best."[36]

For Bob La Follette, Belle Case — with her political ideals, her refusal to compromise on moral issues, and her belief in public service and duty — served as a measuring stick by which he could gauge his own achievements and worth. She was, according to close family friend and journalist Ray Stannard Baker, "as near an alter ego as any person could be." Following Bob La Follette's death in 1925, his widow was urged to pursue his Senate seat. Belle favored women sharing the responsibilities of high office and was deeply mindful that her virtually assured election might pave the way to the Senate for other women. Nevertheless, she stated in no uncertain terms, "At no time in my life would I ever have chosen a public career for myself. It would be against [my] nature for me to undertake the responsibilities of political leadership." The finely honed social conscience and sense of "womanly" duty was no match for her discomfort in the public eye and "womanly" longing to work for the betterment of society comfortably behind the scenes, within the safety and security of home. Belle Case La Follette's life choices were the results of a unique blend of personal and political forces. An assessment of her character far more penetrating than Baker's was offered at her funeral by another journalist and family friend, Lincoln Steffens, who better understood the social, political, and personal crosscurrents perpetually buffeting this complex woman. Calling her "historically and romantically the woman triumphant," he paid tribute to this "great woman, this Belle La Follette, great as great men are great. She too was a statesman, political: she could act but she was content to beget action and actors. She played, herself, the women's part; she sat in the gallery in the Congress or at

*The La Follettes after forty-three years of marriage, Fort Lauderdale, Florida, 1925.*
*(State Historical Society of Wisconsin WHi[X3]48482)*

home with the children and the advisors. She could but she did not often make the speeches or do the deeds." Steffens assessed Belle's life from the time when "a pretty young girl with a gypsy spirit . . . found her man": "She wanted to fly. She inspired flight and she bore fliers, but she herself—Belle La Follette—walked all her life on the ground to keep the course for her fliers. That was her woman's victory; that was a woman's tragedy, too."[37]

# 5: LA FOLLETTE AND THE LAW
## EVERYTHING IS NOT ENOUGH

n Belle La Follette's story "I Married a Lawyer," her fictitious fiancé conferred with her before selecting a profession, "as he always has since, about what . . . was best to do," and the final decision was a joint one. In reality, although Belle was frequently uncomfortable with her husband's subsequent public career (and the perpetual debt it engendered), her approval of a legal career was complete, even enthusiastic. In her ideal scenario, her husband established a flourishing practice, serving the public conscientiously while enabling his family to live in a large, comfortable country home. In truth, her real fiancé saw the practice of law not as a mere profession by which to provide for his family, but as a holy calling — an arena in which he could carry out his crusade to perform so righteously that he would win the approval of his wife and of father figures, including John Bascom. In addition, a legal career provided La Follette with the opportunity to, in his words, "study to know all the ingenious devices which measure man's meannesses to man." Such knowledge could protect him against the Saxtons of the world. Never again did he wish to see himself the helpless victim of false images or devious plans. The practice of law was also a necessary stepping stone toward greater public service. It was, ironically, John Saxton who planted many of these ideas within the mind of his young stepson. "I remember telling my stepfather that I wanted to be a 'statesman,'" La Follette noted. "He told me I had better study law; and so I planned it all in the back of my head to study law and be a statesman before I knew what it meant."[1]

The law school at the University of Wisconsin during La Follette's tenure consisted of fifty-two students and eight professors. In the office of local attorney Robert M. Bashford, La Follette combined this formal training with the old tradition of "reading law." The details of how these endeavors were financed remain unclear, although La Follette received at least one contribution from his brother William. Eager to repeat the personal and financial success of the *University Press*, La Follette concocted a plan of publishing law lectures, which received "the commendation of the Profs as being needed & of double profit" but had to be abandoned because the professors were unprepared to contribute suitably polished material.[2]

La Follette's detailed diary, covering slightly less than a month of the fall of 1879, reveals much about this eager, insecure law student. Its entries are made in the flowery language of a man intent on being sensitive and dramatic. Each day's record begins with a detailed account of the weather which served as a kind of exercise in elaborate phrasing and imagery. The entry for 14 November, for example, reads: "Another one of those uncertain days when the weather gods seem to make a fight along the snow line of winter. Now muffling up the sun with the black front of storm & bringing the cold sweat from the clouds, rendering everything in nature 'clammy'; now beaten and driven back by warriors of fairer promise, armed with bright beams warm from the sun that steal the death-damp from earth & sky."[3]

More than just a sense of the self-importance experienced by many an aspiring lawyer led to La Follette's chagrin following a humiliating experience: "Col. Vilas lectured to us & impressed me with being more facetious than profound — probably because he made everyone who asked for information the subject of a joke, myself among the number." The source of La Follette's sensitivity to such treatment is brought into sharper focus when his deification of the law is understood. The study of law provided La Follette with clearly defined lines of right and wrong. He lauded his Real Property professor because he made reason the ultimate test of every law. The reasonableness of law appealed to La Follette for the same reasons he was drawn to John Bascom and Belle Case: he sought strong, rigid forces to provide guidelines. Had he selected the stage for his career, his performances might have been, to varying degrees, successful, unsuccessful, or merely mediocre. The study and practice of law allowed for no such fuzzy lines and uncertainties. Arguments were either accepted or rejected, cases won or lost. La Follette confided in his journal, "Wish I was ready for work — there is something in a case that demands concentration, that 'puzzles the will,' that taxes invention for a tenable theory, that lends it great attraction." The practice of law promised La Follette the opportunity to lose himself completely in the case at hand, to immerse himself in an activity that would, hopefully, provide a final and definite sense of righteousness.[4]

Just as the certainty of law appealed to La Follette, the uncertainties of life plagued him. During this period he reflected on the quotation, "The dread of evil is a much more forcible principle of human action than the prospect of good." Mused La Follette, "Just now it strikes me that that which furnishes the greatest stimulus a man feels — that which is his strongest moving motive is the prospect of *good* — good to himself & those he loves." Clearly, La Follette wanted to see himself as motivated by good. He worked hard in law school, envisioning his future career as one based on the pursuit of truth and all that was "right." This desire to be motivated purely by altruism caused him to take offense to other attorneys whom he felt did not share his pursuit of righteousness: "Formed a dislike & distrust of Judge Wilson. . . . [H]e lacks the honesty of purpose to be truly effective. Back of all his earnestness will lurk the spirit of insincerity — visible because the larger part of the man — *He will lose*." In contrast, La Follette emphasized his own total earnestness: "Though invited to a lunch party at Prof. Sterling's, my anxiety [concerning] the trial & desire to form an independent opinion based on the testimony, caused me to neglect the cordial invitation."[5]

When La Follette, not yet a member of the bar, was allowed to present his first case before a judge, he recorded, "I do not know how long I spoke. I lost the time & all else save the testimony & the truth in it." La Follette prided himself on his willingness to collect and present all possible evidence with the same thoroughness that had marked his speeches during college. He criticized two fellow law students because "they did not go into court with *all* of the evidence which they might have taken; . . . they thought they had enough," and concluded, "It seems to me that I should always feel that everything is not enough." When he learned, in 1925, that his son Phil had spoken well at a murder trial, he responded, "It gives me great satisfaction to know that he is training himself to make *every* argument in court — whether to judge or jury the subject of the *greatest possible preparation*." Such preparation, La Follette was convinced, led to the greatest possibility of legal success, success that he found enormously rewarding. Upon hearing his first client, James Rogers, judged "not guilty" of intent to murder following La Follette's spirited defense, the ecstatic attorney recorded, "Though not unmindful of the words of honest praise bestowed on my effort by both the judge & lawyers present, the words of gratefulness given by my first client was more than all else & his great joy at the verdict of not guilty returned in an hour by the jury paid me better than would a heavy fee."[6]

La Follette craved praise, but he did not want any confusion as to his motivations. He bridled at the suggestion that he had been motivated by anything other than a desire to do "right" in the Rogers case: "I have been many times complimented for getting him acquitted by Dr. Baker, Col. Keyes & others but I do not like the way they bestow their praise. They seem to consider that I did a smart thing — that I was sharp in the management of the matter & keen in the argument — but they don't seem to think that I did it all because I thought he was innocent — that I was simply fighting a fight for the truth — that his vindication was a *truth*. That is the way I like to think of it & the way I did think of it, else I should not have tried as earnestly to win." The next day Rogers was sentenced to four years after pleading guilty to a burglary charge. "He deserved it I think," wrote La Follette. "I was glad to free him on the first charge (& I do think it was due to the study I gave the case that he was cleared) for he was innocent of that. But he did this crime & must pay the penalty."[7]

Two days after this entry, an introspective La Follette wrote of the difficulties of his childhood. He concluded on an optimistic note, proclaiming:

"There are some things, many things, that I would not have altered, if I could have directed my own future from the first with prophetic wisdom. Out of the responsibilities & cares & privations & struggles of the past I have gathered much good — the very flints I have been dashed against have brought forth living fire from the steel of my nature — have taught me the value of antagonisms." In his search for meaning in the deprivations he had endured, La Follette professed that suffering strengthens and ennobles, repressing any anger. He also admitted, however, "[I]t is hard & growing harder for me to go into society at all and I only feel natural & comfortable at home with the folks — in the society of the immediate few." As a law student, La Follette wanted desperately to feel strong, motivated only by a desire to do right. Doubts plagued him, however. Small wonder he empathized so completely with another man, Judge Bruley, with whom he frequently visited: "Poor man, he seems never to forget his desolation. A starless night has fallen upon him & he gropes his way on & on & on through the darkness alone. Oh how much I pity him."[8]

La Follette proved to be a quick study as a law student and passed the bar in February 1880, only seven months after his studies began. Then, despite his discomfort away from the immediate family few, he plunged into the very public career of a lawyer. Some scholars and La Follette himself cite only the financial reasons behind his decision to run for district attorney of Dane County. True, Madison's abundant supply of established lawyers dimmed the prospects of immediate success for a young attorney just starting out, and the title of district attorney would be a drawing card for potential private clients, facilitating La Follette's long-desired marriage to Belle Case. Also, the position paid the impressive annual salary of $800, plus $50 for expenses. Emotional reasons, however, should not be minimized. La Follette strongly desired to follow in his father's footsteps by holding a public office. He wanted also to gain the approval of Bascom by serving the public and doing "right" and to experience the greater attention that a mere private practice could not provide.

La Follette had already enjoyed some public acclaim before his decision to run for office. Subsequent to his victory at the Interstate Oratorical Contest, he had been a much requested speaker at various events in the communities surrounding Madison. This notoriety complemented a number of other factors, all favoring his entrance into the race for the district attorneyship. The incumbent, James Reynolds, declined to seek a second term, having earned a reputation as a drunkard, procurer for prostitutes, and gambler. Reynolds faced charges of immorality and dishonesty just prior to the convention to select Republican nominees for county office. La Follette enjoyed an unsullied reputation, and his youth, enthusiasm, and idealism in the wake of so much corruption made him particularly attractive. Finally, he was not only a Republican in a Republican county, he was a lifelong resident of that heavily Scandinavian county and spoke some Norwegian.[9]

It was during this initial campaign, according to La Follette, that he first confronted the evils of the political machines that, through party control and the conferring of local patronage, ruled the nation's small towns and big cities. Under this system candidates for the district attorneyship were determined by local caucuses at the county convention. As in virtually all elections from the 1830s through the 1890s, party politics "firmly controlled virtually all access to public office, all aspects of elections and all aspects of policy making." Beginning in 1832, presidential candidates were nominated by their party at national conventions. Some presidential conventions were fairly unified, with the party's nominee selected on a first ballot. Other times, the balloting lasted for days, often deteriorating into near brawls as various interest groups within the party negotiated backroom deals to promote their desired candidates. Russian observer Moisei Ostrogorski called the American system of nominating conventions a "colossal travesty of popular institutions." Although most elected officials at all levels were officially nominated by voters, in reality local party organizers discouraged public participation, preferring to choose for themselves a slate of candidates and the delegates to represent them at party conventions. Ostrogorski noted as late as 1902 that less than 10 percent of the eligible voters participated in public caucus meetings at which voters chose convention delegates, a figure judged by historian Robert Cherny as "probably too low for rural areas but reasonably accurate for most cities." Instead, local nominations, like every other aspect of local politics, were run by a ring, described by British scholar James Bryce as "a small knot of persons who pull the wires for the whole city, controlling the primaries, selecting candidates, 'running' conventions, organizing elections, treating on behalf of the party in the city with leaders of the party in the state."[10]

According to La Follette, the boss of the Wisconsin ring, Elisha Keyes, openly resented La Follette's decision to run without first securing Keyes's approval and warned the aspiring politician that he was "fooling away" his time. La Follette recalled: "Boss Keyes did not know it, but opposition of that sort was the best service he could have rendered me. It stirred all the fight I had in me." This tendency to dramatize, if not wholly fabricate adversity was already an established La Follette characteristic. While such threats were neither rare nor empty during this boss-dominated age of politics, Keyes was unlikely to have devoted much energy to something as inconsequential as a political novice seeking a small office. A skilled old-style politician, Keyes had been remarkably proficient in securing favors for both himself and his friends. In 1870, Keyes was elected chairman of the Republican State Central Committee and manipulated Wisconsin's Republican machine to a remarkable degree. Although tried before an investigating committee in Washington for his role in a whiskey-ring scandal, Keyes was cleared of all charges and resumed his role as political boss with no discernible loss of power. By 1877, however, a group of Wisconsin businessmen (including Philetus Sawyer) frightened by Keyes's weak response to widespread farmers' protest movements, seized control of the state to ensure a political atmosphere and leadership conducive to business concerns. No longer chairman of his party by 1880, Keyes's political star was, in reality, on the wane. However, like the self-told tales of La Follette the college student, struggling as the sole support of his sister and widowed mother, the David and Goliath image of La Follette defying the will of a powerful political boss presented an attractive portrait of a man eager to win out over adversity by doing battle for what was "right."[11]

In truth, La Follette's nomination at the county convention was due in part to the very vocal support of local political leader Eli Pederson, who made a moving speech proclaiming Bob as "our boy" to the Primrose delegates. Once nominated, La Follette conducted his campaign mostly door to door, speaking to virtually every voter. His thoroughness in this case did not constitute wasted effort, for his margin of victory was a scant ninety-three votes. In January 1881, Robert La Follette, age twenty-six, took the oath as district attorney of Dane County.[12]

So inexperienced was La Follette that during his first case as district attorney he did not know how to answer the judge's question as to whether the accused had been "arraigned." Understandably chagrined, La Follette refused to admit his ignorance openly, preferring to stall until he could discover the meaning of the word. Despite this inauspicious beginning, La Follette proved to be a moderately effective district attorney. His zeal, however, cannot be overestimated. According to Belle, "I have heard him say that he could assume the posture and expression of a witness and tell whether he was lying or not." But Bob never relied solely on his dramatic intuition. "At times," Belle wrote, "in anticipation of a trial, a speech in Congress, or a political campaign, I felt he was overzealous, too cautious, in making his preparation. His standard was perfection; he wanted to be sure his proof was invulnerable. Every speech was important to him: it had its moment of dread before he began, its inspirational thrill when he had won the audience, and its satisfaction when his hearers expressed their approval afterward." Although Belle judged her husband overly apprehensive in the preparatory stage of any work, "once engaged in the fray he was alert, aggressive, confident, courteous, ready to meet emergencies and surprises

*Dane County's passionate young district attorney, ca. 1881. Although the State Historical Society of Wisconsin lists this image as a college portrait, it is identified in* Robert M. La Follette, *the biography written by La Follette's wife and daughter, and in* La Follette's Magazine, *as the new D.A. (State Historical Society of Wisconsin [X3]51969)*

with a spontaneous skill and swift decision that made him a dreaded adversary. He seldom failed to make the most of every opportunity to convince a jury or audience. That he was often at his best when speaking spontaneously all who ever observed him well knew."[13]

Although La Follette claimed to admire those attorneys who presented their cases with a "commingling of sentiment & sense with a pleasing yet effective style," in his own trial work he heavily favored the influence and power of emotion and drama over a sensible presentation of the facts. In an impassioned plea during a paternity suit, La Follette implored the jury: "Stop and think what she has borne, poor and ignorant though she be[,] she is nevertheless a woman with womanly feelings and instincts, and I can see her filled with the woe of her sin and his counting the months and weeks and days and hours that hurry by mocking her with their flight — eager to ripen her shame. I can see her tossing in sleepless anguish through the hours when he was taking his undisturbed repose — see her pacing her room the gloomy specter of her happier self — see her looking out through her tears into the night and praying that the day may never break — while every throb of the unfolding life within her — which had he kept his promise — would have been a sweet pain — is now an agonizing stab." This kind of emotional appeal became a La Follette trademark throughout his public career, so much so that on at least one occasion a jury was cautioned not to allow La Follette's eloquence to divert them from the truth. He replied indignantly (and eloquently): "Public opinion is not always the same and is not always right in the first interest [but] when it has been clarified by time and calm dispassionate judgment, it is ultimately righteous and just. But from that dark hour in human history when an overwrought, distempered and misguided public opinion pursued the Son of God with the cry, Crucify Him! Crucify Him! it has never been followed blindly by those charged with the high and solemn obligation of measuring out justice to man in the complex affairs of this life." He concluded by denying any attempt to "stir prejudices" or "appeal to passions," proclaiming, "I shall essay not of the tricks of declaration nor seek to steal upon your judgements with any of the arts of oratory. You have been cautioned against eloquence but the only eloquence counsel need fear from me, Gentlemen, will be the powerful eloquence of fact and truth." When La Follette's histrionic oratory won damages for a client who had lost his hand in an industrial accident, the opposing attorney exclaimed, "He could not have made humanity's case any more desperate if it had been the hand of Providence that was lost."[14]

True to his campaign promises, La Follette did not hire any assistant to help him prosecute at the expense of the county, but he did not, as he asserted in his autobiography, perform the tasks unaided, for several attorneys provided him with free legal assistance. Nevertheless, the district attorneyship offered La Follette the chance to live up to the ideals set by Bascom: to prove himself as prosecutor of evil, a protector of good. He personally swore out the complaint in one murder case, so eager was he to convict the man he suspected of the crime. He was eventually forced, however, to dismiss the charge due to lack of evidence. La Follette rarely showed the slightest leniency in his cases, and many of the criminals he convicted were granted pardons or early releases. Later in life he changed in his attitude toward criminals, professing the more progressive attitude that "the individual criminal is not always wholly to blame; that many crimes grow directly out of the sins and injustices of society." At the time, however, to strengthen his image as ever vigilant, La Follette prosecuted even indigents with a vengeance. In his view, one shared by a great many of his constituents, vagrancy was frequently coupled with drunkenness, and both were an insult to the American Dream of the self-made individual. Just as La Follette resented his stepfather for depending on his mother instead of amply providing for the family, he showed no compassion for any able-bodied man who was not respectable and self-supporting. He praised independent Americans and railed against "human parasites": "They sweep over us like a plague; they haunt the dark lanes, hide in our barns, glide in at open doors, beg, steal, commit an occasional murder, and ruin thousands of homes with nameless violations. . . . Independence is the broad underlying stratum of broad, manly character; dependence is the forfeiture of all natural nobility. Independence develops all our powers; dependence destroys all our worth. Independence is the pure stream starting away up in the mountain, feeling its own course down the valley, cutting its own channel to the sea; dependence is the sluggish pool awaiting an overflow til its dead waters are mantled with the scum of inaction and its foul miasma poisons the air."[15]

La Follette's determined righteousness did not make him an ardent prohibitionist. In contrast to John Bascom's outspoken support of total abstinence, La Follette kept a low profile concerning the issue, only selectively prosecuting saloonkeepers and doing so without his usual blaze of moral outrage, resulting in an uncharacteristic lack of convictions. He enforced the corresponding Sabbatarian laws with similar minimal enthusiasm, but on both issues managed not to antagonize either side, no easy task during a time in which the struggle over prohibition was heated. Suggested reasons for his refusal to commit himself firmly to temperance range from hints that La Follette had been corrupted by the saloon lobby to more convincing arguments that he was already considering running for Congress and had no desire to alienate his voters, the majority of whom were "wets." Following the humiliating drinking incident of his youth, no evidence exists to indicate that La Follette was much of a drinker, but he remained unopposed to light social drinking, and drank alcohol himself for medicinal purposes. Regardless, in 1917, La Follette voted for prohibition, reasoning that the people would be able to decide for themselves when the amendment was submitted to the respective states. His reluctance to commit himself as a "dry" stemmed not only from political expediency but also personal conviction and a reluctance to appear as puritanical as his stepfather.[16]

There are discrepancies between the official record of La Follette's performance as district attorney and his own accounts. His memory of working the sheriff "half to death" to obtain evidence is contradicted by the record, and his boasts of a record number of convictions is only partly substantiated. In the lower municipal court he did indeed set a record with eighty-six convictions of various public nuisances during his first year, but his record in the circuit court was only average: his convictions tended to be in minor cases such as disorderly conduct, and he lost his cases involving murder, extortion, and adultery. Nonetheless, his private practice, with brother-in-law Robert Siebecker as partner, flourished, and at the end of his first term he was reelected, receiving 118 more votes than his Democratic opponent.[17]

Characteristically, La Follette denied his political ambitions, presenting his candidacy for Congress as mere acquiescence to the urgings of others. Belle was certainly not among them, for while she would have welcomed the increase in salary brought by a seat in Congress, she was never supportive of any move that would take her away from her safe, beloved home. According to La Follette, it was his most intimate friend, former classmate and future law partner Samuel Harper, who first introduced the idea that La Follette run for Congress. La Follette asserted that the two friends consulted no one else until La Follette determined to enter the race and that they began the campaign "as though it were a fine game, and with great enjoyment of the prospect." This account minimizes the role of La Follette's "political godfather," Civil War general George E. Bryant, who had replaced Keyes as Madison postmaster. Bryant, a well-known and wealthy farmer and cattle breeder, had previously been a state senator and was the county judge who many years before had prohibited Mary and John Saxton from making further inroads on the sale of the La Follette farm. His actions had not only protected the family's assets, they had directly defied the wishes of John Saxton, thereby doubly meriting the esteem of young Bob La Follette. Bryant was forty-nine in 1882, the year he became postmaster and a substantial personal influence on La Follette. Only six years older than Josiah La Follette would have been, Bryant shared many of the physical and moral characteristics La Follette attributed to his father. Bryant was a large man with an impressive beard and a full head of hair. La Follette called him "a wise man, a good lawyer and judge . . . from a fine old New England family" and considered him "a great moral teacher" who "exerted a powerful influence for good upon the political thought and standards of his time." As with Bascom, La Follette's fondness for Bryant was reciprocated. During Bryant's final illness, the old general wrote to La Follette: "Next to my own two boys, I loved you and Sam Harper better than any one else in the world." Harper and Bryant served as La Follette's most avid supporters and trusted friends (save Belle) until their deaths, which he mourned deeply. Bryant was La Follette's most effective political ally during the 1880s, and he used his substantial influence to help the district attorney enter Congress. La Follette did not allow Bryant's efforts to go unrewarded, using the patronage he so decried in others to repay the judge with an appointive public office following each of his own successful elections over the next two decades.[18]

La Follette claimed that the vigor with which he launched his campaign was not inspired by Bryant's offers of influence but came about as a result, once again, of being challenged by a corrupt authority figure. In his autobiography, La Follette recounts a conversation much like the one he claimed to have held with Elisha Keyes subsequent to his commitment to run for district attorney. He records that Phil Spooner, member of the Madison ring that controlled the congressional district in question, upbraided him for not consulting them, concluding, "Well, young man, you can't go to Congress." La Follette did again "triumph over adversity" by winning this election, but not by virtue of the same personal campaign that contributed to his previous victories. He dropped out of the campaign early due to illness, leaving his aides and supporters to carry on in his stead. Although La Follette liked to present himself as a lone crusader, General Bryant in particular worked steadily and efficiently on his behalf, using his many contacts to promote La Follette's candidacy.[19]

La Follette made no mention in his autobiography of his illness-induced withdrawal from his first congressional campaign, but it was a scenario to be repeated, with some variation, in almost every campaign he entered and at other times of political and personal stress as well. Although La Follette's career was highlighted by enormous energy, enthusiasm, and ambition, it was made possible by periodic bouts of sustained illness. La Follette's frequent retreats from political and personal pressures were the result of a broad variety of common ailments, including colds, nervous indigestion, stomach trouble, digestion trouble (referred to within the family more plainly as diarrhea or "bowel trouble"), La Grippe, exhaustion, liver congestion, and, frequently, gallbladder trouble. Theories abound as to the nature and origin of La Follette's various maladies. That La Follette truly experienced gallbladder ailments is evidenced by the two elective surgeries he underwent at the Mayo Clinic. Jerome D. Oremland, M.D., however, notes that "gall stones rarely cause symptoms [except in] highly definable acute states and only with the wildest imagination could someone call the symptoms that [La Follette] suffered from as being the result of that" and concludes that most of La Follette's various illnesses were somaticizations of his emotions. Granddaughter Sherry La Follette contends that her grandfather suffered from manic depression (bipolar disorder), a biological disorder caused by a chemical imbalance, possibly inherited — and a condition that she herself battles. While the diagnoses differ, the pattern of La Follette's illnesses remains clear: while many were brought on by circumstances clearly beyond his control (for example, diarrhea induced by contaminated waters, virtually unavoidable in his continuous travels), others were neither inevitable, imaginary, or psychosomatic, but rather self-induced.[20]

Throughout his career, despite warnings from physicians, family, friends, and supporters, La Follette refused to voluntarily intersperse his periods of intense work and strain with proper exercise, and he refused to take a substantial rest until forced to do so. "He would forget to eat or sleep," his wife noted, "he would work so long and hard that he would sink exhausted into his desk." La Follette's desire to establish himself as a man so strongly dedicated to pursuing "right" led him to resist any appearance of seeking relaxation merely for pleasure. La Follette's illnesses resulted in a number of gains. The pattern of working until totally exhausted, all reserves spent and natural immunities weakened by factors including a poorly balanced diet, allowed La Follette the "right" to enjoy some guiltless rest once the inevitable illness struck. He reassured himself and others that he would be working still if only his health, which stubbornly remained unaffected by his firm resolve, had held out.[21]

Whatever the illness, treatment was nearly always the same: complete rest — that is, absolutely no exposure to legal or political matters — and frequently a special diet. Often he would insist on his own eagerness to continue working but cite strict doctor's orders as the preventative force. Very often those orders, in keeping with the fashion of the day, included lengthy trips to warmer climates, trips La Follette enjoyed immensely. La Follette specified that the rooms he occupy on campaign tours be warm. He hated the long, cold winters of Wisconsin and Washington and returned repeatedly to San Diego and La Jolla, California, staying as long as six months. He believed in the rejuvenating powers of strong sunshine. He also made several trips to the springs of French Lick, Indiana, to rest and to imbibe the water he described as a "powerful agent" that "acts vigorously upon the stomach, liver and bowels."[22]

La Follette's illnesses also provided a handy rationalization in the event that he lose an election. Rather than be discouraged by the fact that his very best personal efforts were simply not sufficient, he could avoid accepting full responsibility for his failure by reassuring himself he had not been able to give his "all." In addition, not all illnesses were genuine. Claiming illness occasionally bought him vitally needed time, more than once he emerged from a "sickbed," where it had been alleged he had been doing nothing but taking a very much needed rest, only to present a painstakingly researched and masterfully composed speech or bill.

Finally, illness, whether genuine or only professed, offered La Follette a temporary haven when the pressures of his various offices became distasteful or overpowering. For example, as his resentment and distrust of Theodore Roosevelt grew, illness allowed La Follette to avoid their scheduled meetings. By claiming illness, as he did in 1901 when, as new governor of Wisconsin, he was inundated by hundreds of letters of application (with even more corresponding letters of endorsement) for political positions, La Follette gained a brief but much needed respite. Illness not only allowed La Follette to receive extensions on deadlines, it provided an excuse when he performed in a poor or slipshod manner. Such benefits did not go unnoticed, particularly by La Follette's detractors, who occasionally hinted that some of his illnesses might involve more than just sporadic poor health, that he was "sulking in his tent."[23]

For all that La Follette's illnesses were often politically convenient, they served a genuine and far more vitally important, though less obvious, function as well. While his exhaustion was usually referred to as physical in nature, its emotional elements, particularly depression, were frequently obvious to La Follette himself and to those around him. Belle once devoted a column in the family magazine to the topic of "nerves," concluding, "The sense of overwork is nervous, not muscular, for it is more common to those who have no physical labor to perform than to those whose muscular strength is overtaxed. Misdirected nervous force is the secret of most overwork and breakdown." Doctors at the Mayo Clinic in 1920 diagnosed La Follette as suffering from overeating, overwork, and overstrain and advised him to "avoid those types of work which cause irritability and an unstable temper." La Follette himself wrote of his inability to relax and the detrimental affects of emotional strain, noting that anxiety frequently and pointlessly robbed him of necessary sleep. At the onset of his more severe illnesses, La Follette's usual defenses against feelings of despair weakened but did not break down entirely, often taking the form of active concern about his financial status, an anxiety he usually disclaimed.[24]

Genuine physical illness, in short, was an emotional necessity. While ill, La Follette could relax his desperate attempts to be all-knowing, all-powerful, all "right." Sometimes simply being away from his office, surrounded by concerned, sympathetic friends and family members, was sufficiently soothing, and he continued with his daily professional routine in the reassuring surroundings of his home or vacation setting. At other times, the pressures of his work had to be totally removed, and he was isolated from all unpleasant or taxing matters. La Follette's aides realized the importance of such a shield as one of the most efficient ways of hastening his recovery.

Illness brought more than just temporary respite from pressures to do "right." Friends, family, and the public almost universally put aside any personal or political criticisms during La Follette's illnesses and were solicitous and supportive. While some newspapers used his frequent ill health to call for his retirement from politics, causing him to remark in 1923, "The reactionary newspapers have been burying me for thirty years," most provided him with sympathetic coverage. Politicians, even those who opposed his policies, momentarily put aside their differences and tendered sympathy. Letters from friends expressed concern, but the most loving and supportive came from within the ranks of his own family. During one illness his daughter Fola wrote: "Dearest heart, I can't tell you how sorry I am to think of you not well. . . . Any other man but you would have been worn out long ago with such Herculean labors as you have performed the whole winter, yet you would not take a moment's breathing space until nature simply demanded that you should. And now I suppose you think it strange that your tired body, which has for years done the work of two strong men, insists upon having a few weeks rest, don't you? Bless your heart, Papa. [There] are few men like you. Such indominatable will, such lofty ideals and gigantic executive ability — a power of ruling men and yet withal tender and loving." [25]

During lengthy illnesses La Follette enjoyed not just written reassurances but personal attention as well, attention he craved particularly from his wife, to whom he wrote, "We ought to be together every moment." For despite his dependence on Belle, the La Follettes endured many long separations. During their older son's illness in 1918, for example, they were apart for a year. Sometimes financial and familial circumstances did not allow Belle to accompany her husband, but other times it was by her choice, born out of her love for her Wisconsin home and her dislike of Washington. Bob wrote frequently of his desire for her presence, his dissatisfaction with their frequent separations, and his dependence on her letters, for Belle refrained from joining him during many of his countless minor illnesses, preferring instead to write loving letters. During serious illnesses, however, she was at his side and accompanied him on his many journeys to warmer climates.

Belle not only dedicated herself to raising her husband's spirits during those periods with words of praise, she urged her children to do the same, reminding them, "he has a great heart hunger for you," and reporting that their letters brought much pleasure and comfort.[26]

La Follette was also frequently accompanied on these trips by his family physician, of whom he wrote in 1916, "Doctor Philip Fox of Madison is my closest friend." So close was their friendship that the La Follette's second son was named for the doctor. La Follette not only admired Fox deeply, he professed great respect for the whole medical profession and later struck up a personal friendship with Dr. Charles Mayo, one of the famous Mayo brothers. He wrote of medical doctors: "The learning and wisdom of the physician appeals to us most profoundly. It covers everything from the cradle to the coffin. It is nearest to the mystery of birth and knows with prophetic eye the face of death as he makes his silent & insidious approach. We find we trust our physician with our confidences. We lay bare to him our very souls. We whisper in his ear the secrets of our inner lives. We open to him the privacy of our homes. . . . How entirely are we in the hands and at the mercy of the physician. How we watch for his coming — How we search his face as he bends over the bed of our loved one — How we hang upon his every word he utters & cling to every hope he offers." In a pleasant environment, far away from professional pressures, La Follette could enjoy both the medical attention and psychological counsel of his trusted friend.[27]

La Follette's aides and his wife were keenly aware that "kind, encouraging words . . . coming directly from the heart go further to hasten Mr. La Follette's recovery than the treatment of his physician," and they "only wish[ed] the mail were full of them." Away from the public spotlight La Follette gave off not an "air of challenge, of assertiveness . . . of pugnacity" but a "manner of gentleness." His "fleet" expression after a compliment "was amazingly like gratitude," and "his manner had not only gentleness and kindliness, it had moreover a certain wistfulness. As if he would like people to like him." Belle once remarked, "He will be so very much pleased with the beautiful things said in the testimonials. I enjoy and appreciate them too but I always feel that [he] has depths of enjoyment beyond mine." In a reply to a supporter's letter, her husband concurred: "Many times there comes to the public official, desirous to do his duty, a sense of weakness. He is also often overwhelmed by the mass of work which demands his attention. Believe me when I say that letters, of the nature of your communication, coming from men actuated by the spirit in your letter, are most needful to encourage the tired public officer." To another supporter he wrote, "I cannot tell you what a pleasure it was to me to receive your very kind letter. . . . I can assure you that to feel that one has such friends is what makes life worth living, and I know that your words come straight from the heart." Following La Follette's death, Senator George Moses declared, "I have rarely known a man who reacted more fully to friendship. In him lay a deep and rich vein of sentiment."[28]

For La Follette, who knew "how trying it is with the travel, hotel life, sudden changes, and constant attacks upon one's nervous vitality in constantly meeting men and giving out the best there is in you at all times," illness provided an escape from anxiety and depression. "Good health," he noted while emerging from an illness, "brings good spirits." More accurately, it was the initial poor health that eventually brought "good" spirits. As a child, La Follette had discovered the many uses of feigned illness. It allowed him to skip Sunday school and indulge himself. More importantly, it offered him respite from his stepfather and from lessons that taught his father was burning in hell. Illness brought him the uncritical love and care of his mother and sister, providing him with feelings of reassurance and approval. As an adult, he did not feign illness, but, by his actions and lifestyle, often induced it, ultimately recreating those warm, comforting childhood feelings. The prescribed rest and diet allowed him to rebuild his physical health, while the lack of stress combined with the emotional support of others rebuilt what might be termed his spiritual health, allowing him to carry on with his personal and political life.[29]

Despite their candidate's lack of participation due to illness in the 1884 congressional campaign, La Follette's supporters carried out an ambitious campaign presenting him as a bright, self-made young man to a populace weary of professional politicians. La Follette won the election by a slim margin of 491 votes. Boss Keyes is reported to have remarked stoically, "It's the young fellows [in the nominating caucuses] that did it." The election results, however, cannot be attributed to a candidate-based campaign over a contact-based one. Instead, big businessmen throughout Wisconsin were beating the old-style political bosses at their own game. General Bryant, Belle La Follette acknowledged, was "an indispensable factor in Bob's election to Congress." The many contacts Bryant had made in commanding a Wisconsin regiment during the war and in his many years as prominent farmer and county judge helped bring his young protégé the necessary votes to render Robert M. La Follette, age thirty, the youngest member of the Forty-ninth Congress. Belle, who had campaigned indirectly on her husband's behalf, accompanied him to Washington, for General Bryant had advised, "The good people of the Congressional District like to see a man accompanied by his wife."[30]

# 6: CONGRESSMAN LA FOLLETTE
## SO GOOD A FELLOW EVEN HIS ENEMIES LIKE HIM

When Congressman Robert La Follette first arrived in Washington with his wife, the two had graduated from the state university only five years before and had never previously traveled east of Chicago. The La Follettes took advantage of the vast lag time between congressional elections and the seating of those new representatives, arriving nearly a year before La Follette's term began in order for him to observe and "learn the ropes." La Follette's height, five feet, five inches, helped to make the youthful freshman congressman a popular target for the jests of newspaper reporters. The La Follettes, who had left their daughter Fola with Belle's mother in Baraboo, tried to establish, without much success, a stable home life. Their finances obliged them to change their rooms several times. Belle's displeasure at this turn of events was clear. Moreover, the social life was, in her view, "too much influenced by women without any special occupation, whose thoughts were centered on society, dress, cards, and gossip." Belle termed official life "interesting and colorful" but complained that one feeling — "that of being unsettled"— permeated the entire experience: "Officially we met many delightful people and made some close friends; but however pleasantly we were situated, however long we occupied a house, it was never *home*."[1]

To compound her discontent, Belle tired quickly of having to make conversation with constituents on the couple's frequent and lengthy train trips. Her husband, however, was "genuinely interested" in such exchanges and would say "just the right thing," so that "they would soon be calling him 'Bob,'" and by the end of the trip "it was like parting with old friends." La Follette's eagerness to please appeared boundless, and his efforts were frequently noted in the press: "Fascinating personality and manners . . . make 'Bob' seem a synonym of friendship and good fellowship to all whom he exerts himself to please." This personal appeal was one of La Follette's greatest assets during his tenure as a representative: the abrasive self-righteousness that would mark his tenure in subsequent offices was far less pronounced. Following his three terms in Washington, a reporter noted, La Follette "is popular at home, popular with his colleagues, and popular in the house. . . . He is so good a fellow that even his enemies like him." For Belle, the intrusions such popularity generated were not always welcome, and she was relieved when presented the rare opportunity of time alone with her husband.[2]

Belle did enjoy, however, the social functions that included "the entire official group." She distinguished these large, inclusive gatherings from the "insidious," closed inner circles of Washington society, because the bigger events were "necessarily democratic in spirit." While no one enjoyed better than Bob informal gatherings, especially in his own home, he objected to all formal functions, attending only at Belle's request. Once in attendance, however, she noted, "he seemed to be having the best time in the world, though he would never admit it." These opposing preferences are quite representative of the La Follettes. Belle's shyness was not as noticeable at the more formal gatherings where conversation was less intimate and tended to revolve around general, less personal topics. Such events were more "natural" and pleasing to her than those made up of a select and often snobby or gossipy group. Bob appeared able to enjoy himself at almost any kind of gathering, but nevertheless continued to be, as he had confided to his journal during law school, truly comfortable only with the "intimate few." Unlike Belle, he gloried in speaking to small groups, confident in his ability to charm and persuade. Large groups, however, unless part of a formal audience, created too great a challenge to ever be as pleasurable. One aspect of Washington life, however, did appeal to both Belle and Bob. Despite the limited state of their financial affairs, they "never missed a good play" and attended the light operas of Gilbert and Sullivan and others.[3]

La Follette took his seat in Congress in December 1885. Grover Cleveland, the first Democratic president since James Buchanan, had been inaugurated the preceding March. Cleveland championed tariff reduction and civil service reform while opposing unwarranted drains on the national treasury, especially private relief bills and pensions sought by Civil War veterans. Such causes only scratched the surface of the challenges facing Cleveland's administration. The "gilt" of the Gilded Age was glittering indeed: the fantastic lifestyles of individuals who made enormous profits providing steel, oil, meat, timber, and all the other raw materials, manufactured goods, and services vital to a burgeoning nation; the mushrooming cities; the rapidly developing American west. The urban industrial age boasted a rising gross national product, bringing the United States to a new place of importance in world markets. But darkness lurked beneath that dazzling exterior chockablock with such modern marvels as street cars, telephones and electric lights, and inexpensive manufactured goods. The economy, unstable at best, was frequently rocked by depressions. Immigrants poured in from Europe, providing much of the labor force of industrialized America. After long hours in dangerous conditions, workers went home to urban ghettos rife with poverty, crime, and disease. All opportunities for meaningful advancement seemed taken. What remained were menial, often dangerous jobs, so low paying that frequently the labor of the entire family was necessary for survival. Precious, nonrenewable resources were ripped from the earth with no thought to their conservation, let alone preservation. And government appeared at best helpless to curb the harmful excesses, at worst, a willing collaborator. These issues, and many more, would occupy Robert M. La Follette in years to come. But controversy surrounds La Follette's commitment to progressive reform during his tenure as a congressional representative.

During the brief period before illness forced him out of his speaking campaign, La Follette paid all the conventional tributes to the Republican Party. One scholar calls Representative La Follette essentially conservative, "a regular party man," while another refers to him as a "political weathervane" who only later converted to progressivism. Even a contemporary who maintained that the young congressman had been a reformer conceded, "It has been a serious question . . . whether or not, at least in its first years, the La Follette reform movement was inspired by any other motive than the personal ambition of La Follette."[4]

La Follette's years as a representative were not as marked by unlimited attacks on big business or by strong commitments to progressivism as his autobiography indicates or his subsequent career might suggest. He did stray from his party's line when he opposed the unchecked power of big business, especially railroads, and strove to protect farmers, laborers, and all peoples denied basic civil rights. Although he exhibited little leadership, his performance remained basically consistent with reform values already established. In the abstract, he honored only the highest standards of conduct, following his belief that "one deviation, one relaxation, one bending of principle" and a politician "falls, and falls forever." "There is no escape, no appeal," he warned his fellow congressmen, "No! No! Politician or statesman, more than any other man, must . . . ever bend a 'vaulting ambition' to meet the last exaction of the moral law." In practice, he was a little less rigorous. For example, although it was standard practice for politicians to travel courtesy of the complimentary passes supplied to them by the various railroad companies, La Follette paid his own railroad transportation, but he did so quietly, electing simply to file the passes routinely sent to him rather than making a show of returning them.[5]

On 22 April 1886, La Follette made his maiden major speech during a debate on the House floor, opposing (unsuccessfully) a bill to finance improvement of certain rivers and harbors. Like his fellow Republicans, La Follette supported federal funding of waterway development, but this bill, he declared, flagrantly ignored engineers' cost estimates and recommendations. "The tendency of such legislation," he asserted, "is to debauch the country and dull the moral instincts of the American Congress." "Let the committee report a bill for the improvement of only such rivers and harbors," he thundered, "as the interest of national commerce demands." Arguing (again unsuccessfully) to amend the bill a few weeks later, La Follette warned that the people were not fooled by expenditures of their money based upon unsound business principles. "When this snow melteth," he prophesied, "there shall come a flood." "The current corrupt system," he railed, "will break down in this House with a crash that will shake half the members out of their seats." La Follette remembered that this initial speech received much favorable notice. Belle recalled it differently: "He carefully worked out what he was to say, memorized and rehearsed it. Though not striving for perfection, as in 'Iago,' he prepared in somewhat the same spirit, and the address bears the imprint of the college orator. When he rehearsed, the speech had seemed to me quite perfect. But . . . [t]he effect of his formal oration in the large chamber with many empty seats was not so moving as I had anticipated."[6]

This disappointment may have been somewhat ameliorated six weeks later. Sensing that La Follette's support ran deeper than most, Washington's African American community invited the congressman to address the 1886 graduating class of Howard University Law School. "We are one people," he told the graduates, "one by truth, one almost by blood." "Our lives run side by side," he reminded them, "our ashes rest in the same soil." Urging them to seize "the waiting world of opportunity," he railed against separatism: "It is snobbish stupidity, it is supreme folly, to talk of non-contact, or exclusion!" The students' enthusiastic response to his speech and the words of praise from former slave and tireless advocate of his race, Frederick Douglass, deeply gratified La Follette.[7]

Early in his career La Follette earned not only the respect of African American leaders Booker T. Washington, Edgar G. Brown, and G. Victor Cools, he consistently enjoyed the support of important women's leaders as well, including Carrie Chapman Catt and Harriet Taylor Upton. When La Follette advocated votes for women in 1912, he stressed the longevity of his commitment to equality: "I have always believed in woman suffrage, to the same extent as man suffrage, for the reason that the interests of men and women are not superior nor antagonistic one to the other, but are mutual and inseparable. . . . Woman suffrage is but the extension of the principle of democracy. . . . Co-suffrage, like co-education, will react, not in the special advantage of either men or women but will result in a more enlightened better balanced citizenship and truer democracy." "It is so obvious as to hardly admit of argument," he concluded. "We cannot have real democracy while one-half of the population is disfranchised,—and a majority of that

*La Follette's career-long dedication to furthering the rights of women brought him the support of many women's groups. Here women from all states endorse La Follette for the presidency in 1924. (Library of Congress USZ62-090423-90608)*

half have been forced into industry." He also noted approvingly (if somewhat naïvely), "In the states which enjoy suffrage, one of the first results has been equal pay for equal work," and concluded, "The stability of society itself, of all the things we hold most sacred, rests upon this fundamental principle."[8]

La Follette's fervent belief in the equality of all people led him to actively oppose anti-Semitism and discrimination against Asian Americans as well, but in the House he received more notice for his defense of the civil rights of African Americans. In 1889, during the bitterly contested election of an African American representative from South Carolina, La Follette lectured white racists: "There is nothing threatening or portentous in the Negro problem today, excepting as you make it so. The difficulty does not lie with him, but with you instead, in the blind prejudice and stubborn antagonism, ever opposed to his development politically and socially as a citizen." In supporting the so-called Force Bill, designed to guarantee the enforcement of a free, unintimidated ballot to African American southerners, La Follette warned the white South, "[Y]ou can[not] maintain a domestic election system rooted in perjury and fraud and watered with blood and not see it finally blossom and fruit in bitterness and hate and awful retribution." To the applause of fellow House members, he concluded that having "exercised patience for a generation with the people of the South," northern voting constituencies in 1890 "demand that in every part of this country every man shall freely cast his vote and have it honestly counted." La Follette supporters emphasized the very small African American vote in Wisconsin, noting, "He did not need, in order to get votes, to make any statement on the Negro problem which was not sincere." In a statement supporting a federal anti-lynching law in 1924, La Follette stressed his thirty-five years of public promotion of civil rights for all: "My entire public record has made plain that I do not recognize distinctions of race, color or creed. To me an American is an American, no matter what the country of origin in the old world of his ancestors, the religion of his fathers, or his complexion. I had assumed that my every act throughout my long public life, first in the House of Representatives, then as Governor and as United States Senator, had made that clear."[9]

Two days after his Howard commencement address, La Follette delivered a House speech favoring a tax on oleomargarine, which signaled the beginning of his lifelong efforts to protect his home state's powerful dairy industry. La Follette condemned oleo, in typically dramatic fashion, as "fraudulent and unwholesome . . . , as powerful and irresistible as vicious ingenuity can make it. It is as pitiless as a plague." La Follette also began another lifelong interest during his first term in the House — the rights of Native Americans — the result of a circuitous turn of events typical of Congress during this period.[10]

During La Follette's initial term as congressman he first encountered Philetus Sawyer, the multimillionaire lumberman who was senior senator from Wisconsin and leader of the "Milwaukee Ring." According to La Follette, Sawyer promised him a place on the Committee of Public Lands only to ensure that La Follette would not continue to make his predilection for that committee known. Sawyer saw to it, however, that La Follette was assigned to the far less influential Indian Affairs Committee. The young representative later worked against a Sawyer-supported ship subsidy bill, which La Follette considered "a flagrant effort on the part of private interests to get into the public treasury." La Follette's indignant, self-righteous reaction to Sawyer's jabbing him in the chest and calling him a bolter for his opposition to the bill is reminiscent of his reaction to other alleged attempts to intimidate him. As with his confrontations with Elisha Keyes and Phil Spooner, in La Follette's detailed account of his altercation with Sawyer he presents himself as a man of impeccable integrity, unintimidated by the threats of a powerful adversary: "I was furious. I revolted at the whole thing. 'Senator Sawyer,' I said, 'You can't tell me how to vote on any question. You've no business on this floor seeking to influence legislation. You are violating the rules. You get out of here, or I will call the Speaker's attention to you.' I turned toward the Speaker's desk. He knew I would do what I said, and left the floor immediately without another word." The bill was defeated and La Follette suffered no immediate repercussions, but he eventually was to come into open and dramatic conflict with Sawyer.[11]

Once a member of the Indian Affairs Committee, an undaunted, even defiant La Follette used his own money to purchase a small secondhand library on Native Americans, working avidly to protect tribes' property and rights. The notion that Native Americans had rights at all was of dubious credibility to many Americans in the 1880s. The concern over the plight of the Native American, piqued by Helen Hunt Jackson's *A Century of Dishonor* (1881) and *Ramona* (1884), was no match for the belief that the definition of progress was continued expansion and development of urban, industrialized America. Congress blithely deprived Native Americans of traditional lands and continually usurped the oil, mineral, fishing, and timber rights of the lands remaining. On the floor of the House, La Follette called for greater Native American involvement in their own affairs. In reference to "these gentlemen who come here to be delegates for these Indians and to represent their best interests," La Follette claimed, "there is [a] mouse in this meal." La Follette termed Native Americans "entirely capable of making a selection of an agent to participate in the appraisal of their lands," urging that "the privilege of making such a selection . . . be accorded to them." La Follette's career-long efforts to protect the rights of Native Americans were motivated by his staunch belief in America as the land of opportunity for all: "Here the limitations upon the intellectual growth and development, the social place, and the financial success and triumph of each person are fixed by his own character and power alone. I care not what his birth or station, though born to an inheritance of poverty and toil and obscurity, if he be capable, if he be honest, if he be industrious, if he have courage and pluck and persistence, he will win wealth and power and honor and fame [because] all around him lies inviting and unlimited opportunity."[12]

When "the long strain" of the first session ended, the La Follettes returned to Wisconsin, where, according to Belle, "a respite from politics

*Nascent Progressive: Congressman La Follette in 1887.*
(Washington Evening Star *Collection*)

would have been welcome," but was impossible, for they were never "allowed to forget the campaign for renomination and election was at hand." Even when no campaigns were imminent, they found little time for rest or relaxation. The Christmas vacation of 1887, for example, found them both hard at work "cleaning up" various letters to constituents. During campaigns, Belle found herself "unduly anxious over the opposition" as the "persistent efforts to oust him" troubled her much more, she asserted, than they did Bob. She continued her tireless attention to the distribution of campaign literature, while her husband was very much in demand as a speaker, "reaching every voting precinct and acquiring an intimate acquaintance with his constituency." This contact with the people, Belle believed, made it impossible for the machine to defeat his renomination.[13]

La Follette believed it dangerous for a public speaker to gain the reputation of a wit, for nothing he could say would ever be taken seriously, Abraham Lincoln being one notable exception. La Follette therefore usually made few attempts at humor during informal speeches and virtually none during formal addresses to Congress. This unabated seriousness earned him the reputation of something of a humorless drudge. Nonetheless, his persuasive speaking was one of his greatest campaigning assets. Belle professed to most enjoy her husband's speaking when he was "on the stump" (rather than in Congress), for only there would he display publicly, albeit sparingly, the "spontaneous wit which was part of his essential nature." Belle was defensive about her husband's sense of humor. It greatly annoyed her whenever he was portrayed as a grim, unsocial being, for his "unfailing wit," she contended, gladdened their household. La Follette's appreciation of humor and his own frequently self-depreciating wit is evident in his letters and in articles about him, but more often it manifested itself in his love of reading amusing stories aloud, often in dialect, to appreciative audiences of family and friends. Even in real life he saw himself, and other prominent figures, as "actors in a drama full of humor."[14]

In addition to delivering lengthy speeches, La Follette successfully utilized the literary bureau during this and subsequent campaigns — an approach to voters that circumvented the need to depend heavily upon the Republican machine or party. La Follette wrote to various friends in each ward and township in his district requesting that they send him the names of active and potential supporters. La Follette sent out reams of letters, campaign literature, and even garden seeds to his constituents. A "regular" Republican in many of his views, most notably his defense of protective tariffs, such personalized, unconventional tactics were earning La Follette the label of "demagogue."

La Follette, unopposed in his bid for renomination, won the 1886 campaign by a generous margin of 3,500 votes. He and Belle returned to Washington with daughter Fola, whom Belle vowed never again to leave behind, and Bob's mother. Mary Saxton was interested in the congressional debates and, in contrast to her daughter-in-law, thoroughly enjoyed every aspect of Washington life. They all settled in a boardinghouse that Belle found more socially worthwhile than most, at 52 B Street N.E., where the Russell Senate

Office Building now stands, facing Capitol Park. So relaxed and confident was La Follette that following the adjournment in March 1887 he enjoyed his first real vacation in years and, taking his family with him, paid a visit to his half-sister Ellen in South Dakota. There he purchased a 1,000-acre ranch and began planning to stock it with horses. This ranch was the fulfillment of the dream he and Belle had shared of owning their own farm and offered a way for Bob to emulate his father. Unfortunately, it proved a steady drain on the La Follette finances. For eleven years they carried the heavy burden, but finally had to sell just when the price of both land and horses was, according to Belle, at lowest ebb.[15]

A speech that gained him national prominence marked La Follette's second term. Tariff reform had dominated the presidential campaign, and Cleveland strove to fulfill his promises of downward revision. Originally established to raise federal revenues, after 1861 tariffs (government import duties or taxes) were increasingly levied to protect domestically manufactured products from foreign competition. La Follette's rebuttal of the Democratic Speaker John Carlisle's defense of the Mills Tariff bill (a tariff-cutting measure) in July 1888 brought him such undivided attention that he was granted unanimous consent to extend his remarks from the five minutes allotted to the hour and a quarter it took for him to complete his speech. The Democrats argued that high tariffs contributed to the excess profits and increasing power of the nation's trusts and monopolies, furthering the divide between business and the general citizenry, especially laborers and farmers. La Follette charged, "With a reckless indifference to plain and established facts, [Carlisle's] declaration tramples under foot the verified reports of . . . Congress and plays with . . . a vandal hand." To the applause of his fellow Republicans, La Follette thundered that Carlisle's interpretation "transforms a devotee of the American system" of a strong federal role in achieving economic strength and independence "into a heretic and makes him worship the British beast" of rigid class structure. La Follette argued the Republican party line, that what was good for American business was good for America: his eloquent argument that the most marked economic advances were in industries retaining a protective tariff assured him a place on the Ways and Means Committee, the youngest Republican so honored since the appointment of William McKinley.[16]

La Follette was not a party regular in all of his actions, however. In addition to his support of a tax on oleomargarine, he approved agricultural experimental stations. He strove to protect domestic tobacco growers from tariff loopholes and to implement various trust-busting measures. In 1887, he voted for the Interstate Commerce Act, the first federal effort to regulate the all-powerful railroads. All fees, according to the act, must be fair and reasonable, ending the rebates, kickbacks, discriminatory rates, and other practices commonly and openly carried out by the nation's railroads. The five-member Interstate Commerce Commission established to administer the law all too quickly became a virtual tool of the railroads, but, on paper at least, the precedent for governmental control and regulation of business had been set.

La Follette won his 1888 bid for reelection by 3,000 votes. His third term in the House of Representatives was highlighted by a much publicized speech in support of the McKinley Tariff. La Follette continued to denounce unreasonable tariffs as barriers to free and open competition, but he rigorously defended many protective duties, particularly in view of their impact on American labor. The only truly raw materials, he emphasized, were the trees still growing in the forests, the ore lying deep in the earth. "[W]here and how did it get its great value . . . ? Ah, man sought it out." "There is no escape," he warned his fellow representatives, "from the conclusion that labor is the great issue involved here." Years later he noted in his autobiography, "Where there can be shown to be no difference in labor costs, I am for free trade. But the difference must be determined by real experts who understand the use and limits of statistics." This belief in the wisdom of dispassionate experts (rather than the self-serving advice of interested parties) would mark much of La Follette's proposed legislation in subsequent years. To the applause of his fellow Republicans, he asserted, "Whenever foreign products the like of which we can supply our own people with have been taking the market from us, there we have raised the barrier to the protective point, and . . . in so doing we have responded to a patriotic duty." The McKinley Tariff that La Follette so eloquently defended established high tariffs and was sufficiently popular among Republicans to help pave the way for McKinley's presidency.[17]

Representative La Follette also enjoyed his appointment to the powerful Ways and Means Committee, where he garnered the praise of Thomas B. Reed, the Speaker of the House who so dominated that Fifty-first Congress. La Follette and Theodore Roosevelt, then United States Civil Service Commissioner, first met when they worked together during their support of Reed in his struggle against McKinley for the speakership. (Belle La Follette's early dealings with Roosevelt were far less dignified: while gesturing with characteristic vigor during a conversation, Roosevelt accidentally spilled his coffee on her dress.)[18]

Despite his various political triumphs, 1889 found La Follette writing a long letter of protest to the new president, Benjamin Harrison, who had defeated Cleveland's bid for reelection in an extremely tight race. Harrison pledged to uphold a strong protective tariff as a safeguard to domestic industry and stressed his dedication to stability and order. He warned businesses in his inaugural address, "If the educated and influential classes in a community either practice or connive at the systematic violation of laws that seem to them to cross their convenience, what can they expect when the lesson that convenience or a supposed class interest is a sufficient cause for lawlessness has been well learned by the ignorant classes?" Like most of his fellow politicians, La Follette refused to even entertain the thought that such a warning might have application to his own efforts to confer patronage. Instead he appealed to his fellow Republicans for aid, claiming that the Commissioner of Pensions had promised to abide by La Follette's recommendation for physicians to serve on local examining boards within La Follette's own district, only to renege on that decision. La Follette was furious. He depended on such patronage to preserve the loyalty of his vast and intricate network of personal supporters. Over the years, he sent many such letters, varying only in to whom they were sent and which "evil" public official they denounced. La Follette's own meticulously detailed self-righteousness never varied, for he refused to recognize his own carefully molded organization as a well-oiled and efficient political machine.[19]

On 2 July 1890, La Follette's vote helped bring the passage of the Sherman Anti-Trust Act, the first in a series of acts to curb the power and growth of monopolies. Like the Interstate Commerce Act, this precedent-setting legislation was far more powerful on paper than in practice, enabling little actual "busting," despite the high hopes of anti-trust activists. Its supporters assumed that Sherman would break up the powerful trusts, restoring free and open competition. Its vague wording, however, created loopholes big enough for most trusts to pass through unscathed. In reality, it "passed the buck" to the courts, where it was used successfully against labor unions who, their critics charged, constituted a powerful trust by denying their members the right to sell their labor freely.[20]

La Follette's speeches in the campaign of 1890 were well received: "Even Democrats had to admit not only that he was a good speaker, but that he made some points that were hard for them to answer." There seemed to be little doubt that he would be reelected, especially considering the accolades of the press: "Mr. La Follette is one of the best representatives in Congress, an able, painstaking, faithful worker, a ready, clear, and logical speaker, a man equally useful and influential in Committee work and in the debates of the House, and his district, as well as the state at large, may be justly proud to have such a representative." In the face of these optimistic indicators, Belle expressed disbelief when Bob came home and called to her "in a matter-of-fact way, 'Well, Belle, [Allen R.] Bushnell is elected to Congress from the Third District, and I am elected to practice law.'" At the age of thirty-five, La Follette had fallen casualty to the Democratic sweep that included the governor's chair and virtually all of Congress, caused in part by the dissatisfaction of voters with the Bennett compulsory-education bill, put into effect in 1889 by the Republican-controlled state legislature. The large, often foreign-based Lutheran and Catholic populations in Wisconsin resented this mandate that only schools taught in English met state requirements. The law divided Wisconsinites along lines of both ethnicity and religion, and the divisions would be slow to heal. The McKinley Tariff and general hard times also contributed to the Republicans' somewhat predictable fall from grace. La Follette's claim that machine leaders "secretly used all their power against me" is not substantiated by evidence. Rather than actively working against him, the machine instead treated La Follette with benign neglect.[21]

Despite various minor frustrations and setbacks, La Follette's six years as congressman were enormously rewarding. Although he had yet to establish himself as a radical, he was noted (despite his stand on oleo) as a foe of pork-barrel legislation and of lumber companies and railroads seeking land grants and other special favors from Congress. Three times his constituents had entrusted him with power, granting him the opportunity to prove himself an able opponent of prejudice and of the manipulators of power who victimized the weak and the helpless. Although La Follette worked almost ceaselessly during those years, there is no evidence of any debilitating illnesses. It may have been the longest of the very rare periods in his life during which La Follette enjoyed some measure of satisfaction. Compared to Governor La Follette and Senator La Follette, Congressman La Follette was less radical, less flamboyant, less extreme. Nevertheless, as a congressman, he was a hard-working public servant striving to do what he saw as "right."

Their marriage did not permit La Follette to confide directly in his wife all the disappointment and self-doubt he felt when he was voted out of office, but those feelings were expressed in other ways, including illness, immersion into his legal practice, creating crises, and, finally, a return to the political arena. Belle La Follette's reaction to her husband's congressional defeat was one of open anger and resentment that his efforts had been spurned by an ungrateful public. She was "amazed at the way he accepted defeat. There was no break in his habitual good cheer, not a word of complaint, nor one moment wasted in regret . . . [because] he valued life too much to let the ordinary chances of politics spoil it for him." Belle marveled at Bob's "inner peace" and claimed confidence that their "everyday happiness rested on this sure foundation." Although Bob affirmed Belle's belief that "he never blamed his constituency or lost faith in the people," he admitted in his autobiography his "bitter disappointment" at the termination of his congressional career, an admission Belle chose to ignore.[1]

Belle did acknowledge, however, that despite her dislike of much that constituted congressional life, the return to "civilian" life left her unexpectedly depressed. The house seemed desolate, "the hall . . . filled with bags of public documents which must be addressed and sent to constituents." She had a "funereal feeling about the task," noting, "We were poor and in debt; Bob's income was uncertain. We had the problem of the Dakota ranch to wrestle with." Belle's anxiety over debts incurred during her husband's tenure in congress was compounded by the uncertainty surrounding the financial future of the law firm of La Follette, Harper, Roe and Zimmerman, founded in January 1886. According to law partner Gilbert Roe, La Follette produced free of charge "many thousands of dollars of work for what he deemed worthy causes."[2]

Belle chose to interpret her husband's lack of open protest over his political defeat as proof of his intent to withdraw permanently from public life. She maintained that he intended to contribute his share toward making government serve the public interest as a private citizen but would otherwise devote himself to his law practice. Thus ostensibly assured, Belle's interests centered on their home. She was determined to have more children and raise the large family they had always planned.

While his wife pursued a stable home life, La Follette concentrated on his law practice, approaching each case with the thoroughness and energy assigned previously to his congressional work. Partner Roe remembered, "There seemed to be no limit to his endurance." The office joke was that, while La Follette believed in limiting the laboring hours of others, La Follette's own average was eighteen hours, occasionally "stretched to twenty-four . . . when occasion required." When he received a complaint that his fee was excessive, he replied indignantly, "I never worked harder in a case in my life. Possibly more work was done than necessary. It did not seem so at the time. I was very anxious to win the case." He concluded, "It is disappointing and mortifying to me that I estimate my services in this case as of much greater value than does the company. . . . I desire my connection with this case should be rightly understood . . . [for then] nothing further is necessary."[3]

Understandably, La Follette was a strong believer in the jury system. He relished the opportunity to win the approval of the common person and enjoyed pulling out all the stops in his dramatic performances. He represented a vast array of clients during his ten years between public offices, including a railroad company charged by passengers and workers with negligence. That case contradicts the image of La Follette presented by Roe, one of La Follette's closest friends, who claimed, "His labors as a lawyer . . . fitted him for his great service in the larger field of statesmanship. In this field his cause was Equal Rights v. Special Privilege, his clients, the plaintiffs, were the common people of the country." La Follette's defense of a big business might seem to indicate a renunciation of past personal and political policies. Such contradictory behavior has led one historian to call La Follette "a bundle of human inconsistencies," while another offers a more insightful explanation: "He was too much the zealot, considering himself an infallible judge of right and wrong. This conviction served him effectively in battle, but in the long run it led many people to mistrust his judgment and resent his power." La Follette saw no contradiction in his defense of one railroad company against a specific charge despite his record of antagonism toward railroads in general. Instead, he was certain that he, possibly even he alone, could discern right from wrong in all cases and act accordingly.[4]

The speeches La Follette gave on behalf of numerous Republican hopefuls belied assurances that he was truly content with a life divorced from politics. Belle acknowledged that the possibility of a return to politics had never been completely dismissed, for the rank and file of the Republican party of the state regarded La Follette as a future leader. That nonpolitical life did not supply sufficient emotional fulfillment is suggested by the fact that La Follette suffered a severe attack of the grippe following his return from Washington, an illness his brother intimated was self-induced.

In the early afternoon of 17 September 1891, an incident occurred that allowed La Follette to vault back into the political arena. Accounts of the event vary widely. The uncontested facts are these: Enormously powerful lumber millionaire Philetus Sawyer, with whom La Follette had come into conflict in congress, served as bondsman for two former Republican state treasurers. As such, he was liable for up to $200,000 because his clients had been accused by the new Democratic administration of illegally holding back interest on state funds, a practice accepted previously. One of the accused was to be tried in the court of Judge Robert Siebecker, brother-in-law of La Follette. Sawyer sent a letter to La Follette requesting a meeting with him at the Plankinton House, a Milwaukee hotel, where Sawyer offered La Follette fifty dollars, money La Follette insisted was a bribe but Sawyer declared was meant as a retainer.

According to La Follette, he replied, "Senator Sawyer, you can't know what you are saying to me. If you struck me in the face you could not insult me as you insult me now." He concluded, "You haven't enough money to employ me as an attorney in your case after what you have said to me," and indignantly refused to accept any payment for the meeting itself. La Follette claimed that his outrage at this attempt to compromise his integrity and slur his good name stemmed from his mother's insistence that he honor his dead father. His reaction was violent: "I felt that I could not keep my hands off his throat—I stood over him, blindly" before striding out of the hotel.[5]

La Follette spent the next several days relating his version of the exchange to a number of friends and advisers, claiming it his "plain duty to report the matter to the Court." To their protests that the powerful Sawyer would have him "utterly destroyed," La Follette "granted all that, but urged that as a member of the bar, and officer of the Court, I could not be silent; that it was my duty to report to Judge Siebecker exactly what had occurred." By his many conversations, La Follette ensured that his act of courage would not go unappreciated. He presented himself as a man so driven by integrity he would willingly invite the wrath of a man as powerful as Sawyer. Having impressed upon himself and others the magnitude of his bravery and the righteousness of his cause, La Follette notified his brother-in-law of the incident and Siebecker promptly withdrew from the case. Although no official charges were filed against him, Sawyer reacted to the persistent rumors surrounding the incident by telling his version to the *Milwaukee Sentinel*. La Follette contrasted this account with his own honorableness: "I did not point out the weaknesses and inconsistency of Sawyer's statement; I did not note the fact that he could not be ignorant of the relation existing between Siebecker and myself, which everyone knew; and which had been the subject of public discussion and comment when Siebecker was appointed

Circuit judge; I made no mention of the fact that I was constantly practicing my profession in Siebecker's court, and that there could be no impropriety in my accepting a retainer had it been offered upon honorable terms." La Follette denied any vindictiveness, insisting that he made the story public with great reluctance and bore no ill will toward Sawyer.[6]

Despite La Follette's obvious personal animosity toward a variety of individuals encountered during his career (most notably Theodore Roosevelt), he persisted in claiming that he never viewed political enemies as personal ones.[7] However, in a letter opposing the appointment of an individual La Follette believed had subjected him to misrepresentation and abuse, La Follette, despite his vow not to assail the candidate's private character, noted, "He has ruined his own business, destroyed the influence of his paper and put himself generally out of all touch and relation with the people of Madison — all because of his utter lack of judgment, — and this quite apart from his position with respect to political matters. He is commonly spoken of as 'an ass, a fool, a blunderer.'" A La Follette intimate once observed, "Bob La Follette's biggest weakness has been, and is, his hostility toward his opponents and critics." La Follette perpetually believed those with whom he disagreed were incapable of honorable motives, and the intensity of that belief occasionally led him to sacrifice some of his own political goals in order to "punish" those he perceived as evil. Cognizant of the damaging potential of such a weakness, La Follette feared that he would be unable to control even justified anger. Accordingly, he repeatedly denied harboring any such hostilities, claiming, "I do not treasure one personal injury or lodge in memory one personal insult. With individuals I have no quarrel and will have none. The span of my life is too short for that." Belle supported this view of her husband and lauded him for what she chose to view as a purely factual, unemotional response to the entire Sawyer incident. La Follette claimed that death threats were made against him, that he had become a pariah: "I was shunned and avoided everywhere by men who feared or sought the favor of Senator Sawyer and his organization. . . . No one can know what I suffered. As I recall the fearful depression of those months, I wonder where I found strength to endure them." He persevered nobly nonetheless, and his virtue was rewarded: "I found clients who wanted the services of a man who could not be tempted by money. They came to me with their cases, and I found plenty to do. . . . On the street, in my office, and in the courtroom I carried myself so that no one should know how keenly I felt it all. I slept very little and there was fear that my health would give way."[8]

La Follette, "at his best in the storm center," seemed to "thrive while teetering on the edge of political oblivion." The Sawyer incident provided the kind of intensity absent since La Follette's return from Washington. Previous forms of frantic activity, the kind expended in his thoroughness while composing speeches, running campaigns, practicing law, and serving public office, could not always guarantee sufficient personal reassurance. A new method was realized — a crisis that brought a storm of criticism, but also intense support.[9]

La Follette encountered intense partisan hostility in the wake of the Sawyer affair. Perhaps most painful were the letters he received expressing disbelief in the accuracy of his account of the incident. To one critic, it seemed "impossible that a man of Senator Sawyer's breadth and shrewdness should attempt to bribe a court, especially with a paltry 'fifty dollars.'" Despite such denunciations, La Follette took great pride in his handling of the situation. Just as he claimed to have resisted Saxton's attempts to tarnish his father's memory, he felt he had denied Sawyer the opportunity to bring dishonor to the family name.[10]

Moreover, according to La Follette, the Sawyer incident brought him to the greatest revelation of his life. Reflecting on his service in the House, he "had seen the evils singly — here and there a manifest wrong," against which he had "instinctively revolted." Recognizing that he had been "thrown by circumstances" against organized power, his congressional life came back to him "with new meaning" as each piece of legislature was seen in relation to corruption. To ensure that individuals' worth be determined solely by their performance in an open, competitive society, La Follette now advocated that corporate pools and trusts be abolished. The growing number of powerful trusts frightened many Americans, as a handful of companies dominated entire industries by controlling the market, setting prices, and absorbing or eliminating competitors. Increasingly, trusts controlled such modern-day necessities as beef, steel, sugar, oil, and money. Speaking in 1897, La Follette noted that before the rise of big business, a businessman and artisan "gave his business an individual stamp and reputation, making high moral worth an essential element in business life," and was patronized only by those local consumers who were satisfied with the integrity of his products and services. Big business, however, with its powerful pools, cartels, and monopolies, was immune to the discipline of consumers. In the wake of the Sawyer affair, La Follette committed himself to "holding down" and "driving out . . . the mere speculator, or monopolist, or promoter, who wants to take advantage of others under protection of the law."[11]

La Follette claimed that the United States was "fast being dominated by hostile forces that thwart the will of the people and menace the perpetuity of representative government." John Saxton, La Follette believed, used misrepresentation to gain financial control over Mary La Follette. Her son came to rail against other "daring, unscrupulous men [who] plotted in violation of the common law, the criminal statutes and against public right to become masters . . . and take what toll they pleased." In his 1912 autobiography he traced his awareness of this menace back to his years in the House, concluding: "With the changing phases of a twenty five year contest I have been more and more impressed with the deep underlying singleness of the issue. It is not railroad regulation. It is not the tariff, or conservation, or the currency. It is not the trusts. These and other questions are but manifestations of one great struggle. The supreme issue, involving all the others, is *the encroachment of the powerful few upon the rights of the many.*"[12]

With this revelation came a new life purpose: "I determined that the power of this corrupt influence, which was undermining and destroying every semblance of representative government in Wisconsin should be broken." Having felt the "full force" of "the power of the opposition," La Follette noted, "I knew the struggle would be a long one, that I would have to encounter defeat again and again. But my resolution never faltered." The gauntlet had been thrown, "the ten years' fight was on." In Belle's version of the revelation, "What had happened had revealed to him, as a flash of lightning reveals a precipice, the danger that was threatening and undermining our institutions. The evils he had before recognized singly, he now saw as part of the octopus."[13]

La Follette has been accused of exaggerating the impact of the Sawyer affair, which he claimed was the turning point of his career. Contemporaries charged that he continued the feud, which Sawyer would gladly have dropped. The Sawyer incident and La Follette's subsequent claims of political vision became, at that point in La Follette's career, his "principal stock in trade." La Follette had both political and personal motives in keeping the controversy alive. Clearly, he welcomed the opportunity to dramatize convictions that could capture the public imagination and serve to vault him back into the political arena. Approaching the age at which his father died, he was eager to return to public life, where he had found mass reassurance and approval. La Follette's dramatic tale of the impact of the affair not only brought him public attention, it filled some very personal needs as well.[14]

La Follette claimed that he might have gone forward with his law practice quite contentedly had it not been for this event, which "forced [him] into the fight." The dispute, however, provided a convenient way to reenter political life without incurring the wrath of his wife. Determined to convince Belle and himself that he had no choice but to follow the destiny being thrust upon him, he asserted, "Fortunes of birth, temperament and political environment have thrown me into this struggle, and . . . made me in some degree a pioneer in the Progressive movement."[15]

Concerned with reestablishing his Republican credentials lest it appear that he had been read out of the party due to the Sawyer scandal, La Follette recognized that William McKinley's speaking engagement in Madison in July 1892 could not have come at a more fortunate time. As chairman of the Ways and Means Committee, McKinley had drafted and steered to passage the 1890 tariff bill that bore his name. An unsuccessful presidential candidate in 1892, McKinley was nonetheless clearly a "comer" on the national scene. Due to their personal friendship, McKinley was La Follette's house guest, a turn of events that greatly improved the state of La Follette's Republican prestige. Six months later, that prestige was compounded by a reception the La Follettes gave in honor of Theodore Roosevelt, then a former New York State assemblyman in town to address the Wisconsin State Historical Society.

The winds of political change were beginning to blow. The citizens of Wisconsin were rapidly losing faith in the promise of prosperity for all in their increasingly urbanized and industrialized nation. Wisconsinites previously aligned with the Grange and other farmers' alliances were among the more than a million voters nationwide so disillusioned by the inability of either major party to deal effectively with modern problems that they cast their vote for Populist James Weaver in the 1892 election. The Populist (or People's) Party, which emerged victorious in a number of midwestern local and state elections in 1890, advocated a variety of methods to create increased power for voters and decreased power for business, including government ownership of railroads in addition to free coinage of silver to facilitate an inflationary monetary policy to stabilize the economy. Populism enjoyed its greatest popularity in the Midwest, West, and South, especially among farmers suffering from rising expenses (due to the actions of bankers, railroad companies, and crop brokers) and declining crop prices. Populist gains in 1892 were "striking but limited." Most Wisconsinites, like most Americans in 1892, considered the Populists to be the party of disgruntled hayseeds who romanticized the rural past rather than embracing the promise of the urban future. They rejected as too radical the structural changes proposed by the Populists to make government more responsive to the people, including direct election of senators, a single-term presidency, the secret ballot, the initiative, and the referendum. Although the introduction of these proposals was premature, most of them refused to die and would be revived in subsequent elections, ultimately outliving Populism itself.[16]

Grover Cleveland managed a return to the presidency in 1893. Despite Cleveland's promises of stability and prosperity, the depression that began in the banking industry exploded ten days before his inauguration with the Reading Railroad's declaration of bankruptcy. Other companies quickly followed suit as the depression widened, bringing bank failures, unemployment ranging from 12 to 18 percent, and widespread poverty in its wake. Yet the wealth of the rich, who skillfully eluded taxation, seemed only to grow. Tired of policy and elections being determined behind the closed doors of legislators, caucuses, bosses, and the like, and impatient with traditional politicians offering no remedies to modern problems and with powerful lobbyists ensuring even more wealth for the already wealthy, Wisconsinites formed a variety of clubs, leagues, and unions to discuss problems ranging from unemployment to unfair taxation and to promote reform. Divisions along traditional ethnic and religious lines diminished as the depression deepened. Voters grew increasingly willing to consider new types of leadership, especially those promising direct rule and power to the majority rather than the elite. Candidates successfully sought various offices throughout the state on the promise of tax reform and more representative government. Although La Follette would eventually claim these various burgeoning reform movements as his own, in 1894 he was still testing the waters and maintained a low profile in that year's gubernatorial race.[17]

"The first encounter with the organization of Wisconsin," La Follette asserted following the Sawyer incident, "must be one which should compel their respect, even though it resulted in temporary defeat for the reform movement," introducing an often utilized way to view every political defeat as a success by virtue of its triumph of integrity, thereby avoiding depression and doubt.[18] La Follette enthusiastically promoted his friend, Nils P. Haugen, for governor. Haugen ran to gauge the strength of an anti-machine campaign only at La Follette's insistence. La Follette wrote a staggering number of letters on Haugen's behalf — "something like 1200" he acknowledged modestly — and was credited with garnering an impressive one-third of his candidate's delegates. Haugen lost the election, but not before La Follette demonstrated that his persuasive abilities had not faded. An observer wrote, "The devotion which La Follette inspired in the young collegians who fell under his sway amounted to almost fanaticism." La Follette also gained the support of Wisconsin's large Scandinavian population, who noted his relationship with the Norwegian Haugen and who felt increasingly ignored in favor of German Lutherans by the current Republican party leaders, especially in light of the ongoing controversy over the school language law.[19]

La Follette's campaign efforts on behalf of Haugen were abruptly halted by the death of La Follette's mother, aged seventy-six, on 21 April 1894. Until her death, following a brief bout with pneumonia, Mary Saxton had been "of hardy constitution; her faculties alert, her spirit unbroken." According to Belle, Bob "had always worshiped his mother; they had been inseparable." Her death left Bob "overwhelmed and helpless," as "it seemed as though he had never thought she might die, and was wholly unprepared for her passing." La Follette's grief must have been somewhat ameliorated by the disinterment and reburial of his father, ensuring that his parents would remain side by side throughout eternity—without the presence of John Saxton.[20]

Following the burial of his parents, La Follette refused to take on any new cases or speaking engagements, citing ill health and doctors' orders. His recovery from "stomach trouble" took several months. For Bob, whose "emotional nature was intense," according to Belle, and for whom "all family ties were sacred," an effective balm to his grief was the knowledge that, two months after her mother-in-law's death, Belle began her first pregnancy in twelve years. La Follette's joyful anticipation of the birth was somewhat abated by financial concerns. The month before Robert Marion Jr.'s birth in 1895, La Follette sent $35 and a note to his brother William, who was looking after his horse ranch: "I hope this will buy a hundred bushels for feed for the damned horses. . . . I cannot raise money enough to buy a carload of oats any more than I could a corner lot in heaven." Despite the grim state of his finances, La Follette, who had longed for a son, rejoiced at the birth of his namesake. Another son, Philip Fox, followed in 1897, and daughter Mary, named for both her grandmothers, was born in 1899 when her mother was forty, her father forty-four.[21]

During the winter of 1896, La Follette was asked to campaign for William McKinley's presidency. McKinley's strongest Republican challenger, House Speaker Thomas B. Reed of Maine, had the support of Wisconsin's stalwart (old-style, conservative), Sawyer-Payne-Spooner faction. La Follette pledged the support of his friends to McKinley but was himself extremely ill with "another attack of La Grippe." It left him so "very discourag[ed]" that he was unable to take an active role in the campaign himself. He confided in his diary that he felt "very old." Accompanied by friend and physician Phil Fox, La Follette spent months recuperating in Florida, immersed himself in the study of palm reading, followed by several enjoyable weeks at the springs of French Lick, Indiana. His leave of absence totaled over five months. He claimed it left him "entirely restored in health" and convinced him of the "absolute necessity" of rest and recuperation. In addition, it relieved him of many responsibilities, including campaigning for McKinley and legal work, while it allowed him to luxuriate in the pampering he received at French Lick, "a very pleasant and well appointed place to lay by for repairs." It also found him in a grim financial situation, and it became "necessary . . . to call in some ready cash." La Follette's attendants and aides believed worries over his financial status exacerbated his illnesses. His behavior subsequent to this illness followed the usual pattern of immediate immersion into strenuous work designed to recoup the income lost during his absence.[22]

La Follette used some of his newly restored energy to attend the Republican Convention in St. Louis, where he "electrified" the vast assemblage with a brief speech nominating Henry Clay Evans for vice president. Shortly after his return from St. Louis, La Follette admitted to friends that he wanted to be a gubernatorial candidate, citing his desire to avoid any future accusation of cowardice: "I don't want it said that I waited until he [Sawyer] was dead until I dared to hazard the contest." He also worried that people might think him merely politically ambitious or worse yet, a personal glory seeker. Consequently, he took pains to present himself as a man "led to [run] in response to what seemed a very general desire on the part of Republicans in all parts of the state."[23]

Once officially committed to becoming governor in 1896, La Follette declared the righteousness of his cause, proclaiming he would have the support of all the people if the situation could be gotten fairly before them. La Follette did in fact enjoy the support of citizens seeking a governor who would represent their own rather than machine interests. He was greatly aided by former governor William D. Hoard who, like other dairy farmers, enthusiastically lauded La Follette's opposition to oleomargarine. La Follette arrived at the convention with enough delegates pledged to him for a first-ballot nomination. The nomination, however, went to Edward Scofield, whose supporters offered bribes to La Follette delegates the night before the convention, a time-honored last resort of the politically corrupt. La Follette understandably expressed great righteous indignation over this turn of events, making public both his outrage and his nobility in the face of such deceit. When informed that his defeat was inevitable, La Follette claimed "they had [him] beat, but . . . didn't propose to run up any white flag [because he] didn't have one." He even recited William Ernest Henley's *Invictus*, claiming his head to "bloody but unbowed," and thanking "whatever gods there be for my unconquerable soul." "I am the master of my fate," he intoned, "I am the captain of my soul." The stouthearted loyalty of his supporters inspired him to higher resolve, he proclaimed, and he consoled the crowd with assurances that the men who win final victories are those who are stimulated to better fighting by defeat; that the people had not betrayed him or his cause. Like his confrontations with Elisha Keyes, Phil Spooner, and Philetus Sawyer, La Follette's defeat at the hands of corrupt politicians reassured him of his moral superiority.[24]

La Follette rejected all urgings that he run as an independent and instead proved his loyalty to the GOP by speaking for the entire ticket. Nationally, Democratic challenger William Jennings Bryan was no match for McKinley's handsomely financed, efficiently run campaign. And yet the 6.5 million votes garnered by "The Great Commoner" demonstrate clearly that Bryan's crusade tapped into the deep dissatisfaction with the nation's status quo. Bryan's campaign has been often been reduced by historians to his call for abandonment of the gold standard in exchange for free and unlimited coinage of silver in an effort to expand the supply of money and restore economic justice. Certainly, three years into a depression, silverites were more convinced than ever that insistence on the gold standard severely and unnecessarily tightened the nation's money supply, perpetuating the depression. Much of Bryan's popularity hinged on his pro–silver stance, especially after he electrified the nation with his stirring "Cross of Gold" speech, delivered at the Democrats' 1896 nominating convention: "You shall not press down upon the brow of labor this crown of thorns, you shall not crucify mankind on a cross of gold." But even among his supporters there was controversy over the wisdom of bimetallism. What kept them unified behind their candidate was the common thread of anxiety over the nation's course as power flowed from the farms to the cities, from individual farmers and workers to the elite few who headed the giant corporations. Bryan, outspent somewhere between ten and twenty to one, lost by only half a million votes. The Republicans managed to convince sufficient numbers of voters that a Bryan victory would mean moving backward, replacing growth, progress, and prosperity with chaos and confusion, and yet the size of the Bryan vote demonstrated in unmistakable terms that dissatisfaction was not reserved to a few failing farmers or disgruntled workers. Change would be slow in coming, but it would come.[25]

Although La Follette would later align himself with William Jennings Bryan on a number of substantive political issues and make many Populist reform goals his own, in 1896 he still remained a strict party man. Following Bryan's defeat the Democratic party retained its southern stronghold but otherwise was perceived as parochial and anti-industrial, losing much support to the Republicans, who would remain dominant in most key states until at least 1910. La Follette, eager to play a part in this Republican ascendancy, reluctantly returned to his law office, where he complained, "The trouble is we poor fellows who have to earn a living can only occasionally take a hand in politics." Undaunted, he set forth a plan: "We must perfect our organization and hold and strengthen the ground we have gained and be ready for the next opportune time for a party contest. If we have not money or leisure we must work harder and longer. Republicans generally are with us. We must solve the problem of making their sentiments control conventions. Difficult task, but it must be done." La Follette hoped to see his plan enacted despite dire personal financial straits due to work missed first because of illness and then because of the campaign. Although he pledged to safeguard his health, he admitted "straining every nerve to catch up . . . and worked almost all the time without much regard to day or night." Heedless of warnings to take care of himself, he once again fell ill with what was called only his "old trouble," although not so severely as to prohibit him from conducting business completely.[26]

Despite health and financial difficulties, La Follette's political enthusiasm never faltered as he began his battle to legislate the direct nomination of candidates. This goal was certainly in keeping with La Follette's fervent need to believe that he had the approval of "the people" and that his recent gubernatorial defeat was due solely to the treachery of an evil politician. Belle wrote: "When I would suggest that he overestimated the interest of the rank and file, he would always say 'if they understood they would make themselves heard.' Time, for the most part, justified his confidence; but, oh, more often that not, it took long years of abiding faith and patient waiting!" La Follette believed that he knew the people of Wisconsin thoroughly and felt sure they would support him if only political bosses and machines did not intervene.[27]

La Follette believed all he needed to do to ensure the direct primary and his subsequent election was present his case squarely before the people. He perfected a brilliant oration denouncing corruption and promoting the direct primary. He called upon his listeners to eliminate the machine by destroying the caucus and convention system through which the machine controlled the party. "You will place the nominations directly in the hands of the people," he exhorted. "You will restore to every state in the union the government given to this people by the God of nations." "To every generation some important work is committed," he thundered, and put his crusade on a par with Lincoln's freeing of the slaves: "If this generation will destroy the political machine, will emancipate the majority from its enslavement, will again place the destinies of this nation in the hands of its citizens, then 'Under God, this government of the people, by the people and for the people shall not perish from the earth.'" This speech, "The Menace of the Machine," first delivered at the University of Chicago on 28 August 1897, merited La Follette much publicity, as did his refusal to accept President McKinley's offer of the office of Comptroller of Currency. Belle claimed that her husband's refusal of a position paying $6,000 a year probably made a more profound impression on Wisconsin citizens than events of much greater importance. But, as La Follette explained in his letter of refusal to McKinley: "I am poor and could not afford to leave a practice at this time in life which was better than such a salary and further that there was nothing in the position which appealed to my political ambitions."[28]

La Follette found appreciative audiences throughout Wisconsin. The state's population was nearing 2 million. Two-thirds were foreign-born or the children of foreign-born. Increasing numbers lived in cities rather than on farms, but urbanites and farmers alike shared a growing frustration with the political and economic domination of their state by business interests, especially railroads and timber. The timber industry was soon to wane, having depleted Wisconsin's forests in an astonishingly brief period of time, but new industries, led by foundry and machine shops as well as dairying, rose in its place. Grassroots reform movements born of the depression continued to proliferate throughout Wisconsin. The state's politicians responded to such organized protests, both local and statewide, and enacted various reforms to remove some of the more odious practices of corruption and exploitation via inheritance taxes and passed laws regulating railroad passes and lobbying. While these efforts laid the foundation for the more sweeping and radical reforms of the future, prior to 1900 they only scratched the surface. La Follette promised something more.

La Follette attracted huge crowds at county fairs, breaking records for attendance and gate receipts. One newspaper reported that La Follette fully sustained his high reputation as an orator during a local county fair, an exception to the majority of speakers, who found it hard to interest an audience in the face of so many distractions. As La Follette addressed a crowd in Oshkosh, a man who, La Follette alleged, "belonged" to Sawyer, prepared to begin a horse race along the track in front of the speaking platform. La Follette refused to be cowed or bullied into cutting his speech short: "I pulled [off] my coat and told 'em I had not been brought there to be trampled by nothing — horses, or run over by jockeys. . . . 5,000 cheered me to the finish. It was a great break for them to make and scores of the good people congratulated me on having the courage."[29]

Such demonstrations delighted La Follette. He wrote glowingly and gratefully of an appreciative crowd that stayed to listen despite a drenching rain. He enjoyed toying with audiences: his feigned desire to halt at a key moment elicited pleas to continue. One supporter wrote, "The chances are that you would be able to settle the mayor [with] nothing more than a smile and handshake, while we cannot settle him with a crowbar." Another enthused, "Nobody but you can fix matters in this County. 'If Bob La Follette makes a speech in the County everything will be all right' is heard on every side. Them who fought you this fall will be solid for you if you give us a speech." To such flattery La Follette responded, "Thanks! Such letters as yours are an inspiration. A man can work when he feels that his friends are

*La Follette in his element, campaigning country-style in Cumberland, Wisconsin, 1897.*
*(Image Hunters/Pieri & Spring Productions)*

behind him. We are right and will win out." La Follette's rhetoric, however, was not universally well received, and contradictions between his actions and his words did not go unnoticed by the incumbent's supporters: "You have been speaking in many parts of the State as against The Machine in Politics. Why, my dear sir, even your own modesty will not permit you to deny the fact that you and your friends have during the past three years, built as good a Political Machine, and in less time, than was ever known to be built in this State by any Party. It is down right hypocrisy for you or any one to talk against the Machine in Politics, for without it you or any one else cannot succeed politically."[30]

Machine control, as defined by La Follette, was based on misrepresentation and public ignorance, while he viewed himself as a purveyor of truth and knowledge. Furthermore, machines utilized patronage and large sums of money, methods La Follette claimed, despite evidence to the contrary, to eschew. Old party leaders were corrupt and La Follette set out to replace them, confident that his morally superior ends rendered him impervious to the pitfalls of power. Certainly La Follette opposed rather than facilitated the abuse of political power by corporate interests, and his organization lacked the control that conventional machines wielded over legislators. However, even though his contemporaries conceded that La Follette's machine had a more disinterested character and purpose than most, the problem of how to manage his sophisticated, formidable organization without the appearance of either management or machine was never really solved.[31]

Unlike more traditional politicians, La Follette insisted on going directly to the people rather than keeping a dignified, impersonal distance. Few have questioned La Follette's commitment to serve the people of Wisconsin: his eagerness to learn their concerns and to make them understand and support his proposed solutions. Although his early gubernatorial campaigns were unsuccessful, these earnest statewide efforts to reach out to the citizenry established loyal supporters who, for more than a quarter of a century, would follow through fire this short, intense dynamo, convinced that he, and often he alone, had only their best interests at heart. La Follette's plunge back into an extremely demanding speaking schedule was not, however, universally approved by his supporters, who utilized a variety of tactics to persuade him to conserve his strength. His cousin, Charles La Follette, wrote: "Now Bob I have a *scolding* for you. Josie writes me you are working all night, or a large part of each night. You know what that will do for you and you also know you *owe* it to *Belle* and the *children* as well as your friends to take better care of yourself. . . . [You] said you 'would live to see the clods drop on all of your enemies' coffins,' [so] take better care of Bob. . . . And don't forget to *get more sleep.*" Heedless of such warnings, La Follette continued to spread himself thin. In the midst of campaigning, he begged off a speaking engagement because of a legal case: "My client is a poor woman and the case is one against a railroad company for killing an only son. It means everything to her and I must try the case. . . . It is simply a case of *compulsion.*" In a simple and direct way La Follette could defend the helpless triumph over the powerful and corrupt.[32]

During his campaign for the direct primary, La Follette asserted: "If having been 'faithful in a few things,' official honor should come to me, I am frank to say it would be accepted,— but principally and primarily however because it would enlarge my opportunity to do some things that, for the sake of the love we bear for just and equal and honest government, need to be done. . . . I should be more glad to follow than to lead." This thinly veiled ambitious enthusiasm was not echoed at home, where he experienced additional pressures due to a fire that caused heavy losses and tremendous disarray. In addition, the horses at the ranch were sold at a loss and the land rented out. La Follette's extensive investments in a telephone business proved to be another drain on the family's finances. With his health pushed to the limit, he noted, "For sometime I have been threatened with a return of my old trouble which has cost me a portion of each winter since my return from Washington in '91." Despite these pressures, La Follette continued to campaign enthusiastically. In Ann Arbor, Michigan, he warned that "whoever seeks to thwart or defeat" direct nominations "is an enemy of representative government. Let him beware!" "The machine may obstruct, misdirected reform may temporize," he cautioned, "but 'be of good cheer, strengthen thine heart,' the will of the people shall prevail." He concluded in stirring tones, "The fight is on. It will continue to victory. There will be no halt and no compromise."[33]

His vigorous campaigning did halt, however, in March 1898, when La Follette's dear friend, law partner, and trusted adviser Sam Harper fell critically ill with pneumonia. La Follette canceled all speaking engagements during the weeks of Harper's decline, and his death left La Follette dazed and ineffectual. He claimed that no man had ever been so completely a part of his own life as Harper had been. In an unsigned, unfinished, and nearly illegible letter, La Follette spoke of his inability to accept Harper's death. According to Belle, the two men had been "inseparable in mind and heart," and the sympathy between them closer than any ties of kinship. Harper's death left La Follette in deep mourning for a man he had come to love as a brother. Harper shared many of the characteristics La Follette attributed to his late father. Harper "added something for good from his genial helpful gifted mind to every one who came [to know] him." Harper was forty-three when he died, only five years older than Josiah La Follette had been at the time of his death. Like his father, Harper was, in La Follette's eyes, "barely [at] the beginning of his rapidly enlarging sphere [when] he was summoned away. His life was broken off in the middle. But it was filled with good deeds and great thoughts, with noble aspirations and high achievements. 'He was a man, take him for all in all. I shall not look upon his like again.'"[34]

In a memorial address delivered to the Dane County Bar Association two years later, La Follette spoke emotionally of his friend's death, mentioning both the possibility of a glorious afterlife and the reality of the despair of those left behind: "Let us believe that he who so loved to live, found another life where all the virtues and activities of his being, developed so highly here, shall grow and expand through infinite time. Life and Death, the two great mysteries in which we are helplessly involved! How thin and impalpable the veil between, and yet how hopelessly impenetrable! . . . We cannot rend, we cannot reach beyond it. We can only bow in despair, appalled by the dark and tragic doubts which haunt the human soul."[35]

Sam Harper's death added to La Follette's already substantial emotional burdens. Nevertheless, Belle's attempts to persuade her husband to abandon any plans for such an expensive and unpromising venture as another bid for office fell on deaf ears. Despite his previous show of reluctance to commit formally to candidacy, warnings that a second defeat could eliminate him as a viable candidate in 1900, and the knowledge that the wealth of the state was on the side of incumbent governor Edward Scofield, who was ready to spend $400,000 if necessary to defeat him, La Follette officially announced his candidacy for the governorship. He proclaimed in his statement of principles: "I have no contest with individuals and no enemies to punish. . . . I am led to believe on the best authority that it is the wish of a majority of the Republicans of the state that I should stand as a candidate representing principles which the situation demands should be made part of the Republican platform." La Follette pledged equal and just taxation of property and of every corporation transacting business within the state. This was aimed at railroads in particular, which were being taxed on their income rather than on their physical property. He advocated the abolition of the caucus and convention and promoted the nomination of candidates by Australian ballot at a primary election, and the prohibition of the acceptance of railroad passes, sleeping car passes, etc., by public officials. He also called for the prohibition of trusts and other business combinations that destroyed competition and restrained trade.[36]

La Follette did not take part in his own gubernatorial campaign in 1898. The events of the past months — overwork, insufficient rest, illness, financial burdens, charges of hypocrisy, family pressures, the death of Sam Harper, and the fear that he would be rejected in his bid to wrest the nomination from an incumbent — all contributed to the illness that kept La Follette confined to his bed. Despite his absence from the campaign, La Follette's support was sufficiently strong to merit the opposition's using the full range of tactics in the arsenal of various machine leaders intent on his defeat. Railroad workers were warned that support for La Follette in the caucuses could cost them their jobs. Convention delegates were offered bribes totaling $8,300. Once again, despite strong popular support, La Follette was denied nomination at the convention. Typically, he presented this defeat, with some credence on this occasion, as a victory: "We had not fought wholly in vain: we had so stirred the state upon progressive issues that our opponents did not dare risk the rejection of the platform which we presented." "[T]emporary defeat," he asserted in response to Scofield's renomination, "often results in a more decided and lasting victory than one which is too easily achieved."[37]

La Follette, "under the harrow" financially, ensured that his illness, not yet serious, worsened by being in his office "constantly" since the day of his return from the convention, "forced" by the demands of his clients to give up even a few days of much needed rest. He also promised to begin a speaking campaign for the party ticket, and compared himself to a workhorse, complaining that he did "not find it easy to keep even" and had "lost a couple of nights' sleep." He confided to a supporter, "Between professional engagements and political demands I am worked to the very limit." To Belle, her husband's collapse seemed imminent as he made no attempt to alter his self-destructive course. Indeed, he suffered a serious collapse, called variously "the old complaint," "congestion of the liver," "various severe headaches," "nervous indigestion," and, by La Follette himself, "congestion of the liver and stomach."[38]

During this illness of more than six months, La Follette was shielded from the elements that had been plaguing him: business, politics, finances, and even cold weather, for, at Dr. Fox's insistence, the children were farmed out to relatives while Bob and Belle spent several weeks in San Diego, enjoying many day trips to La Jolla. This rather demanding trip west also included a stay in Pomona, California, and side trips to the Grand Canyon, the desert, the petrified forest, Los Angeles, San Francisco, and other points as La Follette's fancy dictated. The traveling party included Dr. Fox and his daughter, plus one additional couple. La Follette enjoyed many a "good lazy day," basking in the sun and in the attention of his wife and friends. Kind words from supporters helped speed his recovery. His letters from Pomona detail his extreme enjoyment of the pleasant climate and scenery but also betray fears that he would be lulled into permanent inactivity: "It is a delightful place, but — I am inclined to think that about three months out of the year is as much as comforts the best development. That is — the higher temperature the year round breeds or begats a lethargy. It requires a touch of extremes to tune the system for its best work." La Follette returned to Madison in April and wrote a letter about his cyclical illnesses that hinted they would continue in the future: "I came home fully restored, good as new, and just as mean as ever. I have sworn all the oaths in my vocabulary to take better care of my health in the future. I believe myself that I cannot pull through many such attacks as I had last winter. Indeed Dr. Fox says I cannot do it again, but I rather think I could fool him if I tried."[39]

After his return from California, La Follette initially claimed to be trying to get proper rest and to work in moderation, and he cited his recent illness when declining speaking engagements. However, he soon admitted to spending "night and day" in court, saying he felt he "owed a duty to devote every practical moment of . . . time" to those who had waited so patiently during his illness. Such frantic behavior elicited fresh warnings from concerned friends to protect his still fragile health. Although his own exhaustive schedule remained unaltered, his letters to friends warning them to guard their health and know their physical limitations strengthen the impression that the previous winter's siege frightened La Follette. Nevertheless, he doubled his efforts to make up for lost time during the summer of 1899. In November, he once again denied any personal desire to run for governor, but by February he declared himself ready to do whatever it was "agreed should be done." He toured the state delivering his popular lecture on Hamlet, which not only kept him in the public eye but added to his income, which he had begun to pour into a new investment, mining.[40]

La Follette initially demurred at urgings that he commit himself to a third try at the governorship. He was preoccupied with his certainty that his mail was being tampered with. Although he insisted on an official investigation, he asked that this request be kept confidential because he believed any charge he made might be attributed in part to prejudice against the present postmaster. His many long letters during this period detail the condition in which his mail had been received. He requested that his correspondents seal each letter with wax and notify him of the design of the seal; mail letters, if possible, upon a train, in order that their postmark not show the exact place from which they were mailed, or enclose letters to La Follette in envelopes addressed to friends of his living in Madison. La Follette claimed that the tampering had become "absolutely unbearable" and that he was "determined that this outrageous wrong shall not continue." However, the chief inspector of the post office in Washington, D.C., found that, of all the letters La Follette was convinced had been tampered with, only one showed evidence of any irregularities. This verdict brought an abrupt halt to La Follette's preoccupation with mail tampering, but it was not to be the last time he would demonstrate behavior bordering on paranoia.[41]

Governor Edward Scofield owed his reelection to the traditional tactics of the old-style "stalwart" politicians: deal making and bribery.[42] Politicians employing such tried-and-true methods were finding themselves now openly challenged rather than congratulated. Scandal as well as squabbles, especially over a U.S. Senate seat available in 1889, had substantially weakened a once seemingly omnipotent machine. Its challengers, reaching new heights of popularity, were on the rise, culminating in a variety of grassroots movements throughout the state. As the members of this new wave of concerned citizenry became aldermen and mayors in a number of communities, La Follette received the flood of letters urging him to run for governor with cautious optimism and wondered, "Is it possible that the sowing of the last six or eight years is at last ripening for the harvest?" Never a politician who suffered from overconfidence near election time, he confessed that he did not know how to account for this new bright political outlook and proposed to exercise the very greatest caution to avoid embarrassing himself or his friends by a third loss. In the midst of La Follette's decision making came the news that Philetus Sawyer was dead, prompting one friend familiar with La Follette's personal animosity toward political enemies to warn him, "Disrespect for the dead is not wise under any condition." La Follette made no "unwise" statements and instead, after much delay, announced his candidacy.[43]

The neutralization of La Follette's enemies combined with the support of powerful former foes resulted in what was called the "harmony campaign." During this third attempt to gain the governor's chair, La Follette for the first time enjoyed the financial support of the wealthy Isaac Stephenson, looked upon as the financial godfather of the movement. Stephenson's generosity, motivated by his own political aspirations, included a newspaper, the *Milwaukee Free Press*, to present the public with editorials and articles favorable to La Follette and his cause. Other members of the "old guard" also recognized that La Follette's political star was on the rise and joined his organization to better advance their own future interests. La Follette countered a powerful corporate enemy by declaring that the railroads should not be singled out for disproportionate taxation but only be asked to carry their fair share. And in a rare nod to foreign affairs, La Follette, who had supported the U.S. war with Spain and the forcible annexation of the Philippines in 1898, defended American expansion in the Caribbean and the Far East, further reassuring traditional Republicans. His campaign speeches, except for the promotion of statewide primary elections, were "almost entirely along national lines," as La Follette emphasized his solidarity with the McKinley and Roosevelt presidential ticket on the major issues of the day. La Follette's already well-known promotion of a legislative program of progressive tax reform, utility regulation, direct primaries, resource conservation, workers' protection, and banking legislation gained increasingly enthusiastic support. His campaign literature presented him as a man of "unimpeachable character," "unsullied fame," "zeal," "enthusiasm," "brilliance," "thoroughness," "extraordinary talent," "unusual power and ability," "personal force," and "without affectation or love of vulgar display." His refusal to respond in kind to Governor Scofield's scathing personal attacks highlighted La Follette's dignity and met with great favor in the press.[44]

Despite La Follette's tremendous popularity, his previous experiences with political conventions left him understandably "awfully anxious." Although he uneasily acknowledged, "It certainly looks now as if it would be impossible to concoct any scheme that would defeat me," he remained at heart unconvinced. He cautioned his core supporters, "I want to feel that the delegates are, every one of them, thoroughly right and grounded in

*From horse-drawn wagons to the whistle-stop campaign of 1900, where La Follette speaks from the rear of his special car. (Image Hunters/Pieri & Spring Productions)*

their allegiance to the principles we are anxious to promote," urging, "I . . . trust that you will see that only those who can be depended upon to pull straight are sent to the convention." When the other candidates withdrew from the race, uniting behind La Follette, he finally allowed himself to consider that victory was at last within his grasp. New anxiety immediately arose from his conviction that, as a consequence of his cinched nomination, the opposition would concentrate every energy toward nominating anti-primary candidates to the state senate. It was, he asserted, a necessity that "the next number of the program . . . be to present a solid front to the common enemy this fall."[45]

La Follette's near physical collapse that summer prompted "Uncle Ike" Stephenson to produce his yacht for a week's cruise of the Great Lakes. A rested and refreshed La Follette conducted a whistle-stop campaign that carried him nearly 6,500 miles in the last three weeks, as he made 208 speeches in sixty-one counties to about 200,000 people. La Follette not only won the nomination but, on 5 November 1900, received the largest majority of votes ever given to a gubernatorial candidate up to that time. In beating Democrat Louis Bomrich, La Follette became the state's first Wisconsin-born governor.

W hether his acts are lauded as courageous political commitment or scorned as selfish obstinacy and hypocrisy, La Follette's first term as governor was a controversial struggle of wills marked by many of his already established behaviors. Even before his election, office-seekers besieged him with requests for appointments. This issue of patronage was a constant thorn in La Follette's side. He promised fervently to fill the offices at his disposal, to the best of an unbiased judgment, with individuals who would accomplish the most good, but at the same time pledged, "I shall not forget my friends." La Follette worried that his inability to reward some of his supporters would test severely their friendships and, in some cases, strain the bonds to the breaking point. Anti–La Follette forces claimed that La Follette abused his patronage. Historian Herbert Margulies agrees: "La Follette's extensive reliance on patronage throughout his career is beyond question. After he became governor, his use of state jobs for political purposes was notorious. Clerks, oil and factory inspectors, temporary personnel such as state fair guards and ticket sellers, but especially game wardens — these were the political leg men. Even before the big gubernatorial victory of 1900, La Follette had more than a worthy cause to offer the deserving." Skillful use of patronage helped La Follette build a powerful political machine, although he answered such accusations with declarations of his piety and dedication. Such denials were undermined, however, when the majority of state employees who later failed the civil service exams La Follette himself had championed were revealed to be his game warden appointees.[1]

La Follette supplemented the power of patronage with skillful appeals to diverse ethnic and interest groups. During his second term as governor, he hosted the governors of several states at a conference dedicated to resolving racial inequalities, contributing to the pro–civil rights reputation he established in Congress. The respect and support of African Americans nationwide led to La Follette's invitation by W. E. B. Du Bois to speak at the national progressive leaders' conference at Atlanta University. La Follette also issued a strong statement of praise for Jews and pledged that Wisconsin would assure them equality and liberty. His perpetual support of woman suffrage and his advocacy of women in state positions earned him much support from women as well. Although women could not yet vote and the number of Jews and African Americans in Wisconsin was small, their support was still valuable to La Follette. The political worth of that support increased after he entered national politics, compounding dramatically when women received the vote.[2]

The state La Follette governed was in considerable turmoil in 1900: Forty-five percent of the farms were mortgaged. Eighty percent of the population owned 10 percent of the wealth, and 1 percent of the population owned half the state's property. "Political and economic power was concentrated in the hands of a few corporations and privileged firms paid little in taxes." In his inaugural speech, La Follette outlined his plans for uniform assessment of taxes. (The speech was the first of three inaugural speeches he gave, all of which he had much difficulty with composing, which prompted one aide to comment, "I am sorry that we are going to have trouble again regarding the governor's message. . . . We have for several years had more trouble than is really necessary.") The taxes he promoted included the instigation of a state income tax and the reinstatement of inheritance taxes, in addition to heavier levies on corporations and penalization of uncooperative corporate officials and negligent assessors. He took special care to assure big businesses that he was not opposed to their largeness but only to their efforts to control prices, stifle competition, and create monopolies. Rather than attempt to implement his wide-ranging program all at once, La Follette stressed two of its most fundamental elements for immediate implementation: a comprehensive primary election law and railroad taxation based on actual property valuation. La Follette delivered this ambitious agenda to the legislature in person, an innovation that was a portent of things to come.[3]

The complexity of the progressive movement is exacerbated by the diversity of programs it encompassed. The spectrum of progressives ranged from those dedicated to only one pet reform (woman suffrage, for example, or conservation of natural resources) to those pressing strenuously for a full slate of reforms. The latter within the Republican Party have been termed insurgents, indicating that they were in revolt against their party. Certainly La Follette belongs on the far end of the progressive spectrum, and he was often at odds with party regulars, but to label him as "insurgent" often provides more confusion than clarification. It is perhaps more helpful to abandon efforts to put a name to the various levels of dedication to progressive reform and acknowledge that there are as many types of progressivism as there are progressive reforms and progressive reformers. As governor, La Follette's particular brand of progressivism was inherent in the famous Wisconsin Idea, which included more than just complete overhauls of the tax structure, voting procedures, and the treatment of corrupt officials and others abusing financial power. In this commonwealth conception of soci ety — which emphasized cooperation between government, the university, and the private sector — public interest transcended all lesser concerns. Vast faith was placed in the experts at La Follette's beloved University of Wisconsin. While La Follette was governor, this meant particular reliance upon the university's president Charles R. Van Hise and two faculty members, economist Richard T. Ely and historian Frederick Jackson Turner, to advise, set standards, and administer Wisconsin's reform laws. The concept of better government through education was hardly new, but La Follette established an unprecedented relationship between the university and the state that would last far beyond his three terms. Progressive leader Frederic C. Howe later characterized the university as the fourth branch of government in Wisconsin, "the nerve center of the commonwealth," impelling it to action in almost every field of activity. The Wisconsin Idea, it was conceded upon La Follette's death in 1925, "probably stimulated more genuine reform in state and national politics that any other influence in the last forty years."[4]

La Follette endeavored to restrict lobbying and campaign expenditures, improve Wisconsin's educational system, curb monopolies, pass laws regulating pure food, child labor, and workers' compensation, and create an industrial commission to regulate the entire working environment based on codes prepared by experts. In short, he set out to make the political machinery more directly responsive to the popular will, to promote equal rights over special privilege. Although much of La Follette's ambitious, innovative reform agenda eventually became the model for other states, many of its elements were not adopted in Wisconsin until after his tenure as governor. Despite his eager determination, confusion and dissent marked La Follette's first term. The "harmony" campaign that put him into office quickly dissolved as old battle lines were redrawn, exacerbated by what has been termed La Follette's "increasingly messianic conception of political leadership." His delays in filling certain key positions infuriated legislators pressured to support his pet bills. His insistence on breaking all precedent and delivering his messages to the legislature in person rather than by messenger helped to earn him a reputation of a browbeater, which was bolstered by his indifference to the advice and demands of others.[5]

La Follette's familiar claims of bravery in the face of threats and bribery attempts continued. He refused to accept any responsibility for the fact that many of his past supporters were becoming disillusioned, and he claimed to be puzzled and shocked by their "betrayal." He attributed gains by his opposition to ruthless corporations and corrupt machine politicians, whom he presented as insidious bribers and whoremongers. He claimed that Emanuel Philipp, then president of the Union Refrigerator Transit Company and later three-term governor of Wisconsin, tried to make an under-handed political "deal" with him; that Lansing Warren, editor of the *Milwaukee Sentinel*, threatened to turn his newspaper against La Follette if certain legislation was not passed, and that a number of federal officeholders, including Wisconsin senator John Coit Spooner, asserted undue influence against him. Although La Follette stressed the incredible pressures that forced some of the legislators to give into bribes and threats, he bragged that he himself remained as uncompromised as ever, declaring, "I will use all the power that the people have given me to fulfill every pledge in the platform," and remonstrating, "You can't violate your conscience." La Follette skillfully used this avowed commitment to morality to curry favor with a number of disparate Wisconsin reformers. He supported legislation for the "proper" observance of the Sabbath as well as the enforcement of several longstanding Wisconsin laws to eliminate or at least strictly regulate prizefighting, cigarette smoking, and the pardoning of state prisoners. La Follette generally believed that people's private behavior should not be subject to legislation. Such "moral" reforms illustrate the differing value systems of various reformers as well as the fact that, far from leading Wisconsinites to a progressive mentality, La Follette's various reform efforts were often in response to his constituents' already established wishes. He was a follower as well as a leader.[6]

La Follette justified his efforts to dominate the legislature: "It was very well known that I was the only man in the capital who could crowd that legislature to do its duty . . . for I could not see honest measures promised to the people beaten by wholesale bribery without doing the utmost I could to prevent it." He refused to acknowledge any personal motivation: "I knew the people of Wisconsin thoroughly. I knew from close contact with them what they were thinking, what they believed. I knew also that I was advocating a sound principle which no amount of abuse or misrepresentation could finally defeat." La Follette used these claims of omniscience to refuse the Hagemeister bill, a primary plan that would apply only to local nominations, despite the fact that such a move would help local like-minded reformers. In his impassioned veto message he did not note that only an uncompromised direct primary bill would virtually assure his own renomination, proclaiming instead, "*no bread* is often better than *half a loaf.*" "My attitude," he acknowledged, "has given me the reputation of being radical and extreme. And if this is radicalism then indeed I am a radical; but I call it common sense. It is simply the clear comprehension of the principle involved, and the clear conception of the utter destruction of that principle if only a part of it is applied. I have always believed that anything that was worth fighting for involved a principle, and I insist on *going far enough to establish that principle* and to give it a fair trial. I believe in going forward a step at a time, but it must be a *full step*."[7]

La Follette was not always as uncompromising as he claimed. When he approved a railroad bill respecting the right of recovery for the benefit of railroad employees, he attached a memorandum: "I am aware that this bill is unsatisfactory to those who expected a more liberal measure, and who in their disappointment would at this time prefer that it should not become a law; but I am impressed with the great difficulties which such legislation encounters and regard it as wise to secure for the present whatever ground has been gained at this session." When a Republican judge, a personal friend of La Follette's, was discovered to have used a railroad pass, La Follette was accused of hypocrisy for not demanding or even requesting the judge's resignation.[8]

Despite such compromises, La Follette's professed belief that it is usually better to fight on for a thoroughgoing law than to have a weak statute written on the books led to the passage of fewer progressive bills in 1901 than had passed when governors had left the initiative to others. "To violate the promises of [the] platform," La Follette scolded the legislature, "is to cheat and betray the voter." In turn, more than half the Republican members of both branches of the legislature signed a manifesto criticizing La Follette for the sanctimoniousness in his encroachment upon the constitutional rights of the legislative branch and organized themselves into a league to fight the progressive movement. When criticized for creating such inner party strife and for publicly denouncing Senator John Spooner, La Follette, although "appreciative" of the embarrassment which the state contest caused some of the representatives in Congress, replied, "I have consistently shown a desire to promote harmony within the party, and shall continue to do so, excepting, always, that it must not be at the cost of principle or in violation of pledges made to the people." His answer to the censure adopted by a senate resolution was to arraign the legislature as derelict of duty, while at the same time claiming, "It is not now, and it never has been, my wish to dictate to any member of the legislature in any way."[9]

Belle remembered this time as one of tremendous strain and anxiety. Active on her husband's behalf throughout his tenure as governor, she too suffered from his political unpopularity. Contrary to the accepted custom of the day, only infrequently was she called upon by the local "ladies." She remembered the first year in the executive residence, one which "should have been a time of triumph and rejoicing," as "the gravest and gloomiest we have ever known." It was the only time she could ever recall when La Follette's humor failed to lighten the seriousness of his struggles.[10]

After the longest session then on record in Wisconsin, the legislature finally adjourned in May 1901. La Follette took personally its failure to pass any of the promised laws and was uncharacteristically openly depressed. The grim financial status of the *Milwaukee Free Press*, whose success was vital to La Follette, brought additional pressure. It was La Follette's unpleasant task to elicit contributions, most notably from Isaac Stephenson. The La Follette–Stephenson correspondence was often bitter and heated. Rather than cajole or flatter his wealthy patron, La Follette chose to shame and bully Stephenson into submission. By emphasizing his own Christ-like suffering, he intimated that generous funding was his rightful due: "After the event with Sawyer, when I was set up as a target in this state to be shot to death and my name made infamous because I refused to be bought or to engage in an attempt to corrupt the court, I accepted the hard part that fate had allotted to me in leading in the struggle against such influence and for decent government in this state. Into it I have put ten of the best years of my life; I have sacrificed a practice worth ten thousand a year; I have loaded myself with debt, made secondary the considerations of my family, which should have been first, and have faced a storm of malignant falsehood, abuse, and vilification, such as I verily believe no man ever before encountered." He denied seeking renomination for his own sake, but rather as a necessary step "toward securing the legislation demanded to insure decent politics and good government in this commonwealth." Although their relationship remained a stormy one, "Uncle Ike" continued to finance La Follette's campaign.[11]

La Follette worked night and day during the legislative session and was exhausted physically as well as emotionally. Pressures over patronage continued and personal debts mounted. He was charged with being a selfish hypocrite and a political trickster who professed to champion the rights of the people only to obtain political power and to compass the defeat of Senator John C. Spooner. Although La Follette claimed, "I have been and am being so persistently lied about that I usually pass it over in silence," and maintained he could endure without protest or denial great personal abuse, he was deeply disturbed by such attacks. A prolonged illness would provide respite and desperately needed assurances in addition to a convenient rationalization if his bid for reelection ended in a humiliating failure.[12]

Beginning in late June 1901, amid torrid heat, La Follette began to suffer from an illness at first considered minor and expected to be short-lived. His condition worsened, however, and his staff canceled his speaking engagements. According to Belle, "Bob was very ill. He suffered intense pain; the source of his illness was obscure and caused grave anxiety. Never did he relinquish the intention, if he lived, to keep on fighting until what he had started to do was achieved." "Depressed in spirit," La Follette lost thirty pounds in three months. Prominent Chicago physician Frank Billings pronounced that the fundamental cause was "an unbalanced nervous apparatus," the result of overwork, and in consequence, "a neurosis of the stomach." La Follette's diet was strictly monitored, and he was allowed only granose biscuits, cream, grain syrup, zwieback, butter, milk, and occasionally a raw egg. Family, friends, and sympathetic members of the public all provided him with much sympathy and praise. After more than eight weeks of loving care at home, La Follette traveled to the farm of physician Phil Fox to convalesce, enjoying the warmth and comfort of his protective friend. When his health improved, he joined his family in a summer-long stay at a small, relatively isolated cottage development on Lake Kegonsa. His beloved sister Josie and her family rented an adjoining cabin, and the two families spent the summer of 1902 rivaling each other in games and stunts. La Follette, "throwing off all care, joined in . . . with the single-minded zest that characterized his pursuit of any object which had once awakened his interest." He also began a series of daily exercises devised to build up and restore a "weakened and deranged digestion." His retreat from politics was marred only by his delivery of four speeches, two of which were in celebration of patriotic holidays.[13]

La Follette took virtually no part in the campaign for his renomination as governor, a campaign that, to him, did not appear at all promising. Debts remained from the previous campaign; former supporters, either out of disillusionment or bribery, had joined the opposition; and La Follette's collapse was being used to support rumors that he was losing his mind. Despite the La Follettes' portrayal of the opposition as extremely formidable, in reality it lacked leadership and focus and was no match for an incumbent with enormous public support running a campaign based on what historian Roger Wyman has called "the most blatant personal use of patronage the state has ever seen." When overwhelmingly renominated at the Republican state convention on 17 July 1902, La Follette attributed his victory to his 145-page "Voter's Handbook," a highly emotional account of his plans and the corrupt methods that had thwarted those plans in the legislature of 1901.[14]

La Follette's renomination ended his illness and retreat of fifteen months. In his acceptance speech he stressed his righteousness and magnanimity and "the sacredness of public obligation." La Follette's public professions of total forgiveness toward his enemies was contradicted less than a month later when he wrote a scathing letter of protest against the return of Henry Payne, an associate of Philetus Sawyer, to the political scene. Two weeks after his nomination, La Follette began a vigorous speaking campaign with a three-hour address in Milwaukee, declaring that political platforms must be upheld if political parties are to be maintained.[15]

As in campaigns past, La Follette believed people would support him if only they understood him. Following a brief stay at the springs of French Lick, Indiana, he adhered to a demanding schedule designed to include as many populous centers as possible and delivered his speech, with its average reading time of three hours, several times a day. Belle remembered that he prepared the part dealing with primary elections and taxation "as though on trial for his life," for he feared if the legislature again failed to pass these measures the people might lose faith. Although La Follette's aides tried to protect his health during this campaign, the strain of such a rigorous schedule was enormous. His health, however, did not give way, a phenomenon Belle attributed to his "extraordinary vitality and will power," but was likely also influenced by appreciative crowds. One audience member wrote: "Thousands will applaud the effort as a great speech, which it is, but the glory of it is the spirit that 'will not bend and cannot be broken.' God give you strength — He has given you courage — to see this contest to the end." Belle noted that, although physically weary, her husband came home from his long hard jaunts refreshed in spirits. His campaign literature presented him as a man who had been through an ordeal worse than any other in the political history of the entire country, but who remained completely objective and totally firm in his resolve. His opponents offered a different view, warning voters of a new, virulent infectious disease, "La Folletteism," whose victims exhibited an "impudent assertion of their own infallibility, an ignoring of their own devious ways and the instant imputation of dishonesty or corruption to any who dare differ with them."[16]

La Follette's unpopularity among his fellow politicians was again no match for his popularity with the public. On 4 November 1902, he beat his Democratic opponent, Milwaukee mayor and conservative machine politician David S. Rose, by 47,599 votes, giving La Follette the second-largest off-year majority received by any Wisconsin governor to that date. Although momentarily bolstered, La Follette succumbed quickly to anxiety over the upcoming legislative session. He wrote to an aide, "The grey wolves [in the state senate] are hunting the ranges. They are out for blood. May the good God give us health and strength for the hard fighting that is still ahead."[17]

Perhaps this appreciation of the difficulties of an overwhelming struggle inspired his remarks, made while still recuperating from his lengthy illness, to the trustees and superintendents of the county insane asylum: "Of all the dire afflictions which may befall mortal man, nothing is so appalling as the overthrow of reason. . . . [T]he most terrifying form of death comes as a sweet haven of refuge and release to the wreck and storm tossed mind." And La Follette's letter to an ex-convict struggling to redeem himself in the eyes of society suggested a method to overcome the taunts of the John Saxtons of the world: "You must make the best of it. You must be brave. You must not falter. *You must conduct yourself as to win the esteem of your fellow men.* You must, by your life, by your every action, constantly work toward the attainment of a place in the community, the peer of your neighbor. . . . You must be more careful than other men, by holding your head erect, by paying no attention to the jibes of others, by being strong and brave, and hewing close to the line, you will make your enemies, those who revile you, those who point the finger of scorn at you, ashamed of that which they do."[18]

La Follette began his second term by publicly reiterating his assertion that legislation had been defeated in 1901 through bribery and corruption, denying any personal responsibility for those failures while asserting his sacred obligation to carry out his party platform. He steadfastly maintained that only faulty digestion induced by lack of exercise was the cause of his own problems, boasting that he suffered neither from oversensitivity nor vanity. As he accepted the nomination, he declared that in matters not covered by the platform, a public official may exercise his best judgment, but that he "has no more moral right to quibble and evade, to say that he will perform a part and repudiate the rest, than he would have to use a part of trust funds committed to his keeping as a private trust."[19]

Aware of the deplorable state of the family's finances, a condition exacerbated by his investment in a failing mining concern, La Follette committed himself to a vigorous speaking campaign of eastern and western states. His efforts were rewarded by attentive audiences, compounded by supportive letters from his wife. La Follette's claims that he was "Busy every minute, day in and day out, Sundays and every day," led Gilbert Roe to criticize his friend for the damaging perfectionism that caused him to lose his sense of perspective and make ill use of his time and energy.[20]

Rather than conserve his energies, La Follette began to openly consider reentering national politics. It was an exciting time in Washington. On 14 September 1901, upon the death of William McKinley following complications from an assassin's bullet, Theodore Roosevelt became president. The reform winds that had swept across the nation's farms, towns, and cities had reached the nation's capitol and were felt by its new, forty-two-year-old president. Roosevelt later said it had been his business "to take hold of the conservative party" and make it "a party of *progressive* conservatives." When he began his presidency, however, Roosevelt's commitment to progressive reform, especially his efforts to put some teeth into the Interstate Commerce Commission, rendered impotent by the courts, so encouraged La

Follette that he declared the people had a "brave, able, and progressive friend" in President Roosevelt, adding "He has declared for them. He cannot be misled. He will not compromise." The swelling tide of reform movements throughout the nation was undeniable. La Follette proudly sent to Belle a news clipping from Colorado Springs, Colorado, which declared him one of the coming men in national life. La Follette also reported that Roosevelt allegedly regarded him as worthy of such recognition in view of La Follette's steadfast and widespread support, his "war with the representatives of the Wisconsin machine, and [La Follette's] determination to fight it out to the death in Wisconsin, and to do it now." Elated by this praise, La Follette was doubly frustrated at the obstacles in his path. Faced with the departure of several of his key aides, La Follette blamed poor finances and even God, indirectly portraying the deserters as mercenaries and himself as an abandoned innocent in his crusade to reform government.[21]

When the smoke cleared, La Follette's second term as governor was highlighted by one great victory — the enactment of his direct primary plan, subject to referendum in 1904 — and a discouraging failure: his inability to pass the railroad rate regulation legislation he had championed all term. "There is nothing to compromise," he had urged the legislature, for "equal and just taxation is a fundamental principle of republican government." The legislature's failure to heed this declaration was not absolute, however. It did pass the taxation of railroads based on the value of their physical property, known as ad valorem taxation. La Follette's plan to set up a powerful railroad regulatory commission met with resounding defeat, proving that La Follette was not, as his critics alleged, an absolute dictator with Wisconsin as his empire.[22]

La Follette and like-minded reformers remained within the GOP, identified as progressive Republicans. They faced opposition from not just the Democrats but their own party's conservative members, the self-named "stalwarts," as well. Although the progressives were too radical for traditionalists, their willingness to reform rather than replace the capitalist system made them too conservative for Wisconsin Socialists and Social Democrats like Victor Berger and Emil Seidel. There were, however, a vast number of voters who sought a more moderate stance between these two extremes. La Follette's shrewd use of patronage and years of struggle, which had honed him into a master politician, culminated in the general consensus that he was a brilliant leader with enormous power within Wisconsin. La Follette's core supporters included Wisconsin farmers, laborers, and citizens from all walks of life who were convinced that La Follette was sincerely dedicated to making their homes and workplaces safer and to providing a more equitable and just distribution of wealth and power. Although the issues facing Wisconsin blurred some traditional dividing lines, La Follette skillfully played on tenacious ethnic identities and loyalties: his longstanding base of Norwegian supporters was enhanced by his increasingly skillful appeal to German voters as well, often utilizing the tried-and-true method of patronage. In light of his growing national reputation, La Follette was advised to run for a third term, push vigorously for desired legislation, then resign and accept the U.S. Senate seat his supporters hoped to obtain when the term of stalwart Charles Quarles, the winner of the hard-fought 1899 campaign, expired.

Despite these indications of support and future promise, February 1904 found La Follette frantic over the mysterious but serious illness (detailed in Chapter 10) of Bobbie, his oldest son. He was also desperate over the state of his financial and political forces: "I could quit living easily, but I *can't quit this contest*. I don't know where the funds are to come from. . . . I have to do everything, plan everything, and look after execution or there is *no execution*. . . . Our whole band is like a flock of frightened sheep now." La Follette claimed that he received death threats and was in great physical danger. Although security forces found no substantiating evidence, Belle contended that the lives of all family members were in jeopardy. Her fears were compounded when a deranged man entered their home, threatening her absent husband. Following the burning of the state capitol on 27 February 1904, the family was warned that the executive residence would be next.[23]

Some of the pressure lifted in April as Bobbie began to recover. Once committed to reelection, however, La Follette redoubled his political efforts, focusing on three main issues: new and back taxes on railroads, a railroad commission to equalize Wisconsin freight rates with those of neighboring states, and primary elections. His continued insistence on tackling issues singlehandedly prompted one supporter to beg: "We don't want to see Wisconsin lose the future president of our country through his total disregard for health and physical strength in a local fight which he has won already. Human nature has its limitations. There is much in your favorite, *Hamlet*, which you can at the present time review with profit. Thousands of us stand ready, and more than willing, to take up your burdens, and . . . we would rather fight than not." But La Follette trusted virtually no one else to perform a task to his satisfaction. He carried out his press campaign personally and without the benefits of selectivity or brevity, omissions that did not go unnoticed. Gilbert Roe went so far as to order, without La Follette's knowledge, that a particularly ill-advised opinion expressed by La Follette for *Collier's* magazine be stricken and replaced with a less inflammatory remark. That manuscript was returned for being overlong, but La Follette's articles did not become more concise with time. The *Saturday Evening Post* printed one as a series, as it was impossible to produce it in a single issue, as originally intended. La Follette refused to relegate even the driest statistical tasks to his staff. To push through his railroad legislation, he took the reams of information on rates covering a variety of states and worked night after night until he wrote a message of 178 printed pages, supplemented by many supporting tables. The legislature, unimpressed, did not pass the bill.[24]

La Follette's lengthy, detailed missives were not always completely accurate. His violent speech against the shabby treatment he allegedly received on an Illinois Central Railroad Company passenger car (ostensibly made not on his own behalf, for he was "made of iron," but for the women and children forced to submit to the same inconvenience) was full of mistakes, the most significant being that the Illinois Central did not run trains anywhere along the route where the incident occurred, a fact that its president happily noted publicly. La Follette made no apology for his misplaced tirade, nor did he even acknowledge his gross error. Shunning the efforts of his staff and friends to protect him from his own overzealousness, La Follette forged on, intent on personally making every voter "fully informed" of his platform. He spoke an average of eight hours a day for forty-eight days and printed enough literature for every voter to receive four copies. Because he claimed to accept no fee for any of his Wisconsin speeches, La Follette refused to cancel his out-of-state Chautauqua engagements, insisting that he must earn money to carry on the fight. He later bragged, "The opposition tried for a time to follow me and catch my crowds, but they were soon worn out."[25]

During that summer La Follette also provided Lincoln Steffens, the influential muckraking journalist, with what La Follette insisted was an unbiased and complete account of his life. Steffens, who had presumed La Follette to be little more than a master manipulator and self-promoter, investigated the governor thoroughly. Steffens's favorable article appeared in *McClure's* magazine in the midst of the campaign and doubtlessly contributed to La Follette's success, prompting him to send Steffens a letter of gratitude and flattery and cementing a lasting friendship between the two.[26]

As the election of 1904 drew near, La Follette began a new form of campaigning, reading legislators' voting records to their constituents. The fact that he could keep audiences riveted to the reading of lengthy roll calls attests to La Follette's magnetic speaking style. In his speeches of three hours and more, La Follette reinforced his image as the only true spokesman for the people, intimating that those who opposed his pet bills were corrupt, yet insisting, "I have no personal feeling against those who do not agree with me but pursue this course solely from a sense of duty to the public."[27]

During the campaign, La Follette denied securing pledges to ensure his

election to the Senate, claiming, "I am not and shall not be a candidate." Privately, however, he admitted, "I should enjoy being back in the old halls at Washington once more." He even denied that he campaigned for his third gubernatorial term simply because it was not mentioned specifically in any of his speeches. Despite all these efforts to appear personally unambitious, a mere servant to the will of the people, La Follette, who had only just returned from his speaking campaign and was frantically composing an acceptance speech, was horrified to discover at the Republican convention that the stalwarts claimed, as did La Follette, to have a majority. To eliminate the opposition in this mid-May convention, La Follette ordered the construction of a barbed-wire passage to force the delegates to enter the red brick gymnasium of the University of Wisconsin at Madison single file. He manned that passage with menacing guards (primarily university athletes). La Follette claimed such measures were necessary to prevent the convention from being taken unfairly and by force. He berated the opposition's employment of bribes and threats in their attempt to defeat him. The stalwarts decried La Follette's strong-arm tactics and, in their meeting at the Fuller Opera House, claimed themselves the legitimate Republican Party convention. La Follette assured his followers that they, not the opera house group, were the rightful delegates and declared theirs a moral as well as a political victory. Although in his acceptance speech he declared, "For a minority to obstruct or delay or defeat the will of the majority is destructive to the principles upon which a republican form of government is founded," one supporter astutely observed. "[You] would undoubtedly feel lonesome if you did not have the gang to fight." The claims of La Follette's opponents gained some credibility, however, when the national credentials committee decided to seat the opera house delegates at the Republican national convention. Representatives of La Follette's Red Gym bloc appealed directly to Theodore Roosevelt. After listening "rather impatiently," the president refused to dignify the squabble by taking a position, bolstering the widely held view that Roosevelt was hostile to La Follette. In the end, the state Supreme Court and Wisconsin Secretary of State Walter Houser ruled in favor of the Red Gym delegates.[28]

Wisconsin voters approved the direct primary by 62 percent, making theirs the first state to require that all candidates for public office be subject to the direct vote of the people. The pledge La Follette made in 1900 had at last been fulfilled: "No longer in Wisconsin will there stand between the

The man behind the Wisconsin Idea, the governor in 1904.
(Library of Congress LC-USZ62-72738)

voter and the official a political machine with a complicated system of caucuses and conventions, by the easy manipulation of which it thwarts the will of the voter and rules official conduct." In this, and in many other matters of reform, including elements of its railroad taxation legislation, Wisconsin became the nationally recognized leader. The state's revenue from railroad taxation increased by 178 percent. Wisconsin voters reelected La Follette, although by only 51 percent. Like many others who sent him congratulatory telegrams on his reelection, William Jennings Bryan, 1896 Democratic candidate for the presidency, expressed his desire to see La Follette in the United States Senate. The flattering messages were enormously appealing: "As you well know, *the people* have very few Senators in that body representing them. The need of a fearless, honest, and able man there to open the eyes of the people which will cause an uprising of the people to compel that body to pass laws favorable to the interest of the people. The man who will do this will become the idol of the people and the highest office in the land will be at his disposal. . . . [He] will be looked up to by future generations, [and] compared to Washington and Lincoln. . . . The man who can do that, (and I believe the only one), is Gov. *Robert M. La Follette as United States Senator*. . . . Though we need you here, I cannot help but feel, there is a much larger field for your services that will benefit not only our State but the whole Union."[29]

Although buoyed by such letters and temporarily reassured by his reelection, La Follette quickly fell back into his pattern of worry and overwork under the stress of the upcoming legislative session and the conflict between his desire to be senator and his need to fulfill his promises as governor. Following a speech in Saginaw, Michigan, La Follette wrote to his wife: "I had a good audience but the house was cold & I could not seem to warm the audience up & it worried me so that I could not sleep. . . . I am not quite right & have a steady pulling across my back." Despite his earlier protests of disinterest in the Senate, he soon canceled his remaining Chautauqua engagements, citing illness, and devoted his full attention to devising a way to become senator without meriting disapproval. Even Belle admitted he was not unwilling to be chosen, but she maintained that he took no part in bringing it about.[30]

The primary law did not take effect until September 1906. On 25 January 1905, the Wisconsin legislature for the last time selected a U.S. senator for the state. A joint session of congress gave La Follette 101 of the 123 votes cast. La Follette, who had been inaugurated governor for the third time just twenty-three days earlier became, simultaneously, Wisconsin's governor and senator. Before he could resign the governorship, La Follette announced, he must complete the task at hand, including Wisconsin's passage of a comprehensive railroad regulatory program, the exclusion of corporations as political contributors, control of trusts and lobbies, extension of the civil service merit system, creation of a civil service commission and a forest conservation program, and the replacement of rural common schools with central schools to which students would be bussed (to ensure uniform, high-quality education throughout the state). Although it was not among his official demands, La Follette also became convinced that an income tax was the only politically effective way to reach the invisible wealth of powerful parasites. He also urged greater cooperation between government and the University of Wisconsin. Finally, in seeking his successor to the governor's mansion, he startled many fellow progressives by promoting the election of long-time supporter Irving Lenroot, Speaker of the Assembly, over La Follette's own lieutenant governor, James Davidson.

The regular legislative session ended without fulfilling all of La Follette's demands. Undaunted, he scheduled a special session for the following fall and spent the intervening summer of 1905 on a Chautauqua tour, a decision that sparked new warnings to guard his health. Just prior to the start of that tour, he and Belle purchased, using the proceeds from the sale of their West Wilson Street home, the Maple Bluff farm on a sixty-acre lakefront lot — at a cost that to Belle seemed far too high. Indeed, the price of $30,000 was a matter of surprise and disapproving comment. But La Follette wanted a farm, with the all the symbolic value it had always held for him, and was intent on instilling in his children the agrarian virtues of responsibility and self-reliance. Ironically, the mortgage on this rather extravagant purchase would be a financial burden for the remainder of his life.[31]

Having reaffirmed his pioneer heritage, La Follette adhered to a grueling speaking schedule all summer. He bragged in a letter to Belle: "Hustle to the hotel. Hustle something to eat. Hustle a shave, wash up and change of linen and then hustle to the Chautauqua grounds. Good big audience and beautiful day. Talked two and a half hours to people who wanted me to keep it up. I threw in two hours and a quarter at night just to make good measure. . . . I know this portion of our country will long remember it." Although aware of her husband's enjoyment of his lecturing "crusades," Belle worried that the travel placed tremendous strain on his heart. His thoroughness obliged him to carry two heavy suitcases, one of them weighted down with documents to substantiate, if need be, every statement made on the platform. When Belle reminded Bob of the great things he had already accomplished and warned him of the potential dangers to his health, he replied, "Belle dear, don't worry about me . . . I should really enjoy every hour of this if you were only with me." According to Belle, Bob ignored her pleas to save his strength by shortening his speeches because he talked to the multitudes as he would to a jury. When he saw earnest faces looking puzzled, he would repeat his arguments in different form and use further illustrations until he saw they understood and were convinced.[32]

La Follette emphasized the vital role each citizen played in shaping the course of the nation, and his earnestness often generated desired results: he expanded a personal following whose loyalty would never falter. One newspaper ran an article entitled "Robert M. La Follette: A Statesman after the Order of Lincoln," and the *Bloomington (Ind.) Daily Bulletin* declared La Follette "universally admired for the fearless manner in which he gives his views and wages his fight." These gratifying public responses were coupled with the expressions of love his absence generated from his children and friends.[33]

Driven to winning people over, La Follette sometimes opted to avoid controversy, rejecting the request of the Chautauqua management for a political address and delivering instead his *Hamlet* speech, much to the puzzlement of his audience. According to one article subtitled "They Can't See What the Melancholy Dane's Got to Do with the Case," the audience "expected the governor to lift the lid and give them something which would make up for all the discomfort they have suffered for a week. They wanted to see the trusts thrown into the mud, after having been held to the ridicule and scorn of every man, woman and child in the state. They wanted tobacco and received milk." The anxiety caused by such disapproval may have been exacerbated, and the loving messages from supporters counterbalanced, by long, unhappy letters from Belle detailing her loneliness, anxiety over finances, self-doubt, and her dislike of the physical and emotional separation from her husband. In early August, La Follette complained of diarrhea so severe he could not eat, and in November he canceled his remaining speaking dates, citing doctor's orders.[34]

Although the special session of the Wisconsin legislature adjourned in December without adopting several of La Follette's demands, his resignation of the governorship took effect — following a storm of confusion, controversy, protest, and derision — on New Year's Day 1906. La Follette rationalized this reneging on his promise to remain in office until all his pet legislation was passed by claiming he would take the issues to the people and they would be settled "right." The *Brooklyn Daily Eagle* echoed this sentiment: "The Governor will bring to the Senate more reputation for courage and capacity than any new member of the body. . . . Mr. La Follette will not acquiesce . . . merely because he will be a new Senator. He is not the submissive sort. He has a great public sentiment behind him. . . . We do not think he is a demagogue. . . . We recognize his unique power. . . . He has stood for what is right within his state and for what should be right the country through. He has that touch of genius which is never withered."[35]

La Follette's tenure as governor was marked by weaknesses, weaknesses which, according to Thelen, "in the end, were those of many insurgent progressive governors, and they resulted from the middle ground those governors held between the old ethnic, job-oriented politics and the new issue-oriented politics." Thelen has termed these politicians who did not move far enough toward the issue politics "victims of the baggage they still carried from the old politics" and claims that by viewing their elections as "the basic reform and not mobilizing public opinion toward legislation, they failed to unleash the real power that existed within insurgency." For these reasons, Thelen concludes, "insurgent governors like La Follette failed to secure truly radical laws that would have transformed American society in the ways implied in their rhetoric. The Senate freed them from these administrative and factional problems, and many of them soon gladly followed La Follette to Washington."[36]

Certainly La Follette's rhetoric during his three terms as governor was not matched by his achievements. But rather than holding a middle ground between job-oriented politics and issue-oriented politics, La Follette used the former to create the latter. Few besides La Follette would deny that his was a formidable political machine, or deny that only a machine of that magnitude had any hope of unseating the entrenched stalwart forces with their large war chest. But, as Lincoln Steffens pointed out, La Follette used his political machine not for self-interest but for the interests of the people of Wisconsin, to bring about a more equitable distribution of wealth and power. La Follette did, in fact, mobilize public opinion, but he did much more: he established a lasting reputation as a shrewd but dedicated and visionary politician, attracting a loyal, even fanatical following, whose faith in La Follette and his principles would outlive even La Follette himself.

Although not all of his promises were fulfilled during his tenure, La Follette achieved some remarkable successes as governor, and it is these successes that serve as the most compelling measure of his governorship: thoroughgoing and efficient reform of railroads and other utilities; civil service reform for state office officials; a stringent anti-lobby law, requiring lobbyists to register with the secretary of state and to publish the details of contacts with legislators; stronger provisions against corrupt practices; several conservation measures, including the forest conservation program; tax reforms; and nominations by primary elections. And his innovation of drawing heavily upon experts from the University of Wisconsin would be one of his most profound legacies.

In six short years, La Follette managed some mighty achievements, and his ability to mobilize public opinion can be measured by the momentum of his reform movement within Wisconsin even when others sat in the governor's chair. In 1911, for example, under Governor Francis McGovern, the legislature passed more significant reform bills in one session than it had in six sessions under La Follette. Certainly McGovern deserves credit for his many accomplishments, but La Follette undeniably paved the way. With good reason could La Follette proclaim in his 1912 autobiography: "Wisconsin is a happier and better state to live in . . . its institutions are more democratic . . . the opportunities of all its people are more equal . . . social justice more nearly prevails . . . human life is safer and sweeter."[37]

Robert La Follette made Wisconsin a leader in the nation's burgeoning progressive reform movement and gained a seat for himself in the U.S. Senate in the bargain, but not without painful compromises — political, financial, and personal. Despite his popular acclaim and many political successes, La Follette's governorship had frequently generated controversy, criticism, and personal turmoil. Belle confessed that their final leave-taking of the executive residence cost her "few heart pangs" and that she would forever associate it subconsciously with unpleasant feelings. Belle's relief and excitement over Bob's opportunity to bring his reform programs to the national arena was tempered by her foretaste of the heavy tolls of such a crusade. For his part, Bob La Follette embraced the "world of problems yet to be resolved." Not content to rest on his laurels, he proclaimed, "[W]e have just begun; there is hard fighting . . . still ahead of us." "The next few years," he predicted, "will test the vital principles of democracy in this country as never before." In the nation's capital, where political change was indeed occurring at a feverish pitch, Fighting Bob, as he was affectionately known, stood poised to leap into the fray.[38]

When La Follette joined the U.S. Senate, Theodore Roosevelt had been president for five years. Critics of Roosevelt's foreign policy (who did not include La Follette) denounced his imperialist tactics and questioned the constitutionality of his actions. An uncontrite Roosevelt revealed something of his views on the centrality of the executive branch when, eight years after he essentially created an independent Panama with which to negotiate an American-controlled canal in 1903, he crowed publicly, "I took the canal zone and let Congress debate, and while the debate goes on, so does the canal." A year after his "taking" of Panama, Roosevelt's Corollary to the Monroe Doctrine provided the justification for much economic and political interference in Latin America. La Follette, who still viewed American expansionism as the best hope of spreading democracy worldwide, applauded such actions. Confident and aggressive in his foreign policy, Roosevelt turned his attention to the complex problems at home.[1]

The nation recovered from the depression of 1896 and was enjoying a period of prosperity, although its fruits were by no means shared equally. For most American workers the cost of living outstripped the rise in wages. Big business got bigger: during the first great merger wave of 1897–1904, one-third of all companies disappeared, swallowed up in combinations with other companies. By 1905, less than 1 percent of manufacturers employed more than one-fourth of all workers in manufacturing and held more than one-third of the nation's capital. Trusts continued to dominate entire industries; conservative values continued to prevail. In coal mining, for example, wages were some of the lowest in the nation, with rates of job-induced injury, illness, and death among the highest. Members of the United Mine Workers struck after their demands for a 20 percent wage increase, an eight-hour day, fair weighing of coal (miners were paid according to individual production), and recognition of their right to bargain collectively were denied. George F. Baer, president of several major coal and iron companies, responded in terms of the Gospel of Wealth: "The rights and interests of the laboring man will be protected and cared for — not by the labor agitators, but by Christian men to whom God has given control of the property rights of the country."[2]

Fearing a cold winter at best, widespread violence and "socialistic action" at worst, Roosevelt personally arbitrated the strike. The results reveal much about Roosevelt's position on the progressive spectrum at that time. The miners made only modest gains: some received a 10 percent pay increase, others a decrease in hours; and while the United Mine Workers did not win recognition, its members were not to be discriminated against in hiring. Conservatives were appalled by this unimaginable precedent of a president cooperating with labor during a dispute. Progressives' joy was tempered by not just the very limited nature of the gains but the knowledge that Roosevelt's prime motivating factor was fear that industrial tyranny sowed the seeds of revolution.

Roosevelt's persecution of a few select trusts was, like his role in mediating the coal strike, both cautious and audacious. In February 1902, he ordered the prosecution of the Northern Securities Company, a giant holding company that included some of the biggest names in American business: J. P. Morgan (banking), the Rockefellers (oil), and James J. Hill and Edward Harriman (railroads). In the next three years Roosevelt initiated only one suit — against the powerful beef trust. In the final years of his presidency he began several more, forcing some of the nation's largest and most visible trusts to break into smaller (although still vast) businesses. Considering the hundreds of trusts in control of much of the nation's commerce that were left untouched during Roosevelt's administration, such accomplishments seem puny indeed. How, then, to explain Roosevelt's reputation as the "Trust Buster," when even his far more conservative successor, William Howard Taft, initiated many more prosecutions than he? As with his action in the United Mine Workers' strike, it was not the extent of Roosevelt's reform activities that set him apart from previous Republican leaders, it was the very existence of such reforms. Even by such limited actions, Roosevelt made clear to the American people that government was not the protector or, worse yet, the mere pawn of corrupt business interests. Roosevelt delineated his vision of reform: "[M]y business is to see fair play among all men, capitalists or wageworkers, whether they conduct their private business as individuals or as members of organizations." But, the president cautioned, this "Square Deal" would not necessarily result in major redistribution of wealth and power: "If the cards do not come to any man, or if they do come, and he has not the power to play them, that this is his affair. All I mean is that there shall not be any crookedness in the dealing."[3]

The problems plaguing modern America, in Roosevelt's view, were abuses of the system rather than the system itself. Many of Roosevelt's domestic reforms as president were driven by a desire to preserve the uncorrupt status quo rather than meaningfully change it. As further evidenced by his mixed record on the rights of African Americans, the success of the Republican party, he believed, depended upon its preserving the middle

*Wisconsin's junior senator in 1906, the beginning of his nineteen-year reign.*
*(Library of Congress LC-USZ62-1736)*

ground between conservatives and radicals, including among the latter in
1906, freshman senator Robert M. La Follette.[4]

La Follette declared that he found amusement in press predictions of his
failure. Before his first public function as senator, his swearing in, he broke
tradition by refusing to request that his state's senior senator, stalwart John
Spooner, escort him to Vice President Charles W. Fairbanks to receive the
oath of office. La Follette gleefully noted Spooner's increasing agitation

over this breach of etiquette. Although Spooner presented the vice president with La Follette's credentials, requested that the oath be administered, and escorted La Follette by the arm to the front of the Senate chamber, La Follette took pride in the fact that, by not formally making such a request of a man he considered to be corrupt, he had not morally compromised himself. The willingness of the two old political enemies to appear so congenially together disappointed the crowd, but La Follette plainly viewed it as a clever moral victory.

That same evening the La Follettes attended a White House reception for the diplomatic corps. Wryly he commented: "We were quite observed during the evening. I think if I had been a wild boar, led about by Mrs. La Follette with a rope fastened to my hind leg, as a pair, we would have not been more observed." La Follette enjoyed the attention that his reputation occasioned him, but he was quickly disappointed when it generated his failure to receive desired committee appointments. The Senate leadership, bestowing even less than the minimal courtesy routinely extended to its freshmen members, ignored La Follette's request for a place on the soon-to-be-revitalized Committee on Interstate Commerce and instead appointed him chairman of the Committee to Investigate the Condition of the Potomac River Front, a position that inspired La Follette to visions of cleaning up the whole Potomac River until he discovered that it was merely a sinecure committee, designed to provide its chair with an office and a clerk. In all its history the committee had never had a bill referred to it, nor even held a meeting. La Follette received appointment to three additional very routine but time-consuming committees: claims, Indian affairs, and pensions.[5]

In spite of these efforts by the Old Guard to keep La Follette busy but ineffectual, Washington observers clearly expected blustering exploits. One predicted: "He has become so accustomed to battle that it is doubtful if he can be happy in the repose and calm of peace; hence the prediction, so often heard of him, that when he gets going in the United States Senate there will be a rattling of dry bones." Portraying him as the "good-humored bad boy of American politics," the *New York Globe* envisioned La Follette "setting fire to his colleagues' whiskers just for the pleasure of seeing the venerable owners cut a few capers." La Follette's fears of failing such enormous expectations were exacerbated by the disadvantage of being a "tenderfoot." Claiming a "bronchial grippy combination" aggravated by cold weather, La Follette spent the first weeks of his senatorship in the reassuring retreat of his sickbed. During his confinement he noted, "I begin my career here in the Senate under somewhat unfavorable circumstances." He reportedly was told that, because the issues he raised and urged in Wisconsin while governor had "infected" so much of the country, he was regarded in Washington as the most unpopular senator who had come to the capitol since Charles Sumner's outspoken abolitionism prior to the Civil War. La Follette finally arose, convinced that he was regarded by every fellow member of the Senate as a crank and a disturber of peace and prosperity. La Follette claimed he received no sympathy, fellowship, or welcome even from fellow Republicans but, undaunted, he devoted himself to consumer issues and to revealing corporate influence within the Senate itself.[6]

Although still outwardly cordial, the relations between La Follette and President Roosevelt had become increasingly strained during La Follette's tenure as governor, when he continually begged off meeting with Roosevelt to discuss transportation rates, citing either illness or overwork. According to Belle, the conflict between the two stemmed from Roosevelt's filling all federally appointed positions in Wisconsin on the recommendation of La Follette's arch foe, John Spooner, resulting in an active organization solidly against La Follette. Publicly La Follette and Roosevelt each professed no personal animosity toward the other. Although Roosevelt privately considered La Follette to be "not evenly balanced and dangerous to the general welfare of the country and party," he proclaimed himself "dee-lighted, over-joyed" upon greeting the La Follettes at the White House, stating that it was one of the greatest pleasures of his life to greet again his old friend. La Follette, who found the Square Deal reforms tepid at best and who privately considered Roosevelt an insincere grandstander, publicly praised the president's contributions to the progressive movement (he once called the president "the dynamic force of moral indignation at crookedness and . . . graft") and maintained that it was his sincere hope that, with closer acquaintance and better understanding, he might aid the president in furthering the progressive cause. Although a facade of cordiality remained between the two for many years, the intensity of their ever-increasing mutual mistrust and dislike was never far below the surface.[7]

Just as La Follette attached great importance to his refusal to request that John Spooner introduce him to the Senate, he took pride in the fact that he refused, despite his expertise in the field, to offer his comments to Roosevelt on the Hepburn Bill unsolicited. The measure, deemed by La Follette to be wholly inadequate, was designed to return authority to the then nearly ineffectual Interstate Commerce Commission. The Hepburn Bill established a uniform bookkeeping system and auditing of railroad accounts but lacked the power to fix rates unilaterally. La Follette claimed that, like the law it was meant to supersede, it would benefit only the shippers, not the "helpless consumer." Lincoln Steffens finally arranged a White House meeting between the senator and the president. La Follette proudly recorded, "It was at a time [10:00 on a Sunday evening] when newspaper reporters were not about, and there was no one to take note of the fact or publish to the country that the President was conferring with so dangerous a person." La Follette's denunciation of the proposed bill and explanation of his own amendments to strengthen federal regulatory powers took two hours. Roosevelt, unimpressed, pointed out the impossibility of the passage of La Follette's proposals and declined to offer support. La Follette responded that getting such a bill through Congress was not the first consideration, to which Roosevelt replied, "But I want to get something through," highlighting the great difference between the two men.[8]

La Follette's first notoriety in the Senate came on 19 April 1906, when he broke the unwritten rule that freshmen should be seen but not heard and began a major speech promoting his nine amendments to the proposed Hepburn Bill. La Follette had spent several weeks preparing his arguments, culminating in a speech that took almost eight hours, spread over three days, to deliver, filling 148 printed pages. "To permit the railroads to control the commerce of the country is, in the final analysis," he charged, "to permit the railroads to control the country." Calling the organized wealth of the country aggressive and unscrupulous, La Follette insisted that nothing less than "the existence of government — real representative government for the people" was at stake.[9]

Belle gave conflicting accounts of the Senate's reaction. In a letter to her daughter she confided that she did "not think that it was altogether intentional — the Senate leaving as it did just as he began to speak." Belle noted that her husband's speech had been preceded by "an exciting controversy" between Senators Benjamin Tillman (D-South Carolina) and Albert Hopkins (R-Illinois). Hopkins claimed that the openly racist Tillman had admitted "that they shot and burned negroes in the South to keep them from voting," a charge Tillman hotly denied. No one wanted to miss the blistering exchange that lasted until after the lunch hour, so many seized the opportunity provided by the change in speakers to break for lunch. Once La Follette began, he was interrupted by a message from the House announcing its passage of an emergency relief bill for the aid of those suffering the effects of the previous day's great San Francisco earthquake and the ongoing fires sweeping the city. Belle admitted, "This news . . . caused excitement and distraction." Nonetheless, she concluded, "It seemed to me that there was a determined effort to discredit the speech." Belle's public account, however, omits any reference to senators' legitimate reasons for leaving and declares only, "As he began to speak a large body of the Senators arose as if by concerted action and left the Senate. There was no mistaking that this was a polite form of hazing." La Follette himself claimed, "I understood perfectly well that I was being rebuked." He broke off from his prepared text to proclaim, "I cannot be wholly indifferent to the fact that Senators by their absence at this time indicate their want of interest in what I may have to say upon this subject. The public is interested. Unless this important subject is rightly settled, seats now temporarily vacant may be permanently vacated by those who have the right to occupy them at this time." Applause from the members of the public seated in the galleries followed this outburst, causing the presiding officer to threaten to have the galleries cleared.[10]

La Follette earned the rancor of his remaining colleagues when Ohio's Joseph Foraker made an attempt to refute some of La Follette's testimony and the freshman rebuffed his elder colleague. Overall, La Follette's speech earned him much public support, and, his wife noted approvingly, he established himself as "the peer of any man on the floor of the Senate,—a *new kind* of leader." His satisfaction, compounded by his wife's rare unqualified approval, remained virtually undampened by his amendments' overwhelming defeat. The names of those senators who voted him down would be read in the roll call La Follette carried, between Senate sessions, directly to the American people in speeches across the nation. La Follette's charge that chairs temporarily vacant would become permanently so proved no idle threat.[11]

As a member of the Indian Affairs Committee, La Follette's actions were reminiscent of those he had taken as a congressman years before. He successfully championed a bill that protected the timber rights of Wisconsin's Menominee from lumber companies. He studied proposed legislation that would sell coal lands of the Choctaw and Chickasaw to mining companies controlled by railroads. He gained much approval from the press and the public when he charged that monopolistic ownership of coal supplies by railroads would mean higher prices to consumers and introduced a measure on 20 June 1906 that would withdraw coal lands from sale until Congress could guarantee competition and lower prices. (This coal reserve bill would later give rise to a major disagreement between La Follette and President Roosevelt.) During the final days of the session, La Follette championed a bill to limit railroad workers to sixteen continuous hours of service. Subject to lengthy debate, the vote was postponed to the next session, as was La Follette's resolution to investigate the grain elevator trust.

Despite much popular support and his own boast that nothing could unnerve or deter him, La Follette privately admitted to great homesickness and loneliness. He sadly noted the difference between being the top-ranking official of an entire state and being merely one of many senators, and a freshman one at that. Although his colleagues were not wholly inattentive, there was no guarantee that he would ever be any kind of a meaningful force among them: "When I have to struggle against all the Stalwarts . . . in an atmosphere that is generally charged with poison, you can realize that it is a good hard proposition for a fellow to go up against single-handed and alone."[12]

The Senate's adjournment at the end of June found La Follette financially strapped. He began an arduous nationwide speaking tour that lasted until the Senate reconvened in December. He wrote plaintively to Belle of the conflict between his guilt at such a long separation from his family and his desire to be a serious political force. Although he urged Belle not to take on any unnecessary duties or needless concerns during his absence, he was himself unable to slacken his own frantic pace or refrain from worrying: "They are too attentive — Luncheons & dinners and committees. I was kept on the go every minute & was too tired to make a good speech at night. I did the best I could & then tossed about like a fool the balance of the night worrying about it." He spent his very few days off sleeping, which he claimed was his restorative. Despite the physical toll of his exhaustive pace, the five months were rewarding. The use of the roll call brought hisses and jeers for his opponents from the large crowds and cheers for La Follette. He carried to the end of his life a watch sent as a souvenir by a supporter.[13]

The summer held some bitter lessons as well. Convinced by his popularity that he could ensure the election of Irving Lenroot to Wisconsin's governor's chair, La Follette campaigned actively for Lenroot throughout the state. La Follette's desire to reduce political battles to terms of good versus evil was ineffective in a contest between two "goods": incumbent James Davidson was a proven progressive and enjoyed the support of some of La Follette's most influential inner ring, including Nils Haugen, General Bryant, and former governor William Hoard. Movers and shakers across the political spectrum were offended by what they perceived as La Follette's attempt to dictate Wisconsin politics. Audiences responded enthusiastically to La Follette's speeches, then cast their votes for Davidson. In September, by virtue of the primary law La Follette himself brought about, Davidson became the first Republican candidate for governor through a direct vote of the people of Wisconsin. Wisconsinites were passionate in their devotion to La Follette, but theirs was not a blind faith. Bowing to the will of the majority, a chastened La Follette campaigned briefly for Davidson, his party's official candidate. The limits of La Follette's personal popularity in Wisconsin had been made evident and the many varieties of progressivism would continue to both strengthen and divide the movement.

La Follette's speaking tour earned $17,000, all of which was swallowed up by the debts of previous campaigns. The lack of any net profit greatly distressed Belle. As their personal debts mounted, she decided to rent their farm land. Her anxiety led her to lash out at her husband when he voted against a salary increase for senators. Belle also attempted to curb Bob's desires to put aside all appearances of party cooperation and work only on measures according to his personal beliefs and needs. When Bob complained, "Sometimes . . . one has to struggle *so much* of the time here against the feeling that the thing which is uppermost and controlling is to *keep up the performances*— not to do some *real thing* but to *seem* to do something," Belle responded pointedly: "The belief that you are working with the President is widespread and pleases your friends. After all, it may be that to win the confidence of the people in your sincerity and power is not less an achievement than to secure the specific legislation I know you feel is so profoundly important. Your growing power is capital upon which to draw for real results in the future."[14]

La Follette's reading of the roll call did little to increase his popularity among his colleagues. He proudly noted upon his return to the Senate: "The air is surcharged —. . . I continue to hear that the subject of 'what we ought to do with La F[ollette]' has been quite fully discussed & is still under consideration by the men who think they are responsible for the Senate." Pleased that he was at least considered a force with which to be reckoned, La Follette was further reinforced when the *New York Times* attributed the passage of the Railway Hours Act to his roll call campaigns. Those senators who were legitimately concerned about the number of consecutive hours served by railway workers had, according to the *Times*, been joined by those who shuddered at the specter of having their names read across the nation in speeches insinuating that they were callous and inhumane at best, if not in the pocket of the railroads.[15]

La Follette continued to be dissatisfied with his relationship with Theodore Roosevelt. The president greeted him very effusively at the session's beginning, but, noted La Follette, "I never know how much he is really *dee-lighted*." Roosevelt privately confided to William Allen White, editor of *The Gazette*: "We are for La Follette when he stands against certain big corporation evils, and against him when he goes to a foolish extreme, or throws away the possible by demanding the impossible. . . . La Follette often does real good in the Senate, and I like him a great deal better this year than last. I became utterly out of patience with his attitude toward the rate [Hepburn] bill last summer. . . . But he often serves a very useful purpose in making the Senators go on record, and his fearlessness is the prime cause of his ability to render this service." Although Roosevelt professed to "have grown to a real liking" for La Follette, confrontations between the president and the senator over coal bills began almost immediately.[16]

Like virtually all issues of the progressive era, the debate over natural resources encompassed a whole spectrum of attitudes and beliefs. Despite his personal friendship with ardent preservationist John Muir and his own reputation as a great outdoorsman and committed environmentalist, Roosevelt, like most progressives, was for the most part a conservationist, advocating the most efficient use of the nation's resources, including grazing lands, water, coal, and timber. Old Guard Republicans balked at any efforts to impede resource exploitation, while La Follette saw federal conservation programs as a way to bring many powerful business interests to heel. Early in 1907, the president and the freshman senator were in agreement that government should hold title to public mineral lands and lease them to businesses, thereby retaining ultimate control. Roosevelt, according to La Follette, gave his heartiest approval to La Follette's comprehensive bill dealing with coal lands belonging to both Native Americans and the federal government and personally assured the senator of his unqualified support. La Follette recorded their discussion as "the most satisfying I have ever had with him. It was quite personal & political — and quite extended and significant." Belle encouraged this cooperative stance, while expressing, perhaps unconsciously, her desire that he abandon any presidential aspirations of his own: "[T]here is [the] possibility of great progress in short time with such an ally. You may be able to accomplish in another session what would have taken years of education and struggle otherwise. It is an opportunity that should be made the most of. . . . If Roosevelt is sincere I believe you could achieve greater things with him [as] President than to be President yourself."[17]

The veneer of friendliness between La Follette and Roosevelt quickly wore thin. On 22 January 1907, Roosevelt, concerned by the lack of support for La Follette's proposal, urged the senator to accept a compromise. Instead, La Follette worked to withdraw mineral lands from corporate exploitation completely. La Follette confided in his family his disappointment in Roosevelt's assertion that the compromise bill La Follette opposed was all that was attainable. He added caustically, "I shall do the best I can to work with him without chasing up and inflicting myself upon him unduly, but at the same time I don't propose to go and jump in the Potomac because he throws me down every day or so — although it is somewhat depressing." La Follette vowed, "I propose to let him know that I am right about the coal matter." Predicting "that the next session of the Senate will be the most stormy since the Adm[inistration] of Andrew Johnson following the assassination of Lincoln," La Follette sent off a condescending, self-righteous letter: "Now, Mr. President . . . I do not like to see this administration make a wrong start. The interests of the public will be better served by temporary defeat of an effective measure dealing with this subject than by compromising on a bill which sounds well in the title but is weak or silent on vital points. The enactment of a law that falls short of reaching the real evil will be a stumbling block for many years to a substantial protection of public interest. It seems to me a mistake to regard leasing the mineral lands as the essential thing to be secured." An indignant Roosevelt, angry at the implication that he lacked integrity and dedication, responded, "[I]t will be a far more difficult matter permanently to keep the coal lands withdrawn when legislation has been refused than it was to withdraw them pending the time when Congress should have a chance to legislate concerning them. . . . I have stood as firmly as a human being can stand for effective legislation. I trust you and your colleagues will give it to me."[18]

La Follette continued his opposition to any compromise bill and later used the issue to demonstrate the "moral" difference between himself and the president. Roosevelt, he maintained, was interested only in what could be passed, not in what was right. To La Follette, Roosevelt's implied acceptance of the maxim "half a loaf is better than no bread" was the cornerstone for all the differences that were to continue to come between them, for La Follette perpetually maintained, "Half a loaf, as a rule, dulls the appetite, and destroys the keenness of interest in attaining the full loaf." Roosevelt countered, "[T]o struggle for one particular bill as against all other bills is to lay into the hands of men who wish to do nothing." Without Roosevelt's support, La Follette's bill died in committee.[19]

La Follette's self-righteousness put enormous strain on his relationship with Roosevelt, a man who had achieved, seemingly effortlessly, all that La Follette coveted: power, mass love, approval, and a stable and high sense of self-esteem. La Follette found some solace in increasingly perceiving Roosevelt as shallow, hypocritical, self-serving, and weak, an undeserving recipient of public adulation. Roosevelt correspondingly viewed La Follette as a self-seeking fanatic and demagogue whose grandiose political notions were completely impractical and potentially harmful. The animosity that would eventually reach titanic proportions began in earnest between the two progressives during this period. La Follette refrained, however, from making public his private view that the president lacked even basic integrity. By keeping his bitterness to himself, he enjoyed widespread speculation that he was Roosevelt's logical successor. La Follette also enjoyed flattering reports presenting exactly the image he wished to project: "[An] isolated and prophetic figure . . . who stands apart and seems to be himself resolutely against all groups and parties. There can be no doubt that the ability and forcefulness of La Follette has taken the Senate by surprise. . . . His speech on railroad rates . . . ; his successful passing of the employers' liability bill . . . , and his overthrowing of a scheme to give three billion dollars' worth of coal lands to a railway syndicate — these were three of the most memorable achievements of the Fifty-Ninth Congress. . . . He has become the bogey-man of the Senate." La Follette's reputation as a fearless fighter was also celebrated: "[T]his newcomer from Wisconsin is in earnest, . . . he is one of the most tireless and successful political figures in public life. This strong-faced man cannot be put aside, . . . either by soft words or intimidations. He is too wily to be tricked, and too battle-hardened to be fought down. Without money — he is the poorest of the Senators; without the aid of any political machine; without the prestige of birth or rank or fortune, this man of destiny has persevered until there is now a State behind him instead of a party. . . . His unique merit as a social reformer is that he has a long record of building up, not tearing down. . . . His idea is not to change American institutions, but to make them work."[20]

La Follette's desire to be seen as a maverick, however, did not always result in words of praise. In March 1907, he wrote a letter to Roosevelt protesting the Indian Office's prejudice against the Mexican Kickapoos, claiming that the Indian Department pursued the tribe into Mexico, resulting in arrests and harassment. F. E. Leupp, commissioner of Indian Affairs in the Department of the Interior, denied the accusation, responding, "Senator La Follette . . . I suspect has been moved by his human sympathies rather than by his knowledge of the details of the case." Concerned about gaining a reputation as a poorly grounded alarmist, La Follette was further disturbed by the claims of Isaac Stephenson, who aspired to fill the Senate seat made available by John Spooner's resignation. Stephenson considered La Follette an ingrate because of his reluctance to promote Stephenson's candidacy and publicly claimed that it had cost him between $500,000 to $1,000,000 to make La Follette governor and senator. La Follette opposed a proposed investigation of his campaign expenditures and attempted to salvage his reputation by splitting hairs: "I should be glad to have Mr. Stephenson state fully and specifically the exact amount contributed to each of my campaigns . . . [but] I do not recognize money invested in Mr. Stephenson's newspaper as contributions to my personal campaigns." The press, however, pointed out that for virtually the entire period of its existence, the *Free Press* had been La Follette's devoted personal organ. In the end, La Follette's vast political debt to Stephenson forced him to promote the millionaire's successful campaign. Although this avoided an ugly split, it was also the traditional culmination of a classic machine-style deal, a turn of events not lost on the citizens of Wisconsin, La Follette's friends and foes alike.[21]

The stress took its toll on La Follette's emotional and physical health. Wisconsin state representative William Bray, in preparing a report for the Wisconsin Assembly committee on Stephenson's bid, included mention of previous dirty campaign tactics by other Wisconsin politicians. Bray cited La Follette's employment, while seeking reelection as governor, of the state game wardens he had appointed to campaign for him and otherwise "follow his political bidding . . . entirely at state expense." La Follette had apparently been briefed on the unpublished report for, according to Bray, the senator accosted him at a train station, shook his fist in Bray's face and threatened to annihilate him politically if Bray made any detrimental references to him in the report. More than fifty years after the confrontation, Bray was still struck by La Follette's inappropriate and ill-mannered aggressiveness.[22]

La Follette's entire body broke out in "lumps," which a skin specialist attributed to uric acid in the blood, and his "bowel trouble" returned. At the short term's end he was bedridden with "severe influenza," and Belle traveled to Washington to nurse him. She noted the mysteriously uneven nature of his symptoms and their link with his emotional state. La Follette had not fully recovered when he began another demanding speaking tour, this time of the West, accompanied by family friend Colonel John Hannon. It was Hannon's responsibility to ensure that La Follette not miss any trains, a duty that once caused him to remove La Follette bodily from a speaker's platform and carry him off to a waiting car, an incident that first enraged then amused the senator. In California, an unusually philosophical La Follette, then fifty-two, reflected: "How small it [Mount Shasta] makes man — how brief his little flutter of life. . . . It made me very homesick to be here without you. It made life seem so short. It made it seem so wrong to be gone all the time. What is left will go so soon." La Follette suffered increasingly from the conflict between his compulsion to appeal directly to the public and his desire to enjoy the company of his family. He viewed the latter as a weakness and concluded, "I am surely growing old and babyish."[23]

La Follette continued to suffer physically as well. Swollen joints led him to suspect he suffered from gout, and he worried that his diet was a contributing cause. He could not be dissuaded, however, from a strenuous speaking schedule. To Belle's horror when she accompanied him for a week, he came off the speaking platform dripping with perspiration. He felt dizzy and almost lost his thread of thought while speaking. His determination to continue was frequently extreme: "I had been talking half an hour when I began to grow sick & to gripe. The house was full of people. I was determined to go on & did to the end but I had to excuse myself *often* & go into a little boarded up room off the stage & vomit into a pail & then use the pail immediately for diarrhea — I don't know how many times I had to excuse myself. The audience was kind — but I was weak when I finished & got to the hotel    a poor enough place without any inside accommodations. The thing went on till about three o'clock. . . . I insisted getting on the way at 6:45 in the morning & rode all day & half the night to get here at Des Moines." Such violent attacks continued.[24]

Although Belle scolded Bob for speaking for too long, she also lavished him with praise: "It is a great achievement to have earned a reputation *really earned*— that creates a spontaneous demand for you from every part of the country. And your message with its high ideals and stirring appeal for better public service is becoming engrafted onto the common thought of the common people. . . .—How glad we should be that your great gifts have been so well used and I am thankful always and ever to have reached the point where we can *realize* the significance of the long struggle — and where we can know the recognition accorded it. It was not long ago when it seemed quite impossible that you should attain anything like Justice." La Follette took pride in his speeches' ability to reach people and "set the *thinking* men of the town thinking more." So reassured was he that he deviated from his usual pattern of filling his entire vacation with speaking commitments and enjoyed, in the fall of 1907, a hunting trip in Colorado accompanied by his oldest son and several friends. During that trip, according to Bobbie, his father was the first man up in camp in the morning, eager to get the party underway, while at night he entertained the group around the campfire, reading tales appropriate to the spirit of the occasion. For all his political dedication, La Follette was also a committed family man. The dedication and intensity he poured into his progressive agenda was matched at least equally by the attention and energy he lavished, despite their many separations, on his children. But like his political agenda for the nation, La Follette's personal agenda for his children, especially his sons, was all the more difficult and demanding by virtue of La Follette's goals of excellence. He would not brook failure, retreat, or compromise.[25]

# 10: THE BURDENS OF A GREAT NAME
## YOU HAVE SET AN ALMOST UNATTAINABLE GOAL FOR US

Robert La Follette claimed, "A life . . . does not terminate with death . . . [but] lives on and on through the generations." He made it clear to his young children — just as his own father, via his mother, had done — that he held high expectations for them. These expectations ranged from small, specific activities to the development of large and demanding personal characteristics. Maintaining that he wanted only the best for all his children, Bob gave his sons in particular sweeping, Herculean directives. When Phil was only eight, Bob wrote, "I love you and expect you to do a lot of good things in this world & help to make everybody happier and happier." His advice ranged in tone from that of a philosopher to a drill sergeant.[1]

Both Bob and Belle manipulated their children emotionally. A standard method was to remind the children of how very fortunate they were to be loved and provided for, then capitalize on their feelings of gratitude and unworthiness by pressing quickly for whatever was desired. The La Follette children were never allowed to lose sight of their blessings and were directed to be constantly appreciative. Bob let it be known that his children's shortcomings and transgressions caused him much disappointment and personal pain. Belle initially shared many of Bob's expectations and confided in her husband, "I pray that my children as they develop may be like you." Even granddaughter Sherry La Follette, who refers to Belle La Follette's character as "crystal pure" concedes, "The one negative . . . was that both she and Bob demanded an unachievable standard of perfection for the next generation." However, as their sons reached maturity, even Belle questioned her husband's determination that they pursue only the career Bob himself had chosen.[2]

Bob's great love of family included his siblings and cousins, but he depended on his wife and children as his main source of strength. Although he spent an enormous amount of time away, Bob's desire for family togetherness was strong. For seven years the children divided each academic year between their Wisconsin farm and a rental house in Washington. Bob wanted to ensure that "they grew up as familiar with politics as children raised on the farm are with its day's work; and in that same spirit of practical knowledge and experience . . . were ready, when it came their turn, to put their hands to the plow and go straight ahead to the end of the furrow." When his daughter Mary was seven, he tried to involve her in his work by writing in terms she could understand: "Did you ever play pussy wants a corner? You know if you have a corner & get away from it some one (who is playing pussy) dives in & gets your corner. Well I have got a game like that with a bill. If I get away from my corner some one else will slip in and get the good corner for his bill. So I just have to keep right in my corner every day & watch that bill."[3]

Belle too desired to keep the children close. During Bob's first term in Congress, Belle recorded that kindergarten "did not seem to agree" with Fola, so Belle taught her herself. Years later, when Bob spent the short winter session of 1907 alone in Washington, Belle allowed Bobbie to attend school, but taught both Phil and Mary at home. Despite Belle's abhorrence of debt, when the family joined Bob in Washington, a teacher was included in the household staff in order to allow the children to remain within the home. Despite such closeness in their daily lives, Belle denied, both publicly and privately, that she or Bob pressured their children as youngsters or were reluctant to allow them true independence as adults. She professed her belief that the greatest gift parents could bestow was to enable their children to care for themselves and urged that "from infancy we parents should guard against any sense of ownership of our children. We are trustees, not proprietors." To her own adult children she vowed, "I [would not] have any of you do otherwise than follow your own convictions," urging, "I want you first of all to do what *you* feel is for your best good," and to "feel free to do whatever you may desire." She pledged, "We want you to have the largest life that we can give you and we don't want you to feel burdened with any sense of obligation or of dependence — and I want you to feel that we *appreciate you*." Although she advised other parents to encourage their children to think and act for themselves, she revealed much when she concluded: "Give them rope, lots and lots of rope — all they can use — more and more as they learn to use it. And when there is a positive need to make it taut, just a little give and take in drawing the slack usually answers the purpose better than a sudden pull." Despite their claims of encouraging their children's independence, Belle and Bob never managed to cut those "ropes," and instead endeavored to keep their children, as youngsters and as adults, on a very tight rein indeed.[4]

Belle acknowledged that it was the hardest thing imaginable to think of leaving the family and made frequent efforts to entice absent members to return, stressing their need for her and insisting that she alone knew what was right even for her adult children. Within the pages of *La Follette's Weekly Magazine*, Belle scorned the notion that a grown daughter is "to stay at home to be our comfort and support or pet and idol according to our needs and circumstances," but before her own daughter, at nineteen, departed on a group tour of Europe, Belle cautioned, "I do not want you to have any un-necessary responsibility. . . . I realize how precious are the years of youth and we agree that it is well to prolong them as long as they naturally can be and I am glad you are to enjoy this trip as a young girl and not as a young lady . . . Enjoy . . . in the sweet and wholesome spirit of sweet and wholesome girl-hood." Not surprisingly, in Belle's story, "I Married a Lawyer," which reveals so many of her fantasies and desires, the oldest daughter voluntarily "came home from abroad . . . cheerfully assuming a large share of the responsibil-ity of the household, and taught the little sister to be a helper also."[5]

Bob shared these visions of their adult children as perpetual youngsters. He was as openly determined as Belle that their children make a conscious effort to perpetuate or at least prolong their dependent childhoods. He could not resist, for example, objecting strenuously to the manner in which Fola, then in her twenties, pursued a career on the stage. He urged her to give up making office calls in favor of spending the winter with him in Wash-ington and went so far as to include a sample letter of protest to send to a stage manager, reminding his daughter, "You know that I only mean, Fola, to save you from the hard things of life." Although publicly he approved Fola's independence, privately he wrote to Belle, "I think of her off by her-self fighting her way single handed among the struggling mass of actors and actresses having to ask [for] recognition & consideration . . . , taking any-thing of a part so [long as] it offers a chance as eagerly as a starved dog would grab a bone. When I think of her alone at night . . . I feel that I can't stand it." He hoped Fola "will be satisfied to demonstrate her ability & then come back to us." Fola resented her parents' lack of faith in her judgment and abilities. When telegraphed, "How could you give such an interview?" in regard to press reports of Fola's comments on her father's political agenda, Fola wired back, "How could you even think I did?"[6]

His children were a major source of comfort and refreshment to Bob. He shared vicariously in their triumphs and defeats and often seemed to view his sons in particular as mere extensions of himself. His dependence upon all his children and delight in their company, particularly during his later years, can scarcely be exaggerated. In 1919, in an effort to entice his twenty-year-old daughter Mary to Washington, Bob offered her a typing job in his office at $100 a month. A few weeks later the sixty-four-year-old father wrote to his family, "Well, what do you think happened to me this after-noon? I was moping away up here in my room when there came a faint tap at the door. . . . I opened the door and there *stood Mary — my Mary!!!!* Do you know what I did? I just cried! That's what I did. I'm an old man all right. . . . Washington is hers. She shall have anything she wants — and do everything she wants to do. Say, I *feel just as if I had been demobilized.* . . . It is so good to talk to one of the family."[7]

As parents, the La Follettes were not above bribery to encourage the family solidarity, which one observer called intense beyond any other he had ever encountered. Bob claimed, "Space and time cannot divide us. The mystic cords of love bind us close together in family communion." During lengthy separations Bob felt listless and dull and expressed his "heart hunger" for "family communion." "The best hour of all the day," he told his family, "is that I spend writing to you." In those daily letters he not only recorded his own thoughts and actions, but speculated, in minute detail, on theirs. He treasured his children's letters, particularly those received during difficult political times. Any gap in communications or even a lack of sufficient detail caused him (and Belle as well), to protest vehemently. Both parents often appeared resentful of their children's attempts at privacy and jealous of diversions such as friends and interests outside the family. "I want to think of my little family," he urged, "as a happy & joyous little group sticking close together, each one trying to make the others have the best possible time." Although he cherished the company of each of his adult children individually, he, like Belle, was never truly content unless the entire family was together and sent frequent reminders that he would not tolerate absenteeism for it was "unfair" to him.[8]

Bob regretted when his children suffered from his unpopular political actions, but, he noted, "I think I should have felt bound to do [the same] if some such thing had been done to my father." The children directed their feelings of family loyalty toward each other as well as their parents. As adults, the siblings exchanged strong declarations of love, approval, and admiration. In a letter addressed to Mary Sweetheart of Mine, Phil, age twenty-two, confided, "I am sorry that you are my sister — simply because I can't marry you." Occasionally these feelings of family solidarity so firmly entrenched within their children backfired on Belle and Bob, as when the children chose to support each other in decisions contrary to their parents' wishes.[9]

All family members were ostensibly encouraged to speak openly on current issues. However, views political or otherwise that ran counter to parental conclusions met with strong disapproval. When Phil was a child and an adolescent, his father was very often irritated with him. The youth stayed almost a year with his maternal grandparents during his father's long illness in 1899 and spent subsequent summers there until his grandmother's death in 1904. As their children grew to maturity, Bob and Belle still found it almost impossible to accept decisions that varied even slightly from their own traditions and values. While Bob's intrusiveness centered around his

*"A happy and little joyous group sticking close together" — the La Follette family in 1910. Phil, holding* The North American, *sits between Mary and Bobbie. Fola (top left) married the following year. Bob and Belle complete the top row. (State Historical Society of Wisconsin image photographed with permission by Elwood Mills)*

sons' career choices, Belle's greatest interferences stemmed from her daughters' decisions to marry. To Phil she wrote, "It is not so much the special attributes of the mate we choose, that ensures a happy marriage as our own attitude toward the union" and, in fact, readily accepted the bride he selected. Her sensitivity to her daughters' choices first became apparent when false reports of Fola's engagement to a family friend circulated. Rather than simply make an effort to correct the misinformation, Belle reacted violently, responding almost rudely to uninformed parties who commented on the story, unable to suppress her feelings of indignation.[10]

Although Belle was disturbed by Mary's criticism, echoed by Phil and Fola, that she always took everything "so awfully seriously," she could not resist interfering deeply into Fola's decision to marry playwright and founder of the Dramatists' Guild, George Middleton, known as Mid. A highly emotional correspondence erupted between Belle and Fola. Although Mid recalled that his "immature political ideas" made a rather poor initial impression on his prospective father-in-law, Belle's chief objection was vague, based essentially on the fact that Mid was not a La Follette, but she was truly distraught and criticized: "It is only fair that you should not act on your own judgement only." She wrote of her own engagement, "I do not think I could of written her [Belle's mother] that I had *decided*. I should have talked it over with her first as I did. She approved of your father. But if she had not would that not be all the more reason why I should have consulted her judgment and promised her I would not act until she knew him better? In your determined attitude Fola you shut your father and me out." In her despair Belle attempted to play on Fola's sympathies and on her sense of guilt, complaining, "I am not as strong as I once was, Fola" and reporting, "The first reading of your letter . . . struck like a blow from your hand."[11]

Belle's lengthy appeals upset Fola enormously, but she refused to bow to her mother's deeply emotional but essentially groundless protests and offered her own impassioned entreaties: "How can you be so *sure*? Why do you close your feeling so absolutely to the possibility of any other understanding of him?" Fola, who was twenty-nine years old and had been working in New York for a number of years, protested her parents' rigidity, an assessment echoed by her brother Bobbie. A visit from a determined Fola and the criticism of a family friend that Belle was being neither understanding nor helpful hurt Belle deeply, causing her to deny emphatically that she resented or opposed her children's independence, only to conclude by renewing her determined view that Fola was about to make a terrible mistake. She implored Fola, "I feel as I should if you had been in [a] burning building and I saw you about to jump and I was powerless to rescue you . . . This goes so deep with me that any attempt to say what it means seems futile. If I fail now all my life fails."[12]

In the end, Belle bowed to the inevitable and accepted Fola's decision to marry Mid, but it was the advice of a trusted family friend rather than the entreaties of her daughter that inspired her apology for not accepting Fola's judgment in the first place. Fola and Mid married in the La Follette's Washington home on 29 October 1911. Mid accepted the position of literary editor for the family magazine, writing a regular column entitled "Snapshots." He proved to be one of his father-in-law's staunchest supporters, even in times of great public controversy. Mid must have curried some favor with Belle as well, for he was a staunch feminist whose depictions of relationships between men and women within his plays received praise from no less than Charlotte Perkins Gilman, author of *Women and Economics*.[13]

Although Fola and Mid's marriage was from all indications a happy one, lasting fifty-six years until Mid's death in 1967, Belle did not seem to learn from her unsuccessful and painful attempt to intrude and control. In 1921, Mary, aged twenty-two, wrote of her decision to marry an old school friend of Phil's, Ralph Sucher, an aspiring lawyer and a La Follette supporter. Although it seemed that Sucher might be a more likely candidate to receive the La Follettes' blessings than the more bohemian Mid, Belle urged Mary to wait indefinitely before marriage. Like her sister, Mary was disturbed by her mother's disapproval and interference, but she refused to allow Belle's objections to affect her decision. Like Mid, Sucher, once part of the fold, was quickly given a position within the family empire. Although only Belle wrote the letters of protest, she claimed that her husband shared her early aversion to their prospective sons-in-law. After each child's marriage, (all but Bobbie married before Bob's death), both Bob and Belle endeavored to keep the newlyweds firmly entrenched within the family — politically, financially, and emotionally.

Considering their parents' enormous expectations, it is no wonder that the children expressed freely their apprehensions that they would fail to measure up. Even as youths they were anxious over meriting approval, and as they grew older, they worried about being worthy of their parents, particularly their father. Phil wrote to Bob, "I know that it will take an almost superhuman effort on any of our parts to even approximate living up to you," and complained, "I do so want to make my life worth while, but you have set an almost unattainable ideal for us." Four years later he concluded more bluntly, "Being a son to you and mother entails an enormous liability: it is almost impossible to be what one ought to with such a heritage."[14]

Despite their children's anxieties about parental expectations and the crises between Belle and her daughters over marriage, Belle publicly portrayed the La Follette family as mutually supportive and conflict-free. Just as Belle and Bob refused to acknowledge any conflicts within their marriage, they would not admit to even the most commonplace of family differences. It was crucial to them to see themselves as "perfect" parents, and their children confirmed that view. Phil in particular, despite many bitter arguments with his father, wrote long letters of praise and admiration. To his father he wrote, "I even feel you are superhuman," and to his mother, "The only person that I know of in history that compares with you is Christ. . . . I am ever the devout worshiper at your shrine of holiness." Such declarations may have helped soften the blow when Phil joined the armed services against their wishes during World War I.[15]

Phil asserted considerable independence in his decision to enter the ROTC training camp at Fort Sheridan, Illinois. Commissioned as second lieutenant in the Infantry, he found his experiences in the military to be, for the most part, rewarding, increasing vastly his confidence. Bob, however, was reluctant to acknowledge his second son's self-sufficiency. Frantic over Bobbie's prolonged illness and the deadly influenza epidemic of 1918–19 (an epidemic particularly virulent in military training camps), Bob insisted that Phil send him the names of his superiors and closest associates and "made Phil agree" to see the medical officer to arrange that Bob be informed of Phil's slightest illness. The intensity of his concern struck even Bob himself, and he confessed, "I suppose he told them I was a nervous old boy — but I don't care." Bob's fears of his second son's poor health were unrealized, however, and Phil's military service merited such a glowing letter of recommendation from his superiors that his father responded, "I sure am proud of the great record you have made but I knew you would do it — my boy." [16]

Phil felt a strong sense of obligation concerning his parents, and during Bob's final illnesses he spoke and worked full-time on his behalf. Following a particularly successful speech in 1924, Phil received the "ultimate accolade" from his father — a warm embrace and the affirmation, "You are my boy." After Bob's death, Phil remained in politics, serving three terms as Wisconsin's governor (1931–33 and 1935–39). Phil, according to his wife Isabel (called Isen), felt the burden of his parents' expectations far less than his older brother, although even Phil insisted he did not enjoy living in the executive residence because it was so inextricably associated with heavy responsibility, both from his childhood when his father was governor and later from his own tenure. As parents themselves, Phil and Isen strove to keep their own children as free of inappropriate responsibilities as possible.[17]

Phil proved to be an aggressive, flamboyant, controversial, and influential leader, "one of the most gifted, creative, and brilliant politicians of the 1930s" whose political style was reminiscent of his father's. Phil's biographer, John E. Miller, contends that Phil was the more natural choice to succeed Bob in the Senate. Upon their father's death, however, only Bobbie had reached the requisite age of thirty. Miller points out that Phil referred to himself as the "second son," apparently resenting the loss of opportunity which was his brother's birthright.[18]

Despite his ambition and dedication, Phil was unable to master a dependable political majority in his attempt to have Wisconsin provide leadership during the Great Depression, although the pioneering unemployment compensation law he signed in 1932 was studied for national implementation. Phil felt his political failures keenly, particularly in view of his father's example and expectations. When he lost the governorship after his initial term, he was acutely aware that he was the first La Follette to lose an election in more than thirty years. "That night . . . I tossed and writhed in anger and humiliation," he recorded, and compared himself unfavorably with his father: "He was the maker of a tradition — I, only the inheritor." Phil served two subsequent terms, but the last was plagued by controversy, especially following his creation of the National Progressives of America

(NPA) in 1938. Previous political successes as well as "the ever present memory of his parents" inspired presidential ambitions, but "the late thirties . . . were not propitious for an isolationist, third-party presidential candidate." His unfortunate choice for the NPA's logo was a blue X in a red circle on a white background, which many, even among his supporters, found disconcertingly similar to the Nazi swastika. Striving to create a new national party while simultaneously running for a fourth term, Phil failed at both. He was only forty-one when he left office for the final time, returning to the practice of law, his professed true career of choice.[19]

Phil served on the staff of General Douglas MacArthur during World War II, then returned to his law practice. Although he continued to participate in public affairs, he deemed himself too old and, mindful of the strain caused by his father's perpetual indebtedness, too "selfish" financially to return to politics. The independence Phil demonstrated by joining the army during World War I allowed him to resist being completely ruled by his father's expectations and desires, but he, like his siblings, certainly felt them throughout his life. Increasingly conservative, he remained politically active despite his denials, promoting MacArthur, Earl Warren, and Dwight Eisenhower in presidential campaigns. He struggled with depression and alcohol and served for five years as president of an electronics corporation in Long Island before returning to Wisconsin in 1960. In the midst of writing his political memoirs, he died in 1965.[20]

Fola and Mary, although less pressured than their brothers to excel in public life, also bore the unique stamp of their upbringing, Fola far more so than her sister. In view of the societal limitations imposed on her sex, Fola lived out her parental expectations in a variety of innovative ways. Like her mother, she was a dedicated suffragist and lifelong political activist. She shared her father's love for drama, culminating in a stage career highlighted by her performance in the brief run of Percy MacKaye's *The Scarecrow* on Broadway. She refused to change her name from La Follette to Middleton. This was not unheard of in theater circles, but Fola publicly advocated the right of all women to retain their own names. She traveled to the Soviet Union in 1928 as a member of the American Education Delegation headed by John Dewey. Although she and Mid struggled financially later in life, she devoted twenty-two years to completing the biography of her father began by her mother. Following its publication in 1953, she began cataloging and organizing the more than 400,000 documents that make up the La Follette collection in the Library of Congress, work that occupied her until her death in 1970 at the age of eighty-seven.

Less is known about the youngest La Follette. Mary did not record any feelings of resentment over her parents' constant political and personal preoccupations but did remember feeling "exceedingly happy" when a bout of scarlet fever made her the sole focus of her mother's attention. Like her siblings, Mary worked for a time in her father's office but broke tradition by deciding against the University of Wisconsin (during the fervor over her father's opposition to American entry into World War I) in favor of art school. She alone rejected a life of political activism, channeling her energies into her family and into her paintings, which were favorably reviewed at their occasional exhibitions. In 1934, her marriage ended when her husband ran off with longtime La Follette family secretary and confidant Nellie Dunn. Like Fola, Mary struggled financially, but managed to support herself and her two children with minor government jobs. Mary never remarried and died at the age of eighty-nine in 1988.[21]

Despite the advantages of being, in his sister's words, the "Crown Prince," it was Bobbie who paid most dearly for his birthright. While his father let it be known that all his children's shortcomings and transgressions caused him much disappointment and personal pain, Bobbie, the oldest son, was warned that he in particular had "no right" to upset his father in any way. The pressure upon him to excel was constant. When Bobbie was six, for example, Belle brought to his attention the pleas from various constituents sent to the family on a daily basis and impressed upon him his personal obligation to ameliorate suffering whenever possible.[22]

By age eleven, Bobbie closely followed his father's political trials and tribulations as a first-term senator and identified with his struggles. "I suppose that the Senate is trying to act like an 'icicle' to you," he wrote to his father. "Never mind, they will have to do something worse than act like an 'icicle' to freeze a *La Follette* won't they?" Bob took his two sons into his complete confidence when they were thirteen and eleven. Bobbie and Phil quickly learned the way to merit Bob's approval, and their interest in legislation sponsored by their father was almost as absorbing as his own. The boys grew increasingly aware of their father's dependence upon them to carry on after his death in his stead. Belle occasionally questioned the wisdom of encouraging Phil and Bobbie to become engrossed in subjects so remote from the thoughts of other children their age, but Bob entertained no such doubts. Phil recalled, "In politics and in public affairs he had no secrets from us. . . . At first some of his progressive callers looked askance at us [during political meetings at the La Follette home] because the subject was thought to be too confidential to trust to young boys. But Dad would assure them that we were to be trusted."[23]

Implicit in this carefully nurtured interest in politics was the expectation that both boys, but Bobbie in particular, would not only follow in their father's footsteps but surpass his already daunting record of accomplish-

"Living on through the generations": Friends and family at the unveiling of Jo Davidson's statue of Robert M. La Follette in the U.S. Capitol's Statuary Hall, 25 April 1929. From left: Senator John J. Blaine, Fola La Follette, and Burton K. Wheeler's granddaughter, Marion Montana Wheeler; Mary La Follette Sucher stands behind her son, Robert La Follette Sucher; Philip Fox La Follette, wearing glasses, stands next to his brother, Robert M. La Follette Jr. (State Historical Society of Wisconsin Whi[X3]46203)

ments. On Bobbie's twelfth birthday his father advised: "Look well to it that you grow in gentleness and tenderness as well as in strength. . . . The boy Bobbie is a mighty important part of the man. . . . Every day and hour of life is precious. Every act lays the foundation for another. I love you dear lad and count on you for many things in the future." When Bobbie reached sixteen, his father praised his "natural abilities awaiting development" but urged "severe discipline to train them for the highest usefulness in life." He concluded: "You have the brain and the constitution and the courage to take high rank in any company and to be a leader of power for good as a man. Every hair of your head is dear to me. Every day of your life is precious. . . . Oh my boy, my boy, I want you to realize *right now* the vital importance of fixing the habits of industry and self-discipline to bring out all your splendid powers. *Now, every hour, every day* of the *next five years* will tell the story of your life to follow." At eighteen came the declaration, "So much depends on your making [it known] . . . that you have the real stuff in you," a message reinforced at nineteen with "I love you, my dear lad,— so much that you must love me enough to do . . . things right." At twenty, Bobbie was instructed to "Get the habit of *mastery — control — discipline—* that is everything. . . . [N]o matter how hard it is, just remember you are at work on the armor and weapons with which to wage a great fight against the wrongs which oppress and the evils and ills which afflict the world in which you live." And as early as 1914, heedless of Bobbie's protests, Bob began urging his oldest son, then nineteen, to begin preparations to run for governor.[24]

Not surprisingly, Bobbie, the most pressured of the La Follette children, was a tremendously insecure youngster who needed constant reassurance. As a little boy, Bobbie, in his father's absence, was especially anxious each night to know if Belle thought he had been good and was the most traumatized of the children by unsettling events. Although older than Mary and Phil, Bobbie suffered most severely by far from separation anxiety during the absence of their parents. (Phil took thinly veiled delight in his brother's misery during such times. When Belle once left Wisconsin suddenly to nurse Bob through influenza, Phil noted gleefully, "How it did surprise Robert to find that Mama had gone. He pretty near fainted.") [25]

As a child, Bobbie was preoccupied with his health. He discovered quickly that people would be "awfully *good*" to him in times of sickness even as "doctor's orders" provided a guilt-free excuse to avoid unwanted burdens. Belle worried about Bobbie's tendency to exaggerate or fabricate illness, but usually her concerns about health won out and made her treat all symptoms, real or imagined, seriously. Bob, too, was very apprehensive about Bobbie's health, and he confided in Belle, "It keeps haunting me that he may get hurt." Bobbie's first serious illness, pronounced "a congestion of the covering of the nerves resulting from poison or infection by the grippe," occurred in 1904 when he was nine years old. Bob, preoccupied previously with the impending gubernatorial campaign, found himself obliged to stay home: "[Bobbie] is so nervous that Belle or I must be with him all the time. . . . It will be weeks before he will be where he will not require constant attendance." Bob noted proudly, "I can soothe and 'steady' him better than anyone else." As Bobbie recovered, the pressures and expectations resumed. Another illness would follow. Although all were marked by much physical pain and suffering, each would also ensure a period of emotional respite and reassurance. The cycle was in motion.[26]

In 1906, Bob and Belle decided to leave their three younger children at Wisconsin's Hillsdale Home boarding school during Bob's first session as senator. According to Bob's sister, Josie Siebecker, whom the children often visited during this period, Phil was "happy as can be," making his envious and wistful older brother comment, "Phil wouldn't be homesick at the north pole." Bobbie, who turned eleven during this separation, wrote to his parents nearly every day, pouring out his misery and loneliness in letters that are literally tear-stained. He complained bitterly of the treatment he received at the boarding school and begged piteously to be allowed to stay with his Aunt Josie. "Oh mama and papa," he wrote shortly after their departure, "5 months seems 10 years. . . . oh if you only knew how homesick I was." A month later he lamented: "Mama and papa, if you only knew how homesick I am you would pity me. Mama and papa, it just seems as though I can't stand it and when I think that I have to — Oh Mama, I am disappearing. My heart is as big as a mountain. . . . Oh, I will be sick. Oh, but I must not. Oh, I am in agony all the time. . . . remember how I love you. Oh Mama, I just can't stand it. Oh, I will go crazy, not really but love crazy, homesick crazy." Even in his misery Bobbie noted shamefully, "Phil and Mary do not mind it much compared with me." Nevertheless, four years later, during a much briefer separation, Bobbie's emotions remained substantially the same. Such overwhelming dependence caused him, when separated from one parent, to cling all the more tightly to the other.[27]

That dependence intensified in the spring of 1912. Following a period of intensification of their already great pressures on Bobbie, then seventeen, Bob and Belle left for a prolonged campaign journey. The very day of their departure Bobbie, enjoying a carefree drive in the family car, struck and nearly killed an African American child, fracturing the boy's skull and necessitating surgery. The child was in a coma for over a week and, owing to a brain injury, was still in the hospital unable to talk more than a month later. Upon hearing of the accident, Bob endeavored to keep the news a secret, even from Belle; he instructed that he be kept informed of the boy's condition and assumed responsibility for all medical bills. The event did not become public and scandal was averted. Bobbie's anxiety and guilt over this incident can only be estimated, but certainly it provided a graphic example of the dangers of independence, enlarged Bobbie's perception of his father's omnipotence, and heightened his anxieties during subsequent separations.[28]

The demands on Bobbie increased after this event, during his studies at the University of Wisconsin, his parents' alma mater. All the La Follette children expressed anxiety about their school performances and feared disappointing their parents. Knowledge of his father's difficulty in reconciling himself to their separation compounded Bobbie's fears of academic failure. Bobbie's election to the presidency of the freshman class pleased his father enormously, but Bob disapproved of Bobbie's membership in a fraternity, insisting he live with Josie and her husband. Although Bob claimed that his disapproval stemmed from concern over Bobbie's academic performance, his letters suggest far more concern that Bobbie stay dependent and carry out his father's will. Bob, whose own university record had been poor indeed and who downplayed the importance of scholastic achievement previously, insisted on nothing but academic excellence from Bobbie, claiming "your *success* in *life* depends on the *thoroughness* and *character* of your work in the University." Belle was better able to accept their temporary separations from Bobbie and the risk that he might find independence. When Bobbie's performance fell below his father's expectations, only Belle's entreaties kept Bob from demanding that Bobbie "pack his trunk and come to Washington and stay here with me."[29]

Bob offered much advice and sent his son self-addressed stamped postcards, instructing him to report daily and in detail on his class work and study habits because, he wrote, "My interest and anxiety are so deep and so constantly with me." When Bob received a form letter declaring Bobbie on academic probation, he reiterated his overwhelming need for Bobbie to be successful. Bob denied any selfish motives in his concern for Bobbie's college career, claiming it only mattered for Belle, who was "not well." Belle, however, begged, "Oh Bobbie, this is a critical time and *you must come out right*. When Papa got those discouraging reports, it seemed to take the gimp right out of him."[30]

Despite her denials, Belle too was far from accepting Bobbie as an independent adult. She wrote soothingly to her "tootsie, wootsie baby boy," that "Mother's heart ached for her baby boy. She knew exactly how he felt over his exams." Belle defended such baby talk: "Although you are twenty tomorrow, there trudges beside you in mother's memory, a beautiful sturdy boy with golden curls and big blue eyes with long curling lashes; he wears a red sweater and red stocking cap and corduroy pants with leather leggings." Refusing to allow Bobbie to assume responsibility for his own actions, Belle visited the university, attended Bobbie's classes, and met individually with each of his professors. Her detailed report to Bob included remarks from both the dean and Bobbie's English professor that Bobbie's imperfect record was not a grave matter, and she expressed resentment when another professor did not seem to take her visit seriously. Like Bob, Belle, despite her baby talk, alternately demanded and pled for academic excellence, though she was less adamantly opposed to Bobbie moving out of his relatives' home and into the fraternity house. Bob, on the other hand, ordering his son to "cut out all entertainment and social affairs," played heavily on Bobbie's sense of familial duty.[31]

Bob wanted Bobbie's professors and classmates to say, "He proves that the second generation can be better than the first!" To ensure that goal, Bob demanded not only that Bobbie notify him of his progress, but that his professors do so as well. Bob rationalized this interference into his son's life to one of Bobbie's professors: "My heart is set on Bobbie's making good in the University. I cannot contemplate having him fail. It will effect all his life. That life is very precious to me. I have a father's hope that it will be useful to society. At the same time I do not forget that, in the main, it rests with him to make it so. . . . I believe his only danger lies in his yielding to the interest which he feels in outside things. . . . I ask no indulgence for him. . . . It is not because I distrust Bobbie [that reports are requested]. He will give it to me straight as he sees it. But he might think he is doing better than he really is doing. And so much is at stake that I must know and know in season." When Bobbie's grades improved, Bob's interference continued unabated. He even requested that one professor confront Bobbie unexpectedly and "make sure he is doing his daily work without any assistance on the side."[32]

Bobbie occasionally protested his parents' refusal to allow him any real independence but never defied them outright. He ignored, for example, his father's transparent effort to dissuade him from motorcycle riding. (Bob claimed that the jarring action of Bobbie's "wheel" could in some way cause liver damage.) Bobbie promptly lost the report cards his father wanted sent daily and occasionally urged his parents not to take his academic performance so seriously. He reminded them that, although his marks were frequently lower than desired, they were passing. For the most part, however, he demonstrated no meaningful resistance. His inability to fulfill parental expectations culminated in a desire to retreat back into the family circle — an understandable response from one for whom a conventional opportunity to assert independence, leaving home for university life, had been so quickly and thoroughly thwarted. He longed to return to the comforts of the family home, since he still bore its burdens. Letters detail his home-sickness during his college years and getting him back to the campus after Christmas vacation "was like pulling teeth."

Only later did Bob admit he might have been wrong in meddling in Bob-bie's college life, but, as with similar admissions, he minimized the significance of such interference. At the time he harbored no doubts what-soever. Bobbie became depressed over the enormous pressures upon him, particularly because they impaired his ability to perform up to his capabili-ties during examinations. Not surprisingly, Bobbie's second serious illness occurred during his sophomore year. Initially his complaints of feeling un-well were greeted with thinly veiled skepticism and derision, but, upon per-sonal investigation, Bob declared his son's illness genuine. This quickly evoked the desired response, as Belle wrote to Bobbie, "Once more I must urge you not to think about your work. It is of no importance compared with your getting well." Bob wrote frantically and in great detail to several doctors and friends, voicing his concern over Bobbie's usually mild but per-sistent fevers. The diagnosis was a streptococcal infection, no small matter during those pre-antibiotic times. When it was determined that Bobbie should have his tonsils removed, Bob brought him to Washington where he could supervise him directly and called in three specialists. For more than two months Bobbie's temperature fluctuated enough to prohibit a tonsil-lectomy, and he suffered enormously from the infection. Once the tonsils were removed, he rallied briefly, then suffered a recurrence of the infec-tion, which for several weeks caused much pain and swelling in his thighs and groin, eventually spreading throughout his body. Family friend and sec-retary Nellie Dunn did not discount Bobbie's physical symptoms, but in her opinion Bobbie was suffering most from depression, a condition noted by Belle as well.[33]

Bob's personal secretary tried to calm Bob's increasing panic over his son's condition. Bob remained attentive to every detail, and he and Belle showered their son with praise and affection. In direct contrast to their scolding over his academic progress, Belle now bathed Bobbie daily and ca-tered to his wants, while Bob praised him for having endured such an ill-ness, calling it "the year of your greatest growth, your greatest development of character and strength, and power and patience." Bobbie's chief physi-cian, Charles Marbury, cautioned the La Follettes that they were "likely to notice every little thing and over emphasize it" and directed that Bobbie be urged to build up strength and resistance. The La Follettes, however, con-sidered this too "risky." Belle noted that Bobbie was "least of all inclined to be rash." Dr. Marbury marveled that, once on the mend, Bobbie experi-enced none of the irritability and depression usual in convalescence. Bobbie's contentment with his impaired condition may be a direct result of his father's cry, "How other things fade away when one of the family gets on the down grade!" and the promise of renewed parental expectations upon his return to health.[34]

As Bobbie recovered, Bob deemed confinement to classrooms a health risk for his son, putting him to work instead in his office at the capitol. Although this arrangement was the fulfillment of Bob's ultimate desire, it was short-lived, and Bobbie soon returned to the university. There he was once again overcome with dread concerning his examinations. Belle, still apprehensive lest he re-injure his health, remained in Madison and indulged him greatly. She once wrote to Bob, "Bobbie was very tired when he got home last night. . . . So I persuaded him to go to bed and I read his lesson to him. . . . He went to a little dance tonight." In the end, Bobbie claimed "doctor's orders" necessitated his dropping out of school. He returned to Washington to assist his father, ostensibly to work on the family magazine. Bob admitted, "I dread to have him leave here." Rather than work on the magazine and recover his health, Bobbie found himself working directly with his father as his private secretary and complained, "I am so tired that I could sleep standing on the toes of one foot."[35]

Although working with his father allowed Bobbie to escape from academic pressures, he suffered even greater strain as he witnessed the vilification of his father over Bob's opposition to American entry into World War I. Bob's leadership of the filibuster to prevent the vote to arm merchant ships was particularly trying for Bobbie, as he felt a sense of responsibility for controlling his almost hysterical father (see Chapter 14). Bobbie took the hatred generated by his father's antiwar stance quite personally. When he learned that all but two of the 423 University of Wisconsin faculty had signed a petition condemning Bob for his disloyalty, Bobbie raged to Phil, "Damn that faculty to hell. I hope that I may live to see each one get what is coming to him if there is any justice in this damn world." Bobbie himself came under fire on 25 January 1918 when he sent a letter defending his father to the *Madison Capital Times*. From its first issue on 12 December 1917, the *Capital Times* was solely dedicated to mounting a vigorous defense of La Follette's position on the war, determined to provide a voice of reason against the rising chorus of pro-war hysteria. Even it did not go far enough for Bobbie, however, who scorned "the weak-kneed sisters that are running that sheet." Privately he derided the paper for having "about as much policy as a piece of wet toilet paper and is and will be just about as useful." The letter went out to forty-five newspapers and earned Bobbie a reprimand for circulating rumors. Bobbie immediately drafted a sharp answer, denying the charge of rumor-mongering, citing sources, and offering to give additional evidence. Then, once again, illness provided a means of escape, a refuge from the ugly emotions generated by his own efforts to emulate his father's activism and commitment to principle.[36]

The illness, a recurrence of the streptococcal infection he first contracted in 1915, began with a very high fever that within a few weeks required surgery to drain pus from the pleural cavity. Family friend Lincoln Steffens noted: "You are gathering unto yourself more than your share of the affection of all of us. That is the effect of sickness and all other forms of unwilling behavior. It makes everybody love you." Like an infant, Bobbie, unable to chew his food, looked to his parents for relief and comfort. Good health became Bob and Belle's only concern for their children, making Phil's academic life far less pressured than his brother's. Belle recorded, "Each day we are engrossed in [the] one thought of what we can do for Bobbie," and Bob's secretary advised outsiders, "Senator La Follette is giving attention only to his son's condition." Belle noted that Bob "has had almost as hard a time as Bobbie. He has been so wrought up over him he will not go to bed nights and hovers about his room. But he will be all right if Bobbie keeps going ahead."[37]

After several months Belle took Bobbie away from the oppressive political and physical climate of Washington to Hot Springs, Virginia. Encouraged when he benefited from the change, she took him next to La Jolla, where "Californians seem so occupied with living that they need not philosophize much." When they came through Chicago, Phil met them at the station "and carried his sick brother in his arms from one train to another." The absence of familial and political adversity coupled with warm weather and the uncritical love and care of his mother and his sister Mary allowed Bobbie to improve, but slowly. Bobbie had been bedridden for so long that the ligaments in his legs had begun to atrophy. Belle noted his unwillingness to push himself, an attitude she encouraged, and his dependence upon her was enormous.[38]

With Bobbie's gradual recovery came the promise of renewed expectations. When Phil's postwar graduation from the University of Wisconsin brought Bob "the greatest possible satisfaction," he pressured Bobbie, "My Bob, it will be a *great joy* to me — I can't tell you *how great*— to *see you and Phil take the law course together*." Alone with Bobbie and Mary, Belle reflected on her oldest son's illnesses. She noted how susceptible he was to the suggestion of others, particularly his father, and his inability to shape his own career or even take an initiative. In response to Bob's urging that they return to Washington as soon as possible, she asserted that Bobbie's health and emotional well-being demanded he be allowed to develop a sense of independence and self-esteem. "Would it be wise," she asked her husband, "would it be safe although he appeared free from [the disease's effects,] to let him go back to the environment and conditions in which he had twice succumbed to the disease?" "Bobbie is deeply desirous of doing what will meet your wishes," she reassured Bob, "but what I feel much more deeply and profoundly that I can ever find words to express, is that it is essential to Bobbie's highest and fullest development that he find something he *wants* to do and can do. It need not be at all the thing he will finally do, or always do — but just to use his own initiative to decide for himself what he wanted to do next year, quite independent of any of us, would in my judgment, do more to put him on the right road, than anything we could do for him."[39]

Ultimately, Belle and Bobbie determined that Bobbie would stay on his own in La Jolla, a decision Belle lauded as his "best foundation for future action," while Bob viewed it with "dread and apprehension." He chided Bobbie, "I hope you don't get so wedded to [La Jolla] that you won't ever want to come home to the family." A month later he confided, "It is positively getting dangerous, this hold that La Jolla and vicinity is getting on you. We will have one time trying to wean you — if ever you give us the chance." Bobbie enjoyed his time alone in La Jolla immeasurably, celebrating it in a letter to his father as "this place [where] one may be lazy and yet it does not seem to give cause to anxiety to you or anyone else," and calling it a "life saver for me."[40]

Upon his return to Madison in the summer of 1919, Bobbie was quickly immersed in old pressures, noting, "I was surprised at how little attachment I have left for this town." The anti–La Follette "'patriots' killed the home feeling." Bob had "hungered" for Bobbie, and his presence seemed to bolster Bob physically. As Bob aged and his health deteriorated, his fear that he would not live long enough to achieve his goals increased commensurably with his desire to have his oldest son and namesake continue in his stead. Bobbie, as political heir, was pressured to keep his father informed of all of his thoughts and activities, no matter how trivial, and Bob made no secret of his ambitious plans for his oldest son: "I have been contrasting him as he is today with myself at 24. . . . You will start life as a man, Bobbie, standing on my shoulders. You have your mother's brain my boy — the best brain in the world. With established health, what a service you can be to your community — your country and humanity!" Bobbie, painfully aware of his father's accomplishments and his own shortcomings, protested, "No dad, I don't start on your shoulders by a long shot. If I did I certainly would set the world on fire."[41]

As Bob aged, he acknowledged more and more openly his dependence upon this son, whom, in many ways, he idolized: "You do not know [how] hard it has been to be separated from you, Bobbie. As you grow toward manhood and a full understanding of my work I find myself wanting you near me all the time." During Bob's many illnesses towards the end of his life he referred to Bobbie as a "son, brother and companion," and they talked frequently of his responsibility and his future, for Bob was "anxious he [Bobbie] should have the opportunity to show the good stuff that is in him." Bob confided in his diary, "I am awfully dependent on that lad and feel guilty at taking so much out of his life to keep me company as the years come on me." He attributed this to a quirk of aging.[42]

It quickly became evident that Belle's efforts to encourage Bobbie's independence had been too little and too late. At one point, Bobbie showed an interest in journalism, but it is impossible to determine if this was of his own volition or merely a fulfillment of his mother's unrealized ambition. Phil La Follette contended that his brother, "under different stars," would have pursued a career in science, probably medicine. Instead, despite his complaints of continued bitterness and resentment over public treatment suffered by the family during the war years, Bobbie succumbed to his father's urging that, "We can never have real mastery of ourselves and a proper development of *willpower* unless we *make* ourselves do something every day of our lives that we are strongly *inclined not to do*." The deep roots of Bobbie's feelings toward his father led to his return to Washington, where he served as an aide, secretary, campaign manager, and successor-in-training. Despite his earlier assertions about the necessity of formal training to Bobbie's success, Bob made no protest when Bobbie neither attended law school nor even completed college.[43]

Although Belle claimed that all were thoroughly pleased with Bobbie's position, one political reporter noted, "Anyone acquainted with [Bobbie] La Follette knows it is his desire to get out of politics, even as his father's secretary, and that it is only his sense of filial duty that keeps him at that task." Bobbie complained to Phil of the identity problems inherent in being "The Senator's son Bob." In addition, Bobbie held himself responsible for his father politically and felt duty bound to safeguard the health and well-being of both his parents. Bobbie's letters to his siblings during the final years of their father's life reveal a dutiful, anxious son constantly urging his parents to conserve their energy. He confessed the strain of trying to protect Bob's failing health while squelching rumors about any such problems.[44]

Bobbie's intense identification with all family members did not fade in adulthood, and he begged them during separations, "Please let me hear often as my heart is wrapped up in each one of you and the time away from home seems too big a sacrifice." When in the company of his father, he longed for the presence of the other family members, remarking, "I sure was not cut out for a wandering Jew or prodigal son (I believe they go away from home don't they?). . . . You don't have to miss me because I do more than enough missing for the whole bunch." At twenty-four he voiced to his parents the same feelings of emptiness and meaninglessness he experienced during their absences as a child: "[I]t just feels as though we were all just sort of existing until you could get back here." During a trip to Europe at the age of thirty, he noted, "Even the famed women of gay Paree do not appeal to me," and complained, "I am suffering from the reaction of getting away from the family and the job and feel as though I am walking and talking in my sleep. I have never felt so washed out in all my life."[45]

Bobbie managed to maintain his delightful, if sardonic, sense of humor as he resigned himself to becoming his father's political heir. (As a child, he and his father had a chance encounter with the corpulent president William Howard Taft. Bobbie wrote to his mother, "We . . . saw his fatness and he spoke!") [46] Reviewing a speech Bobbie delivered on his father's behalf, *The Nation* reported, "That young man has his father's fire along with a comfortable amused humor which his father, if he has it, keeps carefully concealed within the recesses of his most intimate family life. Young Bob captivated the convention. He read with such spirit! He smiled with such charm! He was the perfect picture of youth and gallantry and fun." Bobbie's letters, however, reveal a very different young man, preoccupied with his health, guilt-ridden whenever he enjoyed rest and relaxation, and enormously pressured as he assumed what he deemed to be his responsibility. That sense of responsibility led him to serve, albeit reluctantly, as his father's campaign manager in Bob's final bid for the presidency in 1924.

Following Bob's defeat, Bobbie attended the Chicago Conference for Progressive Political Action to push his father's plan for the individual states to select delegates to a national convention. Writing to his physically failing father, Bobbie confessed, "I dread very much to have to carry alone the responsibility connected with my representing you at Chicago. It is a burden greater than any one man should be asked to carry." Bob, who assured his son of his "absolute confidence in your judgment and ability to meet all requirements tactfully and wisely," rejoiced in reports of Bobbie's warm reception at the conference, for it confirmed his belief in his son's leadership abilities and bright political future.[47]

Bob's death in 1925 offered his oldest son no relief from his feelings of duty to carry out parental expectations. Bobbie's relationship with Belle remained exceptionally close and probably contributed to the fact that he had a reputation for being "distinctly woman shy." Belle transferred much of her energy to Bobbie following her husband's death and acted as his main source of counsel and encouragement. He seldom made an important decision without appealing to her for advice. Mother and son lived together

*Revealing body language: prior to delivering his father's platform to the Conference for Progressive Political Action in Cleveland, Ohio, on 4 July 1924, an obedient son gets some last-minute instructions from Fighting Bob. (Library of Congress LC-USZ62-446)*

until Belle's death, from peritonitis, in 1931. Although Bobbie first met Rachel Young in high school and had expressed his love for her for at least thirteen years, he did not marry her until he was thirty-five, less than a year before his mother's death. In 1925, Bobbie made a successful bid to complete his father's unexpired term, a duty he undertook with a deep sense of obligation and a determination to maintain the principles to which his father dedicated his life. However, when taunted during the special election campaign, "You ain't as good as your pa and you never will be," Bobbie replied, "No one knows that better than I, my friend. No one knows that better than I." At the age of thirty, as the youngest senator since Henry Clay, he embarked upon the service that would last twenty-one years.[48]

The first few years Bobbie spent as an able but rather unimaginative successor to his father, but beginning in 1928 he became more self-assured. Following an illness in 1926 that was both serious and, in the words of his doctors at the Mayo Clinic, "mysterious," he enjoyed fourteen years of relatively stable good health. His Senate attendance record was excellent, and he was noted for his conscientiousness. He served as a transitional figure in the history of modern reform movements, achieving national attention during the Great Depression as one of the first to develop a coherent plan for combating declining purchasing power. He appeared on the cover of *Time* magazine in 1934, the year he abandoned the Republican Party to create the Progressive Party of Wisconsin, and there was talk of his being Franklin Roosevelt's 1936 running mate and/or eventual successor. However, unlike his father, Bobbie harbored no serious presidential aspirations. Although he was a national figure, wholehearted service to the Senate was his goal, not the means to an end. The height of his prominence occurred between 1936 and 1940, when he chaired the Senate Civil Liberties Committee that was investigating industrialists' violations of the civil liberties of unionists. In 1938, he received an honorary doctor of laws degree from the University of Wisconsin. His efforts to modernize the Senate culminated in the La Follette–Monroney Reorganization Act of 1946.[49]

Bobbie's character during his years in the Senate remains elusive. Despite his sometimes brilliant successes, he endured rather than enjoyed public life and increasingly resented the intrusions on his privacy. He managed, however, to retain some of his biting wit. When asked if he could be called "Bob," he answered, "Sure can. Everyone in Wisconsin calls me Bob, or that son of a bitch." Nevertheless, the specter of his father always loomed large, and the fears of failing his father's memory were constant. According to his detractors, Bobbie shared his father's self-righteousness and excessive moralism. Virtually all agreed that he was immensely private about his personal life and found campaigning distasteful. His wife Rachel also resented the intrusions on their privacy. The couple found refuge, when Bobbie's very heavy schedule allowed, in the company of their sons Joseph and Bronson. With such a strong dislike for public life, why did Bobbie continue to "administer this self-inflicted punishment?" His biographer suggests a number of contributing factors but stresses that the most important was his father: "It seemed almost as though father and son had struck a sacred pact, and now Young Bob was driven to carry out his part of it."[50]

Bobbie's obdurate opposition to U.S. entry into World War II vanished

*Senator Robert M. La Follette Jr. (State Historical Society of Wisconsin WHi[X3]46764)*

with the bombing of Pearl Harbor, but the war years marked the steady erosion of his popularity, especially with organized labor. During the war and after, he suffered a number of political disappointments. Bowing to pressure, most of it coming from his brother Phil, with whom relations had become increasingly strained, Bobbie embarked on a demanding political tour of his home state in 1943. Thrust back into an activity that invited only negative comparisons to his father, the burden of carrying that great name was temporarily lifted, yet again, by illness. A bout of bronchopneumonia confined Bobbie to the hospital for six weeks. He devoted decreasing time to Wisconsin affairs.

In 1946, faced with yet another campaign, Bobbie complained of depression and considered retiring from politics. Deciding to return to the GOP, he attributed his reluctance to actively campaign to concerns about his health. He believed his Senate history alone justified his reelection: "My platform is my record. . . . No matter how hard the opposition may try to distort it, they can't make it appear to be anything else than it really is: a good solid record in the public interest." His challengers, Republican Joseph R. McCarthy and Democrat Howard McMurray set out to prove him wrong: both conducted smear campaigns that Bobbie refused to return in kind. He was beaten in the primary by McCarthy by a mere 5,378 votes. Although a number of Bobbie's political positions and activities doubtless contributed to his loss, it can also be attributed in part to his aloofness toward his constituents, underscored by a campaign carried out over a mere six days. Immersed in the promotion of his Senate reorganization bill, Bobbie himself ruefully observed, "I didn't go back to talk to the voters. My father did just what Joe McCarthy did [to win] and I guess I made a mistake."[51]

Following this defeat, Bobbie, at fifty-two, became a director of Sears Roebuck and a successful business consultant. Surprised at how much he missed public life, he seriously considered reentering politics and served in a variety of government-sponsored positions. When urged to run for his father's old Second District congressional seat (although the farm land had been sold, he still owned the family's Maple Bluff home and claimed Wisconsin residency), he made it clear that the burden of his great name remained heavy indeed: "If the people of Wisconsin would be content to let me come to Washington and serve as a Congressman, I would be happy. But they won't let me. They would make me go out and rebuild the Progressive movement. I am not as young as I was. I don't have it in me." His health became permanently compromised following a two-month hospitalization in 1948. As with previous periods of ill health, doctors had difficulty determining a definitive diagnosis, but ultimately suspected coronary disease. Unable to take satisfaction from his lifetime of considerable achievements, Bobbie became increasingly preoccupied by his health (he developed diverticulitis, bursitis, and mild diabetes) and suffered from depression and anxiety attacks. Unlike his early years, however, ill health no longer provided a temporary emotional refuge, so internalized were the pressures and expectations. Illness became an additional ceaseless and overwhelming burden in its own right.[52]

Bobbie complained of memory loss as well as apparently groundless fears that McCarthy intended to summon him to testify about his efforts to stamp out communist influence while chairing the Civil Liberties Committee. He called on select former colleagues once or twice every year, the last visit just three weeks before his death. Friends and family noted a sharp increase in his emotional instability early in 1953, but no treatment was sought. His son Bronson, then aged sixteen, was struck by the vision of his father sitting alone, clearly agitated, but for no apparent reason. The senior La Follette fidgeted nervously and broke into a cold sweat. When Bronson entered the room, his father uncharacteristically hugged him and told him that he loved him. But the love of family and friends and his achievements as senator were no match for the weight of his burdens, which had become intolerable. The expectations associated with the family name prohibited the political future he desired, and illness, his former ally, overwhelmed him. Around noon, on 24 February 1953, Bobbie committed suicide. He left no note. Days before shooting himself in the head, he expressed to friends "how he never should have let McCarthy beat him, how he had let his father down."[53]

New York governor-turned-senator Herbert Lehman maintained that Bobbie's spirit was "crushed by the rejection at the hands of the voters of his party," but the *Wisconsin State Journal* insisted, "He was too big a man to have let political defeat corrode his soul." The La Follette family cited depression brought on by ill health in his later years as the key to Bobbie's suicide. It seems likely, however, that Bobbie's death, like his life, was more the product of his early years — of incredibly high parental expectations, of a boy prohibited from exploring or even discovering his own wants and identity and who found temporary refuge in acute physical suffering. He was, it was noted on the floor of the Senate following his death, "born to serve." His suicide was a tragic end to a distinguished senator and the man who had been his father's pride and best hope. Bobbie's son, Bronson La Follette, an unsuccessful gubernatorial candidate in 1968, served four terms as Wisconsin's attorney general. He too felt the burdens of the La Follette name. Although urged to keep alive the political dynasty begun by his grandfather more than a century earlier, he retired from politics at the age of fifty in 1987.[54]

The La Follette name is not entirely absent from the Wisconsin political scene, however. Bronson's third cousin Doug La Follette (1940– ) was first elected Wisconsin's Secretary of State in 1974, an office he has held in consecutive terms since 1982. He unsuccessfully sought the Senate seat first held by Robert La Follette Sr., his first cousin twice removed (Doug's great-grandfather and Robert Sr.'s father were brothers). Fiercely dedicated to an overhaul of the campaign finance practices that currently bring the American public "the best politicians money can buy," Doug La Follette continues to champion many of the progressive causes spearheaded by Fighting Bob. While he appreciates the instant recognition the La Follette name brings in

Wisconsin, he is mindful of the expectations that accompany such an illustrious heritage. The mixed blessing of name recognition extends even to those family members without political ambitions. When Robert La Follette III (1960– ) was sentenced on arson charges in April 1999, his status as great-grandson of La Follette Sr. was duly noted by the press in the story's lead sentence. Tweed Roosevelt, great-grandson of Theodore, recently reflected on the impact of a great name on subsequent generations. He noted that the burdens on the La Follettes are probably greater than are those placed on his own family. Although the Roosevelts share a heritage with two American presidents, many family members live in either New York or Boston, where the business and political power elite — and their descendants — are so numerous that the spotlight is shared by a great many. Within the confines of Wisconsin, however, the name of Robert M. La Follette remains, through the generations, elevated above all others.[55]

**D**espite her preference for the comforts, peace, and security of life at Maple Bluff Farm, Belle reluctantly acquiesced to her husband's pleas and agreed to reunite the family in Washington late in 1907. Reassured by the presence of his wife and children, ensconced in a furnished rental house at 2229 California Street, La Follette turned his attention to politics. In October, a wave of bank and business failures set off by overextended credit thrust the nation into a financial panic. Conservatives blamed Roosevelt, claiming his persecution of trusts had undermined business confidence. At first the president cooperated with the Morgan banks and others, issuing $150 million in Treasury certificates and bonds to keep banks in the black. But Roosevelt's faith in the Square Deal was beginning to fade. Where before he perceived the corruption of the system at the hands of a few powerful individuals, he became increasingly convinced that vast numbers of profit-driven individuals and businesses, even those acting legally, were responsible for the instability and harsh inequities plaguing the nation. And it was not just Roosevelt whose politics were shifting: increasing numbers of middle-class Americans were also moving toward the more aggressive and interventionist reforms favored by Robert La Follette.

Inspired by the positive press his brand of progressivism was beginning to attract, La Follette began plans to seek the presidency in 1908. Roosevelt was reluctant to step down, asserting, "No other President ever enjoyed the Presidency as I did." No law kept Roosevelt from seeking a third term, but he was bound by the precedent established by George Washington and honored by every subsequent president. And Roosevelt himself reflected, "For the very reason I believe in being a strong President and making the most of the office and using it without regard to the little, snarling men who yell about executive usurpation, I also believe that it is not a good thing that any one man should hold it too long." In a public statement he later heartily regretted, Roosevelt had announced on the evening of his election triumph in 1904 that he would not seek a third term. Although by 1908 Roosevelt and La Follette were somewhat closer on the progressive reform spectrum, the personal animosity between the two was ever increasing. La Follette's campaign nonetheless proclaimed him "logically and necessarily" Roosevelt's successor: "We believe that the pioneer of this movement who was good enough to break the stubborn soil and plant the seed, is good enough to reap the golden harvest and bring it home to the people in its bounty."

*Political pin intimating a Roosevelt–La Follette partnership within the Progressive movement. (Pin from author's collection, photo by Elwood Mills)*

La Follette did nothing to correct the public's perception of the relationship between the scrappy freshman senator and the beloved powerhouse of a president as one of increasingly shared goals and mutual admiration.[1]

La Follette only reluctantly delegated authority during his 1908 bid for the presidency, sacrificing any hope for even a remotely successful campaign for assurances of unwavering devotion. "He works best," it was noted as early as 1902, "with lieutenants who obey without question." Always reticent about appearing personally ambitious, La Follette did little open campaigning, preferring to be promoted by his trusted few. Behind the scenes, however, he showered his committee with suggestions. La Follette did his campaigning on the floor of the Senate, where he devoted himself to furthering his reputation as a fearless progressive by challenging the Aldrich emergency currency bill, a measure supporting the partial backing of United States currency with railroad bonds. In his "Money Power" speech, La Follette mounted a three-pronged attack. He presented the Aldrich bill as proof of yet another attempt by business to use the U.S. government for its own enrichment, charging that government backing would restore public confidence in even worthless railroad bonds. The extra money created by the bill, he argued, would fuel even more dangerous speculation. And finally, harking back to his previous victory of instituting ad valorem taxation of Wisconsin railroads, he demanded that if railroad bonds were to be accepted as security, their value must be based on the actual worth of the physical assets. He rejected proof as a prerequisite for his charges of a conspiracy of business interests, claiming that "any man with ordinary intelligence, who sees the same names repeated over and over again on the various [corporate] directorates . . . will understand how the important business interests are in fact welded and fused together into one mass under one control." The power of the special interests, he insisted, encroached on the rights of every American, becoming the "THING which we must destroy if we would preserve our free institutions," the "real object" of Fighting Bob's "unceasing warfare." The Senate approved several of La Follette's amendments before passing the Aldrich bill on 27 March. But the battle was not quite over.[2]

As the campaign for presidential nomination progressed, La Follette fell ill with what was called variously "an attack of the grippe," "liver trouble," and "influenza." This illness not only provided La Follette with a convenient excuse for any poor showing in his campaign, it allowed him to cancel a meeting with Roosevelt. Away from the Senate floor, he spent some time considering a libel suit against the Publishers Feature Syndicate over the draft of a character study of himself. Incensed over his portrayal as well-to-do, vain, and self-righteous, La Follette was particularly irritated at being described as having presidential ambitions, of being "domineering," "shrewd," a man who "tears his hair, gesticulates and stamps his feet vigorously while speaking [and who employs] prolific use of figures of speech and flowery similes." While the article did contain several factual errors, it was, for the most part, a fairly accurate portrayal. La Follette, however, deemed it "absolutely vile." Although aware that "one in public life is more or less at the mercy of this class of newspaper men" and that it was highly unlikely the publishers would make any of the alterations he demanded, La Follette spent a considerable amount of crucial time neither resting nor working on his campaign but instead revising the proposed portrait, striking out what he deemed offensive or false and substituting material far more flattering. Despite his efforts, including a letter to his attorney instructing him to either "kill all the active members of the syndicate or do whatever is necessary to stop them from publishing the offensive matter contained in the article. . . . Eat 'em alive," the article appeared, in its original form, in 1,200 daily newspapers throughout the country. No legal action was taken.[3]

The Senate was scheduled to adjourn on 30 May. On the previous day, the Vreeland-Aldrich Bill, an emergency currency measure virtually identical to the original Aldrich bill prior to La Follette's amendments, came up for debate. La Follette was furious that his hard-fought efforts to protect the public had been unceremoniously discarded. He began a speech that he hoped would prolong the debate long enough to call forth such an avalanche of protest from independent bankers and businessmen that Congress would be forced to radically change, if not defeat, the bill. At worst, he calculated, his filibuster would prevent the bill from coming to a vote before the Senate adjourned. This dramatization of his already pitched battle against the original Aldrich bill would also, he hoped, give him much needed exposure and vault him into the political spotlight, improving infinitely his chances of nomination.

La Follette began his presentation around noon on the twenty-ninth of May and spoke until seven o'clock the following morning for a total of nearly nineteen consecutive hours. Eleven hours into the speech, which also touched on the need for more comprehensive labor and anti-trust legislation, La Follette took a gulp from a glass containing a mixture of milk and eggs ordered from the Senate restaurant and cried, "Take it away. It's drugged." Subsequent chemical analysis revealed what would have been a lethal amount of ptomaine had he consumed the entire glass. As it was over ninety degrees in the Senate chamber and there were always delays between the time nourishment arrived and when it could be consumed, it is unlikely that La Follette was victim to anything more than natural food poisoning. Nonetheless, the story of La Follette's "attempted murder" still circulates.[4]

La Follette initially feared that the ensuing diarrhea, the fiercest he had ever experienced, might bring the proceedings to a halt, but by forcing roll calls he bought himself enough time to make several hasty trips to the bathroom. La Follette finally relinquished the floor, by prearrangement, to Senators William S. Stone and Thomas Gore. Intent on speaking until their demands were met, Stone and Gore continued alternately for another nine hours. The group's effort met a sudden end when Gore, who was blind, incorrectly presumed Stone to be present and yielded the floor to him. The Aldrich-Vreeland bill passed 43 to 22. La Follette refused to acknowledge defeat, insisting that the aborted effort "at least exposed the character of the conference report . . . [and] added another chapter to the record of the subserviency of Congress to special interests."[5]

Despite Gore and Stone's participation, La Follette persistently referred to the speaking marathon as a significant public service he took on "single handed and alone." La Follette desired to be perceived as a morally superior man who, by his lack of supportive comrades, appeared all the more determined and brave. This was not the view, however, of outgoing president Roosevelt, who wrote privately during the speech, "Congress is ending with a pointless and stupid filibuster by La Follette, who is an entirely worthless Senator. It is sheer idiocy for the Senate to permit such silly rules as will allow this kind of filibuster." Senator Nelson Aldrich agreed and used the occasion to establish several new rules aimed at curtailing filibusters. Moreover, La Follette's extreme efforts did not produce the desired vitalizing effect upon his campaign. A few weeks later La Follette received only twenty-five votes (of Wisconsin's twenty-six) at the Republican national convention. Forced to swallow his pride, La Follette congratulated William Howard Taft, who, as Roosevelt's handpicked successor, swept the nomination with 702 votes on the first ballot. It was the end of what proved to be only the first of La Follette's sometimes embarrassingly ill-fated attempts to win the White House.[6]

Down but not out, La Follette worked to have reforms he considered essential adopted into the Republican platform. Overwhelmingly rejected as "socialistic" were his calls for the direct election of senators, trust and monopoly regulation, exemption of unions from anti-trust laws, the physical evaluation of railroads as the basis of rate making, tariff revision on the basis of the cost of domestic production in relation to foreign, and public reportage of campaign expenditures. The rejection of his proposed party planks and Taft's nomination disappointed La Follette deeply, but, still a party loyalist despite increasing willingness to cooperate with senators across the aisle, he pledged to do all in his power to secure Taft's election. La Follette's endorsement of Taft was hardly wholehearted, however. In a speech in La Crosse, Wisconsin, La Follette praised Democratic candidate William Jennings Bryan. Then, according to Taft supporters, "about four minutes before he finished his speech he had become very worked up and had to take off his collar — for the purpose, some of the boys said, of enabling him to get out the word 'Taft,' which he had been unable to pronounce up to that time."[7]

After the Republican convention, most of La Follette's attention focused on the money trust. Charging that fewer than one hundred businesses affiliated with Standard Oil and the House of Morgan dominated the entire country, La Follette began a vigorous campaign to bring about the end of such monopolies. To promote his ideas, and in the hopes of securing a large profit, he planned the creation of his own national magazine. The financial obligation alone appalled his horrified wife, generating objections that contradict her claims of never having argued with her husband. Belle's opposition went beyond finances: "I saw great difficulty in combining the duties of editor and statesman. I argued that the editor must comment on public affairs as they transpire regardless of consequences; whereas the man in public life, to speak most effectively, must often wait for the right occasion. Bob answered that his life was 'an open book' and that he saw no conflict in his duties as editor and Senator."[8]

La Follette sought to recreate the financial and personal success he enjoyed as owner and editor of his college newspaper. He envisioned his magazine attaining national scope and influence. What better way to leave a lasting testament to his goals and ideals, his righteousness? What better way to give vent to his feelings when opposed or defeated? His magazine provided La Follette with an uncensored forum in which to justify and rationalize, defend and attack, criticize and promote. Unlike public speaking, the magazine did not require La Follette to endure exhausting travels or face hostile audiences, chores he increasingly dreaded. In short, it was the perfect vehicle for La Follette, its appeal overriding the protests of his wife and friends concerning his money, energy, and health.[9]

La Follette planned his weekly, sixteen-page publication to be "the vigilant champion of True Representative Government." As with his college newspaper, he frequently did as much of the work as was possible himself, although his participation over the years was erratic. In the beginning, he wrote, edited, and solicited both literary and financial contributors in addition to advertisers. He even offered advice on the most efficient way to operate the flatbed printing press, despite the fact he had no experience with such a machine. Belle put aside her feelings and cooperated with her husband by running the "Home and Education" department of the magazine. The first issue of *La Follette's Weekly Magazine* appeared on 9 January 1909, featuring articles by progressives Jonathan Bourne and Lincoln Steffens. La Follette, mindful of the criticism he received over its typographical appearance, vowed, "I feel the keenest anxiety for the success of the little paper, and I am going to do everything I can as soon as I can to raise it above criticism." Despite the early encouragement of circulation figures ranging from 30,000 to 40,000 (with about half the subscribers in Wisconsin), Belle's fears that it would be an enormous personal and political drain were quickly realized. During its first few years it lost La Follette more than $1,000 each month. Undaunted, La Follette endeavored to make the magazine a production involving his entire family and, despite massive debts, insisted on its continuance, although he was eventually forced to cut it back to a monthly publication. *La Follette's* offered a mix of homey features, farm news, recipes, fiction, and cartoons as well as a forum for the political views of its editor and his various friends and colleagues associated with a large range of aspects within the progressive movement. La Follette loved his magazine; he refused to acknowledge it as a perpetual drain either politically or personally and willingly made up its deficits out of the family's finances.[10]

Despite La Follette's steadfast popularity in Wisconsin, he grew increasingly concerned about the resurgence of stalwarts in his home state. Wisconsin's senior senator, Isaac Stephenson, now allied with conservative forces within the Senate, was reelected when Francis McGovern and state senator W. H. Hatton split the progressive vote. With Stephenson's men in control, the state's Republican platform excluded planks long endorsed by La Follette. Disappointment over Wisconsin failures was at least partially offset by victories elsewhere. Progressives Albert Cummins of Iowa and Coe Crawford of South Dakota were elected to the Senate, joining the small but growing group of increasingly reformist senators, which included Joseph Bristow, Moses Clapp, Jonathan Dolliver, and Albert Beveridge. The like-minded senators met at La Follette's newly acquired rental home at 1864 Wyoming Avenue on 13 February 1909 to strategize the defeat of a $2 million naval appropriation bill.

To help pay magazine debts, La Follette devoted the Senate recess to writing a series of ten articles for *American Magazine* detailing his political life. The articles, eventually published collectively as La Follette's autobiography, were ghostwritten by Ray Stannard Baker. La Follette's input consisted mostly of criticism for what he considered to be Baker's downplaying of the various evils over which he had triumphed, particularly the intensity and "diabolical character of the plan to destroy the [La Follette gubernatorial] administration by falsehood and treachery."[11]

Once the Senate reconvened, La Follette's attention was absorbed in attempting to push his reforms past an increasingly hostile administration. From the beginning, La Follette considered President Taft a bumbler and compromiser. The very first act of the Taft administration empowered Attorney General George Wickersham to, according to La Follette, "hand over" a great section of New England to the New Haven Railroad by dismissing suits against the railroad. Generally conservative, Taft, like Roosevelt, had gradually come to see the necessity of meaningful change and promoted in particular tax reform and the breaking up of trusts and monopolies. Unlike Roosevelt, Taft was a reluctant president, whose greatest desire was to serve instead on the Supreme Court. In contrast, Roosevelt, the "bride at every wedding, the corpse at every funeral," continued to command the limelight. Graciously, the wildly popular former president departed for a long hunting trip in Africa in 1909, allegedly prompting banking giant J. P. Morgan to cry, "Health to the lions!" Once Roosevelt was half the world away, Taft began to emerge from his predecessor's shadow.[12]

La Follette's preoccupation with Senate matters and his reluctance to contribute articles and editorials to *La Follette's Weekly* on a regular basis infuriated Belle, who was depressed and angry over the tremendous losses incurred. She criticized her husband for working on Senate speeches months in advance while ignoring his immediate obligations to the magazine, upsetting the entire family. Usually tactful and understated in her criticisms, she openly accused him of poor management of his time and energy and threatened that she could not endure it much longer, but to no avail. La Follette, as usual, worked night and day, supplemented by only a few hours of sleep, but the thoroughness and attention to detail that seemed unnecessary and even counterproductive in other situations began to pay off politically. La Follette was convinced that high tariffs strengthened monopo-

*Despite his increasing disdain for Taft, in 1909 La Follette was still willing to benefit politically from his shared party affiliation with the president. On the grandstand at the Wisconsin State Fair in Milwaukee, Taft is third from the right in the front row; La Follette is bareheaded in the last row. (State Historical Society of Wisconsin [X3]34292)*

lies' grip on the economy. The proposed Payne-Aldrich tariff consisted of over 800 amendments to the House rates. Its authors claimed it would bring rate reduction, but La Follette alleged it would sharply boost the tariff rates on a large number of products instead. Payne-Aldrich had no reliable controls, asserted La Follette, producing meticulously gathered evidence to prove his claim. Several senators joined in the crusade, including Joseph Bristow, who commented admiringly that La Follette "never wavers or flinches from any contest, be it ever so arduous or disagreeable." Although officially unheeded, the cooperation of the progressive senators had a dramatic effect on La Follette. Belle wrote to Fola, "I have never known Papa so moved in years and only a few times in our life as he was last night when he came home. He and [Senators] Dolliver, Clapp and Beveridge had had a heart to heart talk, and [they] had assured him that they were in the movement to stay. . . . [H]e was glad, deeply glad of the fellowship, companionship, and understanding." La Follette gloated on the floor of the Senate, "When I came here I stood alone in the chamber. Now there are nearly a dozen men who stand with me." He lectured those who still stood in opposition, "We are not sovereign here; we are but servants. The sovereigns are in the workshops, on the farms, in the factories, in the stores and counting rooms. It is the average interests of the whole people we should serve, not certain special interests."[13]

La Follette surrendered his image as a lone fighter against corruption and inequality for the strength found in numbers, and he did so with no sacrifice of principle. Belle felt as though "something tremendous had happened all at once," which would culminate in "the coming of a new order of things." In 1910, the Senate debated the Commerce Court bill. Originating with Wickersham and proceeding with Taft's approval, the bill was, in typical La Follette hyperbole, "the rankest, boldest betrayal of public interest ever proposed in any legislative body," because it would allow the attorney general and the courts to decide railroad issues previously determined by the Interstate Commerce Committee. La Follette noted proudly that the strong speeches he and other progressives delivered caused the administration senators to abandon entire sections of the bill. When Taft took the credit for the legislation as it finally passed, it was, according to La Follette, "scarcely possible to speak of the course of the administration upon this legislation in temperate language."[14]

La Follette's disgust with Taft grew daily. Like a vast number of his fellow Americans, especially those in the West, La Follette was appalled at Taft's public declaration in Winona, Minnesota, on 17 September 1909, that the new tariff law was "the best bill the Republican Party ever passed." Moreover, the president's Dollar Diplomacy, which marshaled military might to promote American interests abroad, caused La Follette to rethink his own previous support of America's expansionistic foreign policy. Big business, La Follette belatedly realized, had dominated the nation's foreign as well as domestic affairs. The imperialism he had previously endorsed as the key to spreading democracy he now saw as exploitative of less economically developed nations, furthering the excess profits and powers of American multi-national corporations. Dollar Diplomacy, La Follette charged, "was crude, sordid, blighting to international amity and accord," designed to facilitate the "flow without interruption [of other countries' wealth] into the coffers of Wall Street," bringing "our scheme of government into disrepute everywhere in the world."[15]

La Follette's charges notwithstanding, President Taft had not turned his back on progressivism entirely. In 1910, Taft ultimately supported the Mann-Elkins Act, extending the powers of the Interstate Commerce Commission and including the telephone and telegraph under its authority. He vigorously dismantled trusts, including the titanic American Tobacco and Standard Oil companies. But even moderates felt the president's increasingly conservative line to be a betrayal of his campaign pledges. According to William Allen White, "This genial, chuckling, courteous, kindly gentleman was in his heart a deep-dyed political and economic conservative, and bull-headed at that." Word of the widespread frustration ultimately reached Theodore Roosevelt. An anxious La Follette urged "every true friend of the Progressive movement" to "wish that Colonel Roosevelt might stay just where he is — in Africa." "[W]hen Roosevelt returns," La Follette warned, "he will smear over and obscure the issues . . . make principles hazy and exalt personalities," for he is "not a progressive, except with his tongue, and never was." Roosevelt, after bagging hundreds of animals — including five elephants, seven hippos, nine lions, and thirteen rhinos — toured Europe before heading home in 1910 and arrived to adoring crowds who scorned La Follette's gloomy forecasts.[16]

Yet some of La Follette's previous predictions were already proving true. Four years after La Follette proclaimed that the stalwarts' seats in the Senate would be "permanently vacant," William Allen White counted thirty-four senators he considered to be somewhere within the progressive spectrum. Belle La Follette made a prediction of her own: "With this new kind of leadership expressing the public sentiment the outcome is certain." Her husband declared that the national struggle had only begun. Inspired by much favorable attention from the press and the public, he and senators Jonathan Bourne and Joseph Bristow drew up tentative plans for a national progressive Republican league. La Follette's new sense of well-being did not result in even temporary peace of mind. Once again he maintained, although it was never proven, that his mail was being tampered with, and he worked out an elaborate code by which to correspond with his closest associates. Furthermore, he continued to react in a highly emotional manner whenever accused of even the lightest infraction of his rigid moral code.[17]

Greatly heartened by the beginnings of a progressive coalition, La Follette immediately began a speaking tour during the Senate recess to spread the progressive gospel and earn money for his magazine. La Follette's audiences no longer consisted of only the enduring faithful. Growing numbers of the public perceived increasingly conservative Republicans as violating their president's moderately progressive campaign promises and working instead to promote corporate rather than public interests. Many Americans who had rejected La Follette and his progressive agenda as too radical now found both the man and his ideas worthy of a second look.

Always attentive to his physical appearance, a rather jaunty La Follette wrote to his wife: "I bought two pair of elegant duck, *white duck* pants at a *dollar* a pair and you bet I am the swellest looking fellow that ever came down the pike — white collar, white tie, white shirt, white pants, white shoes. I peel off my black alpaca coat immediately after I make my bow and there I stand as fine a figure as you would see in any restaurant or barber shop in the land." But in another letter, more typical of La Follette on such a tour, he complained of illness induced by heat, travel, poor food, and alkali water. A supporter scolded La Follette for sacrificing a strong, condensed speech of two hours for thoroughness so prolonged it wearied its audience and robbed them of the forcefulness of his message. Heedless, La Follette continued to deliver lengthy speeches and was pleased by the enthusiastic reception that they, for the most part, received. According to Belle, "The state of public sentiment, the degree of interest and enthusiasm of the men and women of the country . . . was ever the crucial test in Bob's judgment as to whether the movement was advancing or receding." Despite his denials, La Follette desired personal as well as political approval. He confessed to hating an audience until several of its members complimented him after a speech. He boasted of the large crowds he drew and his ability to win them over. He found encouragement in the praise he received throughout the country for his new magazine and expressed confidence that it would turn a profit in the future.[18]

During the congressional session of December 1909 through June 1910, a warm friendship developed between Louis D. Brandeis and La Follette. Brandeis's legal acumen and progressive sensibilities would later lead Woodrow Wilson to appoint him to the Supreme Court, making him the first Jewish justice on that highest bench. Brandeis initially garnered La Follette's respect as counsel for Gifford Pinchot, chief of the Interior Department's Division of Forestry. Brandeis defended Pinchot's actions to halt Secretary of the Interior Richard A. Ballinger's efforts to open public lands to private business development. La Follette saw Ballinger as selling out hard-fought progressive conservation achievements and was further outraged when Taft quickly sided with Ballinger and removed Pinchot from office.

Brandeis and La Follette enjoyed a relationship reminiscent of that La Follette shared with Sam Harper, and it was one that afforded both men much pleasure and satisfaction. Although the two would later disagree over American entry into World War I, even that divisive issue did not mar their solidly grounded friendship, based as it was on shared beliefs and mutual interests. In all, despite his early concerns, La Follette was no longer "The Lonely Man of the Senate," and his efforts were proving to be rewarding and even, occasionally, enjoyable. Only the absence of Belle and Mary, called to Wisconsin for several weeks by the illness of Belle's father, marred that congressional session.[19]

In June 1910, La Follette traveled to Roosevelt's home at Oyster Bay, New York, for what was to be their last meeting. Roosevelt, still wildly popular, had yet to make his official reentry into politics. Oyster Bay, noted President Taft, had become a mecca for politicians, particularly those of the progressive variety. La Follette's stated mission was to convince the former president that under La Follette's tutelage the progressive cause had made great strides and that nothing could stop or sidetrack it. When Roosevelt ignored the implicit invitation to support La Follette, the relationship between the two politicians, already in its final stages, drew one step nearer to its irrevocable breaking point. According to widely circulated reports, after leaving the meeting La Follette described Roosevelt as "the greatest living American," a quotation used against La Follette in the 1912 campaign. La Follette issued no public denials at the time but claimed privately that he had been misquoted. La Follette believed that Roosevelt wanted very much to be president again but would move slowly and carefully. He also maintained privately that Roosevelt would always be fundamentally undemocratic and a compromiser. In turn, it was probably La Follette as well as Socialist leader Eugene V. Debs that Roosevelt had in mind when he publicly voiced his concern that "unless there is some progressive leadership, the great mass of progressives, for lack of this legitimate leadership[,] will follow every variety of demagogue and wild-eyed visionary."[20]

In the summer of 1910, Roosevelt made a series of speeches delineating his New Nationalism. After denouncing socialism, Roosevelt added, "But this does not mean that we may not with great advantage adopt certain of the principles proposed by some given set of men who happen to call themselves Socialist." Unlike the Square Deal of his presidency, this new plan called for aggressive government action, echoing many of the reforms La Follette had long championed, including graduated income and inheritance taxes, tariff reform, public disclosure of campaign expenditures, labor reform, protection of public lands, and the referendum, initiative, and recall. Similar specific goals did little, however, to establish a shared vision of progressivism or to improve the relations between these two volatile leaders.[21]

Although Roosevelt declined to lend his influential name to the La Follette cause, many progressives did so eagerly. By the end of his first term as senator, La Follette had shaken profoundly the conservative bastion of the Senate, forced a division within the Republican Party, and emerged as the most prominent national spokesman and leader of the rapidly growing, aggressively progressive group of senators and governors. Conservatives worked to oust the progressives in midterm elections. La Follette's opponent in the 1910 primary, Samuel Cook, received enormous campaign contributions from local and out-of-state conservatives. La Follette traveled the traditional campaign route of appearing unconcerned with personal gain while totally consumed by the duties of his office. As soon as the Senate term ended, La Follette, frantic for campaign funds but suffering from intermittent attacks of indigestion and pain, attributed to, among other things, gallstones, planned a strenuous speaking tour. He insisted for several weeks that his lengthening stay at Maple Bluff marked merely a delay in his campaigning but finally acknowledged that doctors' orders demanded that he recuperate from the excessive work of the congressional session.

La Follette did not make a single speech in the primary campaign of 1910. His supporters, including thirteen progressive leaders of national repute who came to Wisconsin at their own expense, waged a low-budget but effective campaign, contributing to La Follette's overwhelming margin of victory in the primary: 142,978 to 40,791. Wisconsinites were proud of the vision and leadership of their favorite son, proud to be increasingly a national model of reform. The La Follette camp rejoiced privately in their success in making their leader's endorsement so emphatic no legislature would dare ignore it, but publicly La Follette reacted modestly, claiming it in no sense a personal triumph but a great victory for the progressive cause. Even Theodore Roosevelt, placing party above personality, said in Milwaukee that every Republican legislator had a duty to cast his vote for La Follette. La Follette swept the final campaign with more than 144,000 votes (78 percent). The progressive cause was further aided in Wisconsin by the election of Francis McGovern as governor.[22]

Belle was distressed that Bob had generated no income during this period, as publication debts, in addition to the expenses normally incurred by the family, continued to mount. Ill health made further inroads on the family's finances. Almost immediately after his victory, La Follette, accompanied by Dr. Philip Fox, checked into the Mayo Clinic, where he underwent an elective operation for gallstones that lasted less than forty minutes. La Follette was confident that this surgery would put an end not only to his bouts with poor digestion and stomach pain but also to the infection of his liver that, he asserted, had poisoned his system, making it impossible to "think clearly" for the preceding five or six years. Reassured by the growing progressive coalition and by the support of family, friends, and the public throughout his illness, La Follette declared himself a new man, but he refrained from doing any public speaking before returning to the Senate, citing doctors' orders. Although he had pledged to be in Washington for the opening session, he remained in Wisconsin with Belle, who was suffering from a bad fall.

Throughout the autumn and winter of 1910, La Follette continued to enjoy favorable press coverage and a growing national reputation. Women and African Americans increasingly looked to him to champion their rights. California's governor-elect Hiram Johnson called him the pioneer of a great patriotic movement and requested La Follette's advice whenever he, as governor, experienced difficult problems. Four years later, an embittered Johnson remembered the zeal of La Follette and his followers during this period differently, exclaiming to Theodore Roosevelt: "There were those with us who thought that the pain of the world was in their special keeping and that we did not with sufficient rapidity apply the remedies that should eliminate this pain. There were others who believed that they bore the weight of the world upon their shoulders and who, after the victory of 1910, in their omniscience, desired to direct the exact political course we should steer."[23]

By December, La Follette, back in Washington, quickly disregarded his doctors' orders to guard his health and was immediately overworked. His energies focused on, among other things, protecting the Alaska territory from private interests and supplementing the Sherman Anti-trust Act to put an end to special pleading and exceptions. He avoided a meeting with Roosevelt, claiming illness, and declined an invitation to meet with President Taft. Diplomatically, Taft sought advice on congressional matters with a variety of political leaders, including La Follette. La Follette's letter to Belle, still detained in Madison by injury, detailed his reasons for not discussing judicial appointments with Taft, for he worried that Belle might disapprove. At first La Follette asserted that he declined so as not to perform a disservice to the progressives by making a move that possibly could be misconstrued as his being in league with the president. More personal reasons soon emerged: "I will not be put in the attitude of rushing to the White House where I have been refused admission and where all the plots to destroy me have been hatched, at the very first opportunity offered. I should feel like a sneak and a bootlick to come at the crook of a finger to be advised with about appointments after all that has happened." As with the previous president, La Follette preferred to correspond in writing and sent Taft his recommendations respecting appointments and legislation, only to be outraged when those recommendations were not heeded. La Follette's dislike for Taft was clearly reciprocated, for Taft viewed the senator as habitually given "to false and misleading statements."[24]

On 21 January 1911, the establishment of the National Progressive Republican League (NPRL) was announced publicly. In addition to the coterie of insurgent senators, the League's charter membership included six governors, including Hiram Johnson and Francis McGovern. The NPRL believed popular government fundamental to all other questions and advocated the following goals:

1. The election of United States Senators by direct vote of the people.
2. Direct primaries for the nomination of elective officials.
3. The direct election of delegates to national conventions with opportunity for the voter to express his choice for President and Vice-President.
4. Amendment to state constitutions providing for the Initiative, Referendum and Recall.
5. A thoroughgoing corrupt practices act.[25]

Left unstated was the League's crusade to deprive Taft of renomination in 1912. Aware of the ever-increasing rift between the former president and the incumbent, La Follette urged Roosevelt to join the NPRL. La Follette was eager to place Roosevelt in open opposition to the Taft administration and commit him to a clear-cut and definite position on the League's five propositions. This last was important because, according to La Follette, it was Roosevelt's political habit to "so state and qualify his positions that you are never quite sure of him." Despite La Follette's clear distrust of the former president, he was willing to benefit from the Roosevelt name, but most importantly, he wanted to remove the threat posed by an independent Roosevelt. Significantly, however, La Follette did not enclose a copy of the draft declaration in his initial request for Roosevelt's support and neglected even to sign the letter.[26]

Roosevelt invited La Follette to his home at Oyster Bay in mid-December to discuss the NPRL. La Follette declined, citing illness, but responded to Roosevelt's invitation for the following week with a promise to attend whenever he could get over to New York. Shortly after Christmas, La Follette found himself committed to a luncheon with Roosevelt, which he canceled, claiming he had slipped and injured his side, perhaps inspired by Belle's recent fall and her subsequent complications. A few weeks later La Follette traveled to New York with Belle to see Fola's performance in *The Scarecrow* but made no attempt to visit Oyster Bay. Upon his return, he found a cordial note from Roosevelt noting his recent presence in New York and complimenting him on his handling of some Senate business. In March another meeting was scheduled, but once again La Follette canceled at the last minute, claiming an attack of grippe brought on by the Senate's night sessions, and sent an aide to present his case.

La Follette sent Roosevelt a series of letters urging him to join the NPRL. The former president, however, began revealing some of his annoyance at La Follette's perpetual postponement of their scheduled meetings. One of the senator's closest aides soothed Roosevelt with assurances that La Follette promised to come over and have a "heart-to-heart talk" with the former president at an early date, a promise never fulfilled. Despite the knowledge that Roosevelt's commitment to progressive ideals was growing along with his hostility toward Taft, La Follette could not bring himself to meet face-to-face with the man he so distrusted and envied. Perhaps he also realized on some level that while it was still unlikely that the former president would join under any circumstances, Roosevelt was guaranteed not to join the NPRL without a number of personal meetings with La Follette. Roosevelt's political value to the NPRL seemed far outweighed by La Follette's aversion to him and reluctance to share the limelight. La Follette's wheedling letters urging Roosevelt to join were frequently condescending and sometimes insulting. Roosevelt professed himself in accord with the League's five propositions but stressed that there should be "carefully modified limitations." Moreover, he warned against allowing "enthusiasm to conquer reason." Eventually Roosevelt made his stand: "Nothing will be gained by making the progressives a small knot of people with advanced ideas which they cannot persuade the bulk of their fellow citizens to adopt." He concluded, "I wish to follow in the path of Abraham Lincoln rather than in the path of [radical abolitionists] John Brown and Wendell Phillips." Roosevelt wrote to La Follette, "It is half amusing and half pathetic to see so many good people convinced that the world can be reformed without difficulty merely by reforming the machinery of government."[27]

Roosevelt was far from alone in his criticisms. Despite his growing popularity and power, even La Follette's closest friends were not always wholehearted in their support during this crucial period. In describing a La Follette speech, William Allen White noted, "He gave the impression of great energy; deep conviction and the fighting capacity—but it did not seem to me to be marked with that largeness, dignity and reserve of power for which one looks in the highest statesmanship. There is no one down here whom I like and admire more than I do Robert La Follette, and I wish—I wish—he also had these other qualities of statesmanship." Despite his shortcom-

*La Follette in 1911, his political star on the rise. (Library of Congress LC-USZ62-34080)*

ings, by 1911 La Follette was clearly the leader of the thirteen insurgent, or most aggressively progressive, Republican senators. Buoyed by their support and the increasingly progressive tenor of congress and the nation, La Follette once again cast longing eyes toward the White House.[28]

Immediately following the adjournment of the extra session of Congress on 15 March 1911, La Follette, who claimed to be working to the full limit of his strength, began a series of lecture engagements postponed previously by illness. In fulfilling those obligations, he laid the groundwork for his as yet unannounced presidential campaign. In keeping with the common social fiction in politics, La Follette wanted the candidacy thrust upon him rather than to make obvious efforts to pursue it. According to La Follette, Taft's course upon tariff legislation raised doubts in the mind of "every real Progressive." La Follette accused Taft of, among other things, "attempt[ing] to foist upon the country a sham reciprocity measure" and surrendering to a reactionary program of discredited representatives of special interests. La Follette claimed the future of the progressive movement demanded opposition to the reelection of the president, calling Taft "the very antithesis of progressivism." (He also claimed, "The whole administration is hostile to me — very hostile," and bragged, "The mention of my name in connection with any matter pending with this administration is enough to bring down upon it the wrath of the present Powers.") In a confidential letter he asserted, "It falls to me to lead this fight." This was precisely what Belle dreaded, and she wrote to a friend what a great relief it would be to her if her husband did not undertake such a campaign.[29]

La Follette expressed confidence in a viable candidacy if only he could be guaranteed organizational and financial support. His set minimum of $300,000 was quickly pledged, but La Follette's suspicion that Roosevelt was looking for someone to "do the Light Brigade act, stop Taft, and get shot about the right time" remained. His fears were slightly ameliorated in April 1911, La Follette claimed, when Gilson Gardner, Washington correspondent for the Scripps newspapers, met with Roosevelt. The former president offered assurances that, although he could not campaign for him openly, he would commend La Follette in the newsmagazine *The Outlook* in his capacity as associate editor. On 16 April, Roosevelt arrived in Madison and praised La Follette in an address to the legislature, stressing that La Follette's was not a blind commitment to progressive ideals but rather a reasoned, "sane," and practical program, which the former president held up for emulation. La Follette was nevertheless still reluctant to commit himself formally as a candidate for fear he would be used as "a mere pawn in the national game." He gave assurances that this concern had nothing whatever to do with his own pride but stemmed from his vocation as protector of the progressive cause.[30]

La Follette combated some of his frustrations by ensuring the soothing, supportive presence of Belle and Bobbie in Washington during the winter of 1911–12. Early in May, La Follette's concern that Roosevelt might usurp his momentum by deciding to run himself was temporarily eased by E. A. Van Valenberg, manager of the *Philadelphia North American*. Van Valenberg stated that Roosevelt's position on La Follette's candidacy was "one of strong encouragement," reaffirming Garner's earlier message. A third-hand account of Van Valenberg's meeting with Roosevelt reached La Follette. Written by a La Follette supporter, it seems more the product of wishful thinking than objective reporting: "T.R. says that [La Follette] is the logical Progressive candidate & should come out *now*, & that he, T.R. will back him up, & agrees not to be a candidate himself! He just *discovered* Wisconsin, says he was blinded by prejudice before & could not recognize [La Follette's] true character,— that if he had done so it would have been better for his own administration — that [La Follette] has educated his state into a true democracy & tried out there on a sound basis the policies that other states are experimenting in blindly, etc. Said he is writing an article on [La Follette] for the *Outlook*— for which look out."[31]

La Follette's fears that he might be used as a stalking horse never totally disappeared. After a meeting with Roosevelt, crusading journalist Fremont Older confided to La Follette on 6 April that the former president believed that La Follette could never be elected and gave the impression that Roosevelt himself hoped to be renominated. La Follette's doubts about the former president were again eased, however, when Roosevelt presented in the 27 May issue of *Outlook* an unqualified tribute to the achievements in Wisconsin under La Follette's leadership. Although Roosevelt avoided mentioning La Follette by name, he called Wisconsin "a pioneer blazing the way along which we Americans must make our civic and industrial advance during the next few decades." According to Belle, Bob appeared to accept the declaration in the *Outlook* as sincere rather than as a possible move on the political chessboard. Armed with initially generous financial contributions, the support of fellow progressives, assurances (albeit questionable ones) of noninterference from Roosevelt, and the firm belief that the people would support him if only they could be reached, La Follette pledged himself formally as a presidential candidate on 17 June 1911.[32]

The purpose of the progressive movement, La Follette asserted, was to restore popular sovereignty, via modification and reform, wherever necessary, including in the courts, statutes, and even the Constitution. He proposed to solve the trust problem by having Congress specifically prohibit all practices that made unfair competition possible. To expand his appeal, however, he deprecated his reputation as a radical. Key progressives endorsed La Follette's candidacy, with the exception of former secretary of the interior James R. Garfield, who qualified his endorsement as a recommendation rather than a firm commitment. Since Garfield was a staunch Roosevelt supporter, La Follette's distrust of the former president intensified. La Follette then made the grave error of naming Walter L. Houser, former secretary of state of Wisconsin, as his campaign manager. Houser accepted the appointment despite his conviction that the progressive movement must be against Taft and not for any particular candidate. A great admirer of Roosevelt, Houser took La Follette at his word and promoted what he considered to be the interest of the cause rather than his candidate. La Follette preferred a campaign manager uncommitted to his candidacy rather than trust the job to someone outside his circle of Wisconsin intimates.[33]

The first months of La Follette's campaign were heady ones, compelling national recognition. As La Follette gained momentum, Roosevelt continued to claim he did not want the nomination but declined, despite La Follette supporters' urgings, to announce that he would refuse the nomination were it offered. Anxiously, John Fackler of Progressive Republican Headquarters claimed the right to know Roosevelt's position. Roosevelt remained noncommittal, creating a difficult situation for all progressives, in particular congressional candidates who were hesitant to endorse La Follette or Roosevelt for fear of alienating their constituents. La Follette continued to be wary of Roosevelt, but most of his attention was divided between Senate sessions, work on the autobiographical *American Magazine* articles, the demands of his own weekly magazine, and preparation of speeches for the active campaigning ahead in what would prove to be one of the nation's most bitter political contests.

# 12: INCIDENT IN PHILADELPHIA
## LA FOLLETTE'S POLITICAL SUICIDE

**A**lthough disturbed by persistent reports that he was about to withdraw from the race, early support so encouraged La Follette that late in October he thought he might win the Republican nomination if Roosevelt "didn't mess things up." It took mounting rumors that Roosevelt would enter the fight to erode La Follette's hopes. Speculation as to the former president's intentions weakened progressive unity in general and La Follette's support in particular, but in public La Follette could do nothing more than reiterate his commitment to candidacy. Privately he was livid over Roosevelt's refusal to make his intentions clear. La Follette was not the only one disturbed by Roosevelt's disruption of party unity, as this period parody of the Apostle's Creed attests: "I believe in Theodore Roosevelt, maker of noise and strife, and in ambition his only creed (my Lord). He was born of the love of power and suffered under William Howard Taft, was crucified, died and was buried. He descended into Africa. The third year he arose again from the jungle and ascendeth into favor and sitteth at the right hand of his party, whence he shall come to scourge the living and the dead."[1]

Despite this campaign's national scope, La Follette persisted in efforts to present every voter with his public record. A reporter who accompanied him on a speaking trip observed that when La Follette's "audience is large and responsive, he talks on and on regardless of train schedules, meals, or sleep, not only in their relation to himself, but to his audience. When La Follette is in the midst of a speech he simply can't stop. He's just got to stick to the finish. . . . He reminded me of Napoleon in his best days, when he could sleep between courses or in the royal coach so as to make possible a night's work with seven or eight secretaries." The *Saturday Evening Post* reported La Follette was thought by so many to be a dangerous man not because of what he said but because of the "thunderous and portentous way" in which he said it, making him, despite his didactic, statistic-laden, interminable speeches, the most popular of Chautauqua stars. The *Post* called La Follette a poet and an artist — and his own best audience: "When he speaks a stirring thing nobody is more deeply moved than he."[2]

La Follette noted proudly that he was occupied fifteen hours a day, every day. Dr. Fox, alarmed by reports of La Follette's shortness of breath, urged him to lose weight and exercise, advice unheeded. Suggestions that he withdraw in favor of Roosevelt caused La Follette to intensify his efforts, but he reiterated his devotion to principle rather than to personal victory. Perhaps

La Follette's frustration at not being able to reach each voter personally led to his critical decision to halt his speaking campaign in favor of polishing his autobiographical magazine articles. La Follette maintained that every line was written "for the express purpose of exhibiting the struggle for a more representative government." During crucial campaign time La Follette was so preoccupied he "could only occasionally look in on the headquarters." Certainly La Follette, committed to a contract, needed the money, and the articles were a way of reaching voters, but they simply were not as effective as an ambitious speaking campaign. However, writing (or rewriting what had been ghostwritten) allowed him the luxury of thoroughness, impossible in public speaking. It was a way of making irrefutable the contrast between his own commitment to candidacy and the waffling of Theodore Roosevelt. La Follette's articles presented a romanticized account of his life. He described himself as a humble pioneer born in a log cabin, almost saintlike in his honesty, virtue, and integrity. While the La Follette faithful received the series enthusiastically, in the opinion of several progressive politicians, La Follette's drive to make a permanent record of his moral superiority cost him crucial momentum. By late fall, progressives increasingly viewed Roosevelt as the only viable candidate to beat Taft, a turn of events that left La Follette alternately angry, frustrated, and depressed.[3]

On 1 January 1912, contrary to La Follette's wishes, his campaign manager Houser accepted a compromise at the Ohio State Conference of Progressives. The conference endorsed La Follette as the logical candidate to carry progressive principles to fruition but endorsed Roosevelt as well. La Follette, deeply troubled by the wavering of many of his supporters, directed Houser to release the statement that "Senator La Follette never has been and is not now a quitter" and that he would be in the running "until the gavel falls in the convention." Significantly, Houser remained La Follette's campaign manager. La Follette appeared unable to acknowledge Houser's disloyalty. As a commentator in the *New Republic* noted near the end of La Follette's life, "He has picked many a lemon in the public garden of politics."[4]

Only five days after La Follette announced his intention to stay in the race, the *New York Globe* reported that, according to unimpeachable sources, La Follette had agreed to quit in favor of Roosevelt. Pressures mounted for La Follette's withdrawal. One Roosevelt supporter declared La Follette's opposition to the former president "as if John the Baptist had objected to Jesus because he put Christianity over . . . although John had baptized people long before Jesus." La Follette reiterated his commitment to remain in the race. In early January, illness brought on by his exhausting schedule briefly incapacitated La Follette. Roosevelt sent best wishes for a speedy recovery and urged La Follette to agree to a meeting, a request that was ignored. Belle wrote that Bob had only been tired and that it gave him new strength to go among the people and find how earnest they were in their support. He received special encouragement on 22 January 1912 when he spoke at Carnegie Hall, which, the *New York Times* reported, never held a bigger nor a more enthusiastic audience. Despite this triumph, amidst a storm of wild, contradictory rumors concerning Roosevelt's candidacy, several of La Follette's supporters urged him to pledge himself to the former president.[5]

Anxiety rendered La Follette unable to sleep, a condition surely exacerbated when word came in mid-January that Roosevelt would run if the Republican nomination appeared to be a public draft. Further tension was brought to bear by several of La Follette's hitherto most faithful supporters, who now believed it impossible for La Follette to be nominated. They urged that progressives unite, regardless of their personal feelings, in support of the enormously popular Roosevelt. La Follette refused. On 29 January, he learned that his daughter Mary was to undergo an operation on 3 February to remove a tubercular gland near her jugular vein. Worried and preoccupied, that same evening he attended a meeting that intensified his fears of betrayal. "When I gave my ultimatum, refusing to abandon the field, Gifford Pinchot left my house and never crossed the threshold again." To one of his few still-loyal supporters, California governor Hiram Johnson, La Follette vowed, "In the interest of the Progressive Movement I must go through to the end." His movement, he insisted, expressed the hopes and desires of millions of American men and women willing to fight for their ideals, to take defeat if necessary, and still go on fighting.[6]

"I eat and sleep in the saddle these days," wrote Fighting Bob, "whether in Washington or out in the field." With rumors of his ill health and imminent withdrawal circulating freely, La Follette believed that any attempt to cancel his speech at the Periodical Publishers Association banquet in Philadelphia on the evening preceding his daughter's surgery might be misinterpreted as a concession of withdrawal. Upon his arrival, La Follette, recovering from ptomaine poisoning, sorely needed some sleep, although he insisted in his autobiography that a "very brief rest" prior to his speech restored him to "full vigor." He later emphasized to friends that his exhaustion stemmed not from simple lack of sleep but from strain over having to "fight a crowd in my own camp who were undermining me every hour to force through a combination with Roosevelt," exacerbated by other campaign, magazine, and legislative pressures. Belle had written to son-in-law George Middleton, who accompanied La Follette to Philadelphia, "Mr. La Follette is dreading the publishers' dinner, as he always does a new audience. His time is so interrupted that it is almost impossible for him to do anything more than outline his ideas for the occasion. I wish he could prepare definitely what he is going to say, as to be sure and keep in the time limit." On the day of the speech La Follette, anxious about his daughter's impending surgery, suffered an attack of indigestion and consumed nothing but a "lukewarm and nauseating" cup of hot chocolate and a shot of whiskey, a drink he sometimes took prior to going on the platform when fatigued.[7]

Mark Sullivan of *Collier's Weekly* promoted this annual prestigious gathering as one including "everybody in the periodical business, . . . all the publishers, editors and writers of the big periodicals . . . together with quite a number of public men." In his autobiography, La Follette provides a very brief account of his performance at the banquet: "I went, arriving after the dinner. It was very late when I began to speak. I was not at my best and did not at once get hold of my audience. It was, I do not doubt, entirely my own fault — but I [was] determined to make them hear me to the end. In my effort to do so I talked too long without realizing." Rupert Hughes, a self-proclaimed anti–La Follette reporter for the *New York Times*, provided an eyewitness account, entitled "La Follette's Political Suicide," an account remarkably in keeping with that supplied by Fola's biography of her father.[8]

According to Hughes, the dinner for 500 or 600 guests had been in progress for approximately three hours when La Follette arrived at the banquet hall around 11:00 P.M. He was scheduled to deliver the next to last speech, following a brief, witty, but profound address by Democratic presidential hopeful Woodrow Wilson. La Follette began his speech with a gracious reference to Wilson, then announced in a hostile tone that he was going to read his forty-five-minute speech for two reasons: first, because his family had requested he do so in order to curb his tendency to lose track of time, and second, because he was tired of being constantly misquoted by the press. Some defensiveness on La Follette's part was understandable. He had been inaccurately and negatively portrayed repeatedly by much of the nation's mainstream press, including the *New York Times*, which alternately ridiculed and vilified him for plotting to subvert American government and business. This audience, however, according to Middleton, felt "instantly the tactlessness of his remark." Its members were appalled not only at La Follette's grossly insulting insinuation but at the prospect of being read to for forty-five minutes at so late an hour with still another speaker on the roster. Middleton was "sure [La Follette] . . . felt the quick unfavorable reaction of the audience. . . . He struck an aggressive attitude at the beginning and this put them in an aggressive attitude toward him." La Follette announced his topic as an attack on predatory interests and, according to Hughes, "again hurled his mental cuspidor in the face of his hosts and fellow-speakers by declaring that many of those present were 'hirelings of the trusts.'" In preparing his papers years later, Congressman Henry Cooper wrote his recollections of the speech on the back of his dinner invitation: "From the very onset his speech was tedious, inappropriate . . . stereotyped, [and] like too many others of his was extreme in matter and especially in manner."[9]

Holding up the press as the single most powerful means of educating the public on political issues, La Follette denounced newspapers for abusing the trust of the people: "[W]herever news items bear in any way upon the control of Government by business; the news is colored." Editorial staffs, La Follette asserted, were increasingly understood by the public to be "hired men who no longer express honest judgements and sincere conviction, who write what they are told to write and whose judgments are salaried." Considering he was at a dinner arranged to bring together newspaper and magazine publishers, La Follette's attack on the subserviency of the newspapers while praising the great educational service rendered by more independent weekly and monthly periodicals could not have been less appropriate. Since the newspaper men were the guests of the periodical publishers, his attack seemed doubly rude and ill-advised. La Follette's prepared text included a detailed history of American industrialization that was painstakingly researched, passionately worded, and quite compelling — on paper. As a late-night speech, it bored his already alienated audience, a fact he attempted to remedy by speaking extemporaneously. This tactic had worked previously with restless audiences in the Senate and on the platform, but on this occasion La Follette's diversion from his text found him shaking his finger at inattentive members of the audience, attacking them as corrupt. "I have the floor," he reminded them defiantly, "those that don't care to listen had better get out." As the tension mounted, he frequently lost his train of thought, returned to his manuscript, and became repetitious. He repeated one portion of his speech seven times, according to one account. So tiresome did La Follette become that, after listening to him paint a picture of dismal conditions and ask, "Is there a way out?" someone in the audience cried, "We hope so!" "With a dejected and disgusted look," La Follette's secretary John Hannon said softly to Henry Cooper, "This is terrible — he is making a d——d fool of himself. It ends him for the Presidency."[10]

Gradually, several hundred members of the audience took up La Follette's invitation to "get out," gathering in the hall to express to each other their disgust and annoyance. Even son-in-law Middleton took a break an hour and a half into the harangue. As audience members returned to their seats, many began to applaud as a way of drowning out La Follette with polite contempt. La Follette, furious, threatened to talk all night if they continued. Resigned, the audience quieted and remained seated through La Follette's concluding remarks, which came more than two hours after he began. Woodrow Wilson, the *New York Times* noted, was probably La Follette's "most respectful auditor," scarcely making a move as he "saw and heard his rival 'talk himself to death' in a political sense." Toastmaster Donald Seitz of the *New York World* rose to state, "I shall not attempt nor have I the time to come to the defense of the newspapers of the country which have just been foolishly, wickedly, and untruthfully assailed." La Follette left the hall, went to his room, and "ill from exhaustion," vomited. Resting briefly on the train to Washington, he was in the operating room when three tubercular glands were removed near Mary's jugular vein during a two-hour-and-twenty-minute procedure. Mary recovered. Her father's campaign did not.[11]

Fola's account of La Follette's notorious speech is peppered with excuses. She noted that he suffered from acute indigestion in addition to physical and emotional fatigue. She acknowledged that it was not just La Follette's strident tone and poor organization that so offended his audience, for "even if Bob had read in his best form, early in the evening, the [briefer] version of his address, the audience might have resented the content of the latter as a premeditated attack." She did, however, minimize her father's abusiveness and complete lack of self-control. Congressman Cooper recalled, "La Follette killed himself politically. . . . It was a shocking scene. He lost his temper repeatedly — shook his fist — at listeners who had started to walk out too tired to listen longer, — was abusive, ugly in manner." Noted another eyewitness, "I had a long talk with . . . other insurgents the next day, and they were pretty well agreed that La Follette had committed political suicide. . . . It seems an entirely silly and trivial idea that a man should make or break himself in a single speech. But it looks as though that were La Follette's situation." Felix Agnus, publisher of the *Baltimore American*, echoed the bewilderment of many: "Poor La Follette. He has killed his chances. Indeed, he will be fortunate if he carries his own state. I certainly believe he is suffering from a mental breakdown."[12]

Ironically, on 3 February, the day after the speech, there appeared in the *Outlook* an assessment of La Follette's speaking abilities written just prior to the incident. It asserted that during the campaign La Follette "would have enjoyed a little vigorous opposition and a few hisses would have added fire to the order of his enthusiasm." It continued, "We are by no means sure that he has the patience which would enable him to endure the vociferations of a hostile audience. . . . Mr. La Follette impressed his hearers as a man of great patience, but not of exhaustless patience." The article prophesied nevertheless, "We do not believe that the mob ever existed which would daunt him."[13]

A Philadelphia editor had remarked in the midst of the speech, "[T]his is shocking — too bad. What ails him?" A multitude of answers to that question quickly found their way into print. According to La Follette, even as he agonized over his daughter's condition, "sensational accounts of this speech and its reception were published throughout the country, and at the same time equally sensational and false reports were spread concerning my physical condition." A *New York Times* article appearing nationwide on 4 February reported an interview with Donald Seitz, the banquet's toastmaster. Although Seitz blamed La Follette's lack of control on aphasia, a medical condition suffered by Seitz's father, he nevertheless rebuked La Follette for his rudeness, accusing him of coming to the dinner with the idea of attacking newspapers and currying favor with magazine publishers. Instead, said Seitz, "He has simply wiped himself off the map," concluding, "I would not be surprised if the man had been seized with a complete mental breakdown."[14]

For days newspapers headlined La Follette's "collapse" and "mental breakdown" and coupled the reports with unauthorized announcements of his withdrawal from candidacy. These stories were supplemented, then and in later years, with a variety of rumors, including that the senator had frothed at the mouth, was totally incoherent, a confirmed alcoholic, and terminally ill. Rumors that he had suffered similar breakdowns both prior and subsequent to the Philadelphia incident were persistent, as were those claiming he had been institutionalized.[15] Despite all denials, it was almost universally accepted among politicians and members of the press that La Follette had suffered a "nervous breakdown," a nonmedical, nonspecific euphemism for a personality disorder.[16] As the rumors grew, La Follette, who admitted only that he had been under a long nervous strain and needed a little rest, fired off letters blaming his performance on exhaustion.[17]

Even reports discounting tales of La Follette's unbalanced behavior were far from soothing. An editorial in the *Philadelphia Public Ledger* concluded, "Mr. La Follette is not suffering, as Mr. Seitz says, from some sort of aberration due to overstrain; he is suffering from too much La Follette." According to the *Milwaukee Journal,* neither La Follette's physical condition nor his remarks on the subserviency of the newspapers to money trusts constituted the "great tragedy of the evening." Rather, it was that La Follette had "no power"; like an athlete who had overtrained, he had "gone stale." Rupert Hughes called La Follette "less a dangerous man than an unutterable bore."[18]

Some La Follette supporters looked for a silver lining around the dark clouds. *Philadelphia Evening Telegraph* editorialist Paul Hanna, present at the banquet, thanked La Follette for "the service rendered a dreadfully deceived but rapidly awakening public by your address. . . . You are creating a sentiment among the people which demands and soon will support a Free Press, from which will spring freedom and genuine democracy in both industry and politics." A witness somewhat less strident in his defense of La Follette dismissed one supporter's assertion that the most vocal members of the Philadelphia audience were plants, prearranged to be antagonistic to La Follette. The witness did, however, comment on the "extraordinary number of stand patters present." La Follette's lawyer and close friend Gilbert Roe even suggested that the speech and its aftermath might work out advantageously, for at last the public would be aware of the newspapers' hostility toward La Follette. La Follette readily agreed, adding that the audience was "stung by my plain truths about the subserviency of the press." He concluded hopefully, "if I am right they won't be able to make their misrepresentations stick." In New Jersey the *Newark News* deemed it difficult to blame La Follette for his sweeping condemnation of newspapers since he had never been treated fairly by the press but suggested that he inspired such treatment because he was much more radical in words and manner than in actions and policies. Another paper noted that, while all that La Follette said was true, he was indiscreet and discourteous and concluded, "We do not want a man for President who forgets what he has said, and repeats several times."[19]

The newspapers' "gross misrepresentation" of her husband's "overtired condition" infuriated Belle. Key La Follette supporters who longed for an excuse to switch to Roosevelt quickly seized the opportunity to declare La Follette broken down. On the morning of 5 February the core members of La Follette's campaign committee, including manager Walter Houser, submitted to La Follette a statement of withdrawal from the presidential race. Belle, despite her personal dislike of Bob's candidacy, stated she would rather see her husband dead in his grave than have him sign the statement. So incensed was Belle that she wrote to family friend Gil Roe: "I know Bob suffers from brain fag all the time because he will not try to rest but to hear these men talk you would think he had been a dead man for several years instead of carrying the whole load of the progressive movement. It needs a man to talk back with them." La Follette directed Houser to issue a denial of any intention of withdrawal but predicted, "I am likely to be attacked in every conceivable and underhanded way by the friends of another candidate in order to force me to quit the field."[20]

Further damage to La Follette's candidacy occurred that same day when

George Record, chairman of the first National Progressive Republican League conference at Chicago, relayed to his fellow progressives the message he had received from Houser (present earlier that day when La Follette had refused to withdraw), announcing the senator's withdrawal due to illness. Despite warnings from still loyal friends, La Follette refused to accept his campaign manager's action as a betrayal and announced, "The attempt of any of my former supporters to justify their desertion of my candidacy by making Houser their scape goat is a cowardly perversion of fact," for "they know that no one had the authority to withdraw me as a candidate." Belief in La Follette's official withdrawal strengthened when Theodore Roosevelt intimate Gifford Pinchot, previously one of La Follette's most influential and financially generous supporters, sent a widely published telegram to the Minnesota Progressive Republican League stating that in his judgment "La Follette's condition makes further serious candidacy impossible."[21]

The impact of all this on Roosevelt was the subject of some debate. In an article entitled "La Follette Now Out of the Race," published only three days after the speech, the *New York Times* noted "there is already a scattering of rats from the sinking ship." The progressive *New York Evening Mail* asserted that the Philadelphia incident put the Republican nomination "very definitely in the hands of Col[onel] Theodore Roosevelt." The *Cleveland Reader* disagreed: "La Follette's collapse will make little or no difference. He was virtually out of the race . . . before he showed any signs of illness or exhaustion and his condition could not affect in any material way the assured swing of the Republican Progressives to Theodore Roosevelt."[22]

The *New York Times* insisted that after La Follette's Philadelphia performance "it will be practically impossible for [Roosevelt] to maintain his sphinx-like attitude and he will be forced to a declaration of his intentions." In fact, Roosevelt confided that he was forced to delay his official entry into the campaign in order to avoid giving "color to the belief that he [was] trying to hustle poor Senator La Follette." Roosevelt stated that he never urged La Follette to become a candidate and denied any role in the mass exodus of key La Follette supporters into his own camp: "It's perfectly silly for him [La Follette] to feel hurt at me . . . I have done absolutely nothing. . . . If ever there was a perfectly spontaneous movement, this is it."[23]

The stories of La Follette's "breakdown" and "collapse" had far greater impact on journalists and political leaders than on voters, who gave little credence to the conflicting statements about La Follette's health and candidacy. A poll of *Kansas City Star* readers showed no change in La Follette's support after the Philadelphia speech. Belle, however, believed that her husband's brief withdrawal from active campaigning following the banquet encouraged rumors of a prolonged breakdown.[24] Although La Follette reiterated his assurances to friends that he had not been in better physical condition for years and needed only sleep, he used this period not to rest but to finish his articles for *American Magazine*. He resolved to "bring the story down to date" by collecting and publishing the articles in book form, announcing, "*I want in the last chapter to give this history of this d——d campaign.*" During that period of "rest," on 26 February 1912, Roosevelt officially announced that his hat was in the ring. Predictably, in the final chapters of his autobiography and in the spring issues of his magazine, La Follette, to the delight of Taft supporters, accused the Roosevelt forces of stooping to treachery in order to make it appear that La Follette had pledged his support to Roosevelt. He even hinted broadly that Roosevelt had been "bought" by railroad money. He did, however, grudgingly admit that he should have campaigned more following the completion of the earlier autobiographical articles but dismissed this major political error quickly with the justification that he had been conscientiously attending to matters pending in the Senate. Having devoted less than a paragraph to his own mistakes, La Follette devoted the remaining pages to the culpability of others. His long list of traitors included Hiram Johnson and Gifford Pinchot. He even included an edited version of the Periodical Publishers' Association speech, ignoring the fact that he deviated far from his prepared text that night.[25]

Roosevelt organizer Gilson Gardner worried over the impact of La Follette's assertions. Gardner reported that Taft supporters were encouraging La Follette forces to make additional attacks on Roosevelt to further split the progressive vote within the Republican Party. Other Roosevelt forces, however, had anticipated La Follette's accusations and advised the former president, "a sick man is not to be held responsible." Moreover, they asserted, even La Follette's staunchest supporters, "except for a few extremists," would not follow the broken-down senator. John Darling's *New York Globe* cartoon "Such Enthusiastic Solicitude!" lampooned the way La Follette's political enemies rushed to utilize rumors of La Follette's ill health.[26]

La Follette initially gave mixed accounts of his performance in Philadelphia. A few days after the banquet he admitted that his "outrageously long" speech had contained serious errors and that his mind had taken refuge in digression. And yet that same day he offered an interpretation more in keeping with what he would ultimately maintain was the true significance of the whole debacle. La Follette told his secretary that he did not regard any aspect of the experience as "anything out of the ordinary, but rather as one of a lifelong series of adventures where he has met opposition and has doggedly stayed with it." "Why," Hannan quoted La Follette as saying, "I

# Such Enthusiastic Solicitude!

*The cartoonist's caption offered the following suggestion to former La Follette supporter Gifford Pinchot, who had recently transferred his loyalties to the Roosevelt camp: "Wouldn't it be safer to quarantine him or lock his clothes up in the fumigator?"* (*John Darling [Ding],* New York Globe and Commercial Advertiser, *17 February 1912*)

have grown fat on that sort of thing all my life." Slightly more than a week later La Follette professed, "The affair in Philadelphia was greatly (and designedly) exaggerated because I aroused the hostility of the press by my criticism." He maintained that his delivery of the speech was insignificant; only the way it was twisted and used against him was important. He was the innocent victim of the immoral treachery of conniving and deceitful men. Furthermore, according to La Follette, this was not the first time the state of his health had been maliciously misrepresented.[27]

La Follette's cryptic account of the speech in his autobiography minimized his own errors, but he devoted considerable attention to attempts to discredit him subsequent to the speech. His own valiant responses, he claimed, disproved completely the stories circulated. He even bragged that such a temporary defeat as the ensuing scandal meant less to him "than to men unseasoned in strife." La Follette's anger and frustration were evident, however, in a Bowling Green, Ohio, speech in which he referred to Roosevelt as an "inconsequential playboy." La Follette did not hold a monopoly on name-calling in the 1912 campaign. Earlier Roosevelt privately referred to Taft as "a flubdub with a streak of the second-rate and common in him" and, as the race grew more heated, publicly called the president a "puzzle-wit" and a "fathead." On 13 May, Taft openly referred to Roosevelt as an "egoist" and "demagogue." All this prompted satirist Finley Peter Dunne's creation, the ever-present political commentator Mr. Dooley, to note, "Ivrybody callin' each other liars and crooks, not like pollytical inimies, d'ye mind, but like old friends that has been up late dhrinkin' together." The mudslinging was fodder for political cartoonists as well. Roosevelt was very careful, however, not to say anything bitter about La Follette in public, for fear of a sympathy backlash, but privately called him "half zealot and half self-seeking demagogue" and called his political goals "impossible." (Roosevelt's contempt for La Follette lives on even today. One of the former president's descendants breezily notes that within the Roosevelt family, "We consider La Follette rather like a buzzing insect.")[28]

Although a majority of the accounts of La Follette's performance at the Periodical Publishers Association banquet were grossly sensationalized and at times fabricated, even the unembroidered facts reveal disturbing and politically debilitating facets of La Follette's personality. La Follette claimed to be unaware of the banquet's purpose to reconcile newspapers with magazines. He believed his speech would please an audience of magazine publishers. This explanation neglects the significance of La Follette's ignorance of the nature of his audience, a grave error for a man who prided himself on his devotion to detail. Although he was personally careless and inadequately prepared, La Follette's poorly organized campaign forces can

*A frazzled GOP hostess strives to keep party unity among her bickering guests, including Roosevelt, La Follette, and Taft. ( John Darling [Ding],* Review of Reviews, *May 1912)*

also be faulted, since the composition of the audience should have been brought to his attention as a matter of course.

Once La Follette learned his audience included newspapermen, he most certainly could have tailored his remarks accordingly: La Follette was noted for his ability to adapt his speeches quickly to fit his listeners. Instead, already harried, he fell victim to the insecurities mounting during the campaign. According to witness Oswald Garrison Villard, "a kind of latent paranoia came to the surface" as La Follette charged his audience with being "reactionary and eager to exploit the public" and "in a conspiracy against him." Even before his ill-fated speech, La Follette was strongly on the defensive, hurt by many recent abandonments. Newspaper accounts of his withdrawal from the race appeared with increasing frequency, reports he considered not just false but malicious. His sensitivity at that point to the slightest opposition, real or imagined, made him an emotional powder keg. In a story headlined "TR Branded 'Traitor': La Follette Manager Declares Treachery Caused Illness," Houser declared that the actions of the Roosevelt camp had "overtax[ed] La Follette's nervous and physical energies."[29] La Follette entered the hall, late and frazzled, only to hear Woodrow Wilson ending a gracious, extemporaneous speech, intensifying his fears of inadequacy. It seems likely that toastmaster Seitz's "aghast" look at his bulky manuscript reinforced La Follette's self-reproachful feeling of ill-preparedness. The powder keg ignited. "At Philadelphia," he confided to his sister, "I felt that the crowd was against me & threw down my manuscript determined to compel them and master them." (In hindsight, one witness offered a simpler solution: "If only he'd had sense enough to tell a funny story and sit down.") [30]

One explanation of La Follette's Philadelphia performance, according to the *New York Times*, was "that for weeks he had been consumed with smoldering rage against the Roosevelt propaganda, and at last vented his rage on the publishers in his audience." La Follette had long resented having to keep his dislike and distrust of Theodore Roosevelt confidential in order not to alienate progressives. For a man who prided himself on being completely honest in addition to morally superior to others, especially Roosevelt, this created an enormous strain. Frustrated and angry, La Follette managed in Philadelphia to refrain from making a personal attack on the popular former president, but could no longer resist venting his general frustration. Overworked and depressed by reports of a failing candidacy, La Follette was unable to control his temper. Refusing to accept responsibility for his decreasing status in favor of Roosevelt, La Follette lashed out at the messenger bearing the bad news, the press. The denunciation of his enemies and determination to win his audience were hallmarks of a great La Follette speech. What made this one different was that so many of the very people he was railing against were in the audience. After feeling so long at their mercy, he now controlled them, and punished them accordingly. For a presidential candidate confronting men with enormous influence over his career, the speech was disastrous. Personally, however, it was cathartic. La Follette, it has been observed, derived a kind of "masochistic pleasure" from his isolation and defeats. In Philadelphia, emotional needs outweighed his desire to perform in a politically expedient manner, for by stressing the vital importance of fair and accurate reporting to the nation's political and economic well-being, he certainly could have maintained his integrity without so completely antagonizing his audience. [31]

Following his Philadelphia speech La Follette suffered financially as well as physically and emotionally. He desired only to complete his autobiography, then retreat for several months of isolated rest. According to Belle, he "worked out in silence and solitude" that which "must be accepted as unalterable failure or sorrow" and did not discuss the incident with his family. This refusal to acknowledge and explore painful emotions is typical of the La Follettes, but perhaps Bob's reluctance to discuss his feelings about this particular issue stemmed in part from Belle's insistence on his continued candidacy. He agreed to a speaking campaign across North Dakota, Minnesota, Nebraska, Oregon, and California only at Belle's urging. Belle confided in their children, "I have felt its great importance in clearing up all this misconception as to the state of his health. It is the best way to give the lie to these deserters who are going about claiming they left him because he was disabled — I don't mind those who come out in the open so much and said they left him because their beloved Theodore Roosevelt could win."[32]

With Belle unwilling to accept without challenge her husband's — and, less directly, her own — tarnished reputation, La Follette pursued the remainder of the campaign with a vengeance, despite the attempts of "everybody . . . outside of the immediate household" to convince him to withdraw. According to Fola, when La Follette reentered active campaigning in North Dakota, "so far as he was concerned the humiliating failure of his speech at the publisher's dinner slipped into the background in due proportion to the totality of his life and work." From then on, La Follette refused to acknowledge publicly the enormity of that "humiliating failure," although the incident and the rumors stemming from it did not fade in the memories of politicians or journalists.[33]

Belle joined her husband during the post-Philadelphia campaign and proved to be a persuasive advocate of votes for women at many meetings sponsored by suffrage organizations. Bob La Follette attempted to refocus attention on politics rather than personalities. The key issues, he asserted, were those he had long championed, including support for the rights to initiative, referendum, and recall; direct nominations and elections; graduated income and inheritance taxes; the parcel post; government ownership and operation of Alaskan railways and coal mines; physical valuation of railways; extension of powers of the Interstate Commerce Commission and a strengthening of the tariff commission. He opposed ship subsidies, excessive defense expenditures, Dollar Diplomacy, the Aldrich-Vreeland currency bill, and Canadian reciprocity plans. Critics noted the absence of any specific discussion of the larger issues of proper relations between capital and labor and the relation of the judiciary to social reform. His supporters reiterated La Follette's contention that such subjects were inherent in his proposed regulation of trusts and in his support for the recall. Detractors countered that La Follette, unable to see the big picture, was flailing at the branches of injustice instead of attacking the roots. Too radical for conservatives, La Follette's policy of reform rather than replacement of the nation's political and economic foundations proved too conservative for radicals.

Although he had rejoiced in 1911 when fellow progressives appointed him their leader, La Follette returned to his status as a "lonely man" in 1912 with some relief. Belle noted, "Bob feels better always when things are straightened out and the decks seem cleared for action, no matter how big a fight he has on his hands." No longer stifled by efforts to please as many progressives as possible, La Follette returned to the style and the image with which he felt the most comfortable — a lone altruistic crusader, fighting bravely against overwhelming odds, unencumbered by annoying compromises. One close friend asserted, "La Follette has not withdrawn, and what is more, he will not do so, and what is still more [is] . . . that he is more anxious to have the thing he is fighting for succeed than he is anxious to be President of the United States." Ten years after these events, *The Outlook* reported a somewhat different interpretation of this lifelong "strength": "His strongest trait is a delight in overcoming obstacles. He would rather have the mass against than with him; he glories in such a contest. . . . He would deliberately choose the road with opposition, provided he did not thereby sacrifice a principle."[34]

An extremely self-righteous La Follette denied the request that he remove his name from the California primary ballot: "I am everlastingly sure of the righteousness of my resolution to fight straight on, never halting, never turning one single step aside to bargain with sham success. Every day strengthens that resolution and the future will vindicate my course. For the present I must endure the pain and mortification attending upon the loss of political followers and even personal friends. But out of many trials I have been taught the lesson of fortitude and patience." Despite the loss of many influential supporters, La Follette's solitary, blustery stance was enthusiastically rewarded by those still loyal. Supporters showered him with reassurance that he was the only rightful candidate. The *Minneapolis Tribune* reported that La Follette, who "had his fighting clothes on . . . plunged into the North Dakota campaign with a vigor which had given him an added right to his title of 'Fighting Bob,'" adding that he "look[ed] anything but a sick man . . . [and was] tense, vigorous, and full of fighting ire." The *Tribune* concluded, "There is an indomitable something in this little fighting man that evokes admiration whether willing or unwilling." La Follette was particularly eager to prove that he "wasn't quite ready for the junk pile" to North Dakotans, for it was in their state that Gifford Pinchot had proclaimed him "a disabled engine" and asserted the need for "another locomotive for the progressive train." La Follette maintained in dozens of speeches that "my drive wheels were good, that my flues were all open and that I had plenty of sand in my sandbox." In contrast, Roosevelt was nothing but a "switch engine," one that "first runs one track, and then on another. Runs forward and then backs up. Makes a heap of noise and never gets anywhere." Those who flocked to his speeches rewarded La Follette with thunderous applause. La Follette had sacrificed the general but less devoted approval of the powerful many for the passionate, sometimes even fanatical approval of the few.[35]

The early primaries confirmed reports that La Follette's alleged debilitated condition had little effect on the voters. He won the North Dakota primary with 58 percent of the vote, compared to 39 percent for Roosevelt and 3 percent for Taft. On 2 April, La Follette triumphed over Taft in Wisconsin by a 3:1 margin, and Roosevelt received only 628 votes. La Follette claimed Roosevelt's overwhelming victory in Illinois, where his own showing was poor, was in no way indicative of progressive sentiment because he did not consider that state to be progressive. In Oregon, where he received few votes and no delegates, La Follette gave a speech that revealed some of the motivations that kept him running in the face of so much adversity: "I ran five times for Governor of Wisconsin and you may just as well make up your mind to elect me President next November. . . . I shall continue to be a candidate for President until our Government is entirely restored to the people. I would rather have the place in history as the man who led such a fight than to have been one of a score of Presidents whose names you cannot remember tonight." La Follette's fellow progressives were not impressed. Roosevelt's eventual vice presidential candidate Governor Hiram Johnson and many of La Follette's other former supporters resented the Wisconsin senator's arrival in California. The local press described La Follette's mission as "one of selfish ambition, selfish revenge, and selfish disregard of the progressive cause." And this assessment was not without justification: La Follette's bitterness continued to divide progressive voters nationwide, increasing the possibility of a conservative resurgence. Johnson, as well as Nebraska congressman George Norris, who was running for the U.S. Senate, earned La Follette's special wrath for their refusal to remain committed to his candidacy. La Follette spent three weeks campaigning in California, denouncing Johnson and his followers. Johnson successfully resisted a conservative takeover, and Norris too would emerge victorious, but Republican unity had been dealt a critical blow.[36]

One week prior to the Republican Convention, hearings were held on contested delegates. Roosevelt asserted, "Taft cannot possibly win now except by deliberate highway robbery," yet he worried that Taft had "all the viciousness and ethical dishonesty" necessary to control the convention if supplied the necessary "ability and nerve" by his "unscrupulous" supporters. The former president traveled to Chicago to protest what he deemed

Taft's fraudulently credentialed delegates. Roosevelt also worked behind the scenes to secure Wisconsin governor Francis McGovern as temporary convention chairman, asserting that if the progressives showed a united front they could stop the Taft forces from seating "fake delegations." The day before the convention opened, Roosevelt electrified 6,000 of his faithful with a speech ending, "We stand at Armageddon, and we battle for the Lord."[37]

La Follette entered the convention with only the thirty-six delegates he had been able to garner in Wisconsin and North Dakota. His alleged breakdown and widespread negative press compounded his reputation as a radical. La Follette, however, refused to concede that his inability to acquire delegates outside his traditional narrow base of support reflected his limited albeit intense appeal, especially against an incumbent president as well as a former one who had been wildly popular. He blamed the nefarious tactics of Taft and Roosevelt. Wisconsin's delegates marched into the convention hall carrying a banner proclaiming:

> We do not need the Taft smile,
> Nor Teddy's toothsome grin;
> La Follette once; La Follette twice;
> La Follette til we win![38]

Under the leadership of Walter Houser, La Follette's forces refused any alliance with Roosevelt supporters and denied support to McGovern. They viewed McGovern's chairmanship as a preliminary step toward all Wisconsin votes being thrown to Roosevelt. La Follette's refusal to unite with Roosevelt even in opposition to Taft further split Republican progressives: Hiram Johnson's earlier charge of selfishness is bolstered by La Follette's refusal to follow the advice of his wife and other staunch supporters that he promote the nomination of Senator Joseph Bristow or some other progressive with whom he could work and support heartily. Such an act would have revealed his greatest concerns to be the success of the progressive cause rather than personal advancement. Instead, the party regulars under the chairmanship of Elihu Root (a "standpat Tory" called to the chair by McGovern) nominated Taft, and 344 Roosevelt delegates marched out.[39]

Five hundred forty constituted a majority, the minimum number of votes necessary to secure the nomination of any Republican candidate. Taft received 561, Roosevelt 107, La Follette 41, other candidates 19, and delegates not voting or absent 350. To his followers Roosevelt repeatedly intoned, "Thou Shalt Not Steal," charging that 72 delegates belonging to him had been wrongly replaced by Taft delegates. Pro-Roosevelt newspapers echoed the former president's assessment of "The Chicago Steal." La Follette maintained that neither Taft nor Roosevelt had a majority of "honestly or regularly elected delegates," while continuing to assert that Roosevelt's candidacy had robbed him of the nomination. Governor McGovern countered that La Follette's own intractability had destroyed his candidacy, contending that if McGovern had been elected temporary chairman, La Follette, with "mathematical certainty," would have been nominated. Even McGovern's friends questioned this assessment: "The idea that the many honest men who were in that convention supporting President Taft would consider Mr. La Follette . . . [who] has never had a decent word to say for President Taft nor for his administration . . . as a possible compromise candidate is . . . preposterous."[40]

La Follette's resentment of Roosevelt remained unabated by Taft's renomination. Two days after the convention he wrote an editorial for *La Follette's Magazine* accusing Roosevelt of attempting to buy the presidency through lavish campaign expenditures and the support of notorious members of the country's largest trusts. Roosevelt supporters countercharged that had it not been for La Follette's jealousy and "dog-in-the-manger attitude at Chicago[,] Mr. Roosevelt might today have been the nominee, and the election would be assured." Despite his still great popularity, Roosevelt's candidacy had in fact been critically compromised long before he reached Chicago. Roosevelt was seeking an unprecedented third term, in violation of his earlier pledge, and his New Nationalism was deemed too interventionist by moderates and conservatives alike. Roosevelt created his own Progressive party, popularly known as the Bull Moose (taken from Roosevelt's characteristically vigorous declaration, "I feel as fit as a bull moose"). But even Roosevelt's popular appeal proved no match for the power of Taft's incumbency. Many Republican progressives felt disgust for both Roosevelt and La Follette. One decried La Follette "and all his socialistic works," while denouncing Roosevelt's third-party movement as "inspired by the personal vanity of its leader," vanity "fostered by the Wall Street and general 'big business' interests."[41]

Roosevelt dominated the headlines on 14 October. While preparing to deliver a speech in Milwaukee, he was shot by a German immigrant bartender who claimed to be acting out desires expressed to him by the ghost of William McKinley. Despite the bullet lodged in his chest, Roosevelt insisted on delivering his speech of almost an hour before allowing aides to take him to the hospital. Even *La Follette's Weekly Magazine*, while noting that Roosevelt's injury was "not regarded as serious," could not help but admire "the spirit with which he met the ordeal." This dramatic show of Rooseveltian panache failed to muster sufficient support, however. Staunch party members cast their lot with Taft; others crossed party lines to support Democratic candidate Woodrow Wilson. La Follette ended his autobiography with a plea to progressives not to break ranks by joining the Bull Moose but refused to officially support or endorse either Taft ("an amiable, easy going fat man, willing but incompetent") or Wilson. He did, however, give Wilson behind-the-scenes support and boasted that Taft had, at La Follette's suggestion, incorporated some of La Follette's ideas into his campaign speeches. In hopes of embarrassing Roosevelt, La Follette also cosponsored Senate resolutions directing an investigation of campaign contributions during 1904, 1908, and 1912.[42]

The personal did not totally eclipse the political, however. Although furious with Francis McGovern for his role in the convention, La Follette nevertheless campaigned on his behalf, calling the reelection of the Wisconsin governor "vital to the progressive cause in this state." "Blind indeed," intoned La Follette during a whirlwind tour of Dane County, "is the man who in this critical hour would endanger all that has taken so much struggle and sacrifice to secure for the poor [in exchange for the] satisfaction of making McGovern suffer."[43]

La Follette was painfully aware of the repercussions of the split between himself and Roosevelt. According to Belle, "[T]he breaking down of the Progressive alliance, which . . . took him so long to build up, is the hardest part of the situation." He continued to blame that breakup solely on Roosevelt's decision to run.[44] Even many longtime supporters found their esteem for La Follette lowered. "Senator La Follette," one complained, "has played high handed politics nearly all his life and I suppose will do so to the end but apparently gets sore when anyone else takes a hand in the game."[45] La Follette lost more in 1912 than just a leading role within a growing progressive movement. He lost more than the Republican nomination for the presidency. He lost forever, at least in the eyes of many key politicians and members of the press, not only the chance of ever becoming president but the chance of ever again being completely trusted and respected. La Follette's insecurities forced him to refuse any possible conciliatory meetings with Roosevelt, needlessly alienating the popular and powerful former president early on. Although La Follette was understandably outraged by Roosevelt's role in the party split, his inability to accept responsibility for his own actions led him to, among other things, maintain a campaign manager of questionable loyalties and attack influential members of the press. The latter culminated in a storm of ugly publicity, to be sure, but also in La Follette's sense of relief at no longer having to share whatever glory came his way. La Follette's personal characteristics — his refusal to accept failure or

to acknowledge the limited support for his political agenda, his unwillingness to compromise or delegate authority, his desire for unqualified approval, and his dedication to his principles no matter what the cost, in short,
the very things that had brought him to the political forefront — ultimately
proved to be his political undoing. In 1912, La Follette's personal needs
were satisfied at great political cost.

# 13: NO SURRENDER
## ONE HARDLY KNOWS WHETHER TO PITY
## LA FOLLETTE OR ADMIRE HIS BRAVERY

Following the break up of La Follette's progressive Republican cohort, Americans at large seemed belatedly receptive to the constant refrain of his progressive ideology. On 10 April 1912, the RMS *Titanic*, then the largest ship in the world, left Queenstown, Ireland, en route for New York on its maiden journey. Like the other members of the White Star Line, the *Titanic*, despite its British flag and crew, was the property of the International Mercantile Marine Company, a shipping trust headed by J. P. Morgan. Business matters forced the cancellation of Morgan's passage, but plenty of other vastly wealthy Americans were aboard, enjoying the fruits of their economic empires in banking, real estate, transportation, brewing, etc. The 46,328-ton ship, eleven stories high and four city blocks long, had a double bottom and was declared "unsinkable." Four days into her transatlantic journey the *Titanic* hit an iceberg. The floating marvel of state-of-the-art engineering and opulence went down in little more than two hours. Although the *Titanic* carried more than the required number of lifeboats, these proved woefully inadequate for the estimated 2,227 passengers and crew members. Had every emergency boat been filled to capacity, 1,178 people could have been saved. Instead, confusion and conflict over who should be allowed to enter the precious few lifeboats resulted in several of the boats' leaving the ship filled to less than half their capacity. Passengers in some of the boats found themselves adrift with insufficient crew members, at risk of being hopelessly lost in the vast Atlantic. In all, some 702 lives were saved, but more than 1,500 people died. Had the liner been loaded to capacity (about 3,000), the death toll would have been even higher.

For many, the sinking of this unsinkable ship was not merely a shocking tragedy but a rude awakening to the hubris of the modern age. Some were horrified by the role that economic status played in who lived and who died. Although American millionaires like John Jacob Astor, Benjamin Guggenheim, and Macy's department store owner Isidor Straus went down with the ship despite their first-class status, steerage (third-class) passengers were nonetheless disproportionately among the victims. For example, of the twenty-nine children traveling first- or second-class, all but one survived, while fifty-three of the seventy-six children in steerage perished. In total figures, the percentage of crew members who went down with the ship (about 76 percent) was only slightly more than that of passengers traveling third-class (about 75 percent), while roughly 58 percent of those traveling second-class and less than 40 percent of those in first class died. Gender too played a large role in who lived and who did not. Two hundred fifty-eight men, including 139 crew members, survived, compared to 393 women, which included all but four of the women in first class. Women's demands for political equality and "Votes for Women," cynics charged, had quickly changed to cries of "Boats for Women" by those demanding special protection by virtue of their sex. In a tart response, Rheta Childe Dorr chose "Women and Children First" as the title for her 4 May 1912 *Woman's Journal* article on the exploitative nature of a Brooklyn sweatshop. The piece concluded, "The law of the sea: women and children first. The law of the land — that's different." The sinking of the *Titanic* brought into sharp focus many of the burning questions of the progressive era: As dependence upon modern machinery ever increased, were human lives, especially those of the poor, to be sacrificed on the alter of modernism and corporate profit? Were some people deserving of special treatment? All during the spring and summer of the 1912 presidential campaign the lessons of the *Titanic* were preached in sermons, debated in newspapers and on street corners. Senator William A. Smith led the American inquiries into the tragedy, calling eighty-two witnesses between 19 April and 25 May. Just as Smith's investigation came to a close, the British Board of Trade's inquiry began, lasting until 3 July. The final recommendations for increased ship safety included a provision for lifeboats for all on board, but such practical preventative measures did little to quell the suspicions of many that the sinking of the *Titanic* was God's judgment on an increasingly proud and overly materialistic people. Robert La Follette's denunciations of corporate injustice and immorality suddenly seemed to be less the rantings of a fanatic and more the reasoned warnings of a long-time expert witness.[1]

La Follette made use of the *Titanic* disaster to further specific legislation, but most of his immediate attention remained fixed on the coming election. La Follette's disappointment at Taft's nomination in 1912 ultimately manifested itself not in lethargic depression or quiet resignation but in greater heights of righteous indignation. He continued to press for presidential primaries to replace nominating conventions and devoted himself, in speeches and magazine editorials, to discrediting Roosevelt. His anti-Roosevelt campaign contributed to La Follette's growing reputation as a self-absorbed tyrant. La Follette's personal bitterness led even his supporters to warn, "Your greatest weakness is your stern refusal to deal with those who at some time may seem to have crossed you." La Follette's contempt for Roosevelt was by no means unrequited. Although the former president refrained from any public name-calling, to political intimates he referred to

La Follette with increasing bitterness as "that vindictive and unscrupulous faker" and "the most contemptible and least conscientious of all our foes."[2]

Disappointed that William Jennings Bryan had not been the Democrats' choice, La Follette nevertheless approved the rhetoric of Woodrow Wilson, especially when Wilson included a dramatic tribute to the Wisconsin senator in his campaign speeches. Wilson depicted La Follette as a lonely, heroic figure: "I have often thought of Senator La Follette climbing the mountain of privilege . . . taunted, laughed at, called back, going steadfastly on." Wilson regretted that he himself had not converted to progressivism earlier, stating, "There was no credit to come in when I came in. The whole nation had awakened." Although appreciative of this recognition, La Follette declared he would "burn no bridges for the present" by committing to any one candidate. The fact that Wilson was a Democrat bothered La Follette less than the fact that he had pledged his commitment to progressivism only a mere eighteen months before, causing La Follette to comment caustically, "I have had some experience with raw progressives who haven't shed their milk teeth."[3]

As governor of New Jersey, Wilson declared war on the bosses and enacted a variety of progressive reforms, including direct primaries, campaign regulation, a public utility commission to fix rates, and the state's first workers' compensation and antitrust laws. The Democratic platform in 1912 included a lower tariff, enforcement of antitrust laws, a federal income tax, states' rights, direct election of senators, a single presidential term, utility regulation, banking reform, workers' compensation, stricter pure food and health laws, and recognition of the independence of the Philippines. Despite its many progressive components, La Follette termed it "a pretty cheap performance." Wilson's southern origins, particularly in view of his deference to state rather than federal rights, compounded La Follette's distrust of Wilson's commitment to progressivism.[4]

Wilson believed that the federal government's task was to "sweep away special privileges and artificial barriers to the development of individual energies, and to preserve and restore competition in business," nothing more. He considered direct federal involvement (for example, giving special protection to workers or farmers) paternalistic and just as detrimental to free enterprise and open competition as the trusts. True economic freedom must be preserved.[5] Wilson was by no means blind to the plight of the human cost of industrial America. He emphasized "the cost of lives snuffed out, of energies overtaxed and broken, the fearful physical and spiritual cost to the men and women and children upon whom the dead weight and burden of it all has fallen pitilessly the years through." But for all Wilson's passionate rhetoric, La Follette found Wilson's proposed "New Freedom" hopelessly naïve: even the proposed restoration of competition could not possibly ensure the social justice measures he felt were necessary to bring about the dignity, decency, and basic fairness lacking in so many American lives. Pessimistic about the Democrats, estranged from the Republicans, La Follette was not quite a man without a party. He remained at least nominally Republican. Shortly after helping to secure Francis McGovern's reelection, however, La Follette was quick to criticize what he deemed the governor's usurpation of power, inspiring one wag to observe that La Follette "should not get sore because 'the pupil excelled the teacher.'"[6]

Not all of La Follette's energies were consumed by the 1912 elections. In August, he delivered a widely reported speech supporting postal employees' right to unionize, based on a personal investigation via a questionnaire sent to more than 12,000 railway mail clerks. The results convinced him that several rules and regulations introduced during the Roosevelt and Taft administrations had been used to deprive civil service employees of fundamental constitutional rights. According to La Follette, his inquiries so panicked officials at the post office that they opened his mail in their efforts to learn the testimony of the railway mail clerks, in a method of espionage he termed "almost Russian." During his speech to the Senate, La Follette had on his desk a package of envelopes similar, he claimed, to hundreds he had received in the same condition, showing "unmistakable signs" of having been opened and resealed. Unfortunately there is no record of those unmistakable signs being examined by an expert, for these charges are reminiscent of ones made twelve years before, when La Follette's outrage over tampered mail disappeared after officials found only one letter with any evidence of irregularities. His proposed amendment to the post office appropriations bill passed in the Senate. He had not lost his political potency entirely.[7]

Despite his indirect support of Wilson in the columns of *La Follette's Weekly*, La Follette cast a blank ballot in November. The night before the election, he proclaimed to a crowd at the famed Red Brick Gym in Madison that he was not "soured, or sore, or unhappy," despite his assertion that it was "put to me as bluntly as it could be [by Roosevelt's managers] that if I'd 'be right' I could have it [the presidency] in 1916." "But this year," he charged, "they simply wanted me to go out and see how thick the ice was." "I was deserted before I broke down," he insisted, a startling admission from a man who had previously denied, with great vehemence, that any breakdown had occurred. He claimed that he would not trade places with Taft or Roosevelt, for he alone possessed a "clean, political score, and that is what I am going to have when the bell rings and the curtain goes down." And yet he could not deny his presidential ambitions: "I may never be president; but I rather think I will."[8]

The following day brought the election of Woodrow Wilson, a man strikingly similar to La Follette in many ways. It was not just the limits of Wilson's reform agenda that would increasingly alienate La Follette. Wilson biographer Arthur S. Link gives a description of the president's brand of leadership that is remarkably in keeping with La Follette's own style: "[H]e conceived himself as the responsible leader of his party, as the only leader who could speak for it and the country. Therefore, he felt himself personally charged with the introduction and sponsorship of important legislation." In his inaugural address Wilson reviewed some of the negative effects of the recent industrial past: "The great Government we love has too often been made use of for private and selfish purposes, and those who used it had forgotten the people." That same day Wilson called for a special session of Congress to begin to remedy these wrongs via tariff reduction, trust restriction, and an overhaul of the nation's banking and currency system. He insisted on addressing the joint session in person, something no president had done since John Adams. This portentous act was reminiscent of La Follette's insistence, as governor, on personally addressing the Wisconsin legislature. Despite their shared commitment to reform, Wilson and La Follette's shared messianic self-perceptions could scarcely be expected to endear one to the other for long.[9]

During their "honeymoon" period, La Follette regarded the Wilson administration with a certain respect, if not cautious optimism. Flattered by Wilson's frequent requests for advice, La Follette rejoiced at the president's investigation into corruption within the congressional lobby surrounding the tariff issue. The president, La Follette noted jubilantly, "hurled his short-fuse missile directly at the insidious interference with tariff legislation . . . [and] it resulted in uncovering the whole works," including the "sinister work" by "evil forces" that La Follette had long charged with controlling Congress and the administration. He was further pleased by Wilson's public words of praise: "[La Follette] is strong because he studies every angle of every question. When he gets up to speak, he knows what he is talking about. When he is finished speaking, it is difficult for a man to vote against him and give any convincing reason for doing so because La Follette has presented the case from the standpoint of the man who knows."[10]

For all his expertise, La Follette was now, once again, a man virtually alone, for he continued to see all things in terms of black and white, not the innumerable shades that color the real world. He believed he was right. Nothing else, including the support of his party, mattered. Historian David

Thelen maintains that Wilson's election to the presidency marked the end of La Follette's tenure as the leader of a powerful force in Congress and caused the La Follettes to withdraw into their "supportive family life." This image of La Follette in retreat is overstated. "The original Republican progressive," reported the press, "finds himself the only real leader on that side of the Senate." Predicted the *Philadelphia Record*, "In the next three years 'Battling Bob' will be very much in the limelight." And the *New York Times* hailed La Follette's relationship with Wilson as a "revolution in politics," arguing that "under the Democratic Administration this Republican Senator will have as much to say about the party politics of the Democracy as any Democrat."[11]

Despite his first-time status as a minority member in the Senate, La Follette was instrumental in passing bills that he had either introduced or long endorsed but which had been considered too radical previously. The Democrats' income tax of 1913, for example, was influenced by La Follette's recommendation of a higher tax bracket for incomes over $100,000. During the debate over federal income tax, La Follette showcased the success of Wisconsin's state income tax. He also reminded his fellow senators of the fate that awaited those who opposed him, referring once again to the predictions he made during his denunciation of the Hepburn bill in 1906: "My warning was scorned, and a goodly percentage of those gentlemen have disappeared from their places upon this side [of the aisle] and many of their seats are occupied by men who realize that legislation must adjust itself to the new industrial conditions of this country."[12]

The 1913 passage of the seaman's bill he first introduced in 1910 brought La Follette great pleasure. In a decision reminiscent of the Dred Scott case, the Supreme Court in 1897 exempted seamen from the Thirteenth Amendment, upholding the contract of merchant sailors as "an exceptional one . . . involving . . . to a certain extent, the surrender of . . . personal liberty during the life of the contract." One of many bills La Follette supported in his efforts to protect labor, the La Follette Seaman's Bill ended this virtual enslavement of sailors. The measure abrogated binding one-year contracts and allowed sailors to quit ships (once they were docked and the cargo unloaded) at their own discretion. Among its many requirements was a provision that every vessel leaving an American port be equipped with sufficient lifeboats and rafts for all passengers and crew members. It also required that the vessel carry enough experienced seamen to assign two to each lifeboat. (The mandatory lifeboat drills aboard cruise lines today are a legacy of this bill.) The debacle of the *Titanic* proved the value of requirements previously deemed prohibitively expensive as well as unnecessary by the major shipping lines. "Travel on a well-officered vessel, manned by able seamen, with lifeboats to bear all on board," La Follette asserted in his impassioned defense of the bill, "should be as safe as travel on land."[13]

The Senate passed the bill on 23 October 1913. La Follette called it an important step in safety and fair employment practices and the best result he had achieved within the Senate excepting the Adamson–La Follette physical evaluation of railways bill, although he conceded that on the "human side [the Seaman's bill] is far and away ahead of all else." The expressions of gratitude from sailors, fishermen, and labor organizations touched him deeply, particularly the reaction of Seaman's Union president Andrew Furuseth, the former sailor who had first brought the plight of sailors to La Follette's attention in 1909 and who had called for such legislation for almost twenty years: "[Furuseth] sprang up . . . crying out — 'This finishes the work which Lincoln began.' Tears were running down his cheeks." Following passage by the House on 27 August 1914, the State Department, citing conflicts with the maritime laws of other countries and urging patience, advised Wilson to veto the bill. La Follette, Furuseth, and Senator Robert Owen made a personal appeal to Secretary of State William Jennings Bryan. Furuseth's impassioned plea persuaded Bryan, who in turn influenced Wilson. After debating the matter "very earnestly indeed," Wilson signed the bill on 4 March 1915.[14]

La Follette spent spare moments during the 1913 Senate sessions on various speaking campaigns concerning current issues. However, he seemed to value personal approval at least as much as political support. When faced with an audience requesting both his lengthy "Hamlet" speech and a political talk, La Follette gladly provided both, noting happily that this satisfied everybody. The tour provided much needed income, although La Follette was troubled by a severe cold and "bronchial trouble." Belle, worried about Bob's physical condition, hoped he could persevere and "get that helpful reaction that usually comes to you from your lecture work regardless of its difficulties."[15]

In late 1913 the La Follettes were asked to leave their rented Washington residence at 1864 Wyoming Avenue because the owner wished to occupy it. They settled in a larger house at 3320 Sixteenth Avenue, where they lived for the next ten years. Despite the family's ever-present financial woes, when La Follette's older brother William was struck by a fatal illness, Bob sent a check and instructed that "Billy" was "not to think about money or expenses *not for* one *moment*."[16]

Although La Follette broke party ranks in 1913 to vote with the Democrats on the Underwood tariff bill, the ideological distance between La Follette and Wilson widened as the president consistently maintained a minimalist approach to federal involvement in social justice issues. Wilson deemed federal child labor laws unconstitutional, for example, and refused to support the woman suffrage amendment. *La Follette's Magazine* described several of the chilly receptions Wilson held for various suffrage groups, whose members included labor leader Rose Schneiderman, minister and physician Anna Howard Shaw, and suffrage leaders Harriet Taylor Upton and Belle Case La Follette. Both Belle and Bob La Follette differed most dramatically with Wilson over issues of civil rights for African Americans. La Follette's 1913 speaking campaign took him through the South, where he observed race relations and studied the economic and educational plight of African Americans living under the iron fist of Jim Crow segregation and oppression. The picture was bleak indeed, yet Wilson's campaign promises to press for civil rights were quickly forgotten following his election. In their place came the racial segregation of federal services, openly criticized by Belle La Follette within the pages of the family magazine. Wilson ultimately succumbed to the pressures of Belle La Follette and like-minded others, taking a more moderate (albeit still racist) stance as segregation in the executive departments was checked and partially reversed by the end of 1914.[17]

In contrast to the president, Robert La Follette shared with his outspoken wife an unshaken belief that the racism of whites was the root cause of the nation's racial inequality and was especially abhorrent because it blocked access to the opportunities that should be open to all Americans. La Follette believed the nation's leaders, including the president, were obligated to formulate programs to remedy past wrongs rather than develop new ways to perpetuate white supremacy. In the following congressional session La Follette and other progressive Republicans denounced the efforts of Democrats to disqualify African Americans from federal aid to southern farmers. Wilson's racial attitudes remained fundamentally unchanged throughout his presidency, however. In 1915, Wilson would praise D. W. Griffith's *Birth of a Nation*. This first epic motion picture glorified the Ku Klux Klan while reinforcing negative stereotypes of African Americans. "It is like writing history with lightning," said the president after screening the film at the White House, "and my only regret is that it is all so terribly true."[18]

Time not taken up with Senate business and travel was consumed by La Follette's autobiography. Abandoned by his ghostwriter, La Follette endeavored unsuccessfully to engage another to create the final chapters. In order to publish the articles as a book, La Follette formed the Robert M. La Follette Company following the cancellation by "mutual consent" of his contract with Doubleday, Page & Company. Alarmed by letters from Gilson Gardner and Francis E. McGovern that contained thinly veiled threats of libel suits, Doubleday asked for and received certain revisions within the text but still made plans for a very small first edition. La Follette was outraged. He mortgaged the family farm in order to buy the printing plates. La Follette also ran his own advertising campaign. It has been generously estimated that more than 40,000 copies eventually sold, but this figure includes those volumes sent for a nominal fee to *La Follette's* subscribers, who totaled 33,708 at that time, although not all subscribers opted to receive a copy.

Even close friends feared that La Follette could not write objectively of his relationship with Roosevelt. La Follette, however, bolstered by Ray Stannard Baker's comment that the work was "a remarkably clear, calm and convincing narrative," claimed that his work was devoid of any personally colored conclusions. A number of reviewers rightly disagreed, although virtually all lauded the first ten chapters — calling them entertaining, insightful, moving, and sincere — and praised La Follette for his courage, high ideals, and devotion to the truth. The final three chapters, however, consisting of a detailed explanation of the 1912 campaign, greatly overshadowed the rest of the book, dampening the enthusiasm of many reviewers. They confessed their amazement at La Follette's assertion that he might have been nominated had Roosevelt not entered the race, and their reactions to La Follette's all-out efforts to vilify Roosevelt ranged from mild distaste to complete disgust. La Follette was branded as bitter, preachy, pompous, and rancorous. A few reviewers, however, praised the last three chapters unreservedly. One predicted, "If this arraignment of Roosevelt gains a wide circulation it will do much to alienate from [Roosevelt] the confidence of thoughtful electors in the United States." Although no libel suits were brought, Roosevelt loyalists Gifford Pinchot and Mendill McCormick publicly declared La Follette's outpourings selfish, absurd, and utterly false. Roosevelt refrained from any public reaction but continued to take potshots at La Follette privately. He confided in Wisconsin governor Francis McGovern, for example, "The worst thing I know about woman suffrage is that La Follette is for it."[19]

Despite their increasing differences, La Follette's approval of Wilson continued as the book's reviews appeared and the controversy over the events of the 1912 campaign rekindled. La Follette was particularly pleased on 31 May 1913 when the direct election of senators, the amendment he had championed for so long, became part of the Constitution. La Follette rejoiced in this important step toward eliminating the power of backroom deal makers and making instead the "will of the people . . . be the law of the land."[20] In February 1914, the relations between Wilson and La Follette remained sufficiently congenial that during a White House dinner Belle La Follette, to her great pleasure, was seated next to the president.

La Follette never completely lost his distrust for Wilson as a "green" progressive, however. The cracks in their early camaraderie, which had widened substantially over civil rights, grew with the passage of the 1913 Federal Reserve Act. The act was intended to regulate business by controlling the money supply, bringing to an end the volatile "boom" and "bust" cycles of the past. La Follette and other Republican progressives saw the measure as wholly insufficient as an attack on the power of investment bankers and proposed a number of strengthening measures, all defeated. In La Follette's eyes, the Democrats, dictated by their fear of the powerful business interests, were giving the monkeys their own banana plantation. When progressives charged that Wilson's nominees to the Federal Reserve Board looked "as if Mr. Vanderlip [president of the National City Bank of New York] has selected them," Wilson shot back that La Follette and like-minded others were irrational in their relentless pursuit of big business — "We have breathed too long the air of suspicion and distrust" — and urged that the goal should instead be for "common understanding . . . for the prosperity of co-operation and mutual trust and confidence." In this and in other issues, Wilson's strategy of working through binding Democratic caucuses prevented La Follette and his fellow progressive Republicans from achieving the balance of power, as they might have had the Democrats, who held the majority in both the House and the Senate, divided ideologically. "The existing tyrannical caucus system must be supplanted," La Follette warned even prior to Wilson's inauguration, "if we are to have real progress."[21]

In the early months of 1914, Belle's behavior increasingly resembled her husband's, as she refused to rest between her various speaking engagements. She complained of ugly squabbles with another speaker who labeled Belle "too serious" and accused her of not having any real affection for anyone save her own flesh and blood. Ostensibly Bob objected to this lengthening speaking campaign out of concern for Belle's health, although he did admit that he missed her, and her wise counsel, enormously. Relief finally came to Belle in the form of a Caribbean cruise as the guest of frequent speaking partner, Elizabeth Evans.

La Follette was troubled by more than just Belle's prolonged absence. Rumors of his poor mental health resurfaced, as did concerns about the impending bankruptcy of his magazine. In February, he suffered a month-long bout with "neuritis," followed by "gout." Upon his recovery, he was immersed in the debate over the Clayton bill, intended to "give teeth" to the old Sherman anti-trust act. Conservatives were able to water down many of the crucial anti-trust provisions, but following strenuous lobbying by American Federation of Labor president Samuel Gompers, they were forced to declare labor unions acting legally as exempt from prosecution. Although the legality of strikes and boycotts remained murky, Gompers declared the Clayton bill to be "Labor's Magna Carta." Progressives like La Follette, however, were far from reassured by Clayton, as it passed on 5 June 1914. Senator James A. Reed remarked bitterly, "When the Clayton bill was first written it was a raging lion with a mouth full of teeth. It has degenerated to a tabby cat with soft gums, a plaintive mew, and an anaemic appearance." As finally passed, the bill was criticized by both businessmen and reformers alike. It was what La Follette loathed most — a classic political compromise. It was nonetheless among the most progressive acts of the Wilson administration.[22]

Wilson, persuaded that merely outlawing trusts was insufficient, became increasingly convinced of the necessity of the kind of direct governmental involvement in business that was outlined in Roosevelt's New Nationalism. Wilson pinned his hopes for constructive interventionism on the Federal Trade Commission (FTC), brainchild of La Follette's good friend Louis Brandeis. Brandeis envisioned a board empowered to respond to public complaints of unfair methods of competition. Hearings could result in the issuance of cease-and-desist orders against businesses that were acting illegally. The commission appointed on 22 February 1915, however, was based on something quite different: Wilson's vision of "a counsellor and friend to the business world." The commissioners selected by Wilson made up what Brandeis termed "a stupid administration." Perhaps worst of all to progressives like La Follette, the FTC marked the end of Wilson's reform efforts, no matter how compromised. As far as the president was concerned, legal barriers to all business abuses had been established and after a brief period of adjustment, the New Freedom could begin in earnest. *New Republic* editor Herbert Croly spoke for many of Wilson's critics when he observed, "Any man of President Wilson's intellectual equipment who seriously asserts that the fundamental wrongs of a modern society can be easily and quickly righted as a consequence of a few laws . . . casts suspicion either upon his own sincerity or upon his grasp of the realities of modern social and industrial life."[23]

In the spring of 1914 the grim state of the La Follette finances and the impending absence of Belle, back from her cruise but scheduled to depart on another lengthy speaking tour, compounded La Follette's worries. La Follette, who had enjoyed relatively good health since his bout of illness four months earlier, was stricken suddenly late in June with an incapacitating illness that led first to the cancellation of a series of lectures and then to La Follette's absence from the Senate until the following December. Although this illness had many early markings of some of La Follette's other, more convenient periods of poor health, it proved to be extremely serious, culminating in dizziness, double vision, partial paralysis on one side, and impaired movement on the other, symptoms common among stroke victims. La Follette was very alarmed by the specter of the potentially debilitating and permanent affects of a stroke. Moreover, he was terrified that, should his condition became public knowledge, rumors of physical and mental incapacity would be impossible to quell. La Follette adamantly maintained that he suffered from a far less serious disorder, which he labeled variously as ptomaine poisoning, liver impairment, faulty digestion, and biliousness. To his daughter Fola, he explicitly denied he had suffered a stroke. Although he confided in her the severity of his symptoms, he also made a concerted effort to minimize his condition, insisting it was temporary and inconsequential.

The secrecy and denial upon which La Follette insisted kept almost everyone from learning of the severity of his illness, but it had its drawbacks as well. Belle could not cancel her prolonged speaking trip without arousing publicity and suspicion, and therefore Bob was forced to endure this long and frightening period without her comforting presence. His distress was compounded by the loss of a much needed $8,000 in canceled lecture fees, resulting in such a desperate state of affairs that he ordered the tenants at the family's Wisconsin farm to sell most of the horses in an effort to pay the interest due on the mortgage.

As in illnesses past, La Follette's aides and physicians endeavored to keep him as free from financial and political concerns as possible. Family and friends unaware of the severity of his condition nevertheless sent messages of unconditional love and support. The greatest comfort, however, came from Bobbie, whose constant companionship during the spring and summer brought his father much happiness and gratification. Bobbie's return to the University of Wisconsin in the fall left Bob in a deep depression, which even Belle's return could not ease, and the senator complained, "Evils are coming upon us in swarms: political disaster—financial destruction—friends growing critical and exacting—and sickness dogging me for months."[24]

Medical bills and other debts overwhelmed La Follette upon his recovery.[25] His magazine proved to be such a drain that Louis D. Brandeis advised La Follette's friends, "We must try to free the Senator from this . . . burden." When Belle suggested that they allow the publication to fold, Bob responded, "Well, if I do I will announce that I am going to quit politics altogether. It is all there is to depend on in Wisconsin." To stop publication would be, Belle reluctantly agreed, a "declaration of surrender and failure which [would be] worse than death to him." La Follette grudgingly agreed to reduce the magazine to a monthly rather than a weekly production. Even at the height of the magazine's popularity the number of subscribers remained less than 40,000, while magazines such as *McCall's* and *Collier's* enjoyed circulations of more than a million by 1914. Nonetheless, by August of that year, according to Gilbert Roe, "next to his family and friends," the paper was "the dearest thing to Bob in life." La Follette continued his efforts to use *La Follette's* to political advantage, directing that editions expressing his position on key issues be delivered free of charge to each member of Congress. His need for a permanent record of vindication — a legacy of explanations of his various positions — outweighed his desire for financial solvency or reduced stress. At least on the pages of his magazine, La Follette was still center stage, an unwavering warrior in the battle to do right.[26]

By September 1914, despair over events in Wisconsin dominated the pages of *La Follette's* and preoccupied its editor. Although La Follette had endorsed Thomas Morris, Governor Francis McGovern won the senatorial nomination. While La Follette's relationship with McGovern had become strained to the breaking point, his greatest distress was reserved for the governor's race. With the progressive vote split nearly equally between two candidates, stalwart Emanuel Philipp emerged as the Republican nominee. A horrified La Follette predicted "*the end of progressive* Wisconsin for a *decade.*" Despite his still fragile health and dismal financial status, La Follette actually considered dropping out of the Senate and running, once again, for the governorship. Many in Wisconsin considered him the "only one" who could "save" the state.[27]

As his dissatisfaction with the Wilson administration increased, so did La Follette's feelings of ineffectualness on the national level, heightening the attraction of a return to the most powerful position in his home state, where people were dependably appreciative of his efforts. In short, although a return to the governorship would have been, to conventional political thinking, a step backward, it remained a temptation for La Follette. It took a strongly worded letter from a horrified Gilbert Roe to convince La Follette of the futility of sacrificing his health and his future in the U.S. Senate for an effort to appoint himself "sole guardian" of the state of Wisconsin. La Follette accepted the logic of such objections and, citing doctor's orders, declined to enter the race, but, observed Belle, the decision was a difficult one: "It is so hard for him to adjust himself to the thought of letting the situation go by default, of not doing the thing that has the greatest chance of saving the state."[28]

La Follette continued to pull no punches in his assessments of Wisconsin politics within the pages of *La Follette's* and wherever else he wielded influence, enraging his political enemies. As one letter to the editor put it, "La Follette won the confidence of our people by his opposition to boss rule and he will meet his Waterloo if he continues to dominate state affairs as a boss. From what appears in the [*Milwaukee State*] *Journal* one would think that the destiny of the state and nation rested on the La Follettes." His critics also charged La Follette with hypocrisy, pointing out that although while governor, "La Follette resented any effort of Senator Spooner to take part in state affairs," once he became senator himself, he refused to honor such separations of power. Francis McGovern complained, "Our Senior Senator has assumed the role of dictator here; and until the question of whether we are political serfs or free men is finally settled here in Wisconsin, no other issue can receive much consideration." This propensity to turn on the loyal lieutenants of a previous era highlights La Follette's inability to share the limelight as well as his tendency to see himself alone as the arbitrator of all things political, especially in regard to his home state. Subordinates who acquired some stature of their own beyond his political patronage ran a very large risk of incurring the wrath of their former mentor and boss over differences real, imagined, or exaggerated. La Follette's repeated attacks contributed to McGovern's loss (by less than 1,000 votes) to Democrat Paul Husting. For governor, La Follette endorsed independent progressive candidate John J. Blaine. The triumph of the conservative Philipp over Blaine was a bitter blow to La Follette, the splintering of progressive Republicans in his beloved state echoing the bitter strife within the national ranks of the party. Theodore Roosevelt went so far as to proclaim that progressivism had run its course and wrote dryly that in Wisconsin the dog "had returned to its vomit!" In fact, surprisingly little was reversed during Philipp's three gubernatorial terms, which were generally moderate in nature.[29]

As La Follette's health improved, he embarked on a vigorous and lengthy speaking tour to fulfill contract obligations and reduce his debts. Belle worried that his stress over their finances might become debilitating and rejoiced when he enjoyed "fine meetings." His tour was marred only by minor throat problems and anxiety over reports of Bobbie's tonsillitis and the beginnings of the boy's mysterious and tenacious streptococcic infection. The 1916 Senate election loomed ahead. Wisconsin, under the administration of Governor Philipp, had become increasingly complaisant, and La Follette was eager to both vindicate his former record and revitalize progressivism in his home state. He worked fourteen-hour days in preparation for the campaign. His thoroughness paid off, as his five-month speaking tour (interrupted periodically by trips to Washington for congressional sessions) found him, he confided in Belle, "feeling good and . . . making good speeches and bringing the old fellows back into line." La Follette's progressive colleagues in the Senate supplied gratifyingly powerful tributes, calling his leadership crucial to the progressive movement. The supportive presence of his two sons bolstered La Follette, but the rewarding campaign was not without its grim reminders of unfortunate speeches past. La Follette's opponent, warhawk M. G. Jeffris, not only denounced the incumbent for his pacifism in light of the war in Europe but quoted a press report stating that La Follette "talks and acts and seems to think like a lunatic in an asylum or an idiot in a home for the feeble minded."[30]

In February 1916, La Follette announced his candidacy for the presidency to a group of progressive Republicans. At sixty-one, the aging La Follette was not wholly content pursuing a variety of smaller, separate issues and seemed compelled to strive for the single highest goal, albeit hopelessly out of reach. Despite his claims to the contrary, on La Follette's scale of values, a presidential candidacy, no matter how slim its chances, placed higher than whatever concrete accomplishments he could achieve as senator. It is unlikely that the perennial nature of La Follette's appearances as a presidential candidate did him any major political harm: his commitment to serve the people of Wisconsin rarely conflicted outright with his efforts to act in ways that he believed enhanced his reputation as a potential president. However, his predictable and fruitless bids for the White House earned him little new respect and certainly cost him time, energy, and money. Former La Follette intimate Nils Haugen termed them "unfortunate" for both candidate and party, for to La Follette such campaigns were never wholly symbolic. When forced to admit that there was no realistic hope for victory, La Follette became a "carping critic" of all other administrations and "entirely incapable of team work." La Follette's personal needs repeatedly superseded political and practical expediency.[31]

La Follette's presidential platform for 1916 illustrates the nation's increasing preoccupation with the Great War raging in Europe. Already on record with an unsuccessful proposal to oppose conscription and broaden exemptions for conscientious objectors, La Follette opposed war profiteering and supported American nonintervention. "It is hardly consistent," he noted, "that we should pray for peace and at the same time supply the ammunition to continue the war." Calling trafficking in arms by American businesses "revolting" and "repugnant in every moral sense," La Follette decried American willingness to "sacrifice human lives for private gain." The La Follette Peace Resolution of 1915 called for nationalization of the manufacture of all war munitions, an embargo on the exportation of arms and ammunition, and a conference of neutral nations to cooperate for peace and establish a tribunal for the settlement of international disputes. Acknowledging it "folly to pretend that the mere calling of [a peace] conference will end hostilities," La Follette nevertheless stridently maintained, "It devolves upon the peoples of the world" still at peace to "bring about a cessation of hostilities through offers of mediation." Despite favorable press attention, the resolution died in committee.[32]

La Follette's antiwar stance was entirely consistent with the record on foreign affairs he had been building as senator. In 1907, he broke ranks with fellow Republicans when he voted for Philippine independence. In 1911, he declared himself essentially a man of peace and began denouncing profit-driven plans to intervene in Mexico, dedicating many pages of *La Follette's* to the issue. Under Wilson's administration, he found plenty to denounce. Both La Follette and Wilson sincerely desired to spread democracy, but only for Wilson did that end justify virtually any means, including commitment of U.S. troops. La Follette's Mexican policy, called "benevolent interventionism" by one scholar, eschewed both armed intervention and territorial expansion while supporting nonmilitary pressure on the Huerta regime by the United States. Although La Follette supported the strengthening of liberal and democratic forces, he proclaimed that the rights of foreigners to govern themselves according to their own standards were as sacred as American sovereignty within U.S. borders.[33] La Follette saw profit as the real reason behind large-scale business support for the Wilson administration's intervention in country after country in Latin America. While La Follette continued to highlight the role of selfish rather than humane American motives and deplored use of the U.S. military, he was not absolute in his pacifism. Once troops were deployed at Vera Cruz, for example, he urged within the pages of *La Follette's*, "Let it be known in every capital of the world that the President has the support of a united nation." But he followed this plea with another, to "withdraw the armed forced at the earliest possible moment consistent with national honor." Less than two years later, La Follette denounced Wilson's actions and their resultant bloodshed: "If the President has the power to order forces of the United States to invade a foreign country, capture a city, and slay its people, as in the case of Vera Cruz, he has the absolute power to make war at will."[34]

When war broke out in Europe in 1914, La Follette applauded the president's stated program of strict neutrality and opposed the conservative Republicans' call for Army and Navy appropriations. By 1916, his assertion that the larger newspapers were influenced by the interests behind the preparedness propaganda merited him much derision and a fresh revival of press stories that he had "barely escaped the asylum." One of his critics, however, acknowledged, "One hardly knows whether to pity La Follette or admire his bravery." The *New York Times* harbored no such mixed feelings: "Wisconsin should get rid at last of this noisy 'reformer' . . . this miscellaneous agitator, this fetterer of American shipping." Urged the *Times*, "Let the Badgers give him back to the tents of the Chautauqua and *La Follette's*

*La Follette in 1917: A senator in search of a cause. (National Archives)*

*Magazine* ... [for] he has ceased to be even amusing." La Follette instead remained steadfast in his pursuit of reform. He was the only Republican to approve the Adamson bill, a measure which, by making the eight-hour day for railroad workers compulsory, averted a nationwide strike and paved the way for general acceptance of the eight-hour workday.[35]

Although La Follette did manage to win a few delegates to the 1916 Republican convention, his real victory came in the Senate race, where he carried sixty-nine of seventy-one counties and won by the largest margin then received by any candidate in Wisconsin. La Follette characteristically denied that he regarded the "splendid endorsement" as personal and instead claimed to view it "merely as an expression of the confidence of the people in the progressive cause." This claim was compromised by the simultaneous reelection of Philipp to the governor's chair, albeit by 58 percent of the vote compared to La Follette's 65 percent. Longtime Wisconsin supporters loved Bob La Follette and admired his unimpeachable integrity and dedication to reform, especially his actions on behalf of farmers and labor. His antiwar stance gained him new support, particularly among Germans. And yet Wisconsin voters were not willing to sacrifice Philipp's proposed tax cuts merely to please their senior senator.[36]

La Follette's enormous personal popularity within his home state was secure. At the federal level, however, his progressive agenda seemed in great danger of stalling out altogether, despite the support engendered by its various individual components. Wilson's New Freedom had usurped (and squandered) much of the progressive momentum that remained even after the Republican debacle at the 1912 presidential election. La Follette's threadbare party loyalties continued to play a weak second to his unique political agenda. When the Republican convention met in Chicago and declined to adopt La Follette's various peace proposals, he refused to endorse the platform or its presidential candidate, Charles Evans Hughes. The rebuff by his own party did not deter him, announced La Follette, noting that of his thirty-one proposals rejected at the 1908 and 1912 conventions, twenty-five had since been enacted into law. La Follette radiated a confident determination that perseverance in pursuing righteous objectives was the key to political success. On the eve of the bitter controversy surrounding the entry of the United States into World War I, La Follette was ripe for a dramatic, righteous cause to revitalize progressive idealism, invigorate his politics, and save himself from potential obscurity.

# 14: WORLD WAR I
## A LITTLE GROUP OF WILLFUL MEN

I n 1916, La Follette assigned much of the blame for the mounting calls for military preparedness to the larger newspapers of the country. He declared them to be under the influence of the advertising dollars of those who stood to profit most from such a program. He supported his accusations by printing in *La Follette's Magazine* a list of the Navy League's sponsors that read "like a Who's Who of American corporate finance." On 21 July, the *Philadelphia Inquirer* derided La Follette's various charges under the headline "Once More the Wisconsin Humbug." The article revived allegations made following his 1912 Philadelphia speech: "From that meeting he went into retirement with his intellect broken"; he "certainly paid the price" for "burden[ing] himself with a pack of lies . . . barely escap[ing] the asylum." Such blatant efforts to bury La Follette persisted but were ineffective. Disappointed with Wilson's limited reforms, La Follette and his fellow progressives tirelessly promoted a myriad of progressive legislative proposals. Despite many stalls at the federal level, progressivism experienced a culmination of sorts in the years just prior to the U.S. entry into World War I: for all its infighting and competing agendas, the movement gathered momentum as it crossed party lines and inspired thousands of reform measures on the local and state levels.[1]

La Follette's pride in his many legislative triumphs rivaled his sense of urgency at how much remained in dire need of reform. Five days after the *Inquirer* article appeared, for example, he decried Frederick W. Taylor's "scientific management" for "grind[ing] the last ounce of sweat" out of American workers, driving them "to the breaking down point." After observing the plight of African Americans in the nation's South, La Follette also decried the evils of racism, concluding, "If the Lord would only let us out of the Filipino mess and keep us out of Mexico, we might in the course of time pay off the own to the black man."[2]

The war that erupted in Europe in 1914 offended all progressive sensibilities. Science, education, and enlightened understanding were expected to solve foreign as well as domestic problems. Treaties were supposed to replace wars as reason replaced force. A horrified Woodrow Wilson urged the American public to be "impartial in thought as well as action" concerning a war "with which we have nothing to do, whose causes cannot touch us." La Follette heartily agreed. Five years earlier La Follette had written, "War and rumors are a dreadful diversion for peoples demanding juster distribution of wealth. War is the money changer's opportunity, and the social reformer's doom." Once the war in Europe began, he believed firmly that the real danger to his country lay not, as his colleagues increasingly asserted, in a lack of preparedness but in the tide of pro-war sentiment based on commercial greed lurking beneath a veneer of patriotism. If America entered the war, he believed it would be at the expense of young lives for the profit of American business. Even the compromised restrictions imposed on businesses by the Wilson administration would be abandoned as winning the war against powers abroad would supersede winning the war at home against monopolies, inhumane living and working conditions, and abuse of political power. Moreover, this foreign war would be financed not by the industries that stood to profit the most but by American taxpayers who could afford it the least. In 1914, La Follette and Wilson were united in their fear that progressive reform would be lost if America entered the war and the struggle for democracy would be set back a generation.[3]

Beginning in 1914, La Follette found himself riding on a new wave of public support inspired by his renewed efforts on behalf of labor, a position strengthened by his antiwar stance, which was shared by most but by no means all of the population. He gained renewed popularity within the Senate as well, as least among those characterized as "peace progressives," an unofficial group whose membership remained almost constantly in flux. Prior to U.S. entry to the war, the peace progressives shared three main beliefs: that a forceful American policy toward East Asia and Latin America served the interests opposed to domestic reform; that imperialism led to costly and unnecessary defense expenditures; and that American involvement in the European conflict should be avoided at all costs.[4]

Officially the United States remained isolated politically prior to 1917, but economically it eagerly profited from the war, with Allied trade far outstripping trade with the Central Powers. When Great Britain instituted an illegal naval blockade, American trade with the Central Powers declined dramatically. At the same time, the United States made tremendous efforts to take over the traditionally European-dominated foreign commerce disrupted by the war, particularly that with Latin America. Loans to the Allied Powers from private sources, including a $50 million loan to France from the House of Morgan in 1915, further eroded American claims of strict neutrality. Such partisan actions did not, of course, escape the notice of the Central Powers. German submarine warfare, stepped up to combat Britain's control of the seas, revealed the antiquated nature of the nineteenth-century international law obligating a belligerent warship to warn a passenger or merchant ship before attacking. German U-boat attacks ultimately provided powerful arguments to advocates of American entry into the war.[5]

Germany announced its submarine blockade of the British Isles on

4 February 1915, stating that it would target even neutral ships to keep supply lines open. Wilson warned Germany that it would be held to "strict accountability" for the destruction of American ships or lives. The following month an American died in the sinking of the British liner *Falaba*. Some advisers urged Wilson to respond with an official, strongly worded protest charging a breach of international law. Others, including Secretary of State William Jennings Bryan, worked to put out the flames rather than fan them. Endeavoring to ensure that no additional Americans fell casualty to further U-boat attacks, they urged the president to prohibit Americans from traveling on belligerent ships in war zones. They were not the only ones eager to keep the United States out of the war: Germany took out space in American newspapers warning that all ships in the war zone were liable to destruction.

On 7 May 1915, a German submarine sank the British luxury liner *Lusitania*. In the greatest loss of life in a marine disaster since the *Titanic*, nearly 1,200 people, including 128 Americans, died in the eighteen minutes it took the ship, unarmed but carrying war supplies, to sink. Anticipating the clamor for war, Wilson responded, "There is such a thing as a man being too proud to fight. There is such a thing as a nation being so right that it does not need to convince others by force." In view of Germany's "murderous offenses," an outraged Theodore Roosevelt responded, "It is well to remember there are things worse than war" and concluded "peace is worth having only when it is the hand-maiden of international righteousness and national self-respect." Roosevelt declared American entry into the war a sacred calling. Years earlier he had proclaimed publicly, "No triumph of peace is quite so great as the supreme triumph of war" and confided privately in a friend, "I should welcome almost any war, for I think this country needs one." In justifying war with Spain in 1899, Roosevelt had warned that an American refusal to fight would mark the end of the nation's greatness: "Are we still in the prime of our lusty youth, still at the beginning of our glorious manhood, to sit down among the outworn people, to take our place with the weak and the craven? A thousand times no." Belle La Follette, reviewing Roosevelt's past pronouncements on the glories of war declared, "The trouble with Mr. Roosevelt is that he is intoxicated with a false idea of War."[6]

By 1915, no longer in the political limelight he so thoroughly enjoyed, Roosevelt divided his considerable energies between advocating American entry into the war and denouncing those "active agents of the devil" who opposed it. While the majority of Americans may have shared Roosevelt's outrage over the loss of American lives, they remained unwilling to commit to war. William Jennings Bryan, for example, fervent in his desire not to exacerbate tensions that might culminate in a declaration of war, resigned as secretary of state rather than sign a note demanding that Germany abandon unrestricted submarine warfare, disavow the sinking, and compensate for American lives. La Follette defended Bryan's actions. Despite all official reports to the contrary, La Follette remained convinced that the *Lusitania* carried munitions. Individuals voluntarily on an armed ship in time of war, he reasoned, shared the same risks with those remaining voluntarily in a foreign land during a revolution. Roosevelt responded, "The United States Senator who [holds such a view] . . . occupies a position precisely and exactly as base and as cowardly (and I use those words with scientific precision) as if his wife's face were slapped on the public streets and the only action he took was to tell her to stay home." The German ambassador's pledge on 1 September that Germany would not attack ocean liners without warning temporarily relieved tensions both at home and abroad. But even as opponents of the war celebrated this victory, they were forced to acknowledge that both trade and travel in the modern age made true isolationism virtually impossible.[7]

La Follette opposed Wilson's 4 November 1915 concession to military preparedness advocates, a call for enlarging and reorganizing the army. Wilson's campaign slogan "He kept us out of war" temporarily placated La Follette the following year. News of poisonous gas, barbed wire fences, flame throwers, and all the unspeakable horrors of trench warfare bolstered the convictions of the anti-interventionists while further inflaming the war advocates. Despite the public's continual exposure to escalating calls for war from the press, especially in interviews with the increasingly vitriolic Roosevelt, La Follette remained convinced that the vast majority of Americans continued to oppose U.S. entry into the war. On 29 April 1916, he introduced a measure authorizing an advisory referendum that would allow the public to make their opinions known to Congress in times of war or impending war. This measure shared the ill fate of La Follette's 1915 peace resolution. As spring turned to summer, he endeavored to squelch continued military, especially naval, preparedness measures, identifying them as serving "the commercial, industrial, and imperialistic schemes of the great financial masters of this country." Here too La Follette's efforts ended in failure. By fall he was asking, "How long can we maintain a semblance of real neutrality while we are supplying the Allies with munitions of war and the money to prosecute war?"[8]

Despite his many defeats, La Follette worked tirelessly to promote legislation, both foreign and domestic, that he deemed in keeping with progressive goals. A rare but limited success came on 6 September 1916 with the passage of a revenue bill ensuring that the bulk of the tax burden for financing the new military buildup would fall on the upper economic classes. In addition to the House provision that doubled the normal income tax (from 1 to 2 percent), the Senate bill increased the surtax on incomes over $20,000 to the maximum 13 percent; increased the estate tax to a maximum of 10 percent; levied a new tax on corporation capital, surplus, and undivided profits; and increased the tax on gross receipts of munitions industries to 12.5 percent. La Follette remained unrelenting in his demands that American industries stop growing in power and wealth at the expense of human lives.[9]

President Wilson too tried to apply progressive ideals to foreign affairs. In his plan for a negotiated settlement between the various belligerents, he proposed on 22 January 1917 a "peace without victory" in which, for once, the victor would not receive the spoils of war. There would be no annexations or indemnities but rather open markets and cooperation. Germany not only rejected this peace overture but, anticipating a quick victory, announced on 31 January its resumption of unrestricted submarine warfare. Wilson responded by breaking diplomatic relations with Germany. As American shipping ground to a near halt, pressures mounted to arm U.S. merchant ships.

Although La Follette led the applause following Wilson's "peace without victory" address, his waning admiration disappeared completely as Wilson's firmly neutral stance gradually gave way. When Wilson announced his breaking of diplomatic relations with Germany on 3 February, La Follette joined with former secretary of state Bryan in an unsuccessful attempt to draft a resolution to discuss the war, which the two hoped would provide a cooling-off period and delay if not prevent American entry. When the vote was called in the Senate to endorse the president's decision, La Follette was temporarily absent from the chamber. He returned just in time, furious at having been denied the opportunity to deliver his prepared speech and raging that he was the victim of a conspiracy to keep him silent. When criticized by the press for his opposition vote, La Follette maintained, "Nothing matters so long as we are doing what is right. That's the only thing that lasts."[10]

On 20 February, Bobbie arrived in Washington to assist his father. The following day the younger La Follette wrote in disgust of Wilson's virtual "executive feudal kingly prerogative in dealing with civilians, making it possible for him to suppress almost any kind of meeting, punish any sort of criticism, and in short do all and more than the Kaiser, Lloyd George and the President of France combined might do under similar conditions." Six days later Wilson asked Congress for authority to arm merchant ships, enabling them to fire upon attackers "to safeguard the rights of peoples at peace." In defending this move almost certain to bring about an exchange of fire between American and belligerent ships and, ultimately, war, the president stressed the disastrous impact of submarine warfare on American commerce. Hearing a plea for what he considered not only an unconstitutional usurpation of congressional powers but a call to war reduced to economic terms, La Follette, vigorously chewing gum to relieve some of the tension of the moment, threw up his hands in despair.[11]

A number of important war-related bills were to be decided by the Sixty-fourth Congress before it adjourned on 4 March. La Follette, flattered at Gilbert Roe's assertion that "the question of peace or war rests more largely with you than with any other man in the country," organized a filibuster among the peace progressives to prevent the armed ship bill from coming to a vote. Aware that a special session would likely be called were he successful, La Follette believed that if American intervention could be avoided during the few weeks between sessions it might be avoided altogether. Also, he desired a special session of Congress during the summer months as a check on any further attempts by Wilson to overstep presidential bounds. Delaying tactics and speeches (La Follette spoke at length on his proposed tax amendments) began on 27 February. Late the next day, La Follette proposed that the Armed Ship Bill "lie over" until Friday, 2 March, while the Senate debated other matters on Thursday, 1 March. His exhausted colleagues agreed.[12]

By the time they reconvened at noon the next day, all hell had broken loose. Anti-German feeling reached a fever pitch as news of the Zimmermann telegram dominated headlines across the nation. In this bizarre communication to the German minister in Mexico, the German foreign secretary offered Mexico much of the territory it had lost in the American Southwest in 1848 in return for Mexico's joining with Germany in a war against the United States. Wilson, aware of the note since 24 or 25 February, chose not to release it to the press until late on 29 February. Outrage over Germany's treacherous attempt to inveigle Mexico into the war contributed to the House's passage of the Armed Ship Bill by a vote of 403–13. The Senate's vote was next.[13]

Almost unbearable tension filled the final twenty-six continuous hours of the session. Never one to shy from conflict, La Follette found himself, in a defining moment of his life, the key player in a showdown between war and peace. The final hours of the filibuster he organized in the early days of March, in a desperate attempt to keep his nation from war, were some of the most emotion laden in American history, capturing the world's attention. Bill supporters, desirous of putting their own views on record, were loathe to speak, for in so doing they inadvertently aided their opponents by using up valuable time. In the end, however, those who favored the bill spoke longer than those who opposed it. In the session's final hours, his fellow insurgents held the floor to allow La Follette the honor of speaking last. La Follette, "looking fresh and eager," wandered around the floor several times during the various speeches, gloating over the success of the filibuster and taunting his opponents by announcing he had a "great speech" to deliver. His attitude even more than his antiwar position so enraged his opponents that they formally introduced a list of speakers to precede him, thereby preventing him the opportunity to take the floor. Tempers, including La Follette's own, were running high. Senators stood toe to toe, screaming at each other as others hissed and booed. Luke Lea of Tennessee, the presiding senator, warned La Follette of the list of speakers. Lea also warned La Follette that he had heard rumors of potential violence on the Senate floor. Recognizing a shutout, La Follette "boiled within" and declared that if he were denied his right to speak under the rules of the Senate "someone would get hurt." La Follette instructed Bobbie to retrieve from his office his traveling bag. Its contents included a revolver, which had for years been carried for protection. Bobbie fetched the bag but opted not to volunteer the information that, fearful of his father's temper, he had removed the revolver before placing the bag just outside the office door.[14]

The rumors of violence were soon substantiated. When La Follette began his official demands for the floor, he was rushed by several Democrats, led by Kentucky's Ollie James. Oregon's Harry Lane also entered the fray. According to the account Lane told La Follette the next day, Lane was gripping a rat-tail file inside his pocket, having procured this potential weapon in response to a tip that James might physically attack La Follette. As James rose from his seat, Lane saw that he was carrying a gun. Although Lane was ravaged by the illness that would kill him three months later, he assured La Follette that he had been prepared to put the file down James's collarbone and into his heart. (La Follette kept the file on his desk for years.) In the midst of the yelling and shoving, La Follette, raising his voice "almost to a shriek," shouted, "I will continue on this floor until I complete my statement unless somebody carries me off, and I should like to see the man who will do it!"[15]

The correspondence between father and son during the final hours of the congressional session demonstrates clearly how close the senator came to a total loss of self-control. One of Bobbie's notes ran, "Please, please, be calm — you know what the press will do — remember Mother," and another pleaded, "Daddy, I expect you to make your protest but there must be a limit to the lengths which you can go. . . . You can not afford to get into a physical argument or be arrested by the Sergeant at Arms for misconduct. You are noticeably & extremely excited. For God's sake make your protest

& prevent passage of [the] bill if you like, but if previous question is made & sustained do not try to fight Senate physically. I am almost crazy with strain." La Follette planned to deliver a highly detailed justification of his antiwar views. According to Senator George Norris, also instrumental in the filibuster, the opposition's success in blocking his speech affected La Follette more deeply than in any other of his historic battles. In the session's final minutes, La Follette clutched a brass cuspidor, "his face contorted with anger, writhed in the humiliation of being unable to get the floor." "I'm going to hit [presiding officer Joseph Robinson, who had replaced Lea] with this spittoon," he cried. Norris grabbed him, shouting, "Don't do it, Bob,— for God's sake, don't do it. They're licked — don't give them the satisfaction."[16]

Although prevented from speaking, La Follette received recognition as the leader of the successful filibuster, a temporary victory nonetheless deeply satisfying. Before finally going to bed, he dashed off a quick telegram to Belle: "Fought it through to finish. Feeling here intense. I must take the gaff for a time." Belle immediately showered her husband with the sweetest of all rewards, her unqualified praise: "It is my heartfelt conviction that you have rendered the world the greatest service it has ever come to you to render and that you have used the power and opportunity that was yours for humanity and democracy. . . . You are sure to be terribly maligned and misunderstood and probably the general public will never get on to the absurdity and dangerous trend of Wilson's usurpation of power, but oh, what a deep satisfaction wells up from within that all these long years of discipline and hardening have made you ready to meet this crisis and stem the awful tide of destruction without fear of its consequences to yourself." Others added to her tribute. Labor leader Eugene V. Debs declared, "Let the Wall Street wolves and their prostitute press howl. The people will sustain you and history will vindicate you." The *New York Mail* predicted, "The twelve men who stood up in the Senate against clamor and ridicule in defense of the Constitution of the United States shall be honored by future generations of Americans when the names of the nondescripts who revile them will only be remembered for their weakness and ignorance." Such words confirmed La Follette's conviction of righteousness and helped to sustain him during even the darkest ensuing days. Confidently he announced, "*Whatever the cost* of my course — never have I been in a better position to render so great a service," and pledged to "*serve the real interests* of *our own country with all my might* as the *call comes.*"[17]

Not everyone shared La Follette's enthusiasm. A frustrated Woodrow Wilson denounced the Wisconsin senator and his associates angrily: "A little group of willful men, representing no opinion but their own, have rendered the great Government of the United States helpless and contemptible."[18] Wilson's phrase "little group of willful men" was intentionally vague, for Wilson desired to indict not only the twelve senators responsible for the filibuster but also to tar with the same brush the members of his own party whom he knew shared in the desire to prevent the measure.[19] The president's open castigation of those who had thwarted his will was calculated to set off a firestorm of denunciation. La Follette, anticipating the tone but not the intensity of the hostile press, warned his family, "You must be prepared for me to get some criticism. . . . I expect it as a matter of course." Such a warning proved woefully inadequate in the face of an onslaught of bitter and voluminous outpourings of criticism and hate seldom matched in the country's history. Across the nation, headlines proclaimed that La Follette's actions united the whole country against him. The primary target of Theodore Roosevelt's seemingly inexhaustible supply of invective, La Follette was, according to the former president, a "skunk" who "ought to be hung." His adversaries compared La Follette to Benedict Arnold and Judas Iscariot, denounced him as a traitor, and declared he should be sent to an internment camp. They portrayed the senator as a pervert, lunatic, madman, and devil who humiliated the nation motivated by his secret pact with Germany. The subject of countless political cartoons, La Follette was portrayed so openly as being in league with Germany that his lawyer uncharacteristically advised he bring a libel suit. Belle called the anti–La Follette reports and cartoons, printed alongside stories of the necessity of American entry into the war, unrepresentative of the underlying sentiment of the masses. She conceded, however, "Just as it is intended to, it *intimidates* folks [and] makes them fearful of seeming to be unpatriotic unless they join in the rush for war."[20]

For La Follette's critics, support for the war quickly emerged as the sole measure of patriotism. According to the *Cincinnati Times Star*, for example, "The vast majority of senators are patriotic Americans. They should use their power and deprive La Follette and his little group of perverts the opportunity of continuing to drag our flag in the dust and to make this great American Republic ridiculous and without honor in the eyes of the world." The press was not alone in its desire to silence La Follette. On 8 March, the Senate passed cloture, establishing that sixteen senators could successfully bring a debate to an end if their motion received the approval of two-thirds of those voting. Only two senators joined La Follette, who called the move "a blow to liberty" and the first step toward the suppression of free speech in war time, in voting against it. The following day, citing an 1819 piracy statute, Wilson announced the arming of merchant ships at his command. A week later, the international tumult grew, as Russian workers, homemak-

*"The Only Adequate Reward": Rollin Kirby's apology for this 7 March 1917 attack on
La Follette in the* New York World *came some sixteen years after La Follette's death. Kirby's
cartoon was one of many depicting La Follette as a traitor to his country.*

ers, and soldiers rose up against Czar Nicholas II and replaced the monarchy with a republic led by Alexander Kerensky. But for Americans the sinking of five U.S. ships in the North Atlantic constituted the month's most earthshaking news. The resulting fury, combined with the advancement of the special session by two weeks, extinguished any hope among La Follette and the other antiwar senators that American entry could be avoided.[21]

On 2 April 1917, Wilson asked the special session of Congress for a declaration of war. La Follette, the American flag pin sported by his pro-war colleagues conspicuously absent from his lapel, chewed gum vigorously throughout Wilson's address and was one of the few to remain seated at its conclusion. If possible, hostility toward La Follette increased on 4 April when he spoke against the war on the Senate floor. His colleagues, already enraged by George Norris's accusation that they were putting "a dollar sign on the American flag," grimly endured La Follette's four-hour denunciation of the various pro-war arguments. La Follette criticized the "irresponsible and war-crazed press" for publishing "the most infamous and scurrilous libels on the honor of the Senators who opposed" the armed ship bill. He also specifically defended himself against Wilson's accusation of "willfulness," claiming "no graver charge could be made" against a senator "than that his official action was the result of a 'willful' — that is, an unreasoned and perverse — purpose." La Follette included portions of his undelivered speech opposing the armed ship bill. Ridiculing charges of unprovoked German aggression, La Follette countered, "Germany has been patient with us." La Follette also highlighted the many different varieties of progressivism when he scoffed at the president's assertion that the war should be entered to "make the world safe for democracy." He attacked the goal of destroying Germany's monarchical government, noting that it was the system that also ruled Great Britain. La Follette read into the *Congressional Record* excerpts from some of the 15,000 telegrams and letters he had received from people in forty-four states. Nine out of ten signatories, he announced, offered an unqualified endorsement of his views, and many included the tallies of various referendums and polls revealing the overwhelming opposition of American voters to entry into the war.[22]

At the end of his speech, according to Amos Pinchot, La Follette "stood in silence, tears running down his face . . . the grief and anger of this despairing man like that of a person who had failed to keep his child from doing itself irreparable harm." Gilson Gardner said to Pinchot, "That is the greatest speech we will either of us ever hear." Mississippi senator John Sharp Williams responded differently — with a scathing attack filling over seven columns in the *Congressional Record*. Williams called La Follette's speech pro-German, anti-American, anti-Wilson, and anti-Congress. He referred to La Follette as a better German than the head of the German parliament and as "a knave or a fool." Scorning La Follette's assertions that the war was sought only by profiteers, Williams thundered, "Wall Street and the money power of the capitalists did not sink the *Lusitania*." Calling La Follette deaf to the "groans of American men and women and children, as they sank after a murderous and unwarned attack," Williams charged, "There are some things worse than war and there are some things worse than death, and one of them is to have self-contempt [because] you are a pusillanimous, degenerate coward." Williams accused La Follette of wanting to "pose as the last, if not the chief actor" in every Senate "drama" and generated derisive laughter at La Follette's expense when he charged that "the man who can not distinguish between the character of the violations of our neutral rights committed by Great Britain and by . . . Germany has not sense enough to distinguish between a prize court and a torpedo."[23]

The following day in the House of Representatives, William La Follette echoed his cousin's plea for nonintervention. The Washington state congressman conceded that Germany's acts of submarine warfare were reprehensible, but he also noted the loss of American lives due to British tactics, asking, "Is a life lost by the destruction of a vessel, coming on contact with a floating mine less dear than one lost on a vessel sunk by a torpedo fired by a submarine? Is the water less cold or wet?" Unmoved, the House approved the declaration of war by a vote of 373–50; the final vote in the Senate was 82–6. Only Senators Gronna, Vardaman, Norris, Lane, and Stone joined La Follette in his opposition to U.S. entry.[24]

Amid the resulting chaos came many messages of support. John Jay Gould praised La Follette as a patriot promoting government by regulation, not domination, and suffragist leader Harriet Taylor Upton assured him that the majority of women in the country supported him despite all the misrepresentation of his actions and motives by the press. A typical letter of support praised La Follette's courage, calling him the spokesman of the inarticulate public, the great majority of whom, the author assured La Follette, opposed the war. California freshman senator Hiram W. Johnson exempted La Follette specifically from his indictment of "the superficiality, the hollowness, the pretense and the hypocrisy" permeating the Senate during the controversy. For the most part, however, Congress, the press, and American business were outraged. Even the public was by no means unanimous in its support of La Follette. Phil La Follette later recalled, "The strange thing about World War I, in terms of public reaction, was that by and large the people who seemed to have lost control of their emotions to a greater extent than any other part of our population were the intellectuals." Others, more dispassionate, seized this opportunity to further their efforts to dismantle progressivism, both in Wisconsin and nationwide, by vitriolic attacks calculated to inflame opposition to La Follette and all that for which he stood. Attacks went beyond formal speeches and angry editorials. Hanged and burned in effigy, La Follette received anonymous hate mail and was spat upon in Washington. Never before had his insistence on remaining uncompromisingly true to his beliefs incurred such bitter and widespread wrath.[25]

Following his speech opposing entry into the war, La Follette was, according to Bobbie, "in fine spirits . . . so splendid in this hour of trial." Noted Fola, "The war clamor and denunciation of the press were as a whisper in his ears compared to the voices which were calling to him throughout the country." This period, for all its trauma and stress, was, in many ways, one of the most fulfilling in La Follette's life. Since he believed the newspapers were prejudiced against him and unrepresentative of the people, all press reports to the contrary did not alter La Follette's certainty that the general public approved his position. Four days after the "willful men" incident, letters arrived at a rate of about 500 a day from all over the country, with at least four to one "strong and beautiful in their support." The German American population was not unanimous in its disapproval of the role of the United States in the war. However, a large portion of that electorate, a number of whom lived in Wisconsin, constituting about 30 percent of the state's population, rewarded La Follette's position with gratitude and life-long loyalty.[26]

During the 1912 presidential campaign, La Follette had felt betrayed and powerless. During the controversy over U.S. entry into World War I, he remained confident, assured of his moral superiority, his righteousness. Harsh accusations served to heighten his feelings of singular courage. Following the filibuster, he wrote to his family: "I couldn't have done anything else unless I went down & slipped into the Potomac & the water's too cold for that now. Lots of people on the street-cars & round the Capitol want to eat me — but conclude I'd be too tough." This was precisely the kind of image in which La Follette gloried — a man who could only do right or die, who remained unmoved when faced with enormous opposition. He was not, however, as confident in his actions and as totally impervious to the violent attacks upon his integrity as he endeavored to appear, for he longed for Belle's advice and reassurance and confessed to her, "It has been an awful trial." Bobbie, overwhelmed by anxiety, begged Belle to come to Washington to help relieve his burden as adviser. Belle ultimately caved in to the combined pressure, but, in a wistful note to Phil and Mary, she expressed her heartache at leaving them and the "quiet and protection of the Farm," concluding almost doubtfully, "and whatever we can do to make the lives of the many happier and freer from pain and stress, we should gladly do — shouldn't we?" Bob found reassurance not only in Belle's presence and in the letters pledging eternal support from other family members but in the renewal of old friendships severed or damaged in 1912. With so much at stake, La Follette could at last be genuinely magnanimous concerning past hurts. He wrote to Gilson Gardner, "Let's close the old books and open a new set. It's a time when friends of democracy should work together to save as much of the wreckage as possible."[27]

Once the United States formally entered the war, La Follette's attention refocused on issues still viable. Wartime concerns, however, completely overshadowed all efforts to further the traditional progressive agenda. In the words of Senator Hiram Johnson, "Our [progressive] group has dwindled to very, very few." Any comprehensive progressive program, Johnson noted, "will die of inanition." La Follette, however, insisted that progressive ideals be upheld. Decrying the expensive large-scale borrowing inherent in the vast number of war bonds sold to an American public frenzied with patriotism, he and his fellow die-hard progressives continued in their efforts to create a permanent tax system based on ability to pay. It included increasing income taxes, lowering exemptions, doubling the levy on all excess profits (not just those war related), and imposing new excise taxes on luxury items, including automobiles. "Our endeavors to impose heavy war profit taxes," Johnson wrote to Theodore Roosevelt, "have brought into sharp relief the skin-deep dollar patriotism of some of those who have been loudest in declamations on war in their demands for blood." Noting in 1917 that the United States taxed war profits at an average rate of 31 percent compared to Britain's 80 percent, La Follette scoffed at the notion that higher taxation would hinder the nation's economy or war production. La Follette's 10 September 1917 amendment in the form of a substitute for the War Revenue Act sought a war profits tax of 76 percent, a graduated income tax, a war income tax, and a war tax on distilled beverages, cigars, and tobacco. La Follette argued that "the war should be paid for as we go forward in its prosecution," for it would be "nothing short of the economic crime of all the ages to permit our financial plans to go one hair's breadth further along lines which violate the principles of sound Government finance." His amendment was defeated 15–65. Senator John Weeks called it "regrettable" that La Follette persisted in "arraying class against class; in creating those animosities which are harmful to the public."[28] The excess-profit tax rates ultimately increased but not to the dramatic levels sought by La Follette, Johnson, and others. And yet World War I marked the achievement of certain long-standing progressive goals. Before the war, nearly 75 percent of federal revenues came from customs and excise taxes; after the war, that same percentage emerged from taxes on incomes, profits, and estates — a profound shift marking the permanent legacy of the surprising union of progressive ideals and the war.[29]

La Follette also persisted in his efforts to protect individual rights, rights he believed were doubly jeopardized in time of war. "Within a few months," he railed during his speech proposing a national referendum on the draft, "under a pretext of carrying democracy to the rest of the world, we have done more to undermine and destroy democracy in the United States than it will be possible for us as a Nation to repair in a generation of time." La Follette's proposal was defeated by a vote of 68–4. On 5 June 1917, the Espionage Act passed, providing for fines and imprisonment for persons obstructing military operations in wartime and for use of the mails in violation of the statute. La Follette, worried about the statute's impact on *La Follette's Magazine*, denounced it as a violation of civil rights, tried to extend the rights of conscientious objectors, and sought protection of the right of Congress to determine the objects and policies of war. Within his own family, he and Belle worked unsuccessfully to dissuade Phil from joining the army but did manage to gain Bobbie a health-based draft exemption.[30]

Despite his preoccupation with war-related issues, other events diverted La Follette's attention briefly. He shared, for example, his wife's fascination with the revolution in Russia as "a blow to all monarchial forms of government. The words Kaiser and King and Czar and hereditary power in government have suddenly been revealed as the insignia of a past order." La Follette skirted the controversy over prohibition, a burning issue of the day, by taking a stand intended to appease people on both sides of the issue. "I have never believed in the principle of prohibition and therefore have never supported it," he asserted. He voted for the constitutional amendment, however, because, he said, "I should be untrue to my convictions in support of democracy if I did not vote to give the people a right to pass upon the pending amendment to the Constitution."[31]

La Follette devoted much of his attention to printing and distributing, at his own expense, thousands of copies of his speeches on the war and related issues. "I am getting the gospel to the hungry just as fast as I can pay the bills to do it," he stated, claiming, "Never before since I have been here [in Washington] has there been such a call for the truth." Although he admitted to occasional depression, in addition to growing anxiety over finances, he vowed, "I can't quit when there is more to fight for and more to fight against than ever before since I entered public office." La Follette's pleasure in Bobbie's company and assistance compounded his joy at having a specific, significant, and clear-cut set of issues to champion. His certainty in the righteousness of his actions, however, undermined his effectiveness. Senator William Stone criticized La Follette for making enormously time-consuming arguments for amendments he submitted on the floor of the Senate, amendments that should have been argued in committee. Hiram Johnson, who shared La Follette's progressive goals and opposition to the war, nevertheless feared that La Follette's name on any measure virtually guaranteed its failure: "La Follette is simply impossible. . . . His attitude upon the war and every question in connection with it has tainted him so that his leadership even in a just cause, or even his advocacy, will militate against that cause."[32]

On 20 September 1917, just three days after Johnson penned this damning assessment, La Follette spoke at the Nonpartisan League's convention in St. Paul, Minnesota. Reports of the address created a fervor that made the previous protests against him appear mild by comparison. La Follette spoke to a packed auditorium of his past struggles against corporate domination, his current opposition to measures repressing civil liberties, and his views on American involvement in the war. The crowd's enthusiasm led La Follette to abandon his prepared speech halfway through and speak extemporaneously. According to the official transcript, he said, amid hearty and prolonged cheers, laughter, and applause: "For my own part I was not in favor of *beginning* the war. I don't mean to say that we hadn't suffered grievances. We had — at the hands of Germany. *Serious* grievances! We had cause for complaint. They had interfered with the right of American citizens to travel upon the high seas — on ships loaded with munitions for Great Britain. . . . I would not be understood as saying that we didn't have grievances. We did. And upon those grievances, which I regarded as insufficient — considering the amount involved and the rights involved, which was the right to ship munitions to Great Britain with American passengers on board to secure a safe transit." "We had a right, a technical right," La Follette thundered, "to ship the munitions. And the American citizens have a technical right to ride on those vessels. . . . I say . . . that the *comparatively* small privilege of the right of an American citizen to ride on a *munitions loaded ship flying a foreign flag* is too small to involve this government in *the loss of millions and millions of lives*!!"[33]

La Follette suggested that American industry aided U.S. entry into the war and that shippers of munitions encouraged the presence of American passengers to give a semblance of safety to the passage of their profiteering cargo. He claimed that four days before the *Lusitania* sailed, Secretary of State Bryan warned Wilson that the ship was carrying explosives and 6 million rounds of ammunition. Finally, in his remarks favoring taxation over bonds as a means to finance the war, he shouted, "*Shame on Congress*" and "Shame on the *Administration*!" Although his audience was wildly receptive throughout the entire speech, the Associated Press was not. The next day, in more than a thousand newspapers coast to coast, La Follette made headlines in reports based on a falsification of his actual speech. The damning misquotation: "We had no grievance against Germany." Two petitions calling for La Follette's expulsion from the Senate were introduced almost immediately.[34]

Although clearly misquoted, that is not to imply (as Fola does in her biography of her father) that the fervor created by La Follette's speech was completely unfounded. William Jennings Bryan publicly denied any knowledge of munitions aboard the *Lusitania* prior to its sinking, despite La Follette's continued (but incorrect) assertions to the contrary. Moreover, the general tone of La Follette's speech was one critical of domestic and foreign policy, and he expressed points of view likely to raise criticism even during peace time. In a time of war, however valid, the speech seemed particularly ill-advised, but certainly not uncharacteristic. Just as La Follette had been unable or unwilling to temper his remarks during the Periodical Publisher's Association banquet in Philadelphia, he refused in St. Paul to give voice to more moderate, politically expedient remarks. There were, however, major differences between the two speeches that merited La Follette such massive amounts of negative publicity. The Philadelphia speech was delivered to a hostile audience, the St. Paul speech to a supportive one. In Philadelphia, an angry and frustrated man lashed out in response to personal disappointment. In St. Paul, a politician expressing controversial political views to an audience who shared those views reigned triumphant. While both speeches made manifest La Follette's need to demonstrate his righteousness, the scene in Philadelphia was a disturbing emotional display, while the event in St. Paul celebrated La Follette's strength of conviction.[35]

La Follette's St. Paul speech earned him far more rancor than his performance at Philadelphia. Theodore Roosevelt repeatedly urged La Follette's expulsion from the Senate, calling him a liar, a "sinister enemy of democracy," a "shadow Hun," and "the most dangerous political leader [of] the analogue to the bolshevik agitation."[36] Roosevelt was enormously bitter that Wilson, that "Byzantine logothete" remained steadfast in his refusal to allow Roosevelt, aged fifty-nine in 1917, to lead troops on the battlefield. "I am the only one he has kept out of war," the former president angrily complained. Roosevelt did all he could on the home front to promote the war, including denouncing La Follette at every opportunity. After St. Paul, other voices added to his chorus. Columbia University president Nicholas Murray Butler said, "You might just as well put poison in the food of every American boy that goes to his transport as to permit La Follette to talk as he does." Butler echoed Roosevelt's call for expulsion, as did former president Taft, Senator Frank Kellogg, and a multitude of associations, organizations, and newspapers. There was talk of having La Follette arrested under the Espionage Act he had tried so hard to liberalize. "If a soapbox orator were to voice the same views," noted the *Omaha Bee*, "he would be promptly arrested."[37]

Even some traditional La Follette critics, however, came to his defense, maintaining, "No informed man can imagine La Follette a corruptionist . . . [for] he has been fearlessly, rashly honest when there was no surfeit of honesty in Washington affairs." Several major papers, while unwilling to endorse La Follette's statements, did suggest that the crusade against him was overdone. Despite the immediate turmoil and threats following the speech, La Follette insisted on fulfilling a speaking engagement in Toledo, where he emphasized the erroneous elements of the Associated Press account of his performance at St. Paul, playing down the accurately reported strong and controversial opinions he had expressed. Belle, ignoring the distorted nature of her husband's presentation, called the enthusiastic reception a great triumph and a demonstration of the true public sentiment of unconditional support.[38]

On 6 October, La Follette, bolstered by the presence of Bobbie and Belle, refuted charges in the Senate calling for his expulsion. He spent nearly three hours delivering not a detailed defense of his controversial remarks but instead a solemn but impassioned plea for the protection of constitutional rights and freedoms, including free speech, during time of war. La Follette invoked Abraham Lincoln, Henry Clay, Daniel Webster, and Charles Sumner to support his claim that "the right to control their own Government according to constitutional forms is not one of the rights that the citizens of this country are called upon to surrender in time of war." It was, according to Belle, his finest speech. Alice Brandeis, however, wrote to her husband Supreme Court Justice Louis D. Brandeis, "It was dignified & would have been effective but for its length." It met with applause from the galleries but also with violent denunciations by several senators and within the press. Senator Frank Kellogg quoted extensively from La Follette's St. Paul speech, denouncing it as "slanderous." According to Kellogg's blistering attack, the St. Paul speech was not an issue of free speech but rather an "erroneous statement of facts" which "aid and encourage the enemy and cast dishonor and discredit upon this Nation." "If I entertained those sentiments," railed Kellogg, "I would apply to the Kaiser for a seat in the Bundesrath." In contrast, Senator Albert Fall granted La Follette's good intentions but defended himself and his fellow senators against La Follette's cries of "Shame! Shame!" by noting, "Some sincere people [mistakenly] become convinced that they are the only honest people." In what the *Philadelphia North American* called "a patent attempt further to [sic] mislead the public," La Follette was described as seeking to create the impression that "he alone is the champion of free speech in the United States and is standing alone for the constitutional rights of individuals against the overwhelming strength of a ruthless war party headed by the president and seeking to destroy those rights." The Senate Committee on Privileges and Elections, chaired by Atlee Pomerene, approved an investigation into La Follette's speeches and antiwar activities. La Follette's letter of response contained half-apologetic explanations, excuses, tentative retractions, and denials concerning his St. Paul speech along with pledges of willingness to cooperate with the investigation, mixed with outright defiance. The investigation began on 26 November, but controversy over witnesses and evidence led to a chain of postponements, giving credence to Belle's assertion, "No one seems to think they will really try to put [him] out of the Senate." La Follette concurred, claiming the committee knew of his innocence, but he declined to publish his St. Paul speech throughout the prolonged investigation, ostensibly because he deemed it improper, but more likely to keep the public from knowing the true nature of his inflammatory remarks.[39]

Despite the renewed criticism generated by his 6 October speech to the Senate, La Follette withstood the strain well. "He is tired," reported Bobbie, "but his spirits are fine and he is wonderful in his faith and confidence in the ultimate outcome of it all." La Follette's confidence was undoubtedly bolstered by the fact that one-third of all the letters he received during his nineteen years in the Senate came in 1917 in support of his antiwar campaign. A sample ran 67:1 in his favor. La Follette's supporters overwhelmingly lauded the Wisconsin senator as the single most influential man in the cause for the common people. Labor leader Eugene Debs wrote that it was to La Follette's glory that the "plutocracy of Wall Street" sought his ouster from the Senate and concluded, "All honor to you for your courage, your manhood and your devotion to the cause of the people in the face of the bitterest and most brutal persecution to which the lawless looters of this nation and their prostitute press ever subjected a faithful public servant."[40]

Although he was buoyed by widespread popular support, anti–La Follette sentiments affected the senator in a variety of ways. Vilification as well as praise was especially intense in his home state. Although petitions and resolutions calling for La Follette's ejection from Wisconsin's clubs and associations abounded, Belle maintained, "Nothing fazes Bob or destroys his faith in the ultimate outcome of all this malign feeling." La Follette himself wrote, "In the midst of this raging storm of hate, I am withal very happy in so far as my own future is concerned. I would not change places with any living man on the record as it stands today."[41] These claims of immunity to intentional humiliations were shattered, however, when all but two of the 423 University of Wisconsin faculty members signed a petition expressing their "grief and shame" at La Follette's "unwise and disloyal utterances giving aid and comfort to the enemy" and denouncing "his failure actively and earnestly to support the government in the prosecution of the present war." This petition hurt more deeply than all other formal actions taken against him during the war, including the Wisconsin joint legislature's condemnation of him for sedition. In his diary he noted, "My picture was taken down from the place where it had been hanging in all of the university buildings and an advertisement for liberty bonds put in its place." In November 1917, La Follette initiated libel suits against the *Madison Democrat*, the *Wisconsin State Journal*, and the directors of the Madison Club, who had voted to eject him.[42]

As the libel suits, and the war, dragged on, La Follette endeavored not only to defend his opposition to the draft, war bonds, and the Espionage Bill but also to publicize his supportive votes on other war-related measures. In his magazine and in letters to influential friends, La Follette stressed in November 1917 that he understood and accepted the obligations that participation in a war entailed and, consequently, opposed only five of the sixty war measures in Congress. Although La Follette invested some borrowed money in government bonds and composed or copied into a notebook a poem complaining of war-induced shortages and expressing hatred for the Kaiser, he continued to be appalled at pro-war enthusiasm, noting, "No one mentions the lengthening death roll." War enthusiasts ignored the bulk of La Follette's record and concentrated on his opposition votes. According to son-in-law George Middleton, the attacks impugning his integrity by lifelong friends hit La Follette hardest. But, at the peak of this frenzied opposition, when Middleton asked if La Follette had any regrets, the senator answered somberly, "I just couldn't vote for this war." Despite the vehemence of his detractors, La Follette's certainty in the righteousness of his position never weakened, and he prophesied to Middleton, "I may not live to see my own vindication, but you will."[43]

President Wilson was relatively restrained in expressing his disdain for La Follette throughout the war, but the two crossed swords in 1918 when former La Follette ally, Irvine Lenroot, sought the Senate seat made available by the death of Paul O. Husting. La Follette's seeking of Lenroot's defeat was the culmination of a long-standing personal and political rift. When Lenroot, who supported Roosevelt as a second choice in 1912, decided that he could not serve as a Wisconsin delegate to the convention because he was not willing to support La Follette to the end, Belle La Follette wrote of her painful realization "that Bob and Irvine can never be the same to each other as before." In a clear rebuke of his former boss, Lenroot announced in 1918 that the sole issue of his campaign was loyalty to the government. Lenroot's denouncement of La Follette's opposition to the war became a major campaign issue in the primary.[44]

With La Follette promoting Republican candidate James Thompson, even President Wilson weighed in on the state campaign. In a widely publicized letter to Vice President Thomas Riley Marshall, Wilson confessed to following "with a good deal of anxiety the critical Senatorial contest in Wisconsin." Urging his vice president to campaign on behalf of the Democratic candidate, Joseph Davies, Wilson cast doubt on the loyalty of Lenroot because of his "questionable support" in Congress of "some test occasions," while discrediting La Follette's entirely: "The attention of the country will naturally be centered upon it [the election] because of the universal feeling against Senator La Follette and the question which will be in every patriotic man's mind [is] whether Wisconsin is really loyal to the country in this time of crisis or not." Although bent on Lenroot's defeat, La Follette was not determined to have it at any cost. He used his magazine as a forum to criticize the platform of the strong Socialist candidate, Victor Berger. Both Wilson and La Follette were disappointed by the election of Lenroot, a man they considered, for entirely different reasons, disloyal and untrustworthy.[45]

The entire La Follette family shared in the abuse heaped upon their patriarch. Phil, a student at the University of Wisconsin where his father was burned in effigy and continually vilified, wrote reassuringly to his parents that, rather than view such actions as a hardship, he welcomed them as opportunities to prove himself. He admitted, however, that a "hypo-martyr-like feeling" plagued him and in his autobiography confessed that during the war period, "I never heard the name La Follette spoken in public places without flinching and bracing myself for some epithet." Mary gave up her plan of entering the University of Wisconsin after, in an intentional slight, her father's name was omitted from the list of dignitaries invited to the annual prom. Throughout the war, Mary and Phil buried whatever resentment and hostility they bore toward their parents, were protective of them, and expressed continually to them their love, appreciation, and admiration. Nevertheless, Bob, who assured Belle in 1917, "It is hard for you and the children, but it is all worth while," felt keenly the pain suffered by his children on his account as the war progressed.[46]

Accordingly, Bob immersed himself in every detail of Bobbie's streptococcic infections, which began early in 1918. He refused throughout Bobbie's illness to give any but the barest minimum of time or attention to political matters. Bob La Follette was absent from the Senate for eight months, in many ways a most timely and convenient retreat. Only a telegram claiming his vote essential to the passage of the women's suffrage amendment that both he and Belle had so long advocated caused his reluctant return on 30 September 1918. Noted a fellow senator, "I believe La Follette's mind was saved during the war by the illness of his son Robert. The Senator's devotion to the boy he loved removed him from the worst of the storm against him." Upon La Follette's return to the Senate, many former foes greeted

*A family portrait (minus Fola) taken during the war. Some of the tension of the period is reflected in Bob La Follette's face. Mary leans against her father. Bobbie flanks Belle and Phil. (State Historical Society of Wisconsin [X3]18450)*

him cordially, echoing the sympathetic sentiments of Boies Penrose, Pennsylvania's Republican "boss," who paused conspicuously before La Follette's front row desk to boom, "Glad to see you, Senator. How's the boy?"[47]

La Follette's vindication came as gradually as his son's recovery and the interventionists' disenchantment with the war. His key libel suit dragged to a conclusion on 23 May 1918, when the Associated Press issued a retraction and apology for their inaccurate reporting of the St. Paul speech. The United Press also apologized. La Follette settled amicably with the *Wisconsin State Journal* and dropped his suit against the *Madison Democrat*. During La Follette's preoccupation with Bobbie's illness, the Committee on Privileges and Elections continued the delays of its investigation despite frequent urging by La Follette and his attorneys that it be completed or dropped. Finally, to La Follette's great satisfaction and Pomerene's chagrin, a committee vote of 9–2 brought the investigation to a halt on 2 December 1918.[48]

As the war drew to a close, the fervor of La Follette's political opposition and public denouncers continued to dwindle. With victory at hand, many forgot past differences, while others began to see the wisdom of La Follette's earlier assertions. Some of his greatest detractors voluntarily retracted their sensationalistic charges and congratulated La Follette on his courage, vision, and steadfast honesty and integrity. Other tributes were a long time in coming. Senator James Reed waited a year after La Follette's death to call his anti-war vote "the most superb act of courage this century has witnessed." Author Irvin S. Cobb's apology for his thinly veiled attack on La Follette came eight years after the senator's death, and not until 1940 did political cartoonist Rollin Kirby confess that he too regretted his wartime attacks on La Follette.[49]

La Follette's concern over Wilson's plans for Versailles and the proposed Fourteen Points quickly tempered his jubilation at war's end. He enjoyed renewed popularity in the Senate. Warned by his family to "lay low," La Follette confessed, "I am like an old horse that has been confined in a box stall all winter. I have gotten out into the paddock. I sniff the fresh air and feel the freedom. I want to kick the bars down and go racing unrestrained over the fields [but] there is real danger that I might run up against the barbed wire fence — for it is *still there*." That "barbed wire fence" remained, in the form of Atlee Pomerene's 15 December presentation of the minority report on the decision to cease the Committee on Privileges and Elections' investigation into La Follette, a report Belle called, "low and mean and cowardly." La Follette was so exhausted from cumulative strain that a few days later he fell asleep on a Washington trolley car.

Nevertheless, as 1918 drew to a close, La Follette faced the future with new confidence, urged by others to, in the words of Louis Brandeis, "take [his] new place of leadership in the struggle for democracy in America." His confidence was reinforced on 16 January 1919, when the Senate voted 50–21 to dismiss the resolution of the Minnesota Commission of Public Safety to institute proceedings to expel La Follette. La Follette was hardly an object of great love and sympathy among all fifty of his fellow senators who voted in his favor. One factor that helps explain their support was a desire to avoid the precedent of expelling senators for voicing unpopular sentiments. Also in La Follette's favor was the fact that the Senate was divided by a 49–47 margin after the 1918 election. The Democratic vice president could break a tie vote in his party's favor to organize the Senate. It was feared that La Follette's ouster would create the possibility of the election of a Democrat, which would ultimately prevent Henry Cabot Lodge (already viewed as crucial to the upcoming debates on appropriate peace terms) from serving as chair of the Senate Foreign Relations Committee.[50]

A scathing attack on his honesty, integrity, and patriotism by his old enemy from Mississippi, John Sharp Williams, somewhat tarnished the day of La Follette's vindication. La Follette claimed he only reluctantly followed the advice of friends who urged him to not dignify Williams's speech with a reply, for he chafed under the humiliation of having to "sit still under an attack for which a man ought to be pounded to a pulp." The sting of the incident faded slowly, for La Follette felt "as if . . . publicly horse whipped by some fool woman." Belle reprimanded her righteously indignant husband: "It has been a terrible long strain and has eaten into your heart more than any one except yourself could realize. And yet as I have said before when we consider what it has cost every one who stood out against war you are perhaps less martyred than most of them."[51]

As the war to end all wars finally ended, La Follette was reinforced by official vindication and a multitude who looked to him with new respect and admiration for his steadfast dedication to righteousness. Nonetheless, he returned to the Senate a somewhat cautious man. What would be his role in the creation of a new world order? Could he resurrect progressivism from the ashes of World War I? Had his stance and demeanor throughout the war alienated even his fellow progressives for good, or was there hope for reconciliation? Wilson's efforts to fashion a lasting peace would provide the first test.

# 15: RESURRECTION
## TIME AND EVENTS ARE BRINGING THINGS YOUR WAY AT LAST

The war La Follette had opposed at all costs finally came to an end on 11 November 1918. Grateful that the killing had finally stopped, he turned his energies to the next great challenges: forging a lasting peace and rehabilitating his own reputation. His desire to expand his magazine was a major irritant to many within his camp, his wife in particular. Moreover, his frequent complaints about members of Congress and the public who still spurned him because of his opposition to the war earned him exasperated replies from even the most loyal of his supporters. "La Follette," noted *The Nation*, "appears to be temperamentally incapable of separating principles from personalities and this incapacity has cost him the Presidency, has destroyed the unity of the progressive movement . . . and has earned [him] the bitter and relentless enmities that beset him." Belle La Follette asked her husband, "Shall we disassociate ourselves from every one who disappoints us and with whom we disagree?" "This war," she scolded, "has shaken the foundations and is changing the face of the earth. Tremendous and unexpected results are following. New issues are arising. If we would preserve our sanity, if we would not be overwhelmed with bitterness, if we are to have any chance for usefulness, must we not co-operate where we can, concentrate mind and heart on the best that can be done and keep faith in the outcome of every rightly directed effort?"[1]

His bitterness over past hurts did not deter La Follette's crusade to shore up the faltering progressive movement. Securing free speech seemed a crucial first step. He continually denounced what he termed "the greatest crime of this war," the Espionage Law. Despite the end of the "war to end all wars," violence was erupting across the globe, from Russia to Egypt, Ireland to India. With eighteen separate wars raging, many of them the result of revolutionary uprisings, Americans hardly felt it the time to relax their vigilance against internal sabotage. Hysteria over domestic radicalism, labor strikes, and bombings increased rather than subsided at war's end. "For whom the Gods would destroy," La Follette reminded the readers of his magazine, "they first make mad. And at this very moment a great campaign is raging with fury and madness throughout the land, for a law to suppress free speech in time of [domestic] peace." The attempts by American authorities to suppress domestic radical activities, ostensibly to stamp out the fires of revolution, outraged La Follette, for they violated the participants' constitutional rights to freedom of expression. As government agents arrested suspected radicals, trampling even the most basic of rights, La Follette cautioned, "Let no man think that we can deny civil liberty to others and retain it for ourselves." To "enlarge the right of free speech in the discussion of matters involved in the Peace Conference," La Follette introduced a resolution to repeal the Espionage Law. It was referred to the Judiciary Committee, proclaimed "the tomb of the Capulets" by a disdainful La Follette. Its eventual defeat did not discourage La Follette from defending civil liberties increasingly under attack.[2]

La Follette redoubled his efforts as watchdog of the public good, concerned that the "temporary" wartime relaxation of rules and regulations governing American business would become permanent and the power of big businesses ever more pervasive. He continued his support of child labor legislation. He denounced bonds as the means by which "wealth is to escape its share of taxes . . . and the people are to sweat and toil in the years to come to pay the interest on bonds, the principal of the bonds, and the higher cost of living." He cast aspersions upon Wilson: "I could say that you wanted to stand in with wealth, that you wanted to curry favor with the big business institutions of the country, that you wanted to let up the taxes on the millionaires in order to finance the future campaign; that you wanted to take it out of the great mass of the people who are not organized, and who have not any wealth nor any power to strike back with." La Follette quickly offered assurances that he personally did not believe such charges, providing his own "kinder" interpretation that the president was more naïve and incompetent than corrupt: "I just think you are going blindly at this business." La Follette maintained that he entertained no illusions that his fellow senators would be any more receptive to his plans for fairer taxation at war's end than they had been at its beginning, but he asserted: "[I]t has been the political and public-service policy of my life to pursue principle, regardless of results; and when I put my hand to the plow I go straight through to the end of the furrow." "I am going to put the lamp at [the senators'] feet," he stated in regard to postwar taxation, "and then let them go blindly on in the other direction if they choose to do so." The Senate, did, in fact, reject La Follette's substitution plan for a war profits tax, but across the nation many Americans were looking to La Follette with renewed respect.[3]

The conference called to establish the terms of the peace following the Great War began on 12 January 1919. Wilson had previously outlined before Congress the fourteen points he deemed necessary to create a nonpunitive, lasting peace. In addition to mandating the end of secret treaties and entangling alliances, his plan included arms reduction, freedom of the seas, and self-determination among nations. The fourteenth point, the es-

tablishment of a league of nations affording mutual guarantees of independence and territorial integrity, was the heart of Wilson's plan to replace
war with enlightened understanding. To his admirers, Wilson's idealistic
plans bolstered his reputation as the consummate progressive. Years after
his own presidency, Herbert Hoover revered Wilson as "a man of staunch
morals . . . more than just an idealist; . . . the personification of the heritage
of idealism of the American people. [A] born crusader . . . [who] brought
spiritual concepts to the peace table."[4] Another former president,
Theodore Roosevelt, perhaps anticipated such remarks when he snapped,
"For Heaven's sake never allude to Wilson as an idealist . . . His advocacy of
the League of Nations no more represents idealism on his part than his advocacy of peace without victory. . . . He is a silly doctrinaire at times and an
utterly selfish and cold-blooded politician always." His disgust for Wilson's
peace proposal ignited some of Roosevelt's old fire, gone since the death of
his son Quentin, an air force pilot shot down over France. His remarkable
exuberance muted, Roosevelt suffered from a variety of ailments, including
recurrences of the malaria and leg infection contracted during explo-
rations of Brazil in 1913–14 when he was fifty-five. A week before the Versailles conference began, however, Roosevelt wrote an editorial for the
*Kansas City Star* denouncing Wilson's proposed League in terms reminiscent
of his old, forceful style. The next morning the Bull Moose was dead at the
age of sixty. A coronary embolism struck the final, lethal blow. The death of
the man La Follette had for so long envied and hated prompted Amos Pinchot to remark to La Follette, "Time and events are bringing things your
way at last."[5]

Like Wilson's, La Follette's commitment to progressive ideals had been
integrated into rather than usurped by his interest in foreign affairs. His
perception of how to best apply progressive ideals beyond U.S. boundaries
differed from the president's, however. In increasingly strident tones La Follette denounced economic and political imperialism while defending self-
determination, even when it meant the establishment of non-capitalist-
based economies under nondemocratic forms of government. He was
outraged when Wilson's plea for $100 million for European war relief was
met by demands within the Senate that none of the funds be allotted to Germany. La Follette characterized the proposed neglect of war-vanquished
Germany as vindictive and inhumane. He believed that Americans should
be concerned with saving the lives of starving peoples rather than demanding contrition or dictating political systems. He asked his fellow senators
to envision "our good old Uncle Sam dispensing charity to the starving
peoples of Europe[:] their hands stretched out to him shrunken with hunger and starvation, little children about his knees, pale, emaciated, their

hands so thin you can see through them." "Think," he urged, "of charity represented in the person of this figure that stands for American benevolence and philanthropy turning away a starving child because it is of German heritage." Passionately he concluded, "Charity . . . is the very spirit of the Christ life. Charity represents and stands for all the principles of His teachings."[6]

La Follette supported Wilson's vision of a peace without victory, but he strenuously opposed the secret nature of the peace negotiations. "The American people," he wrote, "want to know just what is going on in these conferences. We were promised publicity at every step." Wilson's insistence on bringing as his delegation to Paris four political "yes" men enraged all Republicans, who had hoped for at least a bipartisan group of advisers. La Follette contemptuously labeled the entire conference "Willful Wilson's holiday in Europe," and he denounced the president's "autocratic view of executive power" on the floor of the U.S. Senate. Proud of his own triumphs inside the courtroom dating back to his days as Dane County district attorney, La Follette spoke derisively of Wilson's legal and constitutional expertise, depicting the president, "a sort of academic lawyer," as a man who became a professor and politician only after he failed at practicing law. La Follette proclaimed Wilson "guilty of a willful disregard of his constitutional obligations and the honorable precedents of other Presidents."[7]

Worried about the fate of the postwar world, haunted by the lingering controversy over his St. Paul speech, La Follette's spirits were further dampened by the absence of his family, particularly Belle and Bobbie, who remained in California during the latter's long convalescence. La Follette kept much to himself during their absence and urged them frequently to return, complaining of loneliness, boredom, tiredness, and indifference without their counsel, advice, and inspiration. He wrote to them daily and in great detail of his thoughts and activities. He confided his intolerance for those who had so avidly sought the war but were now complaining about its consequences: "I feel sometimes like answering with Richelieu, 'O!, Monk! Leave patience to the Saints — for I *am human*!'" He expressed more personal concerns as well, including his ever increasing awareness of the passage of time, the inevitability of his death, and his fear of the "awful account of *things undone*" that he would leave behind.[8]

Fighting Bob battled on. Among his notable targets was the 1919 coal and oil lands bill which would lease public lands to private corporations. He led a filibuster against it, declaring that the bill would repeal the heart of the conservation program laboriously constructed by progressives. The bill's supporters countered that, by leasing, the government maintained ownership and ultimate control yet could at the same time promote the development and utilization of the nation's natural resources. La Follette asserted that renewable leases would ultimately allow giant corporations to assume title to public lands rich in mineral resources and thereby stimulate monopoly development. In less temperate language, La Follette railed to his family, "These coal & oil vandals . . . have been in this thing until it has made them so sordid and degraded that they would blow up the Holy Sepulcher in their scramble for dirty money." He urged his wife and children to see the Grand Canyon "as God made it" while they could, warning that the heartless exploiters of natural resources already had "a footing in Niagara — [and] they 'got' Hetch Hetchy [sister valley to Yosemite]." Senators Lawrence Sherman and Joseph France also took active roles in the filibuster, while other senators and lobbyists offered support behind the scenes. The group triumphed on 4 March 1919, when the speaking marathon led by La Follette ended the congressional session. Called a willful obstructionist for forcing a call for an extra session of Congress to more carefully examine the appropriations bill as well as advise President Wilson during his drafting of the peace treaty in Paris, Senator Robert La Follette was once again wielding some political clout. Gifford Pinchot credited him with "saving the country from the conspirators for the time being at least."[9]

With the Senate in adjournment, La Follette faced the arduous task of correcting the galley proofs of the filibuster and seven other speeches for the *Congressional Record*. His concerns with perfection and posterity were evident after twelve hours of making corrections: "I always hate a speech *after* I make it and don't see how I or anybody else could ever have thought it even tolerable. . . . [Despite the public's disinterest in the speeches,] *I* may be going over them from time to time after I'm dead — and I know I should feel awfully sore about it to find some sentence awfully bad and past all chance for correction." More than just poor sentence structure worried La Follette. His cousin's son changed his name to Cooper, after his stepfather, because he "couldn't stand the disgrace" of the La Follette name. Some solace, however, was found in the knowledge that many other families, particularly German Americans, were naming their newborn sons Robert La Follette, and in the generous offers from speaking bureaus intent on La Follette's return to the platform.[10]

In May 1919, Belle finally returned to Washington, following Bob's pleas, urgings, and thinly veiled threats. Suffering renewed humiliation over the family's financial distress, coupled with her resentment at having to leave the quiet contentment she had been enjoying with her son for the stress of Washington life with her husband, Belle claimed funds insufficient even to send Bob a telegram announcing her arrival. Bob, who wrote to Bobbie that he was suffering "the sense of *waiting, waiting*, that subconsciously drags at the wheels of time because I know our dear mama is to come," met every train arriving from her departure point until he "caught her trying to slip through the gate," where she "surrendered without a fight." After a separation of almost a year, Belle was struck by her husband's "tired" and "aged" appearance, and she voiced her determination to guard his health. She certainly had her work cut out for her, for he was about to plunge into the special session, formally called for by President Wilson from Paris on 7 May, to do nothing less than draw America's blueprint for the postwar world.[11]

Not all of the special session beginning on 19 May was taken up with foreign affairs. On 4 June the Senate passed the Susan B. Anthony constitutional amendment granting women the right to vote. Bob proudly noted that the applause he started on the floor of the Senate and which swept the galleries was not rebuked by the presiding senator, so widespread was the support for this vote, which had been seventy years in the making. To the great satisfaction of all the La Follettes, Belle helped engineer the effort that ensured that Wisconsin was the first state to ratify the woman suffrage amendment six days later.[12]

There was little time to relish this great triumph, for La Follette was soon consumed by his efforts to defeat a number of propositions emerging from what he termed, "Wilson's Broken Pledges." "We have been lied to so much and for so long," he wrote in *La Follette's Magazine*, "that we hardly know the face of the truth." Like many progressives, he was angered by the bitter wrangling and political chaos wrought by this "war to end all wars." Disillusionment rapidly replaced idealism. "I challenge any man," La Follette declared, "to name one new privilege, one added right which the common people of this or any other allied countries are to gain as the result of this war." La Follette's dislike of Wilson, whom he increasingly viewed as a "selfish, cold-blooded opportunist," contributed to the fervor of his protests. La Follette's views remained consistent with those expressed throughout the bulk of his career: he favored self-determination of peoples over imperialism in any form.[13]

With California's Hiram Johnson, La Follette objected to the presence of American troops in Russia. He scoffed at the official explanation that Allied troops, including 2,500 Americans, were stationed in Russia to defend Allied supplies and prevent Germany from using Archangel (on Russia's northern coast near the Onega River) as a submarine base. La Follette termed the Allied presence an "invasion," Wilson's "private war," and a "war without a declaration of war," actually targeting Bolshevism rather than Germany. "The war is ended," he reminded Congress. "There can be no pretext that the troops of the United States on Russian soil today are fighting anybody but the Russian people." With the United States in the throes of the Red Scare (as the postwar persecution of radicals and alleged radicals was called), in the minds of many Americans Russia was completing its transformation from respected ally to dangerous foe. La Follette had been initially pleased by the overthrow of the czar, envisioning a more enlightened and representative state as a result. Lenin's plans and the potential for a truly socialist state fascinated rather than alarmed La Follette, although he shared Allied concerns when Lenin's decision to withdraw from World War I in early 1918 freed German troops to fight in France. La Follette was also disturbed by reports of Soviet appeals to American workers to stage a revolution of their own, which he felt weakened the forcefulness of arguments for the Soviets' own rights to self-determination. He maintained, however, that "the great organized wealth of all the established governments of the world at this time fears above all things on earth the principles attempted to be established by the soviet government of Russia," rendering it unlikely that "anything approaching the truth with respect to that government or what is taking place in Russia" would be permitted to "reach the ears of the masses of the people of the world." "[W]hether the Russian Government is good or bad according to our standards," he asserted, "it is not up for us to attempt to overthrow it." He reminded Congress, "We have enough to do at present right here in the United States and are likely to have for some time to come in making living conditions more tolerable and in restoring peace and prosperity and self-government to our own people." He noted the hypocrisy of Americans proposing a League of Nations that would make the United States "custodians of peace and instructors in democratic ideals to less enlightened peoples" while at the same time innocent African Americans, among them soldiers who had served with distinction in France fighting to make the world safe for democracy, were being terrorized on the streets of the nation's capital. Although he later denounced Soviet curtailment of personal rights and freedoms, for many Americans gripped by Red Scare hysteria following the war, he emerged a "dead in earnest agent of revolution via Moscow" by virtue of his insistence that Russia's self-determined economic and political state be respected. He continued to protest the presence of American troops in Russia until their final withdrawal in April 1920 and denounced until his 1924 presidential campaign the hypocrisy of his country's policies toward the emerging Soviet Union.[14]

The hottest debate of the extra session was reserved for the peace treaty drawn up at Versailles, particularly the proposed League of Nations. "By ratifying this document [the proposed treaty] in its present form," La Follette declared, "we shall involve this country in the quarrels and dissension of Europe for generations to come . . . [and prevent the U.S. from] turning its energies to the solution of its domestic problems without reference to the bewildering imperialism and diplomacy." "Senators," he warned his colleagues, "if we go into this thing it means a great standing army; it means conscription to fight in foreign wars, a blighting curse upon the family life of every American home every hour." Joining the League would bring "higher taxes, higher prices, harder times for the poor," as well as "greater discontent, a deeper, more menacing unrest." "I shall never vote," he concluded, "to bind my country to the monstrous undertaking which this covenant would impose." He proclaimed the League "from the first sentence to the last . . . a sham and a fraud . . . written in a frenzy of hate to enslave the German people." Although many senators shared his views, he worried about generating public disapproval, for, he maintained, "Not one in a thousand has ever read the League. Not one in ten thousand has ever analyzed it. They are just for a 'League to Stop War.'" La Follette's own wife urged, "Some kind of federated world whose ideal *should* be the best good of all, is bound to come," but added, "the proposed League of Nations may be so bad you can not support it. I am only suggesting the spirit in which I think it should be approached."[15]

La Follette complained bitterly about the Senate's reaction to various compromises reached previously: "We yawp a little as one after another of the vital things go by the board and then settle down to a sullen acceptance of absolute betrayal on the *crux* of the war. How long, oh Lord, how long!" With Republicans outnumbering the Democrats by only two votes, La Follette's status within the Senate, observed the *New Republic*, "was something like that of a daughter who had strayed from the path of virtue, but had been restored to a place in the family circle because the family was in straits and needed help with the housework." The intensity of La Follette's objections to the proposed peace treaty, however, did not render him willing to cooperate unquestionably with other senators who shared his views. When approached to confer on the issues with Wilson's leading foe, majority leader Henry Cabot Lodge, La Follette declined, claiming he had more important business at hand, that of "communicating my thinks to the people who pay me a dollar a year to tell 'em what I'm thinking about twelve times. That's a whole lot better than Henry Cabot will do. What he really wants I suspect is to tell *me* what I *ought* to think." Lodge was probably, at least in part, relieved by this rebuff. The Massachusetts senator had long held La Follette in disdain. In a 1917 letter to Theodore Roosevelt criticizing La Follette's vote opposing a break with Germany, Lodge scornfully characterized La Follette as a Republican who "always votes with the Democrats." La Follette was not wholly incapable of working with colleagues to achieve a shared political goal, however. Although he and Senators Hiram Johnson and William Borah failed to achieve American withdrawal from Russia in the early months of 1919, they did succeed in keeping the issue of intervention before the public and worked, to Lodge's great satisfaction, toward the defeat of the proposed peace treaty.[16]

Although Wilson was intensely disappointed by the nature of the changes written into the treaty by the more vengeful leaders at Versailles, he remained convinced that it remained the world's only real chance to create a lasting peace. Unable to persuade Lodge and the other reservationists within the Senate, he was incapable of negotiation concerning the already compromised treaty. Like La Follette, Wilson found to his dismay that self-righteousness is frequently indistinguishable from arrogance: French president Georges Clemenceau, for one, maintained that Wilson "thinks he is another Jesus Christ come upon earth to reform men." "God gave us the Ten Commandments and we broke them," Clemenceau snorted. "Wilson gave us the Fourteen Points — we shall see." At home, opposition based on Wilson's personal intractability compounded the more serious and far-reaching concerns.[17]

La Follette grew increasingly confident of the Senate's ability to block American entry into what he considered a vast potential for foolhardy forays into foreign involvements, but his relief was dampened in July by the resignation of his personal secretary of sixteen years. Colonel John J. Hannan's resignation led to intensification of La Follette's efforts to persuade Bobbie to return from California to serve as "temporary" secretary. According to his biographer, Patrick Maney, Bobbie "did not realize it at the time, but in the fall of 1919 he made the most important decision of his life . . . [when he] agreed to replace [Hannan]. Having ruled out a political career for himself, he fully intended to work for his father only until he found a suitable non-political job. But for the next six years, circumstances, some of which were probably contrived by his father, and a sense of obligation prevented him from leaving the senator's side. As one family member later described it, every time that [Bobbie] 'made up his mind to break away some crisis — illness or political — seemed to make it impossible for him to leave his father at that particular moment.'"[18]

July brought not only the "desertion" of Hannan but the sudden departure of Belle, who, claiming illness induced by infection following the extraction of two teeth, traveled with Fola to the West Virginia mountains to escape the severe Washington heat. Suspicious that Belle also sought relief from financial worries and his own preoccupation with politics, La Follette minimized political issues in his letters to her, focusing instead on his love for her and on his efforts to find a more affordable place for them to live.

La Follette's efforts to find a new house were half-hearted at best, however; for although they could not afford their current residence, he was "so enamored of that place" he could see "no virtue" in any other.[19]

In August he renewed his commitment to breaking up monopolies, blaming the press, recent chief executives, and both parties for aiding in the entrenchment of "lawless monopoly in business throughout the land." "We must make [a] beginning at once if we would avert disaster," he warned his fellow senators. If given free reign, La Follette mused, his first step would be to "have the Government take back the title to its iron ore and coal and copper and timber and the other natural products." Equal access to these resources would be made through a strict leasing system or through actual governmental control. La Follette continued to oppose leasing public lands, particularly naval oil reserves, to coal and oil companies. Such legislation, he warned his fellow senators, marked "the culmination of a struggle of private interests to control coal and other natural resources of the country as against the interests of the people of the United States and the United States Government." He offered Wisconsin's past as a warning, painting a vivid portrait of the "great lumber organizations, enriched by the despoliation of our natural resources in Wisconsin, [who] became the dictators of the public policy of the State." And it was not only the environmental devastation that he decried: "We have looked on quiescently while these great natural products have been absorbed and have passed under the control of the great monopolies, and then we marvel . . . at the cost of living climbing higher and higher every year. What idiocy that is! What stupidity! What can be expected if the iron, coal, copper and timber, which control the cost of everything else, are in the hands of the monopolies, with the result that they fix the price?"[20]

La Follette denounced the "reprehensible" activities of Standard Oil in particular: "It has driven people all over this country out of business, crushed competition, and driven competitors to suicide." While he stressed that the government should "protect and insure itself future ample reserves of oil for its Navy," he urged that the ultimate goal should be "the emancipation of the people of this country from monopoly control." Bigger than the issues of the League of Nations or the treaty made at Versailles, he argued, "the fundamental problem of the American people [is that] the power that is trying to take the naval reserves is only one of the many that are encroaching upon the rights of the American people and upon their democracy." La Follette used this occasion to vindicate his 1912 Philadelphia speech, touting the wisdom of its prediction that the day was fast approaching when magazines would cease to publish criticism of "this encroachment upon the liberties of the people, this overlordship that controls the industrial and commercial life." That day was nearly at hand, La Follette warned, citing the alarming decrease of such criticism within the pages of major periodicals. He attributed the blame in equal parts to Wilson, Taft, and Roosevelt.[21]

Following endless wrangling, debate, resolutions, and reservations, the Treaty of Paris went down in defeat. It received a majority of votes, but not the necessary two-thirds. La Follette voted against all the various versions of the treaty. Snorted Democratic floor leader Gilbert Hitchcock, "[La Follette] voted against war, now he votes against peace." A desperate Wilson, devastated by the Senate's rejection of the treaty and especially by its refusal to join the League, took his case directly to the American public in an ambitious speaking campaign. La Follette warned the readers of his magazine that "this League and Treaty is nothing but an old, old scheme, modified a little, to fit the times,— of an alliance among the victorious governments, following a great war, by which the conquered enemies may be kept in subjugation and exploited to the utmost." La Follette's tirades against Wilson continued even after a stroke incapacitated Wilson in the midst of his national tour in the fall of 1919, earning La Follette criticism for having no respect for the presidency or sympathy for Wilson.[22]

As the debates raged over what constituted a rightful peace, La Follette enjoyed immensely the Christmas of 1919, for it brought the entire family together, creating "the kind of gay reunion he had been dreaming of and writing about" ever since Bobbie and Belle had departed for California. In January 1920, La Follette was again tempted to abandon the Senate in favor of running for the Wisconsin governorship, but ultimately declined in the resulting storm of dissent, confusion, and renewed rumors of physical and mental illness. La Follette, who had long suffered pains in his side, complained of a severe cold and complications with his teeth. He traveled to Minnesota to undergo a thorough examination at the Mayo Clinic. Although diagnosed as suffering mainly from "over-eating, over-work, and over-strain," La Follette announced he would return to the clinic in the spring for the removal of his gall sac. The successful surgery, in early June, followed by a long convalescence, left La Follette feeling, he claimed, "much more like my old self and . . . free to a large extent from the pain and the dull headaches from which I suffered before."[23]

La Follette was unwilling even during his convalescence to abandon all hope of attaining the presidency in 1920. But when twenty-four of Wisconsin's twenty-six delegates steadfastly voted for La Follette during the balloting at the convention in Chicago, their tenacity was met by boos and jeers from their fellow Republicans. Warren G. Harding was nominated on the tenth ballot, with Calvin Coolidge as his running mate. La Follette, refusing to admit defeat, courted support outside his party, hoping the Labor Party and the newly formed Committee of Forty-Eight (a fledgling party of progressive Republicans dissatisfied with Harding's candidacy) would unite in their platforms and draft him as their leader. According to Bobbie, his father would "be a candidate overnight . . . if someone came along with the money to conduct a campaign . . . and therefore for the first time I will look askance on anyone who comes along and seems to have any indication of carrying money bags." Adequate financing could not be obtained, nor could the Labor Party and the Committee of Forty-Eight reach a workable compromise. Although nominated by the Labor Party, La Follette reluctantly declined to run, finding the platform unacceptable. Despite this failure to create a viable third party, La Follette continued to gain support among farm and labor organizations.[24]

La Follette spent much of the fall of 1920 waging an unsuccessful campaign against the reelection of Wisconsin's junior senator, Irvine Lenroot. La Follette called his former lieutenant's votes in favor of the League of Nations and the Esch-Cummins bill (which returned the railroads to their private owners with a government guarantee of profits) a betrayal of the American people. "Is it rational to believe," he asked caustically while denouncing Esch-Cummins on the floor of the Senate, "that in a few short months a small group of senators and representatives — no one of us an expert in railway transportation — has discovered some magic by which the miserable failures of seventy years are to be converted into a marvelous success?" La Follette waged his campaign mostly through the mails, fearful of the possibility of being misquoted while speaking publicly, but he did speak in Milwaukee, denouncing Lenroot for "*desert[ing] the progressive ranks under fire*" to become "a reactionary and a servant of special interests." While La Follette and Lenroot were split over the war and other significant political issues, the vociferousness of La Follette's attacks are reminiscent of his earlier feud with McGovern.[25]

Following Lenroot's reelection, La Follette, enjoying the company of his family at Maple Bluff Farm, complained of cold symptoms and delayed his return to Washington past the opening of Congress. Bobbie and Belle accompanied him to Washington, where Belle claimed they were all thoroughly pleased and content with Bobbie's position as aide and secretary to his father. Bobbie, however, reported that Belle had taken to her bed in a "very nervous condition." Although Belle cited continued problems with her teeth as the cause, the doctor could find "nothing wrong in any way except her nerves." "This leaves her," noted Bobbie, "with one outlet for her energies . . . and that is through Dad's work. This of course is trying to the extreme as both she and I have so closely identified ourselves with him that we are constantly trying to make him do things as we would and when he does not it is very hard on us." Bobbie urged his mother to take a trip to "restore her confidence in herself and her ability to do good work which . . . she has come to doubt a bit."[26]

Father and son spent the winter's congressional session devoted to amending the Mineral Leasing and Water Power Acts to ensure the regulation of mineral prices. Their proposed legislation was rejected, despite La Follette's dire predictions about both the waste of natural resources and the evils of monopoly control. They also promoted the development of a graduated estate or inheritance tax, which La Follette hoped would pay the interest on the war debt and prevent, or at least retard, the accumulation of immense fortunes in the hands of the few through the generations. In May, La Follette spoke at length on the floor of the Senate, protesting the expense and questioning the utility of proposals to enlarge the U.S. Navy: "[I]f this great Government, the richest and foremost of all the earth, had the courage to dock its Navy and say to the world that it is done with this business, there is not another nation on the face of the earth that could impose upon its people the burden of taxation which is necessary to maintain the military establishments that we are forcing them to build by the insane policy which we are pursuing." He decried the continuing "enormous profits" enjoyed by private industries as a result of government contracts, warning his fellow senators, "You will pay for your loyalty to private business before you get through with it. You can not fool the public forever." During the spring La Follette gradually regained his confidence on the speaking platform beyond the Senate and delivered rousing speeches in his old lengthy and detailed style, warning the public that it was losing its grip on a government increasingly controlled by large corporations.[27]

In the fall of 1921, La Follette began to prepare his campaign for reelection to the Senate. Although his magazine gradually accrued losses, La Follette enjoyed a period of renewed confidence and strength. He gloried in Bobbie's companionship and was elated by Phil's graduation with honors from the University of Wisconsin law school. To his great satisfaction the Committee on Privileges and Elections reimbursed $5,000 he incurred in legal expenses during that committee's investigation during the war. Moreover, a resolution was introduced into the Senate calling for a public burning of the denouncement of La Follette's war record by the faculty of the University of Wisconsin. La Follette discouraged this symbolic act of vindication, replying, "Time is the great sifter and winnower of truth. The formal destruction of that document cannot change the fact of its existence. I stated many times from the public platform in Wisconsin during the recent campaigns that I would not change my record on the war with any man in the United States Senate. History alone can judge impartially. So far as I am personally concerned, I am well content that this document shall remain as a physical evidence of the hysteria attendant upon the war."[28]

Others remained steadfast in their rejection of La Follette. Certainly former president Wilson was in no mood to extend the olive branch, especially after La Follette's 18 October 1921 speech urging the Senate not to ratify the treaty between the United States and Germany, signed in Berlin on 25 August. La Follette went down in defeat, but not before he declared Wilson "guilty of betraying the American people" for not implementing his promised New Freedom and for sacrificing the "proper" interests of the American public and risking the stability of American democracy itself in favor of "European quarrels and dissensions." Wilson appears not to have criticized La Follette by name in the few speeches and documents he completed following his retirement from politics. The *New York Times*, however, in reporting Wilson's Armistice Day speech in 1922, included La Follette in the list of senators denounced by Wilson because they "preferred personal partisan motives to the honor of their country and the peace of the world." According to Wilson, the guilty senators "do not represent the United States, because the United States is moving forward and they are slipping backward." "Where the slipping will end," the former president noted, "God only will determine," but, he predicted, "Puny persons who are now standing in the way [of lasting peace] will presently find that their weakness is no match for the strength of a moving Providence."[29]

Although La Follette still suffered from wartime hurts and ongoing indignities, he was nonetheless gratified by the efforts of many to help heal the old wounds. He was also increasingly aware of the toll of his continued political and personal efforts. He quoted Alice from *Through the Looking Glass*: "Now *here*, you see, it takes all the running you can do to keep in the same place. If you want to get somewhere else you must run at least twice as fast as that." He did not, however, use such cynicism to rationalize a retreat from political confrontation but instead embarked upon what would become a lengthy investigation into the leasing of naval reserve oil lands to private concerns. Less than three months after his inauguration, President Warren G. Harding ordered the transfer of control of naval oil reserves in Wyoming and California from Navy Secretary Edwin Denby to Interior Secretary Albert Fall at Fall's request. La Follette, who had fought hard to preserve those lands, saw this executive order as a dangerous change in policy and began research into the lands' status. "The Senator," reported Louis D. Brandeis, "looks finely and is in great fighting trim. He and his friends are giving the administration headaches. He says, in substance, that the President is an automaton worked by the old guard."[30]

Many Americans, weary from not just the strain of the war, but the many years of fast-paced social, economic, and political change that preceded it, welcomed Harding's administration as a "return to normalcy." Given the rare opportunity to appoint four Supreme Court justices, Harding's choices were conservative, including former president William Howard Taft as Chief Justice. When Taft's court set about rolling back many hard-fought progressive gains, La Follette began to promote a constitutional amendment to allow Congress to override the Court's legislative "veto" power. The willingness to tamper with fundamental elements of the complex system of checks and balances established by the original creators of the Constitution branded La Follette both arrogant and dangerous in the eyes of many.

Harding had called La Follette an enemy to his country during the war not because of his opposition to American entry but, he said, because La Follette attempted to "instill in the hearts of men envy, jealousy, and suspicion of all who succeed" and spread "the impression that wealth and graft are in control of our government and . . . all government agents." Although the newly elected Harding initially treated him with distant respect in 1922, La Follette must have enjoyed some measure of satisfaction when his preliminary investigation of the oil lands' leasings revealed corruption in Harding's cabinet. Wyoming senator John Kendrick, alerted by rumors of secret leasings of oil reserves in his state, introduced a resolution on 15 April requesting that the Secretaries Fall and Denby release all pertinent information. It was reluctantly disclosed that naval reserve number three in Wyoming, known as the Teapot Dome due to an unusual rock formation, had been released on 7 April to Harry Sinclair's Mammoth Oil Company. The value of the oil in number three alone had been conservatively estimated at a half billion dollars. Reminding his fellow Republicans of the harm to the party's conservationist reputation following the 1909 Ballinger-Pinchot controversy, La Follette began his demand for an investigation. "The three great naval reserves have recently become private oil reserves," La Follette announced to a startled Senate on 28 April, "[and] are being sacrificed to private exploitation at the hands of the favored interests." Democratic leader Gilbert Hitchcock, commenting that La Follette "is making some amazing revelations," ensured that a quorum was present to hear La Follette's charges of conspiracy to lease the oil reserves to private companies. La Follette introduced a resolution, passed unanimously, to investigate the entire matter of oil lands in the naval petroleum reserves. Although the investigation languished for a time, La Follette continued to collect evidence and persuaded Montana's Thomas Walsh to pursue the probe. As the Teapot Dome scandal took shape, it greatly enhanced La Follette's reputation as a defender of the public and an enemy of corruption and special interests, galvanizing his position as a powerful radical in the Senate. The scandal forced Albert Fall from office. He resigned on 2 January 1923 (effective 4 March) but staunchly defended his leasing policy. Although he termed the more than $400,000 provided him by oil companies to be loans rather than bribes, after many investigations, trials, and delays, Fall was fined $100,000 and sentenced to a year in prison.[31]

Even among Republicans, La Follette's role in the uncovering of the Teapot Dome scandal revealed him to many not as a traitor to his party but as a man who put the best interests of the American public above petty partisan concerns. Such a reputation was a great asset in the 1922 senatorial campaign, a campaign La Follette decided should rest on four issues: opposition to the Four Power Pact, in favor of an executive policy that would limit U.S. involvement in foreign entanglements; reduction of railroad rates through the restoration of power to state commissions; more equitable taxation; and fair and moral campaign practices. The opposition, spearheaded by junior senator Lenroot, supported college instructor and minister William Arthur Ganfield and denounced La Follette as "obstructionist" in the Senate, anti-prohibition, and pro-German during the war. La Follette led a vigorous speaking campaign in Wisconsin. Enormous, enthusiastic crowds flocked to hear his assertions that the government must revert to the people despite new schemes being promoted by big business.[32] La Follette won the primary with more than 70 percent of the votes cast. He viewed this triumph as a final vindication of his position during the war, although he alone of the six senators Wilson had denounced as "a little group of willful men" remained in office. "Thank God," said Belle, "we have all lived to see him recognized and honored."[33]

The victory gave new impetus to La Follette's presidential ambitions. Following the primary, he traveled to St. Paul, the site of his sensational oration during the war, to deliver to a huge crowd a speech his family agreed would be the climax of the previous five years. Only a few blocks away, incumbent Minnesota senator Frank B. Kellogg, a leader in the fight to have La Follette ousted from the Senate during the war, addressed a much smaller group. Within the pages of his magazine, La Follette had declared Kellogg the "Attorney for Farmers' Enemies" and decried Kellogg's voting record in the Senate. In St. Paul, campaigning for Kellogg's opponent, Farmer-Labor candidate Henrik Shipstead, La Follette delivered a vengeful attack that betrayed his continued bitterness and resentment at the treatment he had received at the hands of Kellogg, who walked with a pronounced stoop, and

*Phoenix rising from the ashes: La Follette in 1922. (Library of Congress LC-USZ62-9467)*

like-minded others during the war: "The best that can be said of . . . [Kellogg] is that he has served . . . powerful trusts just as well in the Senate as he served them in the courts. . . . God Almighty through nature writes men's characters on their faces and in their forms. Your Senator has bowed obsequiously to wealth and to corporations' orders and to his masters until God Almighty has given him a hump on his back—crouching, cringing, un-American, unmanly." Following this speech, La Follette said with a "mischievous grin" to his son Phil: "Your mother will give me hell for saying that about Kellogg." Belle was indeed horrified and deplored the incident, claiming it unworthy and out of character. To add injury to insult, Shipstead defeated Kellogg in the election.[34]

La Follette enjoyed tributes to his own lifelong commitment to integrity and honesty. The *New York Herald* proclaimed his political resurrection: "Once the 'Lonely Man of the Senate,' Robert M. La Follette today is the leader of a faction, a radical bloc, that is likely to hold the balance of power in the House and perhaps in the Senate in the next Congress. In his forty years and more of public life La Follette has never been stronger politically than he is at present." As 1922 drew to a close, press reports provided conflicting portraits of La Follette. *The Outlook* commented on his new "tolerance," "reasonableness," and "mellowing," but the *St. Louis Post Dispatch* maintained that La Follette's "fighting spirit has the same relentless, indomitable quality of two decades ago." He was reelected senator by 278,552 votes, the largest majority ever given to a public official at that point in Wisconsin history. At sixty-seven, his "bodily vigor slightly abated," La Follette faced life with a renewed sense of political and personal confidence and purpose. Noting his continued resistance to being a party regular, the *Raleigh News and Observer* commented, "His success is the most remarkable exhibition of personal power in American politics in the present decade."[35]

# 16: FINAL BATTLES
## I WANT TO DIE . . . WITH MY BOOTS ON

By February 1923 La Follette's circle of influence extended to twenty of the thirty-seven Republican senators. The partisan *Wisconsin State Journal* warned, "Let none mistake the power of Robert M. La Follette. Today no bill can pass Congress without his sanction. It is equally true that no man can become President without his approval." As one journalist phrased it, "The radical bloc kept on forming around La Follette until the original coral insect had formed a coral reef [which was] mighty dangerous." La Follette relentlessly blasted the Harding administration as incompetent and corrupt, concluding, "Two more years of such achievements will bring disaster to [the] American nation and oblivion to [the] Republican Party." The *Washington Post* asserted that higher wages and the current labor shortage belied such "demagogic warnings" and suggested that La Follette's desire for the presidency in 1924 motivated his dire predictions.[1]

La Follette did not publicly acknowledge renewed presidential ambitions in 1923, but in March he planned a tour of Europe to strengthen his authority concerning foreign affairs. In preparation, he traveled to John Kellogg's famous Battle Creek Sanitarium in Michigan for a thorough examination and a long rest, for he was troubled by chest pains, indications of increasing heart disease. The aging process was compounding the toll. Despite his claims of an iron constitution, La Follette's health was deteriorating visibly. Over the previous decade his always stocky physique had softened considerably. His face, particularly his formerly firm jaw, grew fleshy. La Follette's lifelong pattern had been to give everything of himself to meet a challenge until his health collapsed. Once his concerted efforts to achieve candidacy placed him in the spotlight, he could afford no breakdown, no period of convalescence, however brief. His former resiliency diminished, La Follette determined to build up sufficient reserves to carry him through a fast-paced tour of Europe followed by a grueling campaign.

Although La Follette claimed his months at Battle Creek were devoted wholly to regaining his health, he developed presidential campaign strategies during that stay. He also followed the progress of Bobbie, whom he had dispatched to Wisconsin to push a tax reform measure through the state legislature. Bobbie's role in persuading the warring factions to accept the bill overjoyed La Follette, for he perceived it as confirmation of his son's political potential. Many messages of love and of concern for his own health also reassured La Follette, and he extended his stay at the sanitarium rather than conduct a planned campaign for progressive candidates in Minnesota. He cautioned, however, "I must be careful not to have anything go to the public which would give the lying press a chance to represent me as a dead one."[2]

Physician John Kellogg warned the senator he would be dead in two years unless he worked only moderately and with proper periods of rest and relaxation. La Follette replied, "I don't want to — I just can't — live rolled up in a cotton blanket in a damned wheelchair. I want to die, as I have lived, with my boots on. . . . We are going right ahead with our plans, with a full head of steam in the boiler." Despite pleas of family and physicians, La Follette, who for so long "seemed almost to court defeat" in the belief that short-term loss leads to a more smashing victory in the long run, refused to relinquish one final run for the presidency. The obstacle blocking his first step toward candidacy was removed in July 1923 when wealthy admirer William T. Rawleigh, who paid for La Follette's stay at Battle Creek, offered to finance the tentatively planned European tour. Days before his departure La Follette hinted broadly that a third party movement was likely in 1924. Meanwhile, he charged his son Phil to "carry the gospel to the people" on a chautauqua circuit during his absence.[3]

On 1 August 1923, La Follette, whose traveling party included progressives Molly and Basil Manly as well as Belle and Bobbie, sailed from New York on the *George Washington*. The following evening President Warren Harding died of a coronary in San Francisco. At the request of the ship's captain, La Follette conducted a memorial service for the man he had previously denounced as a corrupt reactionary. La Follette concentrated not on Harding's performance as chief executive but, mindful of his own failing health and the warning of his physician, focused on the exhausting nature of the presidency, noting that Harding "literally gave up his life in meeting the exacting demands of his great office." "When we consider that of the last five presidents two have died in office and a third has returned sorely stricken and broken in health," he told the gathered mourners, "we begin to appreciate in some measure the great and ever increasing burdens and sacrifices which those who are elected to this high office are called upon to endure."[4]

La Follette's increasing awareness of the lethal potential of overwork did not hamper his activities once his party arrived in Europe. Their three-month tour included England, Germany, the Soviet Union, Poland, Austria, Italy, Denmark, and France. To Belle's dismay, Bob put aside little time for pleasure and concentrated his energies on meeting with various political leaders. He was nevertheless struck by the wonders around him and confided wistfully, "It was wrong that Belle and I did not go to Europe thirty years earlier. Everyone should go to Europe and go in youth." While in Germany, La Follette sacrificed all sightseeing in order to meet with the nation's new chancellor (and later foreign minister) Gustav Stresemann, Reichstag members, labor chiefs, newspaper editors, industrialists, financiers, and business leaders. The devastating effects of food shortages and inflation overwhelmed La Follette. Upon his return he introduced an unsuccessful bill asking for $10 million in relief to save the German people from starvation and help preserve their infant democracy.[5]

La Follette rested insufficiently in Germany and suffered from exhaustion and a cold. He also experienced frightening chest pains, culminating, to his great disappointment, in the cancellation of a return trip to London. After a period of rest, the party traveled to Moscow, where it was joined by Lincoln Steffens and Jo Davison. Belle expressed relief to be in a place "in which we do not feel obliged to study the conditions." Such relief was short lived, and the careful examination of the Soviet system began. The articles Belle wrote for *La Follette's Magazine* expressed her admiration for the new government. She praised the Soviets for, among other things, quickly enacting the kinds of labor reforms that Florence Kelley and the Consumers' League continued, unsuccessfully, to demand within the United States. Bob's reports were also enthusiastic, but his praise was hardly unqualified. He noted that Lenin, then in his final illness, was "beloved" by the peasants, yet La Follette was greatly disturbed by the lack of free elections and free press, the general suppression of civil liberties, and the exile and "outrageous" treatment of political opponents. He predicted nevertheless, "It may not come in ten years. It may not come in twenty. But I shall live to see Russia one of the greatest democracies on earth," an unrealistic, wishful conjecture in view of the pervasiveness of the conditions he noted and the state of his own health. He also predicted, "Russia is destined to play a large if not dominant part in the international developments of the next ten years." La Follette urged that the "process of awakening Russia to demand the fundamentals of democracy . . . be hastened by the renewal of intercourse with the outside world."[6]

Many on the American left heeded La Follette's call and also came to witness the Soviet experiment firsthand. Progressive educator John Dewey deemed it the near fulfillment of his philosophic hopes: "The main effort is nobly heroic, evincing a faith in human nature which is democratic beyond the ambitions of the democracies of the past." The several hundred economists, labor leaders, artists, leaders of ethnic minorities, social scientists, business leaders, social workers, and reformers, including La Follette, who came to the Soviet Union between 1917 and 1932 and publicized their impressions have been credited with playing a large role in transforming American thought, influencing many intellectual and social leaders to con-

*La Follette and his entourage in the USSR, 1923.*
*(State Historical Society of Wisconsin WHi[X3]51968)*

sider the Soviet Union a kind of "conscience-model" of experimentation for the New Deal. La Follette certainly urged Americans, especially his colleagues in the Senate, to rethink their attitudes toward the young republic. Despite his horror at the control of elections by the elites within the Communist Party, La Follette encouraged the United States and other countries to recognize the Soviet Union and reestablish trade and commercial relations. He even invited the Soviets to send a committee to Wisconsin to study the reforms he had implemented there.[7]

In Rome, La Follette met with Benito Mussolini and expressed his dismay at the lack of freedom of the press throughout Italy. In a series of articles published for the Sunday edition of the Hearst newspapers upon his return to the United States, La Follette contrasted Mussolini's power with the vulnerability of the war-torn citizens of almost every European country. La Follette noted that the common people were "wearied by the ten years of war and turmoil which they have endured, have lost faith in their power to control their destinies and are in a state of mind which makes them an easy prey to the forces of reaction and tyranny." He continued, "I went to Europe five years after the end of the 'war to end war' and 'to make the world safe for democracy'—four years after the so-called peace of Versailles. Instead of peace, I found new wars in the making." The people, according to La Follette, "have come to doubt whether it is possible to achieve international justice or self-government. This fact . . . lies at the basis of the movements to seize control of the machinery of government by force and establish dictatorships." Because the people had forgotten "that their ultimate safety and happiness lies only in themselves," they were "ready to trust their fortunes to any adventurer or would-be Napoleon who offers by force to rid them of the dire conditions that are then irritating or oppressing them."

Conditions in the countries La Follette toured varied, yet certain commonalities remained: "Between the upper and nether millstones of imperialistic and communistic dictatorships — between the fascists and bolshevists of the different countries — the institutions of democracy are being ground to dust." He turned first to Italy, where "the black-shirted fascists have elevated Mussolini to a dictatorship which overrides parliaments and courts of justice. The liberal forces dare not speak." Things were no better in Russia: "the communists, backed by the Red army, have crushed the opposition." Germany, he observed, "is now being rent asunder by civil strife, in which monarchists and communists are simultaneously striving to tear down the republic and erect in its place a dictatorship, resting not on the will of the people, but upon force and arms." Finally he prophesied, with chilling accuracy, "Until that infamous compact [the Treaty of Paris] and its sister treaties have been completely wiped out and replaced by enlightened understandings among the European nations, there will be no peace upon the continent or in the world, and all the pettifogging conferences, councils, and world courts will not prevent or seriously retard the new world war that is now rapidly developing from the seeds of malice, hatred and revenge that were sown at Versailles."[8]

Bobbie called their European trip "profitable," for it allowed Bob to gather information of "invaluable service" to him in his work in the Senate and in the impending campaign. La Follette himself called it "the biggest experience of my life." At the family's new residence at 2112 Wyoming Avenue, he set about organizing the series of newspaper articles. His progress was hampered, however, by his increasingly debilitating heart condition. His family claimed La Follette suffered only from "a grippe cold." La Follette was unable to attend the opening of the congressional session in December. In an article entitled "Senate Progressives Letting One Man's Illness Kill Their Prospects," the *Washington Daily News* claimed La Follette was about to see the fruits of several years' fighting slip out of his hands due to his absence during the crucial opening sessions under the new administration. Two days later, in an effort to squelch reports of broken health, La Follette granted his first interview since his return from Europe. He maintained that, but for a slight cold, he felt fine, that newspapers had been attempting to "bury" him for thirty years and that, borrowing from Mark Twain, the reports of his impending death were "greatly exaggerated." He concluded, "It hasn't been to my liking to sit on the side-lines after the whistle has blown, but there is some hard fighting ahead and I expect to be in it."[9]

Despite all public denials, La Follette suffered a series of heart attacks and took large amounts of nitroglycerine and morphine. He worried about the lackadaisical performance by progressive senators without his leadership. In defiance of doctors' orders, he began a revolt from his sickbed against old guard senator Albert Cummins, who sought to chair the powerful Interstate Commerce Committee. La Follette returned to a warm reception in the Senate on 3 January 1924 and engineered Cummins's defeat and the election of fellow progressive Ellison Smith to the chair. Smith's election marked the first time a Democratic senator had been elected to chair a committee led by Republicans, demonstrating to the Republican majority in particular the force of La Follette's strength. La Follette devised a code by which he could communicate on campaign matters with his staff members without fear of detection. When not developing his campaign, he "determined on a thorough housecleaning" of government departments reputed to be seats of graft and corruption. While these efforts reassured him of his moral superiority and his power within the Senate, they also culminated in renewed exhaustion and illness in March. La Follette's resultant bout with pneumonia brought the entire family to what they feared was his deathbed.[10]

Despite his failing health, La Follette's name continued to appear as a potential third party candidate for president in 1924. President Coolidge's supporters ridiculed any talk of unseating the incumbent, urging Americans to stay the course of peace and prosperity. Coolidge, who beat out La Follette's Wisconsin nemesis Irvine Lenroot for the vice presidential nomination in 1920, committed himself to carrying out Harding's policies, although he was not without his own agenda. Coolidge had managed to distance himself from his predecessor's scandals and, through his quiet, calm demeanor, restored the integrity of the oval office. Perhaps best known for intoning, "The chief business of America is business," Coolidge personified for many Americans contentment with the status quo. Such placid acceptance, even celebration, of the domination of America by business signified to La Follette not the defeat of progressivism, but rather the need for renewed vigor in promoting meaningful economic and social reform. And by no means was La Follette universally perceived as a solitary figure tilting at windmills. The *Philadelphia North American* reported, "Never in the country's history . . . has any other man held so dominating a position in respect to matters of national legislation and national politics." Such a powerful figure, it argued, could play a pivotal role in the next presidential election: "Competent observers everywhere concede that as an independent or third

CAN'T STOP HIM

*Not even the power of Wall Street, supported by both parties, can match the forward momentum of La Follette's progressive movement. (Talburt, Cleveland Press; reprinted in "La Follette and the German Vote," Literary Digest 83 [11 Oct. 1924]: 11)*

party candidate he would carry enough states in the west and northwest to deprive President Coolidge of a majority of the electors, and to capture himself the balance of power in the electoral college." However, even the supportive *North American* was forced to admit that there were limits to La Follette's influence and to the man himself: "He is sixty-eight years old and not in robust health; lacking faith in the Republican party as now managed, he realizes that if it gains a lease of power for another four years his legislative program will be deferred until he is no long able to fight for it." "His influence," the story concluded, "is now at its zenith."[11]

Certainly there were those eager to see La Follette yield that influence, who sought to disrupt rather than protect the status quo. The distress of laborers and farmers stemmed from many sources. The gross national product fell 2.2 percent in 1924, and laborers and their unions had recently lost out to a number of corporate-government alliances. Union membership declined. Farmers suffered as prices in early 1924 remained one-third lower than their 1920 levels. The resentment of both groups was fueled by the role of Treasury secretary Andrew Mellon (the aluminum, oil, and banking magnate) in pushing through large tax cuts for the wealthy. In 1922, a combination of union members, farmers, socialists, and various progressives joined to form the Conference for Progressive Political Action (CPPA). Showing surprising strength in that year's elections, some 140 members of the new Congress representing several states were either officially endorsed by the party or expressed support for its antimonopoly, pro-labor, and pro-election reform platform. Early in the Sixty-eighth Congress they joined as a cohesive voting block. The CPPA agreed to select a presidential candidate if both major parties failed to choose a progressive at their conventions.[12]

La Follette attended the final days of the spring congressional session. Following its completion, despite all Bobbie's efforts to "keep him from over-doing," he devoted himself wholly to preparations for the 1924 campaign. Despite earlier declarations that he preferred to become a candidate by petition, La Follette actively sought the nomination of a major convention, although his efforts did not stir much enthusiasm in the press except among political cartoonists.[13] The *New York Times Magazine* reported, "In the Wisconsin primaries the Republicans named La Follette for the Presidency. An old story. Stick it on the bottom of an inside page. The badger state has been doing that for sixteen years."[14]

La Follette's supporters noted at the Republican National Convention in June that "twenty-six out of thirty-one demands in the platform that the La Follette forces have presented for adoption by their party every four years since 1908 — always contemptuously rejected — have bit by bit become law of the land." Nonetheless, La Follette garnered a mere 34 votes in Cleveland as Coolidge swept the first ballot with 1,165 votes. The Democrats' convention proved to be a far more volatile affair. The deadlock between Democrats Alfred E. Smith and William G. McAdoo at Madison Square Garden resulted in a "bloodbath" requiring 103 ballots. Compromise candidate John W. Davis, member of an eminent Wall Street law firm that included the J. P. Morgan Company among its clients, took the nomination.[15]

La Follette remained in Washington while Bobbie presented his father's statement and platform to the CPPA convention in Cleveland on 4 July 1924. La Follette declared via his son, "The time has come for a militant political movement, independent of the two old party organizations, and responsive to the needs and sentiments of the common people." He criticized the Republican convention for rejecting "the only Progressive platform" and for nominating "the frank defender of the present system of government in the interests of organized wealth." The Democratic Convention received criticism as well for its failure to meet the demands of true Progressives. La Follette formally announced himself as an Independent Progressive candidate for the presidency and provided the same planks he had unsuccessfully introduced to the Republican platform:

1. A thorough "housecleaning" of the Department of Justice, Department of Interior, and other executive departments.
2. The recovery of the naval oil reserves and the creation of a national "super-water-power" system.
3. Repeal of the Esch-Cummins law in favor of railroad rates based on actual, prudent investment.
4. A reduction of federal taxes on individual incomes and legitimate business.
5. A constitutional amendment giving Congress the power to reenact a statute over a judicial decision.
6. Drastic reductions in the schedules of the Fordney-McCumber tariff bill.
7. Abolition of injunctions in labor disputes and protection of the right of farmers and workers to organize.
8. Adjusted compensation for World War I veterans.
9. The construction of a waterway from the Great Lakes to the sea.
10. Nomination and election of the president by direct vote of the people. Extension of the initiative and referendum on wars except in cases of actual invasion.
11. Foreign policy to revise the Versailles Treaty and promote treaties to outlaw war, abolish conscription and reduce armaments.[16]

Plank five, perhaps the most controversial of the entire platform, would, by amendment to the Constitution, give Congress the power to pass and validate federal laws declared unconstitutional by the Supreme Court. In 1906 La Follette had declared, "The people have no need to fear the final judgement of the Supreme Court," for "[a]gain and again it has interposed the strong arm of the law between the people and the unlawful encroachment of corporate power." By 1921 he proclaimed that "The old fight against monopoly and special privilege" had been "brought to ignominious defeat" by recent Supreme Court decisions. The following year, two Supreme Court decisions struck down particularly hard-won progressive achievements. The first, *Coronado Coal Co. v. United Mine Workers*, distinguished manufacturing from commerce and found certain strike practices to be "unlawful restraints of trade." In the second, *Bailey v. Drexel Furniture Company*, the Court declared the Child Labor Tax Law invalid. A month after the *Bailey* decision, La Follette asked on the floor of the Senate, "Which is supreme, the will of the people or the will of the few men who have been appointed to life positions on the Federal bench?" La Follette's proposed remedy, plank five, was similar to the English method of overcoming Parliamentary measures by the House of Commons. It was nevertheless so contrary to the fundamental notions of American government and its system of checks and balances, according to at least one contemporary political analyst, that it destroyed any glimmer of hope for a successful La Follette candidacy.[17]

In addition to controversy over plank five, some progressives were disappointed in the absence of any denunciation of the Ku Klux Klan, then at the crest of its power, although African Americans (and women) were represented at the convention and La Follette issued anti–Ku Klux Klan campaign literature. La Follette's letter to E. W. Scripps denouncing the Klan appeared in the *New York Times* on 9 August, making him the first of the candidates to denounce the Klan by name, but he mentioned the Klan specifically in only one speech. (Coolidge ignored the Klan, while Davis attacked it consistently). La Follette's failure to include planks against Prohibition and for Soviet recognition also generated criticism, as did his assertion that states could dramatically reduce their taxes by cutting down "the exorbitant and wasteful expenditures" for the National Guard. Nevertheless, 1,200 delegates to the CPPA and 9,000 spectators voiced their enthusiastic acceptance of La Follette's platform.[18]

The strength of La Follette's appeal was attributed to four main factors: distressed farmers and laborers, disgust over the scandals of the Harding administration, impatience with Democratic failure to meet ongoing challenges, and La Follette's lively persona, especially in contrast to the incumbent, Coolidge, and to Democratic candidate John Davis, "two colorless, time-serving political straddlers." "Coolidge and Davis," Felix Frankfurter commented to famed journalist Walter Lippmann, "have nothing to offer for 1924; they have no dreams . . . except things substantially as is." The forces behind La Follette, the great jurist concluded, "are, at least, struggling and groping for a dream."[19]

Buoyed by earnest supporters, La Follette began a vigorous campaign with his vice presidential candidate, Burton K. Wheeler, Democratic senator from Montana. For his role in uncovering corruption in the Harding administration, Wheeler shared with La Follette a certain quixotic reputation. It was hoped that he would become a model for other Democrats in his assertion, "I cannot support any candidate representing the House of Morgan," for "I am a Democrat but not a Wall Street Democrat." A contest between a Republican candidate with "reactionary standpat policies" and a Democrat whose claims to progressivism were belied by his actions was, according to Wheeler, no contest at all. Only La Follette offered "fidelity to the interest of the people."[20]

La Follette supporters emerged from unexpected areas throughout the country, and African Americans, motivated by leader Colonel Roscoe Conklin Simmons's statement, "Senator La Follette is the hope of the Negro race," volunteered on a such a large scale there was insufficient personnel to efficiently utilize their support. Oswald Garrison Villard, one of the founders of the National Association for the Advancement of Colored People (NAACP), urged La Follette to appeal directly to African American voters. Although La Follette declined to make the African American cause a campaign issue, his influential supporters included W. E. B. Du Bois and Bishop Hurst of the African Methodist Episcopal Church. Author Zona Gale, feminist Harriet Stanton Blatch, and Hull House founder Jane Addams were some of the speakers recruited by the Women's Division of the La Follette–Wheeler campaign who urged women to put their newly won votes to the best possible use. La Follette's efforts to guarantee equal suffrage, abolish child labor, appoint women to public office, and promote peace were highlighted in the women's speeches. Labor leaders Florence Kelley and Rose Schneiderman voiced their support, as did philosopher John Dewey. Humanitarian Helen Keller wrote to La Follette, "For years I have followed your public efforts with approval and admiration. . . . I am for you because you have courage and vision and unyielding determination to find a sensible, just way out of the evils which threaten this country."[21]

Although the ticket enjoyed early widespread support, it was plagued by mismanagement and poor finances — the same factors that hobbled La Follette in 1912. Twenty-nine-year-old Bobbie La Follette was only reluctantly drawn into the campaign. Noted one reporter, "The spectacle of a man nearly seventy years old and with little organization and no money of his own, relying largely for assistance upon his two youthful sons, setting out to lick both the great national parties, is alone sufficient to command respect." La Follette's underdog status attracted admirers across the political spectrum. Less illustrious supporters included traditionally Republican Francis "Frank" Anthony Nixon, a struggling California lemon grower turned oilfield worker whose children included the thirty-seventh president. Richard Nixon's future father-in-law, a fellow southern Californian similarly down on his luck in 1924, also supported La Follette. (Richard Nixon, aged eleven in 1924, shared his father's admiration for La Follette.

While president, Nixon listed La Follette's *Autobiography* among his three most favorite books.) Like all third party candidates since the adoption of the Australian (or secret) vote, La Follette organizers faced a complex array of requirements to appear on various state ballots. The petition drives to acquire the requisite number of signatures ate up much of his precious funding, the bulk of which had been raised by single-dollar donations. Although there was not enough left to send his "cross-country" rail campaign farther west than St. Louis, La Follette's campaigners did manage to place his name on all but one (Louisiana) of the forty-eight state ballots, but under four different party labels: Progressive, Socialist, Farm-Labor, and Independent.[22]

Some of La Follette's support was inspired less by his specific proposals and more by a desire to retain cohesion among Progressive Republicans. La Follette promoters described their movement as "an honest successor but not a lineal descendant of the Bull Moose Party." This plea for progressive unity had mixed results at best, as many Roosevelt faithful continued to view La Follette as the Judas of the progressive movement. Republican Harold Ickes saw in this split the specter of the death of Republican progressivism, confiding in Hiram Johnson his fears that Coolidge's election would lead to a "natural drifting together of the La Follette Progressives and the Democrats." "The few Progressives that are left in the Republican Party," warned Ickes, "will have no more chance in that Party than the proverbial snowball." Ickes's "inexpressible disgust" for Coolidge led to his "almost overpowering inclination to pack my playthings and go off with the lunatic fringe," culminating in his becoming La Follette's midwestern campaign manager. Ickes and Bobbie La Follette shared management of the campaign with a number of individuals, each operating without the benefit of a strong central organization.[23]

Some found virtue in La Follette's underdog status. One reporter depicted La Follette as the antidote to the self-righteous complacency of Coolidge and termed La Follette's program "the reflection and expression of the salient interests of the members of those classes which the existing system deprives of a sufficient opportunity for liberating activity." Another noted optimistically, "The Englishman [Ramsey McDonald of the British Labor Party] whose war career is most strikingly like that of La Follette now rules England," and looked to La Follette, regardless of the outcome of the election, "to bring the real emancipation of America." Others, however, like an observer for the *Fairmont (Minn.) Independent*, scoffed at such "soft hearted" notions and asked, "How in the name of the pink-toed prophet can an intelligent person expect La Follette to succeed where Roosevelt failed [as an independent candidate]?" Aware that much of the public perceived him as naïve and out of touch with the economic and political realities of the postwar world, La Follette, eternally confident in the wisdom of educated "experts," announced that his candidacy had been endorsed by 63 professors of economics and sociology and 150 professors of history, religion, law, anthropology, languages, literature, psychology, and agriculture.[24]

La Follette sought to offset the Republican slogan of "Coolidge or Chaos," which played on the public's fear that La Follette's election would mean hard times financially. La Follette's campaigners, heeding the directions of *The Nation*'s managing editor, Ernest Gruening, stressed the savings the senator had procured for the American people by preventing the proposed exemption of certain corporations during the war, by exposing the corruption of the Teapot Dome deal, and by demanding fair taxation of railroads. Former head of the Forest Service, Gifford Pinchot, highlighted the "magnificent work" La Follette had done for conservation. La Follette's incorruptibility and his contributions to American workers were also emphasized throughout the campaign.[25]

The campaign officially opened for La Follette on Labor Day in 1924, when he gave the first political address ever delivered exclusively over the radio without a visible audience. Radio was a luxury of the middle class, reaching an audience unlikely to be swayed by La Follette, especially since a lifetime of stump speaking had left La Follette ill prepared for effective radio performances. He preferred the give-and-take of a public meeting, glorying in his ability to read his audience and tailor his remarks accordingly. His constant movement across the stage, which brought vitality to his stump speeches, led only to irregularity of volume in his radio addresses, and his legendary refusal to stick to a schedule was also a huge disadvantage in the rigidly timed world of radio. He lamented, "I like the freedom that comes from not being tied down to a miserable manuscript." Although the first feature-length, "talking" motion picture, Al Jolson's *The Jazz Singer*, did not appear until 1927, short sound films were already attracting large audiences. In August, De Forest Phonofilm recorded the three presidential candidates making campaign speeches and edited them into a single program, which was shown in theaters nationwide, marking another significant campaign "first" in 1924.[26]

Calvin Coolidge spoke in such a quiet monotone during the filming of his speech that the sound crew turned up their equipment in order to capture his voice. Those same settings were preserved when La Follette spoke later that day. With characteristic vigor and volume La Follette so overwhelmed the technology that he had to repeat his speech, "On Responsible Government," after the equipment had been readjusted. In a performance that "offers a rare glimpse of nineteenth century style oratory common in the days before film," La Follette, speaking on the capital steps, looks his

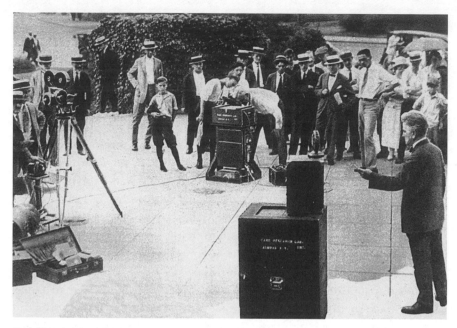

*Speaking on the capitol steps, La Follette is recorded on sound film, 11 August 1924.
(Image Hunters/Pieri & Spring Productions)*

sixty-nine years, his trademark pompadour, still thick, a snowy white. While he appears stocky, he is trimmer than even a few years before, and his voice, though it quavers a bit, is strong. Holding a copy of the speech in one hand, La Follette gestures broadly with the other while speaking in ringing tones. "America," he reminds his audience, "is not made, but in the making." After discussing the "unending struggle" to "make and keep government representative," he charges his listeners to take action themselves, for "mere passive citizenship is not enough. Men must be aggressive for what is right if government is to be saved from those who are aggressive for what is wrong." "There is work for everyone," he urges, "the field is large. It is a glorious service, this service for the country." Every American, he concludes, "should count it a patriotic duty to build at least a part of his life into the life of his country, to do his share in the making of America according to the plan of the fathers." He ends the speech with a little bow and a charming smile. Although the performance lasts only a little over two minutes, it is suddenly easier to understand how even La Follette's reading of the congressional roll call could keep country crowds mesmerized for hours.[27]

The entire La Follette family embarked on speaking tours, with Belle receiving special attention as the first woman ever to "take the stump" for her husband's presidential candidacy.[28] Although his speaking campaign

*Robert La Follette delivers amplified campaign speech at Steuben Day Celebration in New York City's Yankee Stadium, 21 September 1924.* (Washington Evening Star *Collection*)

began in earnest only in September and he spoke in only twenty states, La Follette's speeches were reminiscent of his old "four-pitcher" style. Despite urgent pleas that he keep his speeches to an hour, La Follette, greatly enjoying large, enthusiastic crowds, frequently spoke for two hours or more. His consistent theme was that monopoly constituted the supreme menace to America. Despite advancing age and obvious symptoms of serious heart disease, La Follette asserted, "I never was in better fighting trim in my life." Announcing that one of his ancestors had, at age 100, ridden on horseback from Kentucky to Indiana, he claimed to have the vitality to serve two terms as president, and his campaign literature highlighted the achievements of a variety of men past the age of seventy, including Benjamin Franklin, John Quincy Adams, Henry Clay, and British Prime Minister Palmerston.[29]

La Follette's critics maintained that his self-righteousness prevented him from being objective, that his proposed programs were futile, that he was "out to get" the Supreme Court, and they revived questions about his loyalty during the war. *The Outlook* declared him too short-sighted and provincial to understand national problems. This combination of failings, it was argued, led La Follette to "overemphasize minor issues," "confuse conveniences in the machinery of government with principles of right and justice," and "put in first place things that ought to be subordinated and to forget things that ought to be supreme." In short, "It has prevented him from seeing life in perspective." Yet even *The Outlook* was forced to acknowledge, "His campaign has become so important that it has taken precedence over every other issue presented. . . . He will be at the storm center of every fight, will hold the stage." This view was encouraged by the two major parties, each finding it to their advantage to assert that La Follette was showing great strength at the expense of the other, both crediting him with more support than he really had. They came to believe their own press. The Republican National Committee, for example, paid $10,000 in advertising to ensure the support of the previously pro–La Follette *Omaha Tribune.* Davis's advisers urged the Democratic candidate "not to hammer the Wisconsin senator too hard," as they anticipated he would make deep inroads into the Republican's ethnic support (Americans of German, Irish, and Italian extraction who were opposed to the terms of the Versailles treaty) and take several midwestern states from Coolidge. As the election neared, press reports predicted that La Follette would carry Wisconsin and up to eight, possibly twelve, northwestern states and that his power and influence would divide the Republicans, conceivably forcing the election of the president and vice president into the House and Senate, respectively. The *Richmond Times-Dispatch* was more conservative, predicting, "The fighting Senator from Wisconsin does not stand a chance of election, but he will give the old parties a great deal to think about."[30]

Did La Follette think he could win? According to one study of the 1924 election, most of La Follette's supporters "looked upon the campaign . . . as an opportunity to establish a basis for future farmer-labor political action; some planned, no doubt, to deadlock the Electoral college; but few were so sanguine as to entertain any hopes that La Follette would become President of the United States." For La Follette himself, one historian suggests it was "a fitting climax to his long and consistent career as a champion of progressive causes." But this campaign was more than just symbolic for the "battle scarred warhorse." Although Phil La Follette contended, "None of us for a moment thought we had a chance to win," his father harbored hopes, however unrealistic, of a victory. Many years before, La Follette had warned the people of Wisconsin that they might as well vote for him, because he was determined to be their governor. Buoyed by the optimism of early reports, he saw in 1924 the opportunity to achieve, or at least build toward, that same kind of ultimate success as chief executive.[31]

Despite the largely optimistic reports of the press, La Follette suffered a sharp decrease in support just prior to the election. A study of third party movements observes, "Even though early in the campaign citizens may flirt with minor party candidates, by election day the pull of partisanship, the inevitable 'he can't win — it's a wasted vote' argument, and the wearing off of the third party novelty brings voters home to the major parties." To compound this factor, in the months just prior to the election, farm prices rose dramatically as the nation continued to recover from the postwar depression, aided by poor harvests in Canada and abroad. By early October, "the indications of prosperity were visible . . . where La Follette's greatest hope of victory [previously] lay."[32]

On election day La Follette listened to returns on the radio with Bobbie and Phil at Maple Bluff. Belle remained in Washington to be with their daughter Mary, who was awaiting the birth of her first child. The news that Phil had been elected district attorney of Dane County, the first office to which La Follette himself had been elected in 1880, delighted the senator. La Follette's own results, however, quickly dampened that elation. Slightly more than 50 percent of eligible voters cast their ballots in 1924. La Follette's share was 4,822,319 out of an estimated 28,649,709. Although he ran second in eleven western and midwestern states, this did little to alleviate the disappointment over winning only Wisconsin in the electoral college. Moreover, although his total was 696,298 more votes than Roosevelt had received in his independent bid in 1912, the number of eligible voters in 1924 had nearly doubled, due to woman suffrage and a twelve-year increase in the general population. Proportionately, then, La Follette had received far fewer votes than his old nemesis — and only one state to Roosevelt's six. While Roosevelt had garnered well over a quarter of the popular votes in 1912 (4,119,207, or 27.39 percent), La Follette received about one-seventh in 1924 (roughly 16.8 percent). *La Follette's Magazine* was quick to point out that Roosevelt had the distinct advantage of "a nationwide personal organization through the patronage and prestige which the presidency affords."[33]

La Follette, the analysts agreed, took more votes from Davis than from Coolidge. La Follette secured more votes than Davis in Wisconsin and in eleven primarily western states. About half of La Follette's votes came from farmers and a fifth each from union members and socialists. He averaged 30 percent of the vote in the Pacific and Mountain states, finishing second in all western and four midwestern states. He also carried 9.4 percent of the

GONE DRY

*A dejected La Follette observes the powerful rays of prosperity. Both the river of discontent and his hopes for a political catch have evaporated. (Sykes,* Philadelphia Evening Public Ledger; *reprinted in "Future of the La Follette Party,"* Literary Digest *83 [15 Nov. 1924]: 10)*

vote in the ten largest cities and was especially popular among voters of German and Scandinavian heritage. Despite his influential supporters in the African American community, its members, like most voters nationwide, cast their ballots along traditional party lines.[34]

La Follette's contemporaries attributed his disappointing showing to a variety of factors: his third party status, faulty campaign issues and strategies, rigidly limited demographic and geographic appeal, positions too radical for conservatives and too conservative for radicals, and the general population's relative contentment with the status quo. The issue of monopoly domination seemed rather old-fashioned to vast numbers of Americans. While they appreciated the accomplishments of the progressives since the turn of the century, now that the worst excesses had been curbed they were more eager to celebrate the fruits of the current business economy than to push for further reforms. La Follette's socialist support proved a mixed blessing. American Socialists had established organizations in many cities, and their names appeared on ballots in most states. However, World War I and the Red Scare had substantially weakened the party, vastly diminishing its membership. Yet its reputation as a major threat to democracy persevered. Although La Follette had publicly repudiated communism, urging progressives not to attend the convention of the Farmer-Labor-Progressive due to communist participation, his socialist supporters in the 1924 campaign alienated advocates of more moderate reform. Despite these limitations, La Follette won more than five times the highest previous total for a candidate endorsed by the Socialists. According to this measure, noted a 1999 tribute, in 1924 La Follette conducted "the most successful leftwing Presidential campaign in American history."[35]

The issue of money provides another perspective on the election results. An analysis of third party campaign spending reveals the popular vote for La Follette in 1924 to be an astonishingly impressive achievement. Roosevelt's $665,420 budget in 1912 represented about 60.3 percent of the average spent by the Democrats and the Republicans, and the number of votes he received equaled 84.2 percent of the major parties' average. Thirteen years later La Follette's $236,963 budget reflected only 9.2 percent of the major parties' budget average. Therefore his ability to attract 40 percent of the average of the major parties' votes puts him dramatically ahead of Roosevelt (ahead, in fact, of any third party candidate in the twentieth century), based on dollars spent per vote.[36] La Follette spent 4.9 cents per vote in 1924; Roosevelt spent more than three times that much in 1912: 16.2 cents per vote. These figures reveal the overwhelming importance of La Follette's failure to secure sufficient funding to support a well-oiled and widespread campaign. Although La Follette was the first independent presidential candidate to be officially backed by the American Federation of Labor, his endorsement by Samuel Gompers was halfhearted at best. Finding both Davis and Coolidge unacceptable, an ill and preoccupied Gompers felt "forced to turn to La Follette" since there was "no other way." Ultimately his organization delivered less than 1 percent of the $3 million it had pledged to La Follette's campaign.[37]

The result of La Follette's campaign demonstrated support for his ideas that the *Saturday Evening Post* compared to the famous Powder River, "a mile

*A battered La Follette pulls his beloved Wisconsin from the wreckage of the 1924 campaign, vowing to battle on. (Barryman,* Washington Evening Star, *6 November 1924,* Washington Evening Star *Collection)*

wide and an inch deep." The campaign was, concluded the *Post*, merely a personal adventure and enterprise. La Follette remained on his Wisconsin farm in the comforting presence of his sons following the election. In an editorial for his magazine entitled "Forward Progressives for Campaign of 1926," he refused to concede that the electorate truly endorsed the Coolidge administration. The Coolidge victory was instead the result of the economic thumbscrews twisted down on farmers, wage earners, and independent businessmen during the final days of the campaign. La Follette blamed his defeat on "slush funds," intimidation, technical obstruction, and abuse of power in the placement of independent electors on the ballot and in the counting of the votes themselves. He concluded that while one "skirmish" had been lost, "the Progressives will close ranks for the next battle." He pledged to build a national party on a state-by-state basis, starting with Wisconsin. "His plans and his party make me tired," Lincoln Steffens remarked, "but he, the uncurable, unreformable Bob, is wonderful."[38]

Despite familiar outward signs of unspoiled optimism, privately La Follette burned with mortification over what he considered his humiliating loss. The wolves in both houses of Congress, smelling blood, closed in. A Republican caucus adopted a resolution depriving La Follette and other progressives of committee rank, virtually drumming progressives out of the party. Being replaced on the powerful Interstate Commerce Committee by conservative regular James Watson of Indiana was particularly galling to La Follette. According to one political analyst, "La Follette's defeat not only obliterates him as a Presidential factor and as the founder of a new party . . . it tumbles him out of his dominance in Congress." La Follette's vow to never give up until victorious sounded more wishful than convincing as he reentered the Senate on 1 December. Although he "tried to be a good sport," he confided to his sister, "It was not easy to face the old gang with the election just over and every state lost except Wisconsin. But I sailed [in] my head up & all smiles. You [may] be sure I would not give any outward evidence of the taste in my mouth."[39]

In addition to the blow to his political power, La Follette's final presidential effort failed at enormous cost to his health. His single day in the Senate extracted a large toll, forcing him to return to his sickbed with the warning that the least indiscretion would likely result in pneumonia. Bobbie, frantic with worry over his father's health and his mother's "general depletion of nerve reserve and a consequent increase in her capacity to worry about matters large and small," urged his parents to take a lengthy vacation in a warm climate. They demurred, attempting to regain strength in Washington while enjoying immensely the presence and promise of their first grandchild, Robert La Follette Sucher. Although "not feeling quite up to work," La Follette attended a few hours of Senate sessions later in the month but by January agreed to leave the inclement weather of Washington for a prolonged stay in Florida. At Fort Lauderdale, he reported, "My treatment . . . for two months was to lie on a cot, naked, under the direct rays of that fierce sun from two to five hours daily [which was] very exhausting." Doctors cautioned that his sunbaths should not exceed one hour, but La Follette was confident that the sun would "bake away" all illness.[40]

During this absence, Bobbie reluctantly attended the Chicago CPPA meeting to push his father's plan for individual states to select delegates to a national convention. Bobbie confessed, "I dread very much to have to carry alone the responsibility connected with my representing you at Chicago. It is a burden greater than any one man should be asked to carry but under the circumstances I see no other way out and I trust you will be lenient in your judgment." The CPPA officially ended in Chicago, and a new party was proposed. Through his son, La Follette insisted that the new party not appeal to a particular class or group (i.e., Socialist, Farm-Labor, etc.) but rather be formed on principles more universally appealing. La Follette, who assured Bobbie of his "absolute confidence in your judgment and ability to meet all requirements tactfully and wisely," chose not to dwell on the CPPA's demise and token replacement. He rejoiced instead in Bobbie's success in making "the best of a bad mess" in Chicago, for it served to further confirm his belief in his son's leadership abilities and bright political future.[41]

La Follette looked ahead to the 1926 congressional elections with concern. "National redemption," he insisted, "lies along state by state occupation and conquest" to build a "national base of commanding proportions." As always, in La Follette's view, "Wisconsin is of first importance." Bobbie nonetheless urged his father to remain in Florida until the first of April, partly, confided Bobbie, because "to be here at inauguration [on 4 March] I think would be slightly embarrassing." La Follette returned to Congress on 16 March following urgent messages from Senators Reed and Norris that he was needed to prevent the confirmation of Charles Beecher Warren, whom they suspected as being corrupt, as attorney general. Although La Follette continued to proclaim his lungs completely restored, weakness quickly forced his return to bed and a recurrence of pneumonia was again feared.[42]

La Follette suffered a series of painful heart attacks and depended increasingly on his sons politically and emotionally. He spoke openly of his regrets for involving himself so completely in his career at the expense of his marriage and family. He wrote to Phil, "I am very sorry to see you merge yourself so wholly in your professional work." "It is all very well for you to think that it is only a temporary thing," he warned, adding longingly, "How much I would give if I could make over that part of my life." He warned his son, "It is very wrong and in the long run I am sure that it is very wasteful of the best that is in one. Moreover its tendency is very narrowing in its effect on the cultural side of the individual besides being mighty hard on home life."[43]

La Follette had long been fascinated by the mystery of death, and his notebooks contain many poems, anecdotes, and Bible verses concerning the shortness of life and the finality of death. Death, in La Follette's view, led mourners to reflect upon the departed's "usefulness and service . . . devotion . . . courage and power . . . [and] to rejoice in what he has accomplished and to carry forward the work he has laid down." When speaking at funerals or writing about the deaths of others, he made frequent mention of the dead spending eternity with previously departed loved ones. Certainly in his case that would include the reunion with his father desired since childhood. Nevertheless, he continued to view life as precious and set about enjoying his remaining days. He read mystery and detective stories (a longtime passion previously limited by time constraints) "incessantly" and so lost himself in the thrilling narratives that his night nurse cut down on his supply for fear the excitement would further damage his health. The patterns of a lifetime dedicated to politics could not disappear entirely, however. Even as his health deteriorated, La Follette denied the seriousness of his condition and made a series of ambitious plans. He proposed a conference of progressive leaders and discussed his intention to bring his autobiography up to date. And he insisted on writing editorials for his beloved magazine, overriding Belle's protests with his assertion, "I enjoy writing for the magazine; it never tires me."[44]

La Follette suffered a series of heart attacks in the spring of 1925 and grew increasingly dependent on nitroglycerine and pain medication. In June the family gathered, and Bobbie noted Belle's reluctance to leave her husband's side even briefly. The fourteenth of June was La Follette's seventieth birthday. Four days later, according to their daughter Fola, "We were all in Daddy's room when the end came" at 1:21 in the afternoon. Belle, seated by her husband's bed, held his hand and spoke to him, "pouring out the love and devotion of a lifetime in the last long farewell . . . telling him her vision of the nobility and beauty of his life and work." According to their daughter, "[I]f he could have heard, there has not been and never can be any tribute which would so deeply have satisfied his mind and heart." "His passing," Fola noted, "was mysteriously peaceful for one who had stood so long on the battle line."[45]

# EPILOGUE
## A CHALLENGE TO YOUTH IN AMERICA
## DOWN ALL THE FUTURE YEARS

**L**a Follette's casket was carried by train from Washington to Wisconsin. People gathered in towns and villages all along the route to pay tribute. Newsreel footage shown nationwide features crowds awaiting the senator's body at the Madison station and his casket being carried up the steps of the capitol building. An estimated 50,000 mourners viewed La Follette's body as it lay in the rotunda, where funeral services were held on June 22. "We shall remember him," eulogized the Reverend A. E. Haydon, "as one who in a cynical age loved and kept the faith in humble men and women . . . as a leader of dauntless courage." La Follette was buried under a white oak at Forest Hill Cemetery in Madison. Tributes were sent from a variety of world leaders, including Mexican president Plutarco Eilia Calles and officials of Ireland, Japan, England, and India. Homage and messages of sympathy were delivered to the family from such notables as Jane Addams, Eugene V. Debs, William Jennings Bryan, Clarence Darrow, William Randolph Hearst, Helen Keller, and President Calvin Coolidge. Former enemies as well as old friends expressed their appreciation of his life's work. The House of Representatives adjourned early out of respect, and both houses of Congress held lengthy memorial services. Farmers, laborers, housewives, and other regular citizens declared their great love for the man who, in the words of one writer, "sponsored the cause of the common people to which I belong." Many expressed gratitude for what La Follette had done for their particular occupational or ethnic group. One called La Follette "our greatest American," writing simply, "He inspired me as no other man ever did."[1]

While the presidency eluded his grasp, the approval generated by La Follette's many accomplishments lingered. He was eulogized as "one of those great souls who has made the planet different and better; one of those great spirits who has turned the current in the direction of the ideal dreamed by all the prophets of the ages. . . . The flame of his spirit has passed, but the memory of that magnificent courage, standing loyally in the face of loneliness and isolation, will remain as a challenge to youth in America down all the future years." In a joint resolution to commemorate La Follette's life and services, the Wisconsin senate and legislature concluded, "La Follette is dead. But the soul of him lives in people's hearts wherever men are striving for freedom. La Follette's voice is still, but the spirit that spoke through it is the spirit of brotherhood and righteousness, and is enduring." Lincoln Stef-

*The greatest tribute in Wisconsin since the death of Lincoln: Fighting Bob on his shield at last, 22 June 1925. (State Historical Society of Wisconsin WHi[X3]41033)*

fens called La Follette "a victor, one of the very few; his life is a success." La Follette, noted Steffens, rose above the shallow cynicism of the age: "It is foolish to be honest, it is dangerous to be loyal, it is called cowardly to be brave, it is patriotic to sell out your country, it is demagogic to serve the people, it is a disgrace to be such a hero as Bob was every minute of his fighting life, fighting for the American people whom he trusted as no other leader has ever trusted them."[2]

In a special election shortly after the senator's death, Wisconsin voters chose La Follette's oldest son, Robert M. La Follette Jr., to succeed him—

a dramatic tribute of loyalty to the steadfast progressive who had served them as governor for six years and United States senator for nearly twenty. By unanimous order of the Wisconsin legislature, the statue sculpted by Jo Davidson, for whom La Follette modeled during his 1924 visit to Europe, was unveiled on 25 April 1929 and is still on display in the Capitol rotunda in Washington.

Other legacies, particularly La Follette's contributions to the New Deal, are rarely acknowledged. In his 1936 memoir, however, Republican senator James Watson noted, "If one will take the trouble to examine the platform of 1924 on which Robert M. La Follette ran . . . [one] will find very many of the identical propositions embodied that are now being put into execution by the administration of Franklin D. Roosevelt and, furthermore, a closer examination will reveal the fact that many of the very men who are now engaged in aiding President Roosevelt were in Wisconsin at that time helping La Follette." Harold Ickes's 1924 prediction that the progressives left in the Republican Party after Coolidge's election would have no more chance than a snowball in hell proved correct. Most progressives who supported Theodore Roosevelt in 1912 rejected La Follette in 1924. They remained within the GOP and opposed the New Deal. Many La Follette Progressives tended more toward the Democratic party after 1925. Such appropriation by a major party is often the fate of third parties who, according to one study of third parties in America, "usually lose the battle but, through co-optation, often win the war" by substantially impacting public policy. Ickes himself consistently backed Democrats after 1924. He ultimately converted, becoming secretary of the interior under Franklin D. Roosevelt.[3]

Other key La Follette supporters who subsequently worked to further FDR's goals include Senators George Norris, Robert La Follette Jr., and Burton K. Wheeler. La Follette devotee David K. Niles was Roosevelt's executive secretary, and Basil Manly served on the Federal Power Commission under FDR. Elements found in the 1924 platform (some of which were influenced by La Follette's observations of the Soviet Union the previous year) that came to life in the New Deal include the Tennessee Valley Authority, progressive income and inheritance tax schedules, the Wagner Labor Relations Act, various aid programs to agriculture, the Securities Exchange Commission, and the abolition of child labor. Nearly forty years after La Follette's death, the two Senate votes against the Gulf of Tonkin Resolution, which committed the United States to war in Vietnam, were cast by Oregon's Wayne Morse, a Wisconsin native impressed by La Follette in his youth, and Alaska's Ernest Gruening, a La Follette spokesman in the 1924 campaign. In 1998, Russ Feingold (D-Wisconsin) made the La Follette legacy a part of his successful bid for reelection to the U.S. Senate. Victorious despite being

significantly outspent by his Republican opponent, Feingold told supporters on election nights, "Now we have the chance, one hundred years after the great Fighting Bob La Follette, to send a message to Washington. . . .
Out of the Upper Midwest will come political reform, will come political
changes, will come the principle of one-person/one-vote again." Feingold
traced his own efforts to fight special interests to his father's involvement in
the Progressive movement. A year later, Doug La Follette, one of the founders of Earth Day and then serving in his fifth term as Wisconsin's secretary
of state, credited Robert La Follette Sr., his first cousin twice removed, as the
inspiration for the lifelong activism of many Americans, himself included.[4]

On 12 March 1959, a special committee chaired by Senator John F. Kennedy voted La Follette and senators Henry Clay, John Calhoun, Daniel Webster, and Robert A. Taft the Senate's five greatest members. Their portraits
were put on permanent display in the Senate reception room. Wide publicity about the five honorees heightened Kennedy's visibility just prior to
the 1960 presidential campaign and returned La Follette briefly to the national spotlight. In 1982 La Follette was number one on the "Ten Outstanding Governors of the Twentieth Century" list published in the newsletter
of the National Governors' Association, and as recently as 1986 he placed
fourth among the greatest American senators in a nationwide survey of 400
college professors. La Follette continues to be the subject of dissertations
and scholarly books and articles, but his popular appeal is restricted almost
exclusively to Wisconsin, where on the eve of the year 2000, a panel of experts surveying the state's last century declared him the most significant
person and his election as governor the most significant event.[5]

As noted by William Allen White, La Follette was indeed no "immaculate
white giant." His own self-destructive behaviors were sometimes the most
powerful of all his enemies. His self-righteousness, a quality honed since
early childhood, led to a reluctance to cooperate even with those who
shared his views. His refusal to compromise alienated many, repeatedly curtailing his effectiveness. And yet it was that same certainty in the justness of
his positions that led one scholar looking at La Follette's lifetime of achievements to declare, "It is silly to call a man egotistical in a tone of reproof; what
person who believes in himself and is willing to fight for the prevalence of
his beliefs is not self-centered?" Fighting Bob relentlessly championed, according to his own lights, the rights of the many over those of the powerful
few. Nearly seventy-five years after his death, he was hailed by *Madison (Wisc.)
Capital Times* editorial page editor John Nichols as "the most courageous political leader this nation has ever produced." Moreover, La Follette's battle
to more equitably redistribute the nation's power and wealth continues to
be waged. The true value of La Follette's political legacy may be yet to come

if Martin Luther King Jr. was right, that "somehow righteousness is stronger than evil." "History is a long story of the fact," King insisted, "that goodness defeated is [ultimately] stronger that evil triumphant," for "evil is ultimately doomed by the powerful, insurgent forces of good." Proud, uncompromising, shrewd, resourceful, and inspired, the righteous reformer Robert La Follette was indeed one of the "dull tools" of "Almighty God."[6]

*La Follette's legacy. (Cargill, Central Press Association; reprinted in "After La Follette — What?"*Literary Digest *86 [4 July 1925]: 1)*

# NOTES

ABBREVIATIONS

*Individuals*
AOB     Albert O. Barton
BCL     Belle Case La Follette
FEM     Francis E. McGovern
FL      Fola La Follette
GM      George Middleton
GR      Gilbert Roe
HAC     Henry Allen Cooper
JJH     John J. Hannon
JR      Robert Marion La Follette Jr.
JS      Josephine Siebecker
MEL     Meyer E. Lissner
ML      Mary La Follette
MLB     Mary Livingston Burdick
ND      Nellie Dunne
PFL     Philip Fox La Follette
RML     Robert Marion La Follette
RSB     Ray Stannard Baker
TR      Theodore Roosevelt
WAW     William Allen White


*Periodicals*
CR      *Congressional Record*
LD      *Literary Digest*
LM      *La Follette's Magazine*
NYT     *New York Times*
WMH     *Wisconsin Magazine of History*


*Collections*
ABP     Albert O. Barton Papers
BLP     Belle Case La Follette Papers
FLP     Fola La Follette Papers
FMP     Francis E. McGovern Papers
FP      La Follette Family Papers
HCP     Henry Allen Cooper Papers
JRP     Robert La Follette Jr. Papers
LFC     La Follette Family Collection at Library of Congress, Washington, D.C.
MLP     Meyer E. Lissner Papers
PLP     Phil La Follette Papers

RLP       Robert La Follette Papers
SHSW-H    State Historical Society of Wisconsin, microfilm at Hayward, Calif.
SHSW-M    State Historical Society of Wisconsin at Madison, Wisc.
SUSC      Stanford University Special Collections
WWP       William Allen White Papers on microfilm

Following the date of documents housed in Hayward (SHSW-H) are numbers indicating the reel number, the letterbook number (where applicable), and the frame
number of the microfilm, e.g., 36:775 or 127(23):277. In citations from the La Follette Family Collection at the Library of Congress (LFC) and the papers housed in
Madison (SHSW-M), the designations preceding the name of the collection are the
box and file numbers, e.g., 6-1.

    To improve readability, errors of spelling and grammar found in quotations from
source materials have been corrected.


INTRODUCTION

1. Torelle, *Political Philosophy*, 86; James Sinclair, "Extol La Follette as Great Crusader," *LM* 19, no. 5 (May 1927): 77; Florian Lampert, "Remember La Follette
   for Battles Won," *LM* 19, no. 4 (April 1927): 57.
2. Tattler, "Robert M. La Follette," *Nation* 101 (21 Oct. 1915): 493; "From Colleagues in the United States Senate," *LM* 17, no. 7 (July 1925): 111. See also
   Felix Frankfurter, "Why I Shall Vote for La Follette," *New Republic* 40 (22 Oct.
   1924): 200; MacKay, *Progressive Movement*; and Lowitt, "La Follette and the Waning Insurgent Spirit." See also Glad, *War, a New Era, and Depression*, 293–95, 571–
   88. For an alternative to this traditional view of the New Deal as a logical extension of progressivism, see Graham, *Encore for Reform*.
3. *Janesville Gazette*, 20 June 1925, B-91; RML, Notebook, 5 Sept. 1922, RLP, B-3,
   LFC; BCL to family, 19 May 1925, FP, A-31, LFC.
4. William Hard, "Fighting Bob — Elder Statesman," *Collier's*, 8 Sept. 1923, RLP,
   B-315, LFC. See also "La Follette," *Outlook* 140 (July 1926): 322; "La Follette,"
   *Outlook*, 137 (16 July 1924): 421.
5. Garraty, "Promise Unfulfilled," 85. The American Psychiatric Association currently describes the essential feature of paranoid personality disorder as "pervasive distrust and suspiciousness of others such that their motives are interpreted
   as malevolent." Tsuang, Tohen, and Zahner, *Psychiatric Epidemiology*, 412.
6. Richard Barry, "A Radical in Power," *Outlook* 132 (29 Nov. 1922): 566.
7. Holt, *Congressional Insurgents*, 150; Burton K. Wheeler, *CR* 67, pt. 2:11649; Richard Barry, "They're Out to Get La Follette," *Hearst's International*, Aug. 1922,
   RLP, B-93, LFC. See Lowitt, "La Follette and the Waning Insurgent Spirit," 246.
8. "La Follette," *Outlook* 137 (16 July 1924): 421; Wilder, "Governor La Follette,"
   *Outlook* 70 (8 Mar. 1902): 633.
9. See Lasswell, *Psychopathology and Politics*. See also George, "Power as a Compensatory Value."

10. "La Follette," *Outlook* 140 (1 July 1925): 323; RML to Wm. La Follette, 17 Oct. 1898, 15:657, RLP, SHSW-H; RML, Notebook, 1922, RLP, B-3, LFC; BCL to family, 19 May 1925, FP, A-31, LFC; WAW, unaddressed letter, 27 July 1911, Book M, 11–15, WWP, SUSC. See A. Miller, *Drama of the Gifted Child*, 31–63; Margulies, *Decline of the Progressive Movement*, 282; Thelen, *Insurgent Spirit*, 193–94; Garraty, "Promise Unfulfilled," 76–88. See J. E. Miller, *Governor Philip F. La Follette*, 76–126; Maney, *Young Bob*, 110–32; Lowitt, "La Follette and the Waning Insurgent Spirit," 249–50.

CHAPTER ONE

1. A. Smith, *Exploration to Statehood*, provides a detailed overview of the state's early history. See also Kellog, *French Regime in Wisconsin*; and Current, *Civil War*, 52.
2. See AOB, "Genesis of the La Follette Family in America," 1–5, ABP, SHSW-M.
3. Wm. Barnard Hale, "La Follette, Pioneer Progressive," *World's Work*, July 1911, RLP, B-315, LFC.
4. See L. A. Warren, "The Lincoln and La Follette Families in Pioneer Drama," and RML to Herbert Heiman, 28 Nov. 1904, 127(23):277, RLP, SHSW-H.
5. Assessments of Josiah La Follette's height vary. See Lars P. Myrland, interviewed by AOB, 10 Apr. 1930, and C. A. Harper, interviewed by AOB, 6 Dec. 1928, 6-1, SHSW-M.
6. Charles La Follette to BCL, 15 Dec. 1928; AOB, "Genesis of the La Follette Family in America," 5-1; Clara La Follette Nash to Charles La Follette, 7 Nov. 1930, 5-3, ABP, SHSW-M. David Thelen and Fred Greenbaum each mention only four brothers, but Belle Case La Follette and John H. La Follette both list five.
7. Rippley, *Immigrant Experience*, iii.
8. Lars P. Myrland, interviewed by AOB, 10 Apr. 1930, ABP, 6-1, SHSW-M.
9. PFL, Speech, "Unveiling of the Statue of Hon. Robert M. La Follette," *CR*, 71, pt. 1:532–33; RML, interviewed by AOB, 10 Aug. 1920, ABP, 5-3, SHSW-M. See also BCL and FL, *La Follette*, 1:6–7.
10. Unidentified biographical sketch, *Robert Marion La Follette*, RLP, B-315, LFC. See also Cooper, "Political Prophet," 92. RML, *Autobiography*, 3, 65. In a biographical article based on extensive interviews with Robert La Follette, Lincoln Steffens reported, "When the boy was eight months old the father died, leaving the mother and four children, and, at the age of fourteen, 'Little Bob,' as his followers still call him, became head of the family." Untitled excerpt from *McClure's* by Lincoln Steffens, 1904, RLP, B-315, LFC. See also sketch sent to Alfred Rogers, ca. 1900, 36:775, RLP, SHSW-H.
11. Oliver Osmundsen, 1918, ABP, 6-1, SHSW-M; RML, *Autobiography*, 134; RML to JS, 16 Oct. 1901, FP, A-2, LFC. Bob and William La Follette exchanged congenial letters as adults. Like his younger brother, William was politically ambitious and served as a member of the Railroad Commission of South Dakota. He also ran, unsuccessfully, for lieutenant governor of that state. Bob cut a trip short to be with William just prior to the latter's death. Following their brother's death,

Bob wrote to his sister Jo, "Dear old boy. I know life had been something of a disappointment to him. He had a lot of ability—undisciplined except by trial. He saw the wrongs of the world and hated them—and fought them in his own way. He struck his blows on the right side. 'Strong headed' from boyhood and for the most part having his own way, he came through clean-handed to the finish. I cannot think of him as gone" (RML to JS, 7 May 1913, FP, A-13, LFC). William had been predeceased by his wife in 1911. Following his death, Bob and Belle took responsibility for William's young son, called "Billy," who was in poor health. Bob worked to obtain a suitable career for his nephew and was by his side at the young man's death in 1915. His letter to Billy's surviving siblings was a detailed and comforting account of their brother's illness and death.

12. RML, Diary, 17 Nov. 1879, RLP, B-1, LFC; RML to JS, 8 Apr. 1913, FP, A-13, LFC; MLB, interviewed by AOB, 25 May 1930, ABP, 6-1, SHSW-M; RML to JS and Robert Siebecker, 28 Aug. 1914, A-16, LFC; JS to RML, 15 Oct. 1901, FP, A-2, LFC. Before residing at his fraternity, Robert La Follette Jr. also stayed with the Siebeckers during his brief tenure at the University of Wisconsin. Near the end of his life, Bob took a long-desired trip to Europe, writing to virtually no one, save Jo. A press account of Robert La Follette's funeral noted that only "Mrs. Robert G. Siebecker, sister of the senator's, seemed about to collapse." "Hayden Lauds La Follette in Burial Oration," *Capital Times*, 22 June 1925, 3, RLP, B-266, LFC.

13. BCL and FL, *La Follette*, 1:10.

14. RML to McCannon, 11 Dec. 1903, 124(18):57, RLP, SHSW-H; Oliver Osmundsen, 1918, ABP, 6-1, SHSW-M; BCL to JS, 10 Mar. 1907, FP, A-5, LFC; BCL and FL, *La Follette*, 1:7, 10.

15. RML, *Autobiography*, 65.

16. BCL, "The Farm," *LM* 18, no. 5 (May 1926): 70; BCL and FL, *La Follette*, 1:6, 10; RML, Diary, 22 Nov. 1879, RLP, B-1, LFC.

17. RML, interviewed by AOB, 10 Aug. 1920, 5-3; C. A. Harper, interviewed by AOB, 6 Dec. 1928, ABP, 6-1, SHSW-M.

18. BCL and FL, *La Follette*, 1:10.

19. Thelen, *Early Life*, 11.

20. See Current, *Civil War*, 163–68. In 1915, on the floor of the Senate, La Follette decried the misuse of the land donated by the federal government to aid education, especially the resultant "paltry sum" allotted Wisconsin schools (RML, *CR* 53, pt. 3:2211–12).

21. Carrie Baker Davenport to RML, 6 Apr. 1896, 4:511, RLP, SHSW-H. At one point in their lengthy correspondence, La Follette credited Davenport with "firing his imagination" one day during his childhood when she commented on his "doing things in the world." RML to Carrie Baker Davenport, 25 Oct. 1911, RLP, B-106, LFC.

22. RML, *Autobiography*, 24.

23. RML to J. C. Sarchett, 5 Feb. 1896, 4:366, LFP, SHSW-H; Herbert Quick, "Governor Bob," *Saturday Evening Post* (23 Sept. 1911): 2, RLP, B-263, LFC. See also RML to family, 1 Jan. 1919, FP, A-26, LFC; "Personal Glimpses: When La Follette Carried Water to the Elephant," *LD* 82 (19 Aug. 1924): 40.

## CHAPTER TWO

1. Current, *Civil War*, 320–21. For the distribution of wealth, see Soltow, *Patterns of Wealthholding in Wisconsin*.

2. For more on women's property rights, see Weisberg, *Women and the Law: Social Historical Perspective*; Kanowitz, *Women and the Law: Unfinished Revolution*; and Mc-Bride, *Wisconsin Women*, 5, 21.

3. Marguerite Carpentier Fix to AOB, 19 June 1918, ABP, 5-1, SHSW-M; Current, *Civil War*, 241.

4. BCL and FL, *La Follette*, 1 : 13; RML to family, 16 Jan. 1919, FP, A-26, LFC; RML, *Autobiography*, 129. See Mary M. Saxton, "Expenses Incurred for Robert M. La Follette, Minor," ABP, 5-2, SHSW-M.

5. Loren Ketchum, interviewed by AOB, 27 Nov. 1928, ABP, 6-1, SHSW-M; Thelen, *Early Life*, 13–14.

6. John Z. Saxton to Sir, 15 Jan. 1864, ABP, 5-2, SHSW-M.

7. Thelen, *Early Life*, 15; RML, *Autobiography*, 15.

8. Current, *Civil War*, 573.

9. Current, *Pine Logs*, 94.

10. Rippley, *Immigrant Experience*, 43; Current, *Civil War*, 414.

11. Current, *Civil War*, 566.

12. See James Willard Hurst, *Law and Economic Growth: The Legal History of the Lumber Industry in Wisconsin, 1836–1915* (Cambridge: Belknap Press of Harvard University Press, 1964).

13. Current, *Civil War*, 557.

14. BCL and FL, *La Follette*, 1 : 16–17. Patrick Maney states that La Follette gave the impression that he was an agnostic and cites a lack of Biblical quotations in his speeches as supporting evidence. References to the Bible, to God, and to his own prayers, however, do appear in both La Follette's speeches and his letters. However, as a La Follette supporter once observed, "La Follette is an independent in religion as in everything else" (A.H.R., "La Follette's Religion," *Pearson's*, 1924, RLP, B-315, LFC). When his religious beliefs were once criticized, La Follette caustically responded, "I am not a member of any church. Some of my family are Baptists, some Unitarians. I state the above, not because I think you or any other American citizen has any right to the information, but because I want you to appreciate if you can, the resentment I feel that any man in this country, dedicated to civil liberty and religious freedom, should characterize the religious beliefs of another as 'dry rot.' Do you not think that each one should be permitted to settle this one question directly with his God?" (RML to V. Schach, 15 Dec. 1911, LFC). The La Follettes required their children to say evening prayers and attend Sunday school, but they did not attend services themselves. According to their son Phil, subsequent to attending the funeral of a fellow congressman at the Congregational Church in Washington, La Follette was entertaining a group of visiting clergy, who inquired as to which church La Follette belonged. He replied that he had most recently visited the Congregational Church. Despite his distaste for organized religion, La Follette was an avid reader of the Bible (one of his notebooks is made up entirely of Biblical quotations) and advised his son Phil

that the Bible and Shakespeare "are the two best things in all of literature," adding, "There is no better way to saturate yourself in them than by committing the noble passages [to memory]. They will enrich your mind and inspire your life and color your expression. Soak yourself full on the Bible & Shakespeare." RML to PFL, 27 July 1919, FP, A-27, LFC.

15. RML, unidentified notebook, ca. 1880s or 1890s, RLP, B-2, LFC.
16. BCL and FL, *La Follette*, 1:13.
17. RML, speech, "The World's Greatest Tragedy," 136:615, RLP, SHSW-H. So fascinated was La Follette with the subject that in 1904 he reported that the study, originally intended to last only a year, was still being actively pursued some twenty years later. See John Barrymore to RML, 1924, RLP, B-97, LFC. For a discussion of Hamlet as a man whose "psyche is 'out of joint' because it has to confront the fact that the world in which he had believed has become 'out of joint,'" see Kohut, *Analysis of the Self*, 235–67.
18. BCL and FL, *La Follette*, 1:16. La Follette employed corporal punishment as a form of discipline during his own tenure as a teacher.
19. Ibid., 1:14.
20. John Saxton to Thomas Hood, 5 Nov. 1862, ABP, 5-3, SHSW-M.


CHAPTER THREE

1. BCL and FL, *La Follette*, 1:22. See also BCL, "The Farm," *LM* 18, no. 5 (May 1926): 70.
2. Current, *Civil War*, 588–95; BCL and FL, *La Follette*, 1:22–23.
3. Current, *Civil War*, 595; Burgchardt, *Voice of Conscience*, 66.
4. BCL and FL, *La Follette*, 1:24.
5. Thelen, *Early Life*, 17–18. See also Bogue and Taylor, *University*. A photograph of the Merry Street home is in the visual archives of the State Historical Society of Wisconsin.
6. RML, *Autobiography*, 4.
7. Thelen, *Early Life*, 19.
8. Ibid., 25; Bogue and Taylor, *University*, 17.
9. BCL and FL, *La Follette*, 1:37.
10. Strother, "Death of 'Wisconsin Idea,'" 621; RML, *Autobiography*, 12; BCL and FL, *La Follette*, 1:38.
11. Curti and Cartensen, *University*, 1:251. Bascom published his memoirs, *Things Learned by Living*, in 1913.
12. Curti and Carstensen, *University*, 1:260, 273.
13. RML, *Autobiography*, 12; RML to A. B. Butler, 14 July 1923, RLP, B-57, LFC. Other phrases of the time describing the congenial interchange between the university and state government included "the expert on tap, not on top," "the boundaries of the campus are the boundaries of the state," "the service university," "applying the scientific method to legislation," and "the democratization of knowledge."
14. RML to Alumni, 19 June 1901, 133:65, RLP, SHSW-H; Thelen, *Early Life*, 46.

When the state capitol burned in 1906, La Follette's records, both from his university years and from the law school, were among those destroyed. R. O. Holt, Registrar, to Gentlemen, 18 Dec. 1928, ABP, 6-2, SHSW-M.

15. La Follette later regretted his choice of scientific study. RML to JR, 19 Sept. 1913, FP, A-13, LFC.

16. A notable exception to La Follette's ability to read an audience and deliver accordingly occurred in Philadelphia in 1912. See Chapter 12.

17. Burgchardt, *Voice of Conscience*, xiii.

18. La Follette's denunciation of the fraternities' undemocratic selection process is reminiscent of Woodrow Wilson's abolition of elitist dining clubs during his presidency of Princeton University.

19. Curti and Cartensen, *University*, 1:418.

20. Thelen, *Early Life*, 40.

21. BCL and FL, *La Follette*, 1:30; RML, *Autobiography*, 4. A discussion of La Follette's various illnesses and their significance appears in Chapter 5. For an exploration of the role of illness in creativity, see Pickering, *Creative Malady*.

22. Burgchardt, *Voice of Conscience*, 13–14.

23. Ibid., 14; Thelen, *Early Life*, 35.

24. "Opinions of the Press," *Madison Democrat*, RLP, B-210, LFC; BCL and FL, *La Follette*, 1:34.

25. RML, speech, "Iago," reprinted in unidentified newspaper, 1 Oct. 1911, RLP, B-263, LFC.

26. Burgchardt, *Voice of Conscience*, 6, 30, 155.

27. "Opinions of the Press," *Milwaukee Sentinel*, RLP, B-210, LFC. See also Garraty, "Promise Unfulfilled," 84.

28. BCL and FL, *La Follette*, 1:35; General George B. Smith, speech, 1:6, RLP, SHSW-H.

29. "Don't do it my boy, don't do it," La Follette quoted McCullough. "The actor must fill the eye as well as the mind. Suppose you were playing Iago and I Othello and I took you by the throat! The audience would rise and cry out to me: 'shame — shame — don't hurt the little fellow.'" Jones, "Among La Follette's People," *Collier's* 45 (3 Sept. 1910): 17. Wiesberger's *La Follettes of Wisconsin* is the most recent account to credit La Follette's decision not to pursue a stage career to this admonition.

30. "La Follette Charms Crowds," *Bloomington (Ind.) Daily Bulletin*, 22 Aug. 1905, RLP, B-263, LFC.

31. Burgchardt, *Voice of Conscience*, 14.


CHAPTER FOUR

1. "Wisconsin's Matriarch," *NYT*, 20 Aug. 1931, 18.

2. Ibid. See Unger, "Two Worlds." See also Freeman, La Follette, and Zabriskie, *Belle*; Weisberger, *La Follettes of Wisconsin*; Unger, Review of *La Follettes of Wisconsin*; and Riley, *Belle Case La Follette* and *Votes for Women*.

3. "University Mourns Mrs. La Follette Sr.," *NYT*, 20 Aug. 1931, 19. For a detailed

discussion of Belle Case La Follette in the context of the gender prescriptions of her day, see Unger, "Two Worlds."

4. See Edwards, *Angels in the Machinery.*

5. McBride, *Wisconsin Women*, 31, 60.

6. Thelen, *Early Life*, 41. Belle revisited this theme in 1913 in BCL, "Mother and Daughter," *LM* 5, no. 17 (26 Apr. 1913): 6.

7. BCL and FL, *La Follette*, 1:33.

8. Despite a few striking exceptions, La Follette's existing diaries reveal very little, for entries consist of a single sentence at best, and serve to chronicle insignificant daily events rather than record La Follette's inner thoughts and feelings. La Follette was a great advocate of personal journals and urged his oldest son: "You ought to get you a good sized diary and spend a half hour with it every night — not 'slouching' down all the events of the day — It is all right to 'note' them; — but a few paragraphs of your reflections on the things you have read or heard — such a diary would be worth its weight in gold and would give you a little training & facility in diction and expression. It is by just such use of any faculty of the mind — or any muscles of the body that we get proficiency and ease and grace of expression and movement." Such complete, introspective diaries by La Follette himself did at one time exist. Less than two months before his death a reflective La Follette wrote to his family, "Beginning about the close of my Univesity course, down through the years . . . I kept — not a diary — but a sort of journal which I entitled 'night thoughts.' In this I wrote upon different subjects, my best thinking, in my best form of expression. It was well indexed and was often useful to draw upon in summing up cases to court or jury and in addresses generally. I carried it in my kit-bag when lecturing and it was stolen with the bag and all it contained out of my berth between Chicago and Indianapolis while I was on a lecture trip — some twenty-five years after I began working it up. I prized it very highly, but it was irrevocably lost with many other notes and some manuscripts of value." RML to family, 26 Nov. 1918, FP, A-24; 28 Apr. 1925, FP, A-32, LFC.

9. RML, Diary, undated entry for 1879; 17 Nov. 1879, RLP, B-1, LFC.

10. RML, Diary, 3, 4 Nov. 1879, RLP, B-1, LFC.

11. RML, Diary, 3, 9, 17 Nov. 1879, RLP, B-1, LFC.

12. BCL and FL, *La Follette*, 1:110.

13. McBride, *Wisconsin Women*, 229. Belle's claim to being the first woman to graduate has been the subject of some controversy. Due to a clerical error in a 1921 alumni publication, Elsie Buck has repeatedly been misidentified as the first woman graduate. See Reisner, "First Woman Graduate." See also BCL, "The Law," *LM* 18, no. 6 (June 1926): 89. On Fola's given name, see MLB, interviewed by AOB, 25 May 1930, ABP, 6-1, SHSW-M.

14. Jane Addams, "Woman's Conscience and Social Amelioration," 1908, reprinted in Fink, *Major Problems*, 434; BCL to family, 16 Apr. 1919, FP, A-24, LFC. On the changing roles for women in the Progressive period, see K. K. Sklar, *Florence Kelley.*

15. BCL, speech, "On Segregation," 5 Jan. 1914, BLP, D-40, LFC. See also other BCL speeches: "Women United for Disarmament," May 1921, and "May the Women

of the U.S. Vote in 1920?" Feb. 1920, BLP, D-41, LFC; "The Woman's Peace Party," *LM* 7, no. 2 (Feb. 1915): 10–11. For a discussion of the role of gender in the Progressive peace movement, see Kuhlman, *Petticoats and White Feathers.*

16. Selene Armstrong Harmon, "A New Sort of Woman's Page," *Cincinnati Enquirer,* reprinted in *LM* 6, no. 24 (13 June 1914): 6–7; Link, *Wilson and Progressive Era,* 65; "A Mother's Question," *LM* 6, no. 2 (10 Jan. 1914): 6. See also BCL, "Colored Folk of Washington," *LM* 3, no. 10 (5 Aug. 1911): 10; "The Color Line," *LM* 5, no. 39 (23 Aug. 1913): 6–7; "Segregation in the Civil Service," *LM* 5, 50 (13 Dec. 1913): 6; "Color Line to Date," *LM* 6, no. 4 (24 Jan. 1914): 6–7.

17. BCL, "Color Line to Date," *LM* 6, no. 4 (24 Jan. 1914): 6–7, "Fair Chance for the Negro," *LM* 6, no. 15 (11 Apr. 1914): 6; "Segregation in the Civil Service," *LM* 6, no. 46 (Dec. 1914): 10. See also "Senator La Follette's Wife Addresses Large Audience at Colored YMCA Building," *Washington Star,* 5 Jan. 1914, RLP, B-264, LFC; and three BCL speeches, all in BLP, D-41, LFC: "On Segregation," 5 Jan. 1914; "Segregation in the Civil Service," Dec. 1914; and "A Notable Negro Pageant," Nov. 1915.

18. PFL, *Adventures in Politics,* 2; BCL to family, 1 Aug. 1914, FP, A-13, LFC; BCL, speech, University of Wisconsin, 18 Mar. 1901, BLP, D-38, LFC. Belle punctuated her disapproval of Fola's dress by misplacing the photograph. BCL to FL, 4 Aug. 1904, FP, A-2, LFC. See also MLB, interviewed by AOB, 25 May 1930, ABP, 6-1, SHSW-M.

19. Belle was not completely bereft of a sense of humor, however. Describing a train trip she shared with her husband, for example, she wrote: "We had two evenings at poker. Bob won enough to pay his debts, but I lost enough to make him poor again. Such is the fate of gamblers. . . . Praise the president's message. It is all right, Bob thinks. I have not read it and of course you will not. But praise it." BCL to Samuel Harper, 2 Dec. 1890, 1:585, RLP, SHSW-H.

20. RML, *Autobiography,* 135. Freeman, La Follette, and Zabriskie, *Belle,* 61; MLB, interviewed by AOB, 25 May 1930, ABP, 6-1, SHSW-M; Middleton, *These Things,* 96.

21. MLB, interviewed by AOB, 25 May 1930, ABP, 6-1, SHSW-M; undated article among miscellaneous papers of 1904, 78:797, RLP, SHSW-H; BCL and FL, *La Follette,* 1:56.

22. BCL and FL, *La Follette,* 2:1143.

23. BCL to ML, 26 Mar. 1917, FP, A-20, LFC; BCL to RML, 20 July 1914, FP, A-13, LFC; BCL and FL, *La Follette,* 1:58.

24. BCL, story, "I Married a Lawyer," ca. 1911, BLP, D-38, LFC; RML to A. R. Hall, 6 Nov. 1897, 9:324, RLP, SHSW-H.

25. BCL, speech, "Our Story," 5 Feb. 1916, BLP, D-41, LFC; BCL to RML, 2 Jan. 1907, FP, A-5, LFC. See BCL, "Congressional Children," *LM* 1, no. 15 (17 Apr. 1909): 10; "The Comfort of a Farm," *LM* 1, no. 36 (11 Sept. 1909): 10; "Back to Washington," *LM* 2, no. 1 (8 Jan. 1910): 10.

26. BCL, "What It Means to Be an Insurgent Senator's Wife," *The Housekeeper,* 11 Nov. 1911; BCL, "Washington Society," *Thought for Today,* ser. 4, ca. 1911, BLP, D-38, LFC; BCL, "Home and Education," *LM* 5, no. 51 (20 Dec. 1913): 6; BCL, speech, "Our Story," 5 Feb. 1911, BLP, D-41, LFC.

27. BCL and FL, *La Follette,* 1:165, 184.

28. RML to family, 6 Aug. 1903, FP, A-2, LFC. See also RML to family, 23 Nov. and 16 Dec. 1906, FP, A-5, LFC.

29. BCL to RML, 19 Nov. 1905, 9 Dec. 1906, FP, A-4; BCL, speech, "Our Story," 5 Feb. 1916, BLP, D-41, LFC.

30. PFL, *Adventures in Politics*, 63; BCL and FL, *La Follette*, 2:1033. See also BCL to family, 5 Apr. 1920, FP, A-28; PFL to BCL, 19 Apr. 1919, FP, A-26, LFC.

31. BCL to RML, 16 Aug. 1905, FP, A-3, LFC; RML to BCL, 2 Feb. 1907, FP, A-6, LFC; RML, Diary, 20 Nov. 1879, RLP, B-1, LFC.

32. BCL to Elizabeth G. Evans, 23, 24 Sept. 1914, FP, A-14, LFC; BCL and FL, *La Follette*, 1:72; RML to Sam Harper, 1 Jan. 1888, 1:262, RLP, SHSW-H; RML to BCL, 7 Aug. 1903, FP, A-2, LFC; 30 Sept. 1897, FP, A-1, LFC. See also BCL to JR, 16 June 1919, FP, A-24, LFC. Jerome D. Oremland, M.D., chief of psychiatry at Children's Hospital of San Francisco, maintains that La Follette's fear of relaxing was probably a direct defensive reaction to an intense desire to be taken care of. Jerome D. Oremland, M.D., to author, 12 Mar. 1984.

33. BCL, "A Question of Democracy," *LM* 5, no. 19 (10 May 1913): 6. See BCL speeches: "Twenty-five Years of Women's Progress," ca. 1911, BLP, D-38; "The Business of Being a Woman," 21 Aug. 1912, BLP, D-39; "Women's Suffrage," Fall 1912, BLP, D-39; "Working Women and Prison Labor," 17 May 1913, BLP, D-40; "Suffrage School," Dec. 1913, BLP, D-40, LFC.

34. Ruth Story, "Success of Suffrage Is Shown Here, Declares Mrs. La Follette: Asserts She Is Not Campaigning for Husband but for Good of Principles," *Los Angeles Evening Herald* (26 Apr. 1912): 3, in MLP, 40-717, SUSC.

35. BCL and FL, *La Follette*, 1:x; BCL, "What It Means to Be an Insurgent Senator's Wife," *The Housekeeper*, 11 Nov. 1911, BLP, D-38, LFC; RML to BCL, 2 Feb. 1907, FP, A-6, LFC.

36. BCL to JR, 14 Oct. 1914, FP, A-14; BCL to RML, 3 Aug. 1903, FP, A-17, LFC; BCL and FL, *La Follette*, 1:138; BCL, "What It Means to Be an Insurgent Senator's Wife," *The Housekeeper*, 11 Nov. 1911, BLP, D-38; RML to family, 12 Dec. 1918, FP, A-24, LFC.

37. Undated notes, Papers of RSB, Stanford University Microfilm Collection, Reel 53; BCL to Edna Chynoweth, 28 July 1925, FP, A-31, LFC; Lincoln Steffens, "The Victorious Mother," *The Progressive* 2, no. 49 (Belle La Follette Memorial Edition, 7 Nov. 1931): 2.

CHAPTER FIVE

1. BCL, "I Married a Lawyer," ca. 1911, BLP, D-38; RML, Diary, undated entry 1879, RLP, B-1, LFC; BCL, "The Law," *LM* 18, no. 6 (June 1926): 88.

2. RML, Diary, 28, 29 Oct. 1879, RLP, B-1, LFC.

3. RML, Diary, 14 Nov. 1879, RLP, B-1, LFC.

4. RML, Diary, 27 Oct., 13 Nov. 1879, RLP, B-1, LFC.

5. RML, Diary, 29 Oct., 14 Nov. 1879, RLP, B-1, LFC. "The simplest plainest moral rules," wrote La Follette, are "purity & truth." RML, Diary, 19 Nov. 1879, RLP, B-1, LFC.

6. RML, Diary, 17, 19 Nov. 1879, RLP, B-1, LFC; RML to family, 28 Apr. 1925, FP, A-32, LFC. See GR, "Practicing Law with La Follette," *LM* 18, no. 8 (Aug. 1926): 121.

7. RML, Diary, 20 Nov. 1879, RLP, B-1, LFC.

8. RML, Diary, 14, 20 Nov. 1879, RLP, B-1, LFC.

9. La Follette gained particular acclaim for an address made at Sun Prairie, Wisconsin, on 4 July 1879, praising home and country and vilifying vagrants.

10. Cherny, *American Politics in Gilded Age*, 5, 7.

11. RML, *Autobiography*, 6–7; Thelen, *Early Life*, 52–61. See also Nesbit, *Wisconsin*, 403; Thelen, "Boss and Upstart"; and Hantke, "Bismarck of Western Politics" and "Keyes and Radical Republicans."

12. BCL and FL, *La Follette*, 1:47.

13. GR, "Practicing Law with La Follette," *LM* 18, no. 8 (Aug. 1926): 121; BCL and FL, *La Follette*, 1:75–76.

14. RML, Diary, 14 Nov. 1879, RLP, B-1; undated entry for 1879, RLP, B-1; undated entry ca. 1880s or 1890s, RLP, B-2, LFC; Thelen, *New Citizenship*, 297.

15. RML, *Autobiography*, 18–19; RML, Speech at Sun Prairie, 4 July 1879, RLP, B 210, LFC.

16. A remedy for La Grippe found in one of La Follette's diaries consisted of three cents worth of bitter apple mixed with one half pint of whiskey. Even less temperate in his use of tobacco than alcohol, La Follette smoked, at various times in his life, a pipe, cigars, and cigarettes. There are conflicting reports as to the extent of his tobacco usage. La Follette gave up cigars in 1878 but began again in 1894. By 1921, he smoked enough to necessitate buying his preferred cigars, rat-tail stogies, in bulk. Following his stay at the Battle Creek Sanitarium in 1923, however, he claimed to have cut out all forms of smoking.

17. See Thelen, "La Follette, Public Prosecutor."

18. RML, *Autobiography*, 20–21, 149. Belle made no mention of the income generated by La Follette's booming private practice but pointed out that the $800 salary of the district attorney did not seem quite so magnificent when one took into account "the difference between the cost of living in town where everything is to buy and on the farm where there is usually something to sell." BCL, Speech, "Our Story," 5 Feb. 1916, BLP, D-41, LFC.

19. RML, *Autobiography*, 20–21.

20. Jerome D. Oremland, M.D., to author, 12 Mar. 1984; Freeman, La Follette, and Zabriskie, *Belle*, 241.

21. BCL, "The Law," *LM* 18, no. 6 (June 1926): 88. Shortly before he died, La Follette stated he had earned the right to a good long rest, "virtually the only one," it was noted in his obituary, "he ever took." *Newark Star Eagle*, 20 June 1925, RLP, B 91, LFC.

22. RML to GR, 24 Apr. 1896, 4:550–53, RLP, SHSW-H.

23. AOB, untitled three-page note on RML's illnesses, ABP, 6-3, SHSW-H.

24. BCL, "Thought for the Day," ser. 5, ca. 1911, BLP, D-38, LFC; John M. Stokes, M.D., to RML, 13 Feb. 1920, RLP, B-86, LFC.

25. "Newspapers Have Been Burying Me Thirty Years," *Capital Times*, 7 Dec. 1923, RLP, B 265; FL to RML, 1901, FP, A-2, LFC. An article in the *Washington Daily*

*News* carried the headline "Senate Progressives Letting One Man's Illness Kill Their Prospects." *Washington Daily News*, 5 Dec. 1923, RLP, B-266, LFC.

26. RML to BCL, 20 July 1903, FP, A-2, LFC; BCL to family, 11, 12 Oct. 1910, FP, A-9, LFC.

27. RML to Wm. McAdoo, 9 Oct. 1916, RLP, B-110, LFC; RML, Diary, 1880s or 1890s, RLP, B-2, LFC.

28. Unsigned to H. W. Rood, 24 Nov. 1898, 17:89, RLP, SHSW-H; Zona Gale, "La Follette Planned for the Government of Tomorrow," *LM* 17 (July 1925): 99; BCL to family, 12 Oct. 1910, FP, A-9, LFC; RML to W. E. McPherson, 23 June 1904, 125(20):315, RLP, SHSW-H; RML to I. J. Schaefer, 26 Jan. 1899, 17:822, RLP, SHSW-H; AOB, untitled tribute to RML, ABP, 11-2, SHSW-M.

29. RML to W. D. Hoard, 26 Dec. 1904, 128(25):2391–92, RLP, SHSW-H; RML to James J. McGillivray, 26 Dec. 1902, 118(6):426, RLP, SHSW-H.

30. BCL and FL, *La Follette*, 1:58–59; BCL, speech, "Our Story," 5 Feb. 1916, BLP, D-41, LFC.


CHAPTER SIX

1. BCL and FL, *La Follette*, 1:61–62.

2. Ibid., 71; Thelen, *New Citizenship*, 292. See also A. S. Hearn to Sam Harper, 16 Oct. 1888, 1:332, LFP, SHSW-H.

3. BCL and FL, *La Follette*, 1:67–68; BCL, story, "I Married a Lawyer," ca. 1911, BCL, D-38, LFC.

4. Maxwell, *Great Lives*, 3; Nesbit, *Wisconsin*, 402. See also Thelen, *New Citizenship*, 291–92; and Maney, *Young Bob*, 5.

5. Torelle, *Political Philosophy*, 59–60.

6. RML, *CR* 17, pt. 3–5:3747–48, 4244; BCL and FL, *La Follette*, 1:68. In Belle's story "I Married a Lawyer," she provides a less guarded account: "My greatest disappointment was the cold reception given his maiden effort, a carefully prepared speech that I had expected to take the House of Representatives by storm." BCL, "I Married a Lawyer," ca. 1911, BLP, D-38, LFC.

7. Torelle, *Political Philosophy*, 362.

8. RML, Comments, 1912, RLP, B-215, LFC. See "Our Weakness and Not Our Strength," *LM* 1, no. 40 (9 Oct. 1909): 5; RML, "The Attack on the Jew," *LM* 12, no. 11. (Nov. 1920): 179; RML, *CR* 50, pt. 3:2951.

9. RML, *CR* 21, pt. 9–11:468–69; pamphlet, "La Follette and the Negro," 1924, RLP, B-99, LFC; untitled, undated statement, 1924, RLP, B-230, LFC. Only in one personal letter, written in 1905 in dramatic style for humorous effect, did La Follette refer to an African American as a "coon" and a "blamed nigger" (RML to family, 9 July 1905, FP, A-4, LFC). Belle, a more active supporter of racial equality, also exhibited a rare lapse into the racist rhetoric of the day when she wrote to her husband of the amusement she and the children enjoyed when La Follette sent them a box of wigs and theatrical makeup, particularly when Bobbie applied "coon paint" and sang, "If the man in the moon were only a coon." BCL to RML, 14 May 1907, FP, A-12, LFC.

10. Burgchardt, *Voice of Conscience*, 29.

11. RML, *Autobiography*, 36–37.

12. RML, *CR* 19, pt. 1–2:1934–35; *CR* 21, pt. 1–2:4474. See RML, *CR* 52, pt. 5:5134–61.

13. BCL and FL, *La Follette*, 1:69. Belle's conscientiousness sometimes resulted in such anxiety that she became "nervous" and unable to sleep. Even though her husband ran unopposed in 1886, she maintained, "During his six years in Congress there was no let-up in the opposition of the political machine to Mr. La Follette's renomination." BCL, speech, "Our Story," 5 Feb. 1916, BLP, D-41, LFC.

14. BCL and FL, *La Follette*, 1:70–71; Herbert Quick, *Wisconsin State Journal*, 20 Nov. 1911, RLP, B 268, LFC. The stories of Lewis Wolfville and the tales of Darby O'Gill and the Little People were frequent favorites. Max C. Otto, "Two Views of the La Follettes: Washington, the '20s," *WMII* 42–43 (Winter 1958–59): 111; BCL to family, 1 Nov. 1918, FP, A-23, LFC. See also Unger, "Robert M. La Follette," in *Biographical Dictionary of Literary Influences*.

15. La Follette could not afford to buy his own horses and eventually leased them from General Bryant over a five-year period, providing the taxes and feed in return for one-half share of the breeding profits.

16. RML, *CR* 19, pt. 6–8:6309.

17. RML, *CR* 21, pt. 1–2:4475–76; RML, *Autobiography*, 47.

18. Although Belle was unhurt and completely forgiving, Roosevelt sent her flowers and a "charming" note the next day and later would confide: "I blush when I wake up in the dark and think about spilling that coffee over Mrs. La Follette's dress." BCL and FL, *La Follette*, 1:86.

19. Degregorio, *U.S. Presidents*, 337.

20. See Painter, *Standing at Armageddon*, 36–71.

21. J. J. Fruit to Samuel Harper, 28 Oct. 1890, 1:542, RLP, SHSW-H; *Milwaukee Sentinel*, 12 Aug. 1890, 1:784, RLP, SHSW-H; BCL and FL, *La Follette*, 1:88; RML, *Autobiography*, 58–59; Cooper, "Political Prophet," 94.


CHAPTER SEVEN

1. BCL and FL, *La Follette*, 1:90; BCL, "What It Means to Be an Insurgent Senator's Wife," *The Housekeeper*, 11 Nov. 1911, BLP, D-38, LFC.

2. BCL and FL, *La Follette*, 1:90; GR, "Practicing Law with La Follette," *LM* 18, no. 8 (Aug. 1926): 124.

3. GR, "Practicing Law with La Follette," *LM* 18, no. 8 (Aug. 1926): 121; RML to Burton Hanson, 22 May 1895, 3:127–28, RLP, SHSW-H.

4. BCL and FL, *La Follette*, 1:94; Nesbit, *Wisconsin*, 399; Garraty, "Promise Unfulfilled," 84.

5. RML, *Autobiography*, 64. In an interview many years later La Follette called attention to both his willingness to fight and his inherent decency when he said, with a "menacing" expression, "'If he hadn't been an old man —' and then with a wave of the hand dismissed the scene." Henry Beach Needham, "La Follette's Ideas," *Saturday Evening Post*, 8 July 1911, RLP, B-315, LFC.

6. RML, *Autobiography*, 65–66, 69–70. For all of his concern about propriety, La Follette never expressed any concern about the possibility of favoritism or prejudice inherent in practicing in his brother-in-law's court. Sawyer's biographer returns a verdict of "not proven" concerning the charges of attempted bribery, but leans toward La Follette's version.

7. The 1902 voter's handbook proclaimed La Follette "by nature and training a courteous gentleman with a keen sense of propriety and self-control. As a lawyer . . . he never resorts to personal abuse or the brow-beating methods sometimes employed, but always relies on the merits of his case and the force of his argument for success. In the political contests he has fought, he has, indeed, attacked bad methods, false principles, and indefensible policies, boldly and unsparingly with voice and pen, but no single word of personal abuse or of personal attack can be found in all his campaign speeches or in any of his public addresses, extending over a period of more than twenty years." Voter's Handbook of 1902, 35, 133:377, RLP, SHSW-H. La Follette copied the following into one of his notebooks: "He who voices his hate is almost certain to loose some verbal inaccuracies as a by-product — which is another way of saying that Malice is sure to outrun the Truth." Unidentified, undated notebook, RLP, B-1, LFC.

8. RML to unidentified, May 1906, 92:965, RLP, SHSW-H; Margulies, *Decline*, 96; BCL and FL, *La Follette*, 1:152; RML, *Autobiography*, 70–71.

9. "Messages of Appreciation from Individuals," *LM* 17 (July 1925): 107; Nesbit, *Wisconsin*, 419. Supportive letters expressing admiration of La Follette's heroic honesty and integrity vastly outnumbered those voicing disbelief or criticism.

10. Harry Coleman to RML, 31 Oct. 1891, 1:746, RLP, SHSW-H. Another writer scoffed, "Your true character has at last come out. Everybody would hiss you. Why such an error?" Anonymous to RML, 30 Oct. 1891, 1:747, LFP, SHSW-H.

11. RML, *Autobiography*, 71–72; RML, "War Against the Machine," *Chicago Record*, 28 Aug. 1897, RLP, B-263, LFC. See also RML, *Autobiography*, 51–59.

12. RML, "War Against the Machine," *Chicago Record*, 28 Aug. 1897, RLP, B-263, LFC; RML, *Autobiography*, 321, 325.

13. RML, *Autobiography*, 72; BCL, Speech, "Our Story," 5 Feb. 1916, BLP, D-41, LFC.

14. Nesbit, *Wisconsin*, 406. For a study of the anniversary syndrome of adults following the death of a parent in childhood, particularly the attempt to "live out" the deceased parent's life, see Hilgard, Newman, and Fisk, "Strength of Adult Ego," 796–97.

15. RML, *Autobiography*, x, 61–62.

16. Cherny, *American Politics in Gilded Age*, 110. For a concise explanation of the political upheaval in the last decade of the nineteenth century, see 94–126.

17. See Thelen, *New Citizenship*.

18. RML, *Autobiography*, 72.

19. Margulies, *Decline*, 21.

20. BCL and FL, *La Follette*, 1:109. La Follette himself wrote of his mother's death, "However much one may anticipate it, you are never ready for it." RML to Irvine Lenroot, 28 Mar. 1911, RLP, B-106, LFC.

21. BCL and FL, *La Follette*, 1:110. RML to Wm. La Follette, 21 Jan. 1895, 2:709, RLP, SHSW-H. La Follette also sent a wishful letter to his uncle Harvey La Fol-

lette: "While I might make a [great] deal more money looking after business matters with the speculative side, I cannot let loose long enough to do so." RML to Harvey M. La Follette, 14 Oct. 1895, 3:636, RLP, SHSW-H.

22. RML to M. E. Walker, 7 Jan. 1896, 4:259, to George F. Baker, 5 May 1896, 4:569; RML to C. C. Pease, 10 June 1896, 4:684, RLP, SHSW-H. RML, Diary, 13 Mar. 1896, RLP, B-1; RML to FL, 22 Apr. 1896, FP, A-1, LFC. It was probably La Follette's friend Gilbert Roe who wrote during one of La Follette's lengthy illnesses: "It seems to us that when he is sick business matters worry him more than at any other time. I know no reason except that he has more opportunity to think." Unsigned to Jefferson Crawford, 29 Oct. 1898, 16:880, RLP, SHSW-H.

23. BCL and FL, *La Follette*, 1:115; RML to B. F. Dunwiddie, 6 July 1896, 4:17, SHSW-H.

24. RML, *Autobiography*, 83–85. La Follette further claimed, "My candidacy stood for something besides my personal success, and though I was not nominated we gained ground which must be held and fortified for the next contest." RML to James A. Stone, 22 Aug. 1895, 5:192, RLP, SHSW-H. This sentence is repeated in nearly every letter sent to supporters following the convention. See also Graham, *Encore for Reform*, 70; "After La Follette —What?" *LD* 86 (4 July 1925): 9; Thelen, *Insurgent Spirit*, 21.

25. Cherny, *Righteous Cause*, 60. See also Cherny, *American Politics in Gilded Age*, 124–25.

26. RML to A. Beckwith, 17 Aug. 1896, 5:172; RML to Geo. B. Clemenston, 25 Aug. 1896, 5:236; RML to W. A. Jones, 21 Dec. 1896, 6:45, RLP, SHSW-H.

27. BCL and FL, *La Follette*, 1:130.

28. Torelle, *Political Philosophy*, 29, 56–57; RML to BCL, 18 July 1897, FP, A-1, LFC. Later in La Follette's career his fear of being misquoted and need for thoroughness led him to prefer print over speech.

29. RML to BCL, 30 Sept. 1897, FP, A-1, LFC.

30. Frank Ostrander to RML, 22 July 1898, 13:47; E. F. Conley to RML, 19 Oct. 1898, 16:683; RML to H. E. Tickner, 11 Aug. 1897, 8:109; Frank Pooler to RML, ca. summer 1898, 15:62–63, RLP, SHSW-H.

31. On the complex evolution of both La Follette's reform agenda and the shifting membership of core campaigners, advisers, strategists, policy makers, etc., who made up his inner circle see Acrea, "The Wisconsin Reform Coalition."

32. Charles La Follette to RML, 29 Mar. 1897, 6:699; RML to T. L. Harrington, 9 Mar. 1898, 11:243, RLP, SHSW-H. See also Henry Favell to RML, 28 Aug. 1896, 5:258–60; Charles La Follette to RML, 6 Apr. 1897, 7:26; Nils Haugen to RML, 25 Feb. 1897, 8:476, RLP, SHSW-H.

33. RML to A. J. Turner, 7 Sept. 1897, 8:430; RML to George Hazleton, 1 Feb. 1898, 10:402, RLP, SHSW-H; Torelle, *Political Philosophy*, 31.

34. RML to D. James, 18 Mar. 1898, 11:331; RML to G. H. Dickey, 26 Mar. 1898, 11:332; RML to Wm. Gender, ca. Mar. 1898, 11:393–94, all in RLP, SHSW-H; BCL and FL, *La Follette*, 1:125; RML, Speech to Dane County Bar Association, 1900, RLP, B-211, LFC.

35. RML, Speech to Dane County Bar Association, 1900, RLP, B-211, LFC.

36. RML, Address to the Republicans of Wisconsin, 18 July 1898, 12:798–802;

unidentified news clipping enclosed in letter from Geo. F. Hawes to RML, 3 Aug. 1898, 15:453, RLP, SHSW-H.

37. RML, *Autobiography*, 95; Geo. F. Stickney to RML, 1 Oct. 1898, 16:405, RLP, SHSW-H; Thelen, *Insurgent Spirit*, 29–30.

38. RML to Jim C. Kerwin, 21 Sept. 1898; RML to E. Labuwi, 7 Oct. 1898, 16:480; RML to Gideon A. Newman, 29 Sept. 1898, 16:358, RLP, SHSW-H. In a more humorous attempt to convey his busy schedule and personal stress, La Follette wrote, "I enclose you the document you ask for. Please keep it, and never, under any circumstances, let me have it again. I have spent half a day looking for it, and have come near dying of heart disease besides." RML to Jerre C. Murphy, 17 Oct. 1898, 16:652, RLP, SHSW-H.

39. Unsigned [RML] to M. T. Williams, 14 Feb. 1899, 17:974; RML to Alfred Rogers, 15 July 1899, 17:985; RML to Nils Haugen, 6 Apr. 1899, 18:563, RLP, SHSW-H.

40. Unsigned [RML] to Jefferson Crawford, 19 Apr. 1899, 18:349; RML to Dwight T. Parker, 27 June 1899, 18:963; RML to W. D. Hoard, 8 Feb. 1900, 20:581, RLP, SHSW-H.

41. RML to W. D. Hoard, 8 Feb. 1900, 20:581; RML to Henry Casson, 16 Mar. 1900, 21:104, SHSW-H.

42. Although many recent historians maintain that the degree of the corruption of Gilded Age politicians has been exaggerated, no one denies its existence. See Cherny, *Politics in Gilded Age*, 1–4, 15, 53–56; and Charles W. Calhoun, "The Political Culture: Public Life and Conduct in Politics," in *The Gilded Age: Essays on the Origins of Modern America*, edited by Charles W. Calhoun (Wilmington, Del.: Scholarly Resources, 1996), 185–213.

43. RML to A. R. Hall, ca. Mar. 1900, 21:221; O. G. Munson to RML, 30 Mar. 1900, 21:297, RLP, SHSW-H.

44. Barton, *Winning of Wisconsin*, 161; Evening Wisconsin Company to Alfred Rodgers, 1900, 35:775, RLP, SHSW-H. La Follette's imperialistic rhetoric was not merely calculated to reassure traditional Republican voters. Contrary to the popular belief that La Follette was either a life-long isolationist or pacifist, he exhibited little personal interest in imperialism prior to 1900 but carried on in his early career what has been termed an "imperialist flirtation," rendering him "at the very least agreeably acquiescent" to the "imperialist surge." Kennedy, "La Follette's Imperialist Flirtation," 141–42.

45. RML to Wm. Stroud, 28 June 1900, 30:390; RML to D. W. Hutchin, 10 July 1900, 32:55; RML to M. J. Labuwi, 11 July 1900, 32:178; RML to Jos. G. End, 10 July 1900, 32:12; RML to M. A. Barry, 27 July 1900, 33:31, RLP, SHSW-H. See also RML to Frank B. Dorothy, 10 July 1900, 32:25; RML to L. J. Cornelius, 19 July 1900, 32:10, RLP, SHSW-H.

CHAPTER EIGHT

1. RML to David E. Williams, 25 Apr. 1900, 23:426, RLP, SHSW; Margulies, *Decline*, 22. See also RML to Walter J. Wilds, 11 June 1901, 45:597, RLP, SHSW-H; RML

to C. A. Pinney, ca. spring 1900, 45:798, RLP, SHSW-H; Garraty, "Promise Unfulfilled," 84.

2. For La Follette's subsequent support for Jews, as well as his attitudes toward immigrants, see P. C. Kennedy, "La Follette and the Russians," 190.

3. Greenbaum, *La Follette*, 51; Henry C. [Illegible] to Mr. Hanna, 2 Dec. 1905, 88:837, RLP, SHSW-H. La Follette joined his brother in protesting against those who held the "almighty dollar greater than honorable humanity," but he was not against wealth "rightfully" earned and spent. Wm. La Follette to RML, 21 Aug. 1898, 15:620–21; RML to Harvey La Follette, 21 Feb. 1903, 122(13):255, RLP, SHSW-H.

4. Current, *Wisconsin*, 427, 438; Thelen, *Insurgent Spirit*, 108–9; Strother, "Death of the Wisconsin Idea," 622. For a summary of the lively debate over the origins, definitions, and legacy of the Wisconsin Idea, see Buenker, *Progressive Era*, viii–ix, 569–610. See also Hoeveler, "The University and the Social Gospel."

5. Thelen, *New Citizenship*, 306.

6. RML, *Autobiography* 109, 114. See Thelen, *New Citizenship*, 11–22.

7. RML, *Autobiography*, 115–17. See "Governor's Ringing Message," *Outlook* 68 (25 May 1901): 199–200.

8. RML, Memorandum to Bill Number 238A, 22 May 1903, 62:682, RLP, SHSW-H.

9. Torelle, *Political Philosophy*, 46; RML to Mr. Van Norman, 2 Aug. 1902, 55:936; RML to B. F. Hagemeister, 2 Jan. 1902, 39:812, RLP, SHSW-H.

10. BCL, speech, "Our Story," 5 Feb. 1916, BLP, D-41, LFC.

11. RML to Isaac Stephenson, 25 Jan. 1902, 49:6, RLP, SHSW-H. See also T. J. McGovern to RML, 11 May 1901, 44:596; RML to Isaac Stephenson, 25 Feb. 1901, 116:1:394; Isaac Stephenson to RML, 17 Jan. 1902, 49:912, RLP, SHSW-H.

12. RML to Edward O. Brown, 7 Dec. 1901, 188(5):134, RLP, SHSW-H.

13. BCL and FL, *La Follette*, 1:146; Thelen, *Insurgent Spirit*, 36; RML to Wm. Lachenmaier, 22 Nov. 1902, 121(11):337, RLP, SHSW-H.

14. Wyman quoted in Buenker, *Progressive Era*, 467. La Follette received 790 votes to opponent John Whitehead's 266.

15. RML, speech, Acceptance of Nomination, 17 July 1902, 59:854, RLP, SHSW-H.

16. BCL and FL, *La Follette*, 1:157, 267; John T. Kelley to RML, ca. autumn 1902, 57:8, RLP, SHSW-H; *Milwaukee Journal*, 1 May 1902, in Buenker, *Progressive Era*, 469. See campaign document, "The Battle Half Over," Aug. 1902, 133:492; pamphlet, "Governor Robert M. La Follette: Some Facts of His Life," 58:766–86; W. J. McElroy to RML, 3 Oct. 1902, 57:69; W. A. Hayes to RML, 5 Oct. 1902, 57:147, RLP, SHSW-H.

17. RML to A. H. Hall, 9 Dec. 1902, 121(12):1, RLP, SHSW-H.

18. RML, Address of Welcome to Trustees and Superintendents of the County Asylum of Wisconsin, 1 Dec. 1903, 65:298; RML to James Clark, 9 Sept. 1903, 123(16):408, RLP, SHSW-H.

19. Torelle, *Political Philosophy*, 25.

20. RML to GR, 18 Jan. 1904, 124(18):318, RLP, SHSW-H.

21. Gould, *Progressive Era*, 61–62; Maxwell, *La Follette and Rise of Progressives*, 79; RML to GR, 28 Dec. 1902, 124:18:138; RML to Wm. Scallon, 13 July 1903; RML to Jerre Murphy, 14 Nov. 1904, 127(23):92, RLP, SHSW-H. For assessments of Roo-

sevelt, including his commitment to progressivism, see Morris, *Rise of Roosevelt* and "Theodore Roosevelt, President"; Brands, *Last Romantic*; and Mowry, *Era of Theodore Roosevelt*.

22. Torelle, *Political Philosophy*, 64, 72.

23. RML to GR, 24 Feb. 1904, 12(19):65, RLP, SHSW-H. Wisconsin's current capitol building was begun almost before the ashes of the previous one had cooled. With a central dome only slightly smaller than that crowning the nation's capitol, it is a spectacular structure which cost nearly $8 million in 1905 — an accomplishment, legislators proudly noted, achieved without graft.

24. Charles F. Clark to RML, 2 July 1904, 73:266, RLP, SHSW-H.

25. RML to J. S. Campbell, 12 July 1904, 124(20):425, RLP, SHSW-H; RML, *Autobiography*, 131, 144. This claim of declining any fee is contradicted by a letter that discusses the profits of a La Follette lecture in Superior, Wisconsin; C. A. Marshall to I. L. Lenroot, 9 Dec. 1903, 65:383, RLP, SHSW-H.

26. See Garraty, "Promise Unfulfilled," 76–78.

27. Greenbaum, *La Follette*, 59. See BCL and FL, *La Follette*, 1:172; BCL, Speech, "Our Story," 5 Feb. 1916, BLP, D-41, LFC.

28. BCL and FL, *La Follette*, 1:187; RML to Byron Andrews, 4 Mar. 1904, 125(19):132, RLP, SHSW-H; Torelle, *Political Philosophy*, 25; J. M. Kerr to RML, 25 June 1904, 73:116, RLP, SHSW-H; Barton, *Winning of Wisconsin*, 379–85.

29. Torelle, *Political Philosophy*, 36; D. A. Jones to RML, 9 Dec. 1904, 77:651, RLP, SHSW-H. See also A. R. Hall to Nils Haugin, 14 Nov. 1904, 76:790, RLP, SHSW-H. Such recognition was not always completely deserved. Historian John Buenker points out that, despite its reputation, "Wisconsin emerges more as a follower than a leader in railroad legislation" and that "even La Follette acknowledged that his measure owed much to the advice of reformers in Texas, Iowa, and Minnesota." Noting that La Follette "clearly promised more than he delivered — and claimed more for his achievement than it deserved," Buenker nonetheless concedes, "Still, given the enormous wealth and political influence opposing railroad regulation, perhaps little more was possible." Buenker, *Progressive Era*, 487–88. This long awaited volume is a meticulous recounting of Wisconsin political history during this vital period. La Follette scholars will find chapters 9–14 of particular interest.

30. RML to BCL, 14 Dec. 1904, FP, A-3, LFC. See Margulies, "La Follette Goes to the Senate," for the behind-the-scenes machinations that led to La Follette's senatorship.

31. BCL, "The Farm," *LM* 18, no. 5 (May 1926): 71. See also "Extraordinary Gain of State Officers," *The Germania*, 27 Nov. 1905, James Davidson Papers, 4-1, SHSW-M.

32. RML to BCL, 9, 10 July 1905, 28 June 1905, FP, A-4, LFC.

33. "La Follette Charms Crowds," *Bloomington (Ind.) Daily Bulletin*, 22 Aug. 1905, RLP, B-263, LFC.

34. "La Follette's Tale Sadly Disappoints Kansans," 6 July 1905, newspaper clipping enclosed in Wagner to unidentified, 8 July 1905, RLP, B-61, LFC.

35. "An Accession to the Senate," *Brooklyn Daily Eagle*, 26 Jan. 1905, RLP, B-263, LFC.

36. Thelen, *Insurgent Spirit*, 51.

37. RML, *Autobiography*, 157.

38. Ibid.; Torelle, *Political Philosophy*, 189.

CHAPTER NINE

1. Frost, *Bully Pulpit*, 183.

2. Painter, *Standing at Armageddon*, 177, 182.

3. Frost, *Bully Pulpit*, 182, 227.

4. Ibid., 188.

5. RML to Alfred Rogers, 7 Jan. 1906, RLP, B 5, LFC. For a discussion of "working" vs. "non-working" Senate committees, see Byrd, *Senate*, 2:238–42.

6. Greenbaum, *La Follette*, 69; Charles Merz, "The Senator from Wisconsin," *New Republic* 43 (8 July 1925): 173; RML to A. M. Lewis, 14 Jan. 1906, 89:759, RLP, SHSW-H.

7. TR to Nicholas Murray Butler, 21 May 1904, and TR to Henry Cabot Lodge, 22 July 1904, both in TR, *Letters*, 4:802, 863–64; RML to Alfred T. Rogers, 7 Jan. 1906, FP, A-5, LFC; RML, "'Righteous Unrest' or Unrighteous Rest," *LM* 1, no. 10 (13 Mar. 1909): 3.

8. RML, *Autobiography*, 174–75.

9. RML, *CR* 40, pt. 6:5687.

10. BCL to FL, 24 Apr. 1906, FP, A-4, LFC; RML, *CR* 40, pt. 6:5519, 5688; BCL, speech, "Our Story," 5 Feb. 1916, BLP, D-41, LFC; RML, *Autobiography*, 176.

11. BCL to FL, 24 Apr. 1906, FP, A-4, LFC; Paul Munter to RML, 20 Apr. 1906, 91:891; Wm. Marks to RML, 21 Apr. 1906, 91:902, RLP, SHSW-H.

12. RML to Isaac Stephenson, 6 June 1906, 92:1101, RLP, SHSW-H.

13. RML to family, 17 Nov. 1906, FP, A-5, LFC.

14. BCL to RML, 29 Jan. 1907, FP, A-5, LFC; RML to family, 30 Jan. 1907, FP, A-6, LFC; BCL to RML, 12 Feb. 1907, FP, A-5, LFC. See also BCL to RML, 14, 27 Jan. 1907, FP, A-5, LFC. Belle's assertion that the public saw Roosevelt and La Follette as working together for the same goals was reflected in the press. Political buttons featured a joint portrait of the two leaders. See "An Accession to the Senate," *Brooklyn Daily Eagle*, 26 Jan. 1905, RLP, B-263, LFC.

15. RML to family, 5 Dec. 1906, FP, A-4, LFC.

16. RML to family, 16 Dec. 1906, FP, A-5, LFC; TR to WAW, 5 Jan. 1907, in TR, *Letters*, 5:540–41.

17. RML to family, 18 Dec. 1906; BCL to RML, 23 Jan. 1907, FP, A-5, LFC.

18. RML to family, 30 Jan. 1907, FP, A-6, LFC; RML to TR, 19 Feb. 1907, RLP, B-103, LFC; TR to RML, 19 Feb. 1907, RLP, B-62, LFC.

19. RML, *Autobiography*, 165–66; BCL and FL, *La Follette*, 1:223.

20. Newton Dent, "Senator Robert M. La Follette," *Munsey's Magazine*, Feb. 1907, RLP, B-315, LFC. See RML, *Autobiography*, 166–67.

21. F. E. Leupp to James R. Garfield, 19 Mar. 1907, RLP, B-62, LFC; unidentified news clipping, *Milwaukee News*, 1907, RLP, B-263, LFC. R. I. Dugdale claimed that La Follette showed him, in 1909, the canceled check for $20,000 made out by Standard Oil to Spooner that was secretly responsible for the senator's mys-

terious and rapid retirement. Dugdale intimated that the check had been acquired in 1907 by Alfred Rogers, "who often undertook such jobs for La Follette." R. I. Dugdale, statement, 23 Mar. 1954, RLP, 204–5, SHSW-M.

22. "[H]ad I had time to gather my wits together before he rushed away," Bray recalled, "I believed I would have twisted his nose for him. His pompadour seemed to reach about to my chin." Wm. M. Bray to SHSW, 8 Aug. 1961, RLP, 205–6, SHSW-M.

23. RML to family, 14, 26 Apr., 27 Mar. 1906, FP, A-6, LFC.

24. RML to BCL, 27 Mar. 1907, FP, A-6, LFC. See also John Bingham Hurlbut, "The Loss of a Great American," *LM* 18, no. 11 (Nov. 1926): 168.

25. BCL to RML, 17 July 1907, FP, A-5; RML to family, 14 Apr. 1907, FP, A-6, LFC.

CHAPTER TEN

1. RML, speech, "Tribute to Albert H. Hall," 1905, RLP, B-212, LFC; RML to PFL, 1 Sept. 1905, FP, A-4, LFC. For more on RML's views on life after death, see RML, Diary, 11 Dec. 1924, 30 Mar. 1925, RLP, B-1, LFC. For RML as philosopher, see RML to PFL, 14 Feb. 1907, FP, A-6, LFC. For RML as drill sergeant, see RML to JR, 13 Mar. 1915, FP, A-18; 15 May 1919, FP, A-27; and RML to PFL, 30 Jan. 1916, FP, A-19; 30 July 1923, FP, A-30; 28 Apr. 1925, FP, A-32, LFC.

2. Freeman, La Follette, and Zabriskie, *Belle*, 142; BCL to RML, 3 Aug. 1903, FP, A-2, LFC. See BCL, "Bobbie's Lesson," 1901, BLP, D-38, LFC; BCL to children, 27 Mar. 1904, FP, A-2, LFC.

3. BCL and FL, *La Follette*, 1:111; RML to ML, 11 Dec. 1906, FP, A-5, LFC. See RML to family, 4 June 1920, FP, A-28, LFC.

4. BCL and FL, *La Follette*, 1:81; BCL, "Mother and Daughter," *LM* 5, no. 17 (26 Apr. 1913): 6; BCL to family, 15 Nov. 1917, FP, A-20, LFC; BCL to PFL, 8 May 1919, FP, A-24, LFC; BCL to ML, 13 Mar. 1921, FP, A-29, LFC; BCL to FL, 4 July 1909, FP, A-7, LFC; BCL, "Apron Strings—A Substitute," in "Thought for Today," ca. 1911, BLP, D-38, LFC.

5. BCL, "Mother and Daughter," *LM* 5, no. 17 (26 Apr. 1913): 6; BCL to FL, 11 June 1901, FP, A-2, LFC; BCL, Story, "I Married a Lawyer," ca. 1911, BLP, D-38, LFC.

6. RML to FL, 8 Oct. 1906, 95:531–34, RLP, SHSW-H; RML to family, 13 Feb. 1907, 14 Apr. 1907, FP, A-6, LFC; Middleton, *These Things*, 85.

7. RML to family, 25 Mar. 1919, FP, A-26, LFC. For children as extensions of RML, see PFL, *Adventures in Politics*, 39–39.

8. RML to family, 28 Dec. 1918, FP, A-24; 13 Jan., 4 Feb. 1919, FP, A-26; RML to PFL, 14 Feb. 1907, FP, A-6; RML to family, 14 Apr. 1907, FP, A-6, LFC. For bribery, see RML to FL, 29 Jan. 1910, FP, A-9, LFC; unsigned to Apeda Studio, 21 Nov. 1910, FP, B-105, LFC; RML to A. A. Franklin, 24 Sept. 1911, RLP, B-106, LFC; RML to family, 29 July 1906, FP, A-8, LFC; 14 Apr. 1907, FP, A-6; BCL to JR, 16 May 1914, FP, A-13, LFC. For family closeness, see RML to family, 14 Feb. 1907, FP, A-6, LFC.

9. RML to family, 16 Mar. 1919, and PFL to ML, 23 July 1919, both in FP, A-26, LFC. See also PFL to JR, 13 July 1819, FP, A-23; PFL to ML, 2 June 1919, FP, A-26; JR to PFL, 24 June 1921, FP, A-29; JR to PFL, Apr. 1916, FP, A-19; JR to FL, 1 Aug. 1911, FP, A-11; BCL to RML, 20 Oct. 1918, FP, A-22, LFC.

10. BCL to PFL, 6 Jan. 1919, FP, A-24, LFC. For PFL's difficult relationship with his father, see PFL to JR, 25 Mar. 1916, FP, A-19, LFC. For RML's reaction to FL's reported engagement, see RML to BCL, 30 Jan. 1907, FP, A-6, LFC.

11. BCL to RML, 6 Feb. 1919, FP, A-24, LFC; Middleton, *These Things*, 89; BCL to FL, 12, 15 Mar. 1911, FP, A-10, LFC.

12. FL to BCL, 14 Mar. 1911, and BCL to FL, 28 Mar. 1911, both in FP, A-10, LFC. Fola complained to her brother Bobbie about their parents' closed-mindedness and the fact that they "never let up and play for a few glad hours" (Thelen, *Insurgent Spirit*, 165). He comforted her, "It seems to me pretty damn small of them if they won't even get acquainted with him to see if they like him. . . . After you have tried [to get them acquainted] and . . . it doesn't work out go ahead anyway. Don't sacrifice your happiness too long." JR to FL, 1 Aug. 1911, FP, A-11, LFC.

13. Charlotte Perkins Gilman, "George Middleton's Plays about Women," *The Forerunner*, reprinted in *LM* 6, no. 12 (21 Mar. 1914): 8.

14. PFL to RML, 10 Mar. 1917, FP, A-20; 12 June 1921, FP, A-29, LFC.

15. PFL to RML, 10 Mar. 1917, FP, A-20; PFL to BCL, 11 Mar. 1916, FP, A-19, LFC. See also PFL to RML, 12 June 1921, FP, A-29; 14 June 1916, FP, A-19; 22 May 1919, FP, A-26; 13 Apr. 1923, FP, A-30, LFC; and PFL to BCL, 24 July 1919, FP, A-26; 16 June 1910, FP, A-9; 8 May, 19 Apr., 18 Mar. 1921, FP, A-29; 24 July 1919, 3 Jan. 1919, FP, A-26; 8 May 1918, FP, A-23, LFC. For the senior La Follette's attempt to dissuade PFL from joining the service, see BCL to PFL, 11 Apr. 1917, FP, A-20, LFC.

16. RML to PFL, 11 Oct. 1918, and RML to family, 25 Oct. 1918, FP, A-23; RML to family, 31 Dec. 1918, FP, A-24, LFC. Even after PFL's discharge, RML continued to advise his son to protect his health: "Now Phil dear laddie do this just for dad. *I am begging you hard my boy.*" RML to PFL, 10 Jan. 1919, FP, A-36, LFC. For details on Phil's military service, see PFL, interviewed by Edward M. Coffman, PLP, SHSW-M.

17. Freeman, La Follette, and Zabriskie, *Belle*, 220.

18. Feinman, Review of *Governor Philip F. La Follette*, 410. For PFL's political life, see J. E. Miller, *Governor Philip F. La Follette*.

19. PFL, *Adventures in Politics*, 178–79; J. E. Miller, *Governor Philip F. La Follette*, 184. See Raushenbush, "Starting Unemployment Compensation in Wisconsin."

20. PFL's manuscript, edited by Donald Young, was published in 1970 as *Adventures in Politics*.

21. Freeman, La Follette, and Zabriskie, *Belle*, 128. For more on the lives of the La Follettes after the death of their patriarch, see Weisberger, *La Follettes of Wisconsin*, 277–318.

22. BCL, "Bobbie's Lesson," 1901, BLP, D-38, LFC.

23. JR to RML, Dec. 1906, FP, A-5, LFC; PFL, *Adventures in Politics*, 21. See BCL to RML, 14 Jan. 1907, FP, A-5; 3 July 1905, FP, A-3; 27 Jan. 1907, FP, A-5; 28 Oct. 1918, FP, A-24, LFC.

24. RML to JR, 5 Feb. 1907, FP, A-6; 29 July 1911, FP, A-11; 7 Oct. 1913, FP, A-13; 4 Mar. 1914, FP, A-16; 13 Mar. 1915, FP, A-18, LFC.

25. Freeman, La Follette, and Zabriskie, *Belle*, 87. Travel and excitement exhausted Bobbie and upset his stomach, while the other children suffered no such ill effects.

26. JR to RML and BCL, 17 Jan. 1906, Dec. 1906, FP, A-5; RML to family, 30 Aug. 1909, FP, A-8, LFC; RML to GR, 24 Feb. 1904, 125(19):65, RLP, SHSW-H. See also RML to family, 20 Aug. 1909, FP, A-8; 14 Apr. 1907, FP, A-6, LFC.

27. JS to RML and BCL, 7 Feb. 1906, FP, A-5; JR to RML and BCL, 21 Jan. 1906, 17 Feb. 1906, FP, A-5; 5 Jan. 1906, FP, A-4, LFC.

28. Except for ND to Alf, 17 May 1912, RLP, B-107, LFC, a few cryptic notes and telegrams in the La Follette family papers constitute the only evidence of the entire affair. See also ND to Alf, 11 Apr. 1912, and ND to RML and BCL, 18 Apr. 1912, RLP, B-107; BCL to family, 8 Apr. 1912, FP, A-11, LFC. Bobbie continued to view driving as a rare opportunity for independence. See JR to family, 5 Dec. 1918, FP, A-23, LFC.

29. RML to JR, 29 July 1911, FP, A-11, LFC; RML to Alfred T. Rogers, 7 Aug. 1911, RLP, B-106, LFC. See also RML to JR, 9 Nov. 1914, FP, A-16; 29 July 1911, FP, A-11; 4 Mar., 9 Nov. 1914, FP, A-16, LFC.

30. RML to JR, 1 Oct. 1914, FP, A-16; RML to Alfred T. Rogers, 7 Aug. 1911, RLP, B-106; BCL to JR, 29 Oct. 1914, FP, A-14, LFC. See also RML to JR, 12 Oct., 9 Nov. 1914, FP, A-16, LFC.

31. BCL to JR, 23 Jan. 1914, FP, A-13; 5 Feb. 1915, FP, A-17; RML to JR, 9 Nov. 1914, FP, A-16, LFC. See RML to JR, 18 Nov. 1914, FP, A-16, LFC.

32. RML to JR, 18 Nov. 1914, FP, A-16; RML to F. W. Roe, 22 Oct. 1914, RLP, B-109; RML to Voyta Wrabetz, 20 Aug. 1911, RLP, B-106; RML to JR, 31 Mar. 1914, FP, A-16, LFC. See also BCL to Prof. Dowling, 13 Nov. 1914; BCL to Carl R. Fish, 29 Oct. 1914, FP, A-14, LFC.

33. BCL to JR, 26 Mar. 1915, FP, A-17, LFC. See RML to JR and PFL, 23 Jan. 1917, FP, A-21, LFC. Nellie Dunn's assessment is noted in JJH to RML, 25 May 1915, RLP, B-77, LFC.

34. RML to JR, 29 June 1915, FP, A-18; BCL to FL, 28 Sept. 1915, FP, A-17; BCL to family, 13 Sept. 1915, FP, A-17; RML to family, 16 Oct. 1915, FP, A-18, LFC. When unavoidably separated from Bobbie, La Follette insisted that he be informed of his son's temperature twice daily. He predicted enthusiastically, "Give Bob back his health and he is a winner in anything he goes after." RML to family, 3 Oct. 1915, FP, A-18, LFC.

35. BCL to RML, 29 Jan. 1917, FP, A-20; RML to family, 14 July 1917, FP, A-21; JR to FL, 10 Oct. 1917, FP, A-20, LFC.

36. JR to PFL, 16 Jan. 1918, FP, A-23, LFC.

37. Lincoln Steffens to JR, 5 Feb. 1918, RLP, B-83; BCL to PFL, 5 May, 5 Apr. 1918, FP, A-22; JJH to John S. Donald, 18 Feb. 1918, RLP, B-112, LFC. See PFL to family, 18 Feb. 1918, FP, A-23; JJH to Charles H. Crownhart, 3 Aug. 1918, RLP, B-83, LFC. In direct contrast to Bobbie's weak protests against parental expectations and interference, Phil proclaimed during his college years, "Life is too blamed short to worry so much about one or two papers . . . and if . . . I flunk, why that

will be hard luck, but just because I've flunked the exam, that is no sign they can take away from me what I have learned during the semester and anyway, we are coming here to learn and not to be examined." PFL to family, 19 Jan. 1916, FP, A-10, LFC.

38. BCL to family, 27 Oct. 1918, FP, A-22, LFC; BCL, "Great Is La Jolla," *LM* 11, no. 5 (May 1919): 74. Bobbie put off trying crutches, preferring to move about the house by leaning directly upon his mother. In addition, he called her frequently in the night for her to rub his back for a half an hour at a time when he was unable to sleep. Belle's indulgence as Bobbie recuperated included the purchase of a car because he so enjoyed driving, which was therefore a "good investment" as "the use of his feet running the car is a constant stretching exercise." BCL to RML, 3, 16 Dec. 1918, FP, A-22, LFC.

39. RML to PFL, 8 May 1919; RML to family, 24 Dec. 1918; BCL to RML, 6 Feb. 1919, FP, A-24, LFC.

40. BCL to JR, 8 May 1919, FP, A-24; RML to family, 25 Mar. 1919, FP, A-26; RML to JR, 14 Apr. 1919, FP, A-27; JR to RML, 21 May, 29 June 1919, FP, A-26, LFC. See also RML to family, 31 Mar. 1919, FP, A-26; RML to family, 14 Apr. 1919, FP, A-27, LFC.

41. JR to BCL, 30 July 1919, FP, A-26; RML to family, 6 Feb. 1919, and JR to RML, 12 Feb. 1919, FP, A-26, LFC. See RML to JR, ca. 1919, FP, A-27, LFC.

42. RML to JR, 20 Aug. 1911, FP, A-11; RML to Professor Roe, 19 Sept. 1914, RLP, B-189; RML, Diary, 2 Apr. 1925, RLP, B-1, LFC.

43. RML to JR, 15 May 1919; JR to BCL, 30 July 1919; JR to RML, 30 July 1919, FP, A-26, LFC.

44. Roger T. Johnson, *La Follette Jr.*, 7.

45. JR to family, 6 Feb. 1915, FP A-18; 20 Feb. 1917, FP, A-20; JR to BCL and ML, 5 Oct. 1919, FP, A-26; JR to Rachel Young, 30 Apr. 1925, FP, A-32, LFC.

46. JR to BCL, June 1910, FP, A-9, LFC. See also JR to family, 5 Dec. 1917, FP, A-20; JR to family, 11 Apr. 1919, FP, A-26; JR to Rachel Young, 30 Apr. 1925, FP, A-32, LFC. Although many of Bobbie's letters reveal his dry wit, controversy continues over the true nature of his temperament. His biographer concludes his tendency to show different aspects of himself to different people allowed one acquaintance to describe him as the least introverted, least depressed man he ever knew, while another friend called him a "gloomy Gus," and his sister-in-law recalled him as humorless. Maney, *Young Bob*, 150, 312–13.

47. Wm. Hard, "That Man La Follette," *Nation* 119 (16 July 1924): 65; JR to RML, 17 Feb. 1925, and RML to JR, 19 Feb. 1925, FP, A-32, LFC. Bobbie noted in a letter to his family, "I still have ¾ of a degree of temperature today." JR to family, 21 Jan. 1925, FP, A-32, LFC. See RML to family, 20, 22 Jan. 1925; RML to JR, 19 Feb. 1925, FP, A-32; JR to RML, 9, 19 Feb. 1925, FP, A-32, LFC.

48. Maney, *Young Bob*, 80; Freeman, La Follette, and Zabriskie, *Belle*, 242.

49. See Auerbach, "The La Follette Committee."

50. Maney, *Young Bob*, 150, 153. See JR to BCL, 7 May, 12 Feb. 1929; JR to Rachel Young, 26 July 1929, FP, A-37; PFL to JR, 14 June 1943, FP, A-48, LFC.

51. Kades, "Incumbent Without a Party," 14; Roger T. Johnson, *La Follette, Jr.*, 159.

52. Roger T. Johnson, *La Follette, Jr.*, 160.

53. Maney, *Young Bob*, 311, 314.

54. *CR* 99, pt. 2:1560, 1562–63.

55. "La Follette Gets 60 Days for Restaurant Fire," *La Crosse Tribune*, 9 Apr. 1999; Doug La Follette, interviewed by author by telephone, 3 Feb. 1999; Tweed Roosevelt, interviewed by author, 26 Apr. 1999.


CHAPTER ELEVEN

1. Frost, *Bully Pulpit*, 183; Henry F. Cochems, "Nominating Senator Robert M. La Follette for President at the Republican National Convention, Chicago, Illinois," 18 June 1908, Henry F. Cochem Papers, 186–89, SHSW-M.

2. Wilder, "Governor La Follette," *Outlook* 70 (8 Mar. 1902): 632; Burgchardt, *Voice of Conscience*, 75–76.

3. Herman Blum to RML, 3 Apr. 1908; RML to GR, 6 Apr. 1908, RLP, B-103, LFC. La Follette enclosed the entire text of the offending article and Blum's letter in his letter to Gilbert Roe.

4. RML to family, 1 June 1908, FP, A-7, LFC. See Richard Shenkman and Kurt Rieger, *One-Night Stands with American History: Odd, Amusing, and Little-Known Incidents* (New York: Quill, 1980), 198; Byrd, *Senate*, 2:117; and Alexander, *Famous Five*, 147.

5. RML, *Autobiography*, 202.

6. RML to Leland S. Wilson, 5 June 1908, 105:554; RML to Henry Moore, 6 June 1908, 105:564; RML to A. Walter, 10 June 1908, 105:659, all in RLP, SHSW-H; TR to Theodore Roosevelt, Jr., 29 May 1908, in TR, *Letters*, 6:1044. For more on Roosevelt's views of La Follette during this period, see TR to Lincoln Steffens, 5 June 1908, in TR, *Letters*, 6:1050–53. See also Margulies, "La Follette as Presidential Aspirant." On the efforts to curtail filibustering, see Byrd, *Senate*, 2:108–11, 117.

7. Pringle, *Taft*, 1:373.

8. BCL and FL, *La Follette*, 1:263.

9. La Follette rationalized his unwillingness to campaign for Taft by assuring the candidate that two issues of *La Follette's Magazine* devoted to urging his election would be more effective than a speaking tour and its press reports.

10. Form letter by RML, 8 Oct. 1908, RLP, B-103, LFC; RML to Frank A. Harrison, 27 Jan. 1909, 106:844, RLP, SHSW-H. Even when they were very young, the La Follette children were encouraged to submit articles. *La Follette's Weekly Magazine* became *La Follette's Magazine* when published on a monthly basis. After La Follette's death, it became *The Progressive*, a monthly magazine still in publication. The January 1999 issue offered a number of highlights from the first ninety years of the magazine's publication as well as a tribute to its founder, including a cartoon of La Follette returning to life for one day to chastise business and political leaders Bill Clinton, Bill Gates, and Rupert Murdoch for their greed and hypocrisy.

11. RML to RSB, 9 Dec. 1911, RLP, B-107, LFC.

12. Boller, *Presidential Anecdotes*, 199. Following his presidency, Taft's heart's desire was fulfilled: he served as Chief Justice of the Supreme Court from 1921 to 1930.

13. BCL and FL, *La Follette*, 1:275; BCL to FL, 12 June 1909, FP, A-7, LFC; RML, *CR* 44, pt. 3:3013, 3021. For struggles between RML and Taft over the tariff and other issues, see Coletta, *Presidency of Taft*, 62–66, 148–50.

14. BCL and FL, *La Follette*, 1:275; RML, *Autobiography*, 180–81.

15. BCL and FL, *La Follette*, 1:282; RML, "Dollar Diplomacy," *LM* 5, no. 13 (29 Mar. 1913): 1. See also "Dollar Diplomacy," *LM* 3, no. 9 (4 Mar. 1911): 3.

16. Painter, *Standing at Armageddon*, 254; Herbert Quick, "Roosevelt's Treachery to Progressivism," *LM* 7, no. 7 (July 1916): 8.

17. BCL to JS, 4 July 1909, FP, A-7, LFC.

18. RML to family, 20 Aug. 1909, FP, A-8, LFC; BCL and FL, *La Follette*, 1:285.

19. See "The Pinchot Ballinger Controversy," *LM* 1, no. 33 (21 Aug. 1909): 3; "Pinchot or Ballinger —Which?" *LM* 1, no. 40 (9 Oct. 1909): 3; "Pinchot's Dismissal" *LM* 2, no. 2 (15 Jan. 1910): 3. Even after La Follette's death, the friendship between the two families remained close. The Brandeis family subsidized the two-volume biography of La Follette that Belle began and Fola completed.

20. BCL and FL, *La Follette*, 1:303; Painter, *Standing at Armageddon*, 257. La Follette's views of Theodore Roosevelt as a great politician rather than a great statesman are echoed by historians Richard Hofstadter, John Chamberlain, and Russel B. Nye in their comparisons of the two leaders. See Hofstadter, *American Political Tradition*, 27–28; Grantham, *Theodore Roosevelt*, 144–51.

21. Frost, *Bully Pulpit*, 227.

22. Buenker, *Progressive Era*, 522. Among La Follette's prominent supporters during that campaign were Senator Joseph Bristow, Representative Charles A. Lindbergh, and American Federation of Labor president Samuel Gompers.

23. Hiram Johnson to TR, 20 Aug. 1915, FLP, E-80, LFC.

24. RML to BCL, 5 Dec. 1910, FP, A-9, LFC; Mowry, *Era of Theodore Roosevelt*, 247. To one family friend La Follette denied that he was consulted by Taft at all. See also Manners, *TR and Will*, 98.

25. RML, *Autobiography*, 212. See RML, "The Beginning of a Great Movement," *LM* 3, no. 5 (4 Feb. 1911): 7–9, 12.

26. RML, *Autobiography*, 213; RML to TR, 27 Dec. 1910, RLP, B-105, LFC.

27. TR to Jonathan Bourne, 2 Jan. 1911; TR to RML, 29 Sept. 1911, RLP, B-70, LFC. In his last letter to Roosevelt, La Follette made a thinly veiled accusation that Roosevelt was a "bungler" who could give the progressives a bad reputation. RML to TR, 4 Oct. 1911. See also RML to TR, 19 Jan. 1911, RLP, B-106, LFC. For Roosevelt's responses, see TR to RML, 3, 24 Jan. 1911, RLP, B-70, LFC.

28. WAW to unknown, 27 July 1911, WWP, Book M, microfilm, SUSC.

29. RML, *Autobiography*, 204–5; RML to E. Clarence Jones, 6 Aug. 1911; RML to Gertrude Allen, 5 Oct. 1911, RLP, B-106, LFC. See also RML, "Little Brother to the Payne-Aldrich Law," *LM* 3, no. 29 (22 July 1911): 4–8, 13; and unsigned, "Where Taft Stands," 3, no. 36 (9 Sept. 1911): 3.

30. RML to Fremont Older, 18 Apr. 1911, RLP, B-106, LFC; "Roosevelt Lauds Wis-

consin," Apr. 1911, ABP, 8-1, SHSW-M; RML, *Autobiography*, 223. *The Outlook* was known to be Roosevelt's unofficial forum. He served as its associate editor between 1910 and 1914.

31. RML, *Autobiography*, 224; BCL and FL, *La Follette*, 1:332–33.

32. TR, "Wisconsin: An Object Lesson for the Rest of the Union," reprinted in *LM* 3, no. 22 (3 June 1911): 6–7.

33. For specific proposals, see "Senator La Follette and His Policies," "Senator La Follette on the Trust Question," and "Senator La Follette in the Tariff and Other Questions," *Outlook* 100 (13 Jan. 1912): 57–58.

CHAPTER TWELVE

1. BCL and FL, *La Follette*, 1:356–57; Greabner, Fite, and White, *History of the American People*, 610. Fite cites Mississippi senator John Sharp Williams as the author of this ditty, which first appeared 26 Apr. 1912 in the *Chicago Record-Herald*. Gilbert C. Fite to author, 16 Apr. 1998.

2. P. J. Watrous, "Between Sandwiches and Pullmans," *Milwaukee Free Press*, Nov. 1911, B-268; Herbert Quick, "Governor Bob," *Saturday Evening Post*, 23 Sept. 1911, RLP, B-263, LFC.

3. RML, *Autobiography*, ix, 237.

4. Ibid., 255; Eyewitness, "Dickey DeLion's Delight," *New Republic* 39 (6 Aug. 1924): 298.

5. George Sylvester Viereck to GM, 3 Oct. 1917, RLP, B-82, LFC.

6. RML, speech, Nov. 1912, ABP, 6-3, SHSW-M; Francis Heney to RML, 29 Jan. 1912, FLP, E-80, LFC; RML to Hiram Johnson, 30 Jan. 1912, RLP, B-107, LFC.

7. RML to Albert Beveridge, 29 Jan. 1912, RLP, B-107, LFC; RML, *Autobiography*, 259; RML to Charles Zueblin, 15 Feb. 1912, RLP, B-107, LFC; RML to Charles A. Lindbergh, 20 Feb. 1912, RLP, B-107, LFC; BCL to GM, 29 Jan. 1912, FP, A-11, LFC.

8. Mark Sullivan to HAC, 23 Jan. 1912, HCP, 2-3, SHSW-M; RML, *Autobiography*, 259. Although Hughes's account appears to be generally accurate, it was included in the file La Follette accumulated in 1917 when he considered instigating several libel suits.

9. BCL and FL, *La Follette*, 1:400–401; Rupert Hughes, "La Follette's Political Suicide," *NYT*, 21 Oct. 1917, RLP, B-322, LFC. For Cooper's complete memorandum, see Maxwell, *Great Lives Observed*, 112–13, or Cooper's handwritten notes on Mark Sullivan to HAC, 23 Jan. 1912, HCP, 2–3, SHSW-M.

10. "La Follette Ill; Makes No Excuses," *NYT*, 4 Feb. 1912, sec. 1A, 7; BCL and FL, *La Follette*, 1:402; HAC, handwritten note on letter from Mark Sullivan to HAC, 23 Jan. 1912, HCP, 2–3, SHSW-M.

11. "La Follette Ill; Makes No Excuses," *NYT*, 4 Feb. 1912, sec. 1A, 7; "Calamity Ends Meeting," *Daily Northwestern*, 3 Feb. 1912, RLP, B-268, LFC; RML, *Autobiography*, 259.

12. BCL and FL, *La Follette*, 1:403; unidentified letter, MLP, 40-717, SUSC; "La Follette Ill; Makes No Excuses," *NYT*, 4 Feb. 1912, sec. 1A, 7.

13. "Mr. La Follette as Seen from the Gallery," *Outlook* 100 (3 Feb. 1912): 255.

14. HAC, handwritten notes on letter from Mark Sullivan to HAC, 23 Jan. 1912, HCP, 2–3, SHSW-M; RML, *Autobiography*, 259; "La Follette Ill; Makes No Excuses," *NYT*, 4 Feb. 1912, sec. 1A, 7; Angus McSween, "Overwork Cause of La Follette Scene; Doctors Urge Rest," *Philadelphia North American*, 4 Feb. 1912, RLP, B-322, LFC. Less than six months later, Seitz unexpectedly became a La Follette supporter.

15. See RML, "A Malicious Lie," *LM* 6, no. 2 (Dec. 1914). 2. Without actually naming him, President Taft publicly referred to La Follette as a "neurotic."

16. A "personality disorder" is defined in the American Psychiatric Association's *Diagnostic and Statistical Manual* (*DSM-III-R*) as "inflexible and maladaptive personality traits that cause either significant functional impairment or subjective distress . . . conceptualized as long-term characteristics of individuals that are likely to be evident by adolescence and continue through adulthood" (Tsuang, Tohen and Zahner, *Psychiatric Epidemiology*, 407). Despite the vagueness and obsolescence of the term "nervous breakdown" in professional psychiatric terminology, it is included in relatively recent works mentioning La Follette.

17. La Follette's secretary stressed La Follette's tiredness but reported that the senator was also "a little depressed." ND to Dr. Charles McCarthy, 15 Feb. 1912, RLP, B-107, LFC. See also RML to unidentified, 20 Feb. 1912, RLP, B-107, LFC; RML to JS, FP, A-12, LFC.

18. BCL and FL, *La Follette*, 1:405; Rupert Hughes, "La Follette's Political Suicide," *NYT*, 21 Oct. 1917, RLP, B-322, LFC. The *Journal* termed La Follette's remarks about the newspaper men the most "interesting and characteristic" of his speech. "Collapse of La Follette," *Milwaukee Journal*, ca. Feb. 1912, RLP, B-268, LFC.

19. Paul Hanna to RML, 3 Feb. 1912, RLP, B-71, LFC; unidentified letter, MLP, 40–717, SUSC; RML to JS, 5 Feb. 1912, FP, A-12, LFC; Dr. George Keenan to RML, 4 Mar. 1912, RLP, B-71, LFC. Even the supportive Hanna, however, made mention of La Follette's poor physical health.

20. BCL and FL, *La Follette*, 1:407–8, 412; RML to GR, 6 Feb. 1912, RLP, B-107, LFC.

21. RML to Rudolph Spreckles, 17 Apr. 1912, RLP, B-107, LFC; John Commons to RML, 24 June 1912, FLP, E-81, LFC; RML, "A Perversion of Fact," *LM* 4, no. 16 (20 Apr. 1912): 3; La Follette, *Autobiography*, 261. See ND to GF, 15 Feb. 1912, RLP, B-107, LFC.

22. "La Follette Now Out of the Race," *NYT*, 6 Feb. 1912, 1; "Mr. La Follette, as Seen by His Party Press," *LD* 40 (Feb. 17, 1912): 319.

23. "La Follette to Rest, But Won't Quit Fight," *NYT*, 5 Feb. 1912, 4; TR to Gilson Gardner, 8 Feb. 1912, FLP, E-80, LFC; TR to Callan O'Laughlin, 8 Feb. 1912, in TR, *Letters*, 7:499.

24. Support for this claim can be found in Charles A. Lindbergh to TR, 13 Feb. 1912, FLP, E-80; Walter F. Cushing to TR, 9 Feb. 1912, FLP, E-80; Fremont Older to Walter Houser, 20 Feb. 1912, FLP, E-81, LFC.

25. RML to GR, 17 Feb. 1912, RLP, B-107, LFC. La Follette published the text of his Philadelphia speech in his magazine as well. See RML, "The Undermining of Democracy," *LM* 4, no. 23–24 (23 and 30 Mar. 1912).

26. C. D. Willard to TR, 16 Feb. 1912, FLP, E-80, LFC.

27. RML, statement, ca. 6 Feb. 1912, RLP, B-107, LFC; Hannan quote in "La Follette Now Out of the Race," *NYT*, 6 Feb. 1912, 2; RML to George Keenan, 12 Feb. 1912, RLP, B-107, LFC. See also RML to John S. Phillips, 4 Feb. 1912, RLP, B-107, LFC.

28. RML, *Autobiography*, 260; Manners, *TR and Will*, 230; Frost, *Bully Pulpit*, 235; footnote to TR to Sturges Bigelow, 10 May 1912, in TR, *Letters*, 7:541; Gould, *Progressive Era*, 75; TR to John Strachery, 26 Mar. 1912, in TR, *Letters*, 7:531; Tweed Roosevelt, interviewed by author, 26 Apr. 1999.

29. P. Smith, *America Enters World*, 296–97; "TR Branded Traitor," dateline Minneapolis, 15 Feb. 1912, enclosed in MEL to Walter Houser, 16 Feb. 1912, 3–54, MLP, SUSC.

30. RML to JS, 5 Feb. 1912, FP, A-12, LFC; unidentified letter, MLP, 40-717, SUSC.

31. "La Follette to Rest, but Won't Quit Fight," *NYT*, 5 Feb. 1912, 4; Holt, *Congressional Insurgents*, 143. Theodore Roosevelt declined the invitation to the banquet. Perhaps some of La Follette's wrath would have been directed squarely at Roosevelt had he been in attendance.

32. BCL and FL, *La Follette*, 1:406–7; BCL to children, 11 Mar. 1912, FP, A-11, LFC.

33. RML to GR, 6 Feb. 1912, RLP, B-72, LFC; BCL and FL, *La Follette*, 1:415, 417.

34. BCL to GM, 6 Mar. 1912, FP, A-11, LFC; George Keenan to John Darling, 4 Mar. 1912, RLP, B-71, LFC; Richard Barry, "A Radical in Power," *Outlook* 122 (29 Nov. 1922): 566. La Follette's secretary sent out a form letter describing La Follette as a man who "refused, as he always has, to make any deals or combinations that would confuse the issues, or mislead the people, who looked to him as the unswerving, uncompromising leader of Progressive principles." Form letter by JJH, ca. Feb. 1912, RLP, B-71, LFC.

35. RML to Wm. Kent, 15 Feb. 1912, RLP, B-107, LFC; BCL and FL, *La Follette*, 1:427–28; RML, speech, Nov. 1912, ABP, 6-3, SHSW-M.

36. BCL and FL, *La Follette*, 1:431–32. See also Pinchot, *History of Progressive Party*, 136–57.

37. TR to FEM, 28 May 1912, FMP, 7-3, SHSW-M; Painter, *Standing at Armageddon*, 268.

38. "Wisconsin and the McGovern Incident at National Convention," 1912, FMP, 7-5, SHSW-M.

39. See Walter L. Houser, "A Betrayal of Wisconsin Voters," *LM* 6, no. 35 (29 Aug. 1914): 5.

40. Erwin A. Holt to FEM, 8 Oct. 1912, FMP, 9-1, SHSW-M; RML to Fred McKenzie, 24 June 1912, RLP, B-107, LFC; RML to GR, 8 July 1912, RLP, B-107, LFC; RML, *Autobiography*, 280–85; unsigned to W. E. Lipke, 13 July 1912, FMP, 7-5; G. D. Jones to FEM, 31 July 1912, FMP, 8-3, SHSW-M.

41. Wm. A. Ernst to *La Follette's*, 2 Aug. 1912, FMP, 8-3, SHSW-M; G. D. Jones to FEM, 6 Aug. 1912, FMP, 8-3, SHSW-M. Roosevelt explained, unconvincingly, that he had meant to say that he would seek no *consecutive* third term.

42. "The Shooting of Roosevelt," *LM* 4, no. 42 (19 Oct. 1912): 3; "La Follette Tours Dane County," Oct. 1912, FMP, 7-5, SHSW-M; RML, speech, Nov. 1912, ABP, 6-3, SHSW-M.

43. "Vote for McGovern," *LM* 4, no. 43 (26 Oct. 1912): 3; "La Follette Tours Dane County," Oct. 1912, FMP, 7-5, SHSW-M.

44. BCL to Emily Bishop, 20 Feb. 1912, BCL, D-11, LFC. Historians George E. Mowry and Henry F. Pringle concur with La Follette's assessment, while more recent scholar Herbert F. Margulies convincingly refutes it. Mowry, *Roosevelt and the Progressive Movement*, 208; Pringle, *Theodore Roosevelt*, 548; Margulies, "La Follette, Roosevelt, and the Republican Nomination of 1912."

45. J. J. Burke to FEM, 20 Jan. 1913, FMP, 10-3, SHSW-M.

CHAPTER THIRTEEN

1. Biel, *Down with the Old Canoe*, 103; Ann E. Larabee, "The American Hero and His Mechanical Bride: Gender Myths of the *Titanic* Disaster," *American Studies* 31 (Spring 1990): 15–16. Of the first- and second-class women who perished in the *Titanic* disaster, at least two remained on board of their own volition. No woman had to plead for special consideration, for Captain Edward J. Smith's order of "women and children first" met with "unanimous approval." Archibald Gracie, *Titanic* (Toronto: Academy Chicago Publishers, 1986, 1996), 41. On the *Titanic* sinking as a sign of God's displeasure with the modern age, see Alma White, *The Titanic Tragedy: God Speaking to the Nations* (Bound Brook, N.J.: Pentecostal Union, 1912). Totals of both survivors and casualties conflict, as do numbers within the various classifications. The British Board of Trade's Inquiry, for example, concluded that the casualties among the first-class passengers included four women but no children, while the U.S. Senate hearings list a total of eleven lost in the category of first-class women and children. Most scholars of the *Titanic* find the British figures generally more convincing but not without error. See Walter Lord, *Night to Remember* (New York: Holt, Rinehart & Winston, 1955; reprint, New York: Bantam, 1956), 140; and Spignesi, *Complete Titanic*, 112, 162–63.

2. Richard Lloyd Jones to RML, 23 May 1914, RLP, B-75, LFC; TR to Gifford Pinchot, 28 Mar. 1912, in TR, *Letters*, 7:659; TR to Hiram Johnson, 16 Nov. 1912, in TR, *Letters*, 7:716. See also Maxwell, *Great Lives*, 113–15.

3. Torelle, *Political Philosophy*, 11; RML to Rudolph Spreckels, 12 July 1912, RLP, B-107, LFC; RML to JR, 8 July 1912, FP, A-12, LFC. See also RML, "Presidential Primary," *LM* 5, no. 51 (20 Dec. 1913): 1.

4. RML to GR, 8 July 1912, RLP, B-107, RLP, B-216, LFC. See also Unsigned [RML], Comments on Wilson's Acceptance Speech, 2 June 1912, RLP, B-216, LFC. New Jersey's antitrust laws were repealed after Wilson left office.

5. Link, *Wilson and Progressive Era*, 20. For discussion of the New Freedom, see 1–80.

6. Degregorio, *U.S. Presidents*, 418–19; J. J. Burke to FEM, 20 Jan. 1913, FMP, 10-3, SHSW-M.

7. BCL and FL, *La Follette*, 1:447.

8. RML, speech, Nov. 1912, ABP, 6-3, SHSW-M.

9. Link, *Wilson and Progressive Era*, 35; Degregorio, *U.S. Presidents*, 419.

10. BCL and FL, *La Follette*, 1 : 460, 474.

11. Thelen, *Insurgent Spirit*, 100; *Philadelphia Record*, "The President Courting the Progressives," quoted in *LD* 46 (29 Mar. 1913): 423; *NYT*, 14 Mar. 1913, in Holt, *Congressional Insurgents*, 82.

12. RML, *CR* 50, pt. 4 : 3820.

13. La Follette–Wheeler National Committee, "La Follette and the Seaman's Act of 1915," RLP, 1–2, SHSW-M; RML, *CR* 50, pt. 6 : 5718. For La Follette's invocation of the *Titanic*, see RML, *CR* 49, pt. 5 : 4409–10; *CR* 50, pt. 6 : 5516–786. See also "Congress Should Act upon the Seaman's Bill," *LM* 5, no. 35 (30 Aug. 1913): 1.

14. RML to BCL, 24 Oct. 1913; RML to JR, 24 Oct. 1913, FP, A-13, LFC; Link, *Wilson and Progressive Era*, 63. See also RML, "Battle for Freedom of Sailors Begins in La Follette's Office," *Washington Daily News*, 18 Sept. 1924, RLP, B-230; BCL to RML, 25 Oct. 1913, FP, A-12; ND for RML to GM, 30 Oct. 1913, FP, A-13, LFC.

15. BCL to RML, 10 Nov. 1913, and RML to family, 2 Nov. 1913, both in FP, A-13; ND to Louis Edelman, 31 Oct. 1913, RLP, B-13, LFC.

16. RML to JS, 8 Apr. 1913, FP, A-13, LFC. However desperate the state of his own family's finances, La Follette was always quick to offer help to others in need. See RML to James Manahan, 4 Nov. 1915, RLP, B-110, LFC.

17. Heckscher, *Wilson*, 292. See also Lewis, *Du Bois*, 509–11.

18. Wilson quoted in James W. Loewen, *Lies My Teacher Told Me* (New York: New Press, 1995), 18. See RML to family, 10 Nov. 1913, FP, A-13, LFC. For a classic discussion of progressivism in the South, see Woodward, *Origins of the New South*, 369–95.

19. RSB to RML, 10 Aug. 1912, RLP, B-71, LFC; W. T. Allison, "The Book of the Week," *Winnipeg Telegram*, 24 May 1913, RLP, B-264, LFC; TR to FEM, 21 Apr. 1913, 11-4, FMP, SHSW-M. See also Clyde H. Tavenner, "La Follette's Work Shows Power of People When Acting Together," *Moline Daily Dispatch*, 28 Apr. 1913, RLP, B-322, LFC.

20. From the letterhead of the National Republican Progressive League.

21. Link, *Wilson and Progressive Era*, 77; Thelen, *Insurgent Spirit*, 103–4; Holt, *Congressional Insurgents*, 85. See RML, "Legalizing the 'Money Power,'" *LM* 5 (27 Dec. 1913): 1; and Holt, *Congressional Insurgents*, 21.

22. Painter, *Standing at Armageddon*, 277; Link, *Wilson and Progressive Era*, 72–73.

23. Link, *Wilson and Progressive Era*, 74, 79–80; Painter, *Standing at Armageddon*, 278.

24. RML to GR, 17 Sept. 1914, RLP, B-16; BCL to JR, 17 Nov. 1914, FP, A-14, LFC. The true nature of La Follette's condition was kept a secret even from his half-sister Ellen Eastman, Fola's husband George Middleton, and close family friends Gilbert Roe, Alfred Rogers, Rudolph Spreckels, and Phillip Fox.

25. La Follette's physical and financial status made it impossible for him to qualify for medical insurance. RML to Alfred Rogers, 5, 13 Jan. 1915, RLP, B-110, LFC.

26. Louis D. Brandeis to GR, 18 Sept. 1914, RLP, B-76, LFC; BCL and FL, *La Follette*, 1 : 511–12; GR to Rudolph Spreckels, 6 Aug. 1914, Gilbert Roe Papers, H-4, LFC. See also E. E. Garrison to RML, 20 May 1913, RLP, B-73; Alfred Rogers to RML, 12 Apr. 1915, RLP, B-78, LFC.

27. BCL and FL, *La Follette*, 1 : 506; Richard Lloyd Jones to RML, 23 May 1914, RLP, B-75, LFC. See also RML, "E. L. Philipp, Lobbyist," *LM* 6, no. 31 (1 Aug. 1914): 1.

28. BCL to JR, 22 Sept. 1914, FP, A-14, LFC.

29. Splinters to the Editor of the *Wisconsin State Journal*, FMP, 11-2, SHSW-M; Maxwell, *La Follette and Rise of Progressives*, 192; Doan, *La Follettes and Wisconsin Idea*, 76; RML, "The Leopard's Spots," *LM* 6, no. 42 (17 Oct. 1914): 3; Buenker, *Progressive Era*, 661.

30. Thelen, *Insurgent Spirit*, 123; BCL and FL, *La Follette*, 1:579. See "The Terrific and Unscrupulous Fight against La Follette Has Been in Vain," *LM* 8, no. 9 (Sept. 1916): 10.

31. Maxwell, *La Follette and Rise of Progressives*, 194. See RML, "La Follette for President," *LM* 8, no. 3 (Mar. 1916): 7, 14–15; Margulies, "La Follette as Presidential Aspirant."

32. RML, *CR* 52, pt. 4:3631, 6333. See "Compare These Platforms," *LM* 8, no. 6 (June 1916): 4–5.

33. For more on La Follette's "decidedly ambivalent" Mexican policy, see Kennedy, "La Follette's Foreign Policy," 289–91.

34. Doan, *La Follettes and Wisconsin Idea*, 77–78; RML, *CR* 53, pt. 4:3887.

35. "Once More the Wisconsin Humbug," *Philadelphia Inquirer*, 21 July 1916, RLP, B-265, LFC; Doan, *La Follette and Wisconsin Idea*, 82.

36. RML to Charles H. Butler, 9 Nov. 1916, RLP, B-110, LFC.


CHAPTER FOURTEEN

1. Holt, *Congressional Insurgents*, 129; "Once More the Wisconsin Humbug," *Philadelphia Inquirer*, 21 July 1916, B-265, RLP, LFC.

2. Torelle, *Political Philosophy*, 131–32; RML to family, 10 Nov. 1913, FP, A-13, LFC.

3. RML, *LM* 1 (24 Apr. 1909): 4.

4. See Robert Johnson, *Peace Progressives*, 34–69.

5. Kennedy, *Over Here*, 38.

6. TR, *Fear God*, 355–56; Frost, *Bully Pulpit*, 82, 256; BCL, "Mr. Roosevelt's Attack on the Woman's Peace Party," *LM* 7, no. 5 (May 1915): 5.

7. TR, *Fear God*, 23, 35.

8. RML, *CR* 53, pt. 11:11330; RML, "Neutrality," *LM* 7, no. 9 (Sept. 1915): 1.

9. Link, *Wilson and the Progressive Era*, 195.

10. RML to family, 15 Feb. 1917, FP, A-21, LFC. Vice President Thomas Marshall maintained that while the call for the vote had come without warning, there was no conspiracy. La Follette remained unconvinced and indignant. Ryley, *Willful Men*, 68.

11. JR to family, 21 Feb. 1917 [dated incorrectly as 20 Feb.], FP, A-20, LFC.

12. GR to RML, 27 Feb. 1917, RLP, B-81, LFC. "The chances [of avoiding war] are small," Belle agreed, but "[e]very day gained is a possibility of hope" (BCL to family, 19 Mar. 1917, FP, A-20, LFC).

13. There is much debate on Wilson's motives concerning the timing of the note's release. Arthur S. Link maintains that Wilson was not trying to pressure Congress, but evidence to the contrary is strong. See Ryley, *Willful Men*, 86.

14. *Baltimore Sun*, 5 Mar. 1917, RLP, B-265, LFC; Ryley, *Willful Men*, 120; RML to Family, 6 Mar. 1917, FP, A-21, LFC.

15. Ryley, *Willful Men*, 127; RML to family, 6 Mar. 1917, FP, A-21, LFC; *Baltimore Sun*, 5 Mar. 1917, RLP, B-265, LFC. See also Paul S. Halbo, "Senator Harry Lane: Independent Democrat in Peace and War," in *Experiences in a Promised Land*, edited by G. Thomas and Carlos Schwantes (Seattle: University of Washington Press, 1986), 252.

16. JR to RML, 4 Mar. 1917, FP, A-20, LFC; Norris, *Fighting Liberal*, 181; John Craig Ralston, manuscript, p. 173, John Craig Ralston Papers, Box 6, SHSW-M. La Follette printed a variation of the aborted speech in his magazine: RML, "The Armed Ship Bill Meant War," *LM* 9, no. 3 (Mar. 1917): 1–4.

17. RML to BCL, 5 Mar. 1917, FP, A-21; BCL to RML, 5 Mar. 1917, FP, A-20; Eugene V. Debs to RML, 7 Mar. 1917, RLP, B-80; *New York Mail*, 8 Mar. 1917, clipping enclosed in Fred McKensie to RML, 8 Mar. 1917, RLP, B-265; RML to PFL, 27 Mar. 1917, FP, A-21, LFC. See also Amos Pinchot to RML, 6 Mar. 1917, RLP, B-81; PFL to RML, 10 Mar. 1917, FP, A-20, LFC.

18. Ironically, in the same speech, in a passage almost universally ignored, Wilson also offered partial vindication of those "willful men" by his admission, "Armed neutrality is ineffectual at best. It is practically certain to draw us into war without either the rights or effectiveness of belligerents." Link, *Wilson and the Progressive Era*, 272–82.

19. Like La Follette, Kenyon is included in the twelve, although he did not speak. Senators Kirby, Lane, Cummins, Clapp, Gronna, Works, Vardaman, Stone, Norris, and O'Gorman complete the roster.

20. RML to family, 7 Feb. 1917, FP, A-21; GR to RML, 7 Mar. 1917, RLP, B-81; BCL to RML, 8 Mar. 1917, FP, A-20, LFC. See also BCL to RML, 10 Mar. 1917, FP, A-20, LFC. For cartoons, see Rollin Kirby, "The Only Adequate Reward," *New York World*, 7 Mar. 1917, in BCL and FL, *La Follette*, 1:630; "Gulliver's Plight," *Baltimore Sun*, 7 Mar. 1917, and "Iron Crosses for Twelve," *Dallas Morning News*, 6 Mar. 1917, in RLP, B-265, LFC.

21. News clipping, *Cincinnati Times Star*, 5 Mar. 1917, RLP, B-265, LFC; RML, *CR* 55, pt. 1:40.

22. RML, *CR* 55, pt. 1:224–34.

23. Pinchot, *History of Progressive Party*; John Sharp Williams, *CR* 55, pt. 1:235–38.

24. Wm. La Follette, *CR* 55, pt. 1:371.

25. Phil La Follette, interviewed by Edward M. Coffman, PLP, SHSW-M. Phil La Follette cites the National Security League as an example of a political group determined to use the anti–La Follette sentiment to "smash" progressivism in Wisconsin. See cartoon entitled "For Services Rendered," in Peterson and Fite, *Opponents of War*, 7. Johnson was "appalled" at his colleagues' "lack of understanding of the great world problems." J. J. Fitzpatrick, "Senator Hiram W. Johnson," 55.

26. JR to family, 4 Apr. 1917, FP, A-20, LFC; BCL and FL, *La Follette*, 1:652; RML to family, 8 Mar. 1917, FP, A-21, LFC. Various polls confirm La Follette's assertion of public opposition to the war. Entry into the war muted that opposition, but

the intensity of the pro-war propaganda confirms that Americans were far from uniform in supporting the war. See Thelen, *Insurgent Spirit*, 131–32. For more on La Follette and German-Americans, see O'Connor, *German-Americans*, 409; Frank Perry Olds, "Wisconsin in the Balance," *Outlook* 117 (14 Nov. 1917): 412; H. M. Kallen, "Politics, Profits and Patriotism in Wisconsin," *Nation* 106 (7 Mar. 1918): 257–59; "Lenroot and La Follette: A Contrast," *Outlook* 115 (18 Apr. 1917): 691; "La Follette and the German Americans," *New Republic* (1 Oct. 1924): 108–10; "La Follette and the German Vote," *LD* 83 (11 Oct. 1924): 10–11.

27. RML to family, 8 Mar. 1917, RLP, A-21, LFC; BCL to PFL and ML, 12 Mar. 1917, FP, A-20, LFC; Thelen, *Insurgent Spirit*, 143. See RML to family, 10 Mar. 1917, 8 Feb. 1917, FP, A-21, LFC.

28. Kennedy, *Over Here*, 41, 108; RML, *CR* 55, pt. 6:6202; John Weeks, *CR* 55, pt. 6:6210. For war tax rates, see Thelen, *Insurgent Spirit*, 138. For La Follette's war-related positions, see RML, "Turning Light on the Food Bill," *LM* 9, no. 8 (Aug. 1917): 3, 14; RML, "The People Lost—Wealth Won," *LM* 9, no. 9 (Sept. 1917): 1–2.

29. The war left additional economic legacies, not all of them in keeping with progressive goals. Some 42,000 Americans joined the ranks of the millionaires, while salaried workers between 1916 and 1919 lost 22 percent of their purchasing power.

30. RML, *CR* 55, pt. 2:1355. For World War I as the origin of the modern draft, see Chambers, *To Raise an Army*.

31. BCL to family, 18 Mar. 1917, FP, A-20, LFC; RML, *CR* 55, pt. 6:5660.

32. RML to family, 19 June, 10 July 1917, FP, A-21, LFC; RML to GR, 17 July 1917, RLP, B-111, LFC; Kennedy, *Over Here*, 109–10. La Follette tried a variety of ploys to prolong Bobbie's stay in Washington indefinitely. See RML to family, 14 July 1917, (two letters), FP, A-21, LFC. For Stone's criticisms, see Wm. Stone, *CR* 55, pt. 7:7174. La Follette defended his actions at length within the *Congressional Record* later that day: *CR* 55, pt. 7:7177–78.

33. RML, speech, St. Paul, Minn., 20 Sept. 1917, RLP, B-220, LFC.

34. Ibid.

35. For Bryan's denial, see Frank Kellogg, *CR* 55, pt. 8:7887.

36. TR, "'Shadow Huns' Is Right Name for Traitors," *Philadelphia North American*, 1 Oct. 1917, RLP, B-322, LFC; "'Lesser Microbe' Name T.R. Gives to Lundeen," *St. Paul Pioneer Press*, 29 Sept. 1917, in FLP, E-81, LFC; TR to TR Jr., 29 Nov. 1917, in TR, *Letters*, 8:1256–57; "La Follette as Foe to Democracy," *LD* 55 (6 Oct. 1917): 15; "The Case of Senator La Follette," *Current Opinion* (Oct. 1917): 289–90.

37. Boller, *Presidential Anecdotes*, 200; BCL and FL, *La Follette*, 2:772; "In the Case of Senator La Follette," *Current Opinion* 63 (Nov. 1917): 291. See also "La Follette as Foe to Democracy," *LD* 55 (6 Oct. 1917): 15.

38. "La Follette Is Caught in a Typhoon of Indignation," *New York Tribune*, 7 Oct. 1917, RLP, B-322, LFC.

39. RML, *CR* 55, pt. 8:7878; Louis D. Brandeis to Alfred Brandeis, 7 Oct. 1914, in Brandeis, *Letters*, 4:314; Frank Kellogg, *CR* 55, pt. 8:7887–89; Albert Fall, *CR*

55, pt. 8:7894; Angus McSween, "La Follette Defy in Senate Brings Patriotic Replies," *Philadelphia North American*, 7 Oct. 1915, RLP, B-322, LFC; BCL to family, 15 Nov. 1917, FP, A-20, LFC.

40. JR to PFL and ML, 10 Oct. 1917, FP, A-20, LFC; Eugene V. Debs to RML, 15 Oct. 1917, RLP, B-80, LFC.

41. BCL to JS, 3 Jan. 1918, FP, A-20, LFC; RML to James C. Kerwin, 5 Jan. 1918, RLP, B-112, LFC. See State and County Councils of Defense to RML, 9 Oct. 1917, and University of Wisconsin Club of Philadelphia to RML, 17 Dec. 1917, in RLP, B-82; GR to Charles H. Crownhart, 29 Dec. 1917, RLP, B-81; GR to John D. Moore, 4 Jan. 1918, RLP, B-112, LFC. Efforts were also made to force La Follette to lose the mortgage on his family home.

42. BCL and FL, *La Follette*, 2:842–43; RML, Diary, 19 Apr. 1918, RLP, B-1, LFC. See Faculty of the University of Wisconsin to RML, 16 Jan. 1918, RLP, B-82, LFC; "La Follette Condemned at Home," *LD* 56 (23 Mar. 1918): 17–18.

43. RML to JR, 14, 15 Oct. 1918, FP, A-23, LFC; RML, Notebook, 1918, RLP, B-2, LFC; Middleton, *These Things*, 173–74.

44. BCL and FL, *La Follette*, 1:424, 2:859.

45. Wilson, *Papers*, 46:119; BCL and FL, *La Follette*, 2:869.

46. PFL to family, 12 Dec., 15 Oct. 1917, FP, A-20, LFC; PFL to BCL, 13 Mar. 1918, FP, A-23, LFC; PFL, *Adventures*, 51–53; BCL to ML, Oct. 1917, FP, A-20; RML to family, 27 Apr., 16 Mar. 1919, FP, A-27; RML to ML, 18 Mar. 1919, and RML to PFL, 17 Mar. 1919, in FP, A-26, LFC.

47. Barry, "A Radical in Power," *Outlook* 132 (29 Nov. 1922): 566; BCL and FL, *La Follette*, 2:892.

48. See "A Tardy Vindication," *LM* 10, no. 12 (Dec. 1918): 2–3.

49. James Reed, *CR* 67, pt. 2:11651.

50. RML to family, 26 Nov. 1918 (two letters), FP, A-24; BCL to family, 16 Dec. 1918, FP, A-22, LFC. See Nesbit, *Wisconsin*, 453.

51. RML to family, 16 Jan. 1919, FP, A-26; BCL to RML, 26 Jan. 1919, FP, A-24, LFC.


CHAPTER FIFTEEN

1. H. M. Kaller, "Politics, Profits and Patriotism in Wisconsin," *Nation* 106 (Mar. 7, 1918): 257; BCL to RML, 6 Feb. 1919, FP, A-24, LFC. See also Fred Holmes to RML, 7 Jan. 1919, RLP, B-84, LFC.

2. BCL and FL, *La Follette*, 2:936; RML, "Ballots Not Bonds," *LM* 11, no. 5 (May 1919): 1; RML, *LM*, Mar. 1920, reprinted in "Where La Follette Stands on Fifty Living Issues," RLP, 1–3, SHSW-M. For a concise summary of postwar global affairs, see Painter, *Standing at Armageddon*, 352. La Follette was also concerned that the repression of radical expression created the "worst possible condition" for a Supreme Court decision favoring La Follette supporter Eugene V. Debs, who was on trial for violating the Espionage Law.

3. RML, *CR*, 57, pt. 3:819, 824.

4. Degregorio, *U.S. Presidents*, 427.

5. Ibid.; Pinchot quoted in RML to family, 6 Jan. 1919, FP, A-26, LFC.

6. RML, *CR*, 57, pt. 2:1983.

7. RML, "We Are Waiting, Mr. President," *LM* 11, no. 1 (Jan. 1919): 1; RML to family, 16 Jan. 1919, FP, A-26; 9 Apr., 5, 9 May 1919, FP, A-27; RML to P. B. Noble, 26 Sept. 1921, RLP, B-115, LFC; RML, *CR* 57, pt. 1-5:4980–85. For Wilson's views on the presidency, see Stid, *President as Statesman*.

8. RML to family, 10 Feb., 26 Jan. 1919, FP, A-26; RML to JR, ca. 1919, FP, A-27, LFC. See also RML to family, 1 Jan., 25 Mar. 1919, and RML to FL and GM, 26 Jan. 1919, FP, A-26; RML to family, 29 Dec. 1918, FP, A-24; 29 Apr. 1919, FP, A-27, LFC.

9. RML, *CR*, 58, pt. 5:4760; BCL and FL, *La Follette*, 2:944, 949–50. In 1913, following thirteen years of opposition spearheaded by naturalist John Muir, Congress granted permission to convert California's Hetch Hetchy Valley, the "sister valley" to Yosemite, into a reservoir. None other than Gifford Pinchot approved the plan, arguing that it served the needs of the most people and was therefore the best use of valuable natural resources. One of many increasingly expensive and complex measures to bring water to thirsty western cities and "make the desert bloom," the project, which included a dam and a 200-mile aqueduct to deliver water to San Francisco, was completed in 1934.

10. RML to family, 14, 16 Mar. 1919, FP, A 26, LFC.

11. RML to JR, 11, 12 May 1919, FP, A-27, LFC.

12. La Follette had Lieutenant Governor Edward Ditsmar's telegram announcing the amendment's ratification by both Wisconsin houses read into the *Congressional Record*. See *CR* 58, pt. 1:894. Ironically, because previous efforts to grant Wisconsin women the vote had failed, Wisconsin woman suffrage seekers remained sufficiently active and organized to pull off this political coup. McBride, *Wisconsin Women*, 234–63.

13. RML to PFL, 24 July 1919, FP, A-27, LFC; RML, "The President and Profiteers," *LM* 11, no. 8 (Aug. 1919): 117–18; Arthur Warner, "La Follette in Washington," *Nation* 119 (20 Aug. 1924): 181. See also RML, "Wilson's Broken Pledges," *LM* 11, no. 7 (July 1919): 101–2.

14. "La Follette and Kenyon Demand Truth about Expedition," *Washington Post*, 8 Jan. 1919, B-265; RML, speech, ca. 1919, RLP, B-221; RML, speech, "Withdraw Troops from Russia," RLP, B-222; RML to family, 1, 4, 13 Feb. 1919, FP, A-26, LFC; RML, "Why?" *LM* 11, no. 7 (July 1919): 101–2; RML, *CR* 57, pt. 2: 1102–4; RML, "Murdering Negroes," *LM* 11, no. 8 (Aug. 1919): 118–19.

15. RML, speech, "The War in Retrospect," ca. May 1919, RLP, B-222, LFC; "La Follette Says German Treaty Will Entangle Us," *Washington Capital Times*, RLP, B-224, LFC; Torelle, *Political Philosophy*, 252; RML to JR and PFL, 21 June 1919, FP, A-27, LFC; BCL to RML, 22 July 1919, RLP, B-84, LFC. See also RML, "The War in Retrospect," *LM* 15, no. 24 (Apr. 1920): 70–71.

16. RML to family, 1 Feb. 1919, FP, A-26, LFC; John W. Owens, "La Follette," *New Republic* 33 (20 Dec. 1922): 78–80; RML to family, 9 May 1919, FP, A-27, LFC; TR and Lodge, *Correspondence*, 494.

17. Degregorio, *U.S. Presidents*, 427; George Brown Tindall, *America: A Narrative History*, 3d ed. (New York: W. W. Norton, 1992), 1008.

18. Maney, *Young Bob*, 29.

19. JR to PFL, 24 June 1921, FP, A-29, LFC.

20. Torelle, *Political Philosophy*, 123–24; RML, *CR* 58, pt. 5:4739, 4741–42.

21. RML, *CR* 58, pt. 5:4741–57.

22. Thelen, *Insurgent Spirit*, 152; RML, "President Wilson Campaigns for the League," *LM* 11, no. 9 (Sept. 1919): 134.

23. BCL and FL, *La Follette*, 2:898; John Stokes to RML, 13 Feb. 1920, RLP, B-112; RML to R. F. Paine, 19 Oct. 1921, RLP, B-116; unidentified to Harold I. Johnson, 17 Aug. 1920, RLP, B-113, LFC. Since his initial surgery nine years earlier, removal of the gall sac had become a standard preventative procedure for all gallstone sufferers.

24. JR to GR, 2 Aug. 1920, RLP, B-113, LFC.

25. Torelle, *Political Philosophy*, 100; BCL and FL, *La Follette*, 2:1016–17.

26. JR to PFL, 2 May, 21 Sept. 1921, FP, A-29, LFC. See also BCL to family, 25 Jan. 1921, FP, A-29, LFC.

27. RML, *CR* 61, pt. 2:1744, 1752. At one gathering, reported Bobbie, "Dad didn't get on to speak until 9:30 P.M. He spoke until 11:20. He only had time to use about ⅓ of his speech." PL to family, 24 Mar. 1921, FP, A-29, LFC. For La Follette's predictions on natural resources, see RML, *CR* 60, pt. 4:4237–38.

28. RML to Henry Huber, 9 Feb. 1923, RLP, B-118, LFC.

29. RML, *CR* 61, pt. 6:6435; Wilson, *Papers*, 68:186–87.

30. RML, Diary, 1922, RLP, B-1, LFC; BCL and FL, *La Follette*, 2:1044; Brandeis, *Letters*, 5:487.

31. Warren G. Harding to Wm. E. Arnold, 10 Oct. 1917, RLP, B-80, LFC; RML, *CR* 62, pt. 6:6041–51. See also Warren G. Harding to RML, 28 Mar. 1922, RLP, B-89, LFC. Fall's fine remained unpaid, and, due to ill health, Fall served less than ten months of his sentence, emerging from prison on 9 May 1932. Permanently disgraced as the first cabinet member to serve time for a felony committed while in office, Fall died in 1944.

32. Of the Wisconsin campaign, Bobbie noted, "He has never had such meetings in his life. There is literally nothing to it as far as he is concerned and the only thing that will hurt is the feeling on the part of the voters that he has a walkaway." RML to Ralph Sucher, 27 July 1922, FP, A-29, LFC. See also "Workers of Wisconsin, Vote for 'Bob,'" *Labor*, 5 Aug. 1922, RLP, B-265, LFC. La Follette did not limit himself to political speeches. To at least one audience of 4,000, he delivered his *Hamlet* oration.

33. "Mrs. La Follette Chief Aid in Husband's Fight," *Wisconsin News*, 9 Sept. 1922, RLP, B-265, LFC.

34. "Kellogg's Bad Record" and "Kellogg Attorney for Farmers' Enemies," *LM* 14, no. 10 (Oct. 1922): 147, 149; BCL and FL, *La Follette*, 2:1063; PFL, *Adventures in Politics*, 77.

35. Donald Craig, "La Follette Rises Again," *New York Herald*, 26 Nov. 1922, RLP, B-265, LFC; "Harding Administration Paving Way for a New Party, Says La Fol-

lette," *St. Louis Post Dispatch*, 17 Sept. 1922, RLP, B-265, LFC; *Raleigh News and Observer* quote from "La Follette for President?" *LD* 74 (23 Sept. 1922): 12.

CHAPTER SIXTEEN

1. "Third Party Ideas in the Northwest," *LD* 81 (19 Apr. 1924): 15; RML to *LD*, 6 Mar. 1923, RLP, B-118, LFC, Polis, "The Presidency in 1924?" *The Forum*, Feb. 1923, RLP, B-315, LFC. See Louis Seibold, "La Follette's Crowd's Bark Drowned in Wisconsin by Prospering Trade Song," *Washington Post*, 10 Apr. 1923, RLP, B-265, LFC.
2. RML to Wm. T. Rawleigh, 16 June 1923, RLP, B-118, LFC. La Follette wrote to Bobbie, "[The] *personal* significance *to me* is *the fact* that you have been able to go into a perfectly chaotic condition there, after the bickering and back-biting had reached the knifing stage and bring out a bill & put it through the Assembly with an overwhelming majority is the *highest* test of *generalship* in a bitter conflict of ideas and ambitions. It is simply *great!*" RML to JR, 16 June 1923, FP, A-30, LFC.
3. PFL, *Adventures in Politics*, 89; Polis, "The Presidency in 1924?" *Forum*, Feb. 1923, RLP, B-315; RML to PFL, 30 July 1923, FP, A-30; RML, to A. B. Butler, 14 July 1923, RLP, B-118, LFC. Kellogg's three-pronged health program stressed healthful diet, exercise, and sexual abstinence. See Money, *Destroying Angel*.
4. RML, Memorial Address, 5 Aug. 1923, RLP, B-227, LFC. See "President Harding's Death," *LM* 15, no. 6 (June 1923): 115. For more on Americans seeking social reform ideas in Europe, see Rodgers, *Atlantic Crossings*.
5. BCL and FL, *La Follette*, 2:1086.
6. Ibid., 2:1082; RML, Article 4, 1923, RLP, B-227, LFC; RML, unidentified article, 1923, RLP, B-227, LFC.
7. Lewis S. Feuer, *Marx and the Intellectuals* (New York: Anchor, 1969), 100–140.
8. RML, Article 1, 1923, RLP, B-227, LFC.
9. International News Service to Unidentified, 26 Sept. 1923, RLP, B-95; Washington Bureau Universal Service to Unidentified, 8 Nov. 1923, RLP, B-96; JR to Phil and Isen La Follette, 12 Nov. 1923, FP, A-30; "Newspapers Have Been Burying Me Thirty Years; Feeling Fine," *Capitol Times*, 7 Dec. 1923, RLP, B-265, LFC. See JR to Dante Pierce, 23 Nov. 1923, RLP, B-118; McClure Newspaper Syndicate to RML, 17 Nov., 20 Dec. 1923, RLP, B-95, LFC. La Follette wrote to several fellow senators that he was confined to his home by the orders of a "hard hearted" doctor.
10. One press account noted, "He is not as young as he used to be, and is less able to stand the strain of the intense activity to which he subjects himself." "The Prudent Course," *La Croque Tribune*, 23 Mar. 1924, RLP, B-265, LFC.
11. "The Shadow of La Follette," *Philadelphia North American*, 4 Apr. 1924, RLP, B-266, LFC. For fears concerning the vote going to the House of Representatives, see Havig, "Disputed Legacy," 54–55.
12. Rosenstone, Behr, and Lazarus, *Third Parties*, 93–94.
13. JR to Elizabeth G. Evans, 5 June 1924, RLP, B-119, LFC. See Herbert Johnson,

"Playing Indian," unidentified newspaper, ca. 1924, and untitled cartoon, *Portland Oregonian*, in RLP, B-265, LFC; De Mar, "It's a Shame to Wake Him," *LD* 82 (19 July 1924): 11.

14. "Wisconsin Political Pioneer," *NYT Magazine*, 4 May 1924, RLP, B-265, LFC. See "Never Speak Ill to a Stranger: He May Be a Presidential Candidate," *Washington Daily News*, 6 Apr. 1924, RLP, B-265, LFC.

15. Arthur Warner, "La Follette in America," *Nation* 119 (27 Aug. 1924): 214.

16. Statement and Platform of RML, 4 July 1924, RLP, B-230; "Eleven Planks in La Follette Platform," *Capitol Times*, 17 Mar. 1924, RLP, B-256, LFC.

17. RML, *CR* 40, pt. 6:5687; *CR* 61, pt. 6:6435–36; *CR* 62, pt. 9:9081. La Follette's willingness to break down whatever he perceived as a barrier to progress, no matter how sacred or longstanding the tradition, was hardly new. On 5 Aug. 1912, he introduced a resolution intended to make amending the Constitution easier. "Amend the Amending Clause," *LM* 5, no. 8 (22 Feb. 1913): 4. In 1912, Theodore Roosevelt advocated the popular recall of judicial decisions at the state level. See Havig, "Disputed Legacy," 53–54.

18. RML, "Where La Follette Stands on Fifty Living Issues," RLP, 1–3, SHSW-M.

19. "What La Follette Is After," *LD* 81 (7 June 1924): 17; K. Thompson, *Lessons from Defeated*, 30. An unswayed Lippmann supported Davis.

20. MacKay, *Progressive Movement*, 136. See "What Wheeler Brings to La Follette," *LD* 82 (2 Aug. 1924): 9–11; John Gunn, "Burton K. Wheeler Rises from Poverty," *LM* 15, no. 8 (Aug. 1924): 121. La Follette's first choice for a running mate, Supreme Court Justice Louis Brandeis, refused. BCL and FL, *La Follette*, 2:1115.

21. See Edgar G. Brown to John M. Nelson, 31 July 1924, and John M. Nelson to JR, 8 Aug. 1924, RLP, B-110; Statement, "La Follette and the Negro," ca. 1924, RLP, B-99; Statement on Lynch Laws, RLP, B-230, LFC. Keller noted bitterly, "I have hesitated to write to you because I know that the newspapers opposed to the Progressive Movement will cry out at the 'pathetic exploitation of deaf and blind Helen Keller by the "motley elements" who support La Follette.'" Helen Keller to RML, 1924, RLP, B-98, LFC. Keller expected the 1924 election to be the "swan song" of the old parties, and after La Follette's disappointing performance, she refrained from participating in politics, making no public political endorsements until she supported Franklin Roosevelt in his bid for a fourth term in 1944. Joseph P. Lash, *Helen and Teacher* (New York: Delacorte, 1980), 529.

22. BCL and FL, *La Follette*, 2:1145; Richard M. Nixon to Rachel La Follette, 21 Mar. 1923, JRP, C-31, LFC; Roger Morris, *Richard Milhous Nixon: The Rise of an American Politician* (New York: Henry Holt, 1990), 207–8; Stephen E. Ambrose, *Nixon: The Education of a Politician* (New York: Simon and Schuster, 1987), 59, 430. See also "How 'Dangerous' Is La Follette?" *Nation* 119 (3 Sept. 1924): 229.

23. Havig, "Disputed Legacy," 57; Robertson, *No Third Choice*, 302–3. See also MacKay, *Progressive Movement*, 175–76.

24. Herbert Croly, "La Follette," *New Republic* 40 (29 Oct. 1924): 221–24; "La Follette to the Front," *Nation* 18 (11 June 1924): 668; "Third-Party Ideas in the Northwest," *LD* 81 (19 Apr. 1924): 15–16; La Follette–Wheeler Progressive Campaign Headquarters, "63 Professors of Economics and Sociology Endorse La Follette's Economic Policies," RLP, 1–3, Release 138, SHSW-M.

25. Havig, "Disputed Legacy," 59.

26. BCL and FL, *La Follette*, 2:1136. See MacKay, *Progressive Movement*, 213–14. For the text of the Labor Day address, see RML, "La Follette Affirms Lincoln's Stand," *LM* 16, no. 9 (Sept. 1924): 133–35. La Follette also commissioned an official campaign song and authorized a number of slogans.

27. RML, speech, "On Responsible Government," 11 Aug. 1924, in Payson, *Great American Speeches* (videotape), vol. 1. The text to this introduction to La Follette's speech "The Making of America," appears in Torelle, *Political Philosophy*, 111–12. On the morning of 8 October La Follette made a series of sound films for the Fox Movietone News. Footage of La Follette also appears in a variety of earlier silent newsreels.

28. This distinction is undeserved however, as Jessie Benton Fremont had established the precedent in 1856, speaking on behalf of her husband, John C. Fremont.

29. RML, speech, Minneapolis, 16 Oct. 1924, RLP, B-228, LFC; La Follette–Wheeler Joint National Committee Publicity Bureau, "La Follette Has Enough Vigor to Serve Two Terms as President," *Leaflet #16*, RLP, 1–3, SHSW-M.

30. "La Follette," *Outlook*, 137 (16 July 1924): 421; "La Follette Takes the Stage," *Outlook* 138 (15 Oct. 1924): 212; K. Thompson, *Lessons from Defeated*, 27; "The Significance of La Follette," *LD* 82 (19 July 1924): 9; MacKay, *Progressive Movement*, 191.

31. MacKay, *Progressive Movement*, 113; PFL, *Adventures in Politics*, 88. See RML to family, 17 Nov. 1923, FP, A-30, LFC; Maney, *Young Bob*, 35; RML, "The Prospect of a Progressive Victory," *LM* 16, no. 9 (Sept. 1924): 129–30.

32. Rosenstone, Behr, and Lazarus, *Third Parties*, 41; MacKay, *Progressive Movement*, 205–6.

33. "Lessons for Progressives from 1924," *LM* 17, no. 1 (Jan. 1925): 5. In 1968, third-party candidate George Wallace also garnered about one-seventh of the vote. Ross Perot managed about one-fifth in 1992. See Gillespie, *Politics at the Periphery*, 80. Sources vary slightly on La Follette's 1924 vote total.

34. Rosenstone, Behr, and Lazarus, *Third Parties*, 97; MacKay, *Progressive Movement*, 218.

35. John Nichols, "Portrait of the Founder, Fighting Bob La Follette," *The Progressive* 63, no. 1 (Jan. 1999): 10. See "Senator La Follette's Pre-Convention Statement" and "Press Comment on the La Follette Statement," *LM* (June 1924): 84–85. Wisconsin remained something of a Socialist stronghold. Victor Berger regained his House seat in 1923, and Socialists remained in various positions of political power in Milwaukee until 1960. See Gillespie, *Politics at the Periphery*, 185, 189

36. By this measure, La Follette far outdistanced both Henry Wallace and Strom Thurmond in 1948, George Wallace in 1968, John Anderson in 1980, and Ross Perot in 1992. Campaign expenditures in the nineteenth century are more difficult to gauge due to both inflation and inconsistencies of record-keeping. See Gillespie, *Politics at the Periphery*, 3–4, 82.

37. MacKay, *Progressive Movement*, 152.

38. Samuel G. Blyth, "Future of Radicalism," *Saturday Evening Post* (10 Jan. 1925): 13; RML, "Forward Progressives for Campaign of 1926," *LM* 16, no. 11 (Nov. 1924);

165; Lincoln Steffens to Frederic C. Howe, 24 Nov. 1924, in L. Steffens, *Letters*, 2:674.

39. "Future of the La Follette Party," *LD* 83 (15 Nov. 1924): 10; RML, Diary, 1 Dec. 1924, RLP, B-1; RML to JS, 27 Dec. 1924, FP, A-31, LFC. For actions against La Follette–Wheeler supporters in the House, see *CR* 66, pt. 3:2642–51, 2712–19, 2803–6.

40. JR to FL, 3 Dec. 1924, FP, A-31; JR to Wm. T. Rawleigh, 6 Dec. 1924, RLP, B-119; RML, Diary, 18, 19 Dec. 1924, RLP, B-1; RML to Wm. Borah, 14 Jan. 1925, and RML to Rudolph Spreckels, 25 Mar. 1925, RLP, B-119, LFC. See RML, Diary, 5 Mar. 1925, RLP, B-1; John J. Blaine to RML, 3 Mar. 1925, RLP, B-102, LFC.

41. JR to RML, 17 Feb. 1925, FP, A-32, LFC; BCL and FL, *La Follette*, 2:1156–57. See JR to RML, 9, 19 Feb. 1925, and RML to JR, 19 Feb. 1925, FP, A-32, LFC.

42. BCL and FL, *La Follette*, 2:1158, 1168; JR to family, 12 Feb. 1925, FP, A-32; RML, Diary, 15 Mar. 1925, RLP, B-1, LFC. Coolidge offered the appointment to Warren despite the Senate's refusal to confirm him. Warren declined.

43. RML to PFL, 28 Apr. 1925, FP, A-32, LFC. See also RML to family, 29 Apr. 1919, FP, A-27, LFC.

44. RML to Mrs. George Loftus, ca. July 1916, RLP, B-111, LFC; BCL and FL, *La Follette*, 2:1165–66. La Follette concluded one eulogy with these words: "[A]cross the silent tomb our loved ones call to us and we are sure that we will find the way." RML, Funeral Address, ca. 1903, RLP, B-211, LFC. See RML to Guy, Fred, Ralph, and Maude La Follette, 13 Jan. 1915, FP, A-18, LFC.

45. BCL and FL, *La Follette*, 2:1169.


EPILOGUE

1. "La Follette Comes Home to Rest!" Grinberg Film Libraries, 26 June 1925; A. E. Haydon, "Funeral Sermon"; Alburn Lippitt, David K. Niles, "Messages of Appreciation from Individuals," *LM* 17, no. 7 (July 1925): 102, 105. In Madison, the banks and stores were closed by proclamation, and the university suspended graduation ceremonies until after the funeral. "Since Lincoln, at least, no such tribute has been paid any man as was offered at his funeral here." Stanley Frost, "The Scramble for 'Fighting Bob's' Shoes," *Outlook* 140 (29 July 1925): 461.

2. A. E. Haydon, "Remarks — Funeral Services for Senator Robert Marion La Follette" (22 June 1925): 5, RLP, B-316, LFC; Legislature of Wisconsin, "Memorial Resolution to Commemorate the Life and Services of Robert Marion La Follette," RLP, 1–4, SHSW-M; "Messages of Appreciation from Individuals," *LM* 17, no. 7 (July 1925): 104.

3. MacKay, *Progressive Movement*, 258–59; Rosenstone, Behr, and Lazarus, *Third Parties*, 44.

4. Nichols, "Portrait of the Founder," *Progressive* 63, no. 1 (Jan. 1999): 12; Doug La Follette, interviewed by author via telephone, 3 Feb. 1999. Although more liberal than his father on several issues, Bobbie La Follette never joined the Democratic Party. After abandoning the GOP in 1934, he remained independent until his return to the Republicans in 1946. For more on La Follette Sr.'s political

legacy, see Altmeyer, "Wisconsin Idea and Social Security"; Havig, "Disputed Legacy," 63–64; Graham, *Encore for Reform*; and Glad, *War, a New Era and Depression*. Brett Flehinger's forthcoming study will provide detailed insight into the family's political legacy.

5. La Follette's life is recreated by an actor at the living-history site of Old World Wisconsin, and in 1998 the Madison Theater Guild premiered the musical production "Fighting Bob: A Love Story." See also Jim Stingl, "La Follette Shaped Century in State, Experts Say," *Milwaukee Journal Sentinel*, 30 Dec. 1999.

6. John Chamberlain in MacKay, *Progressive Movement*, 129; Nichols, "Portrait of the Founder," *The Progressive* 63, no. 1 (Jan. 1999): 14. The January 1999 issue of *The Progressive* also includes a cartoon illustrating La Follette's actions if allowed a one-day return to confront current American problems. Sound recording of Martin Luther King Jr., on *Pride* by Hapa, produced by Barry Flanagan, Coconut Grove Records, Inc., 1997, compact disc. Martin Luther King Jr., speech, "The Death of Evil Upon the Seashore," 17 May 1956, in *The Papers of Martin Luther King, Jr.*, edited by Clayborne Carson, vol. 3 (Berkeley: University of California Press, 1997), 259. Both La Follette and Taft were initially suggested by Kennedy. "The Immortals for the United States Senate," *Life* 42 (6 May 1957): 73–74. While campaigning for the presidency the following year, Kennedy invoked the memory of La Follette in a Milwaukee speech. See "Wisconsin Caucuses," WTMJ-TV performance, 31 Mar. 1984, ABC News VideoSource.

# BIBLIOGRAPHY

PRIMARY SOURCES

*Documents*
Hayward, California
  California State University, Hayward
     Robert M. La Follette Papers of the State Historical Society of Wisconsin
       (microfilm)
Madison, Wisconsin
  State Historical Society of Wisconsin
     Albert O. Barton Papers
     Victor L. Berger Papers
     John J. Blaine Papers
     Charles Boardman Papers
     Henry F. Cochems Papers
     John Commons Papers
     Henry Allen Cooper Papers
     James O. Davidson Papers
     Herman L. Ekern Papers
     Richard Ely Papers
     William Evjue Papers
     Albert R. Hall Papers
     Nils Haugen Papers
     William D. Hoard Papers
     La Follette Family Photo Collection
     Philip Fox La Follette Interview
     Robert M. La Follette Papers
     Robert M. La Follette Photo Collection
     Francis E. McGovern Papers
     Herbert Margulies Manuscript
     Emanuel Philipp Papers
     John Craig Ralston Papers
     Gwyneth King Roe Papers
     John C. Spooner Papers
     Isaac Stephenson Papers
     Charles F. Stout Papers
     The Progressive, Inc., Records
     Albert G. Zimmerman Papers
Stanford, California
  Stanford University Special Collections
     Meyer E. Lissner Papers
     William Allen White Papers

Washington, D.C.
 Library of Congress
  Albert Beveridge Papers
  La Follette Family Papers
  La Follette Photo Collection
  Belle Case La Follette Papers
  Fola La Follette Papers
  Mary La Follette Papers
  Philip La Follette Papers
  Robert M. La Follette Papers
  Robert M. La Follette Jr. Papers
  National Progressive Republican League Records
  Gilbert E. Roe Papers
  Alfred T. Rogers Papers
  Theodore Roosevelt Papers
  William Howard Taft Papers
  Woodrow Wilson Papers
 National Archives Photo Collection

*Periodicals*
*Congressional Record*, 1885–1953
*La Follette's Magazine*, 1914–1926
*La Follette's Weekly Magazine*, 1910–1914
*Literary Digest*, 1912–1925
*The Nation*, 1900–1932
*New Republic* 1922–1925
*New York Times*, 1880–1926
*The Outlook*, 1900–1926
*Washington Evening Star*, 1906–1924

SECONDARY SOURCES

*Books*
Aaseng, Nathan. *America's Third Party Presidential Candidates.* Minneapolis: Oliver,
  1995.
Alexander, Holmes. *The Famous Five.* New York: Bookmailer, 1958.
Amchan, Arthur J. *The Kaiser's Senator: Robert M. La Follette's Alleged Disloyalty During
  World War I.* Alexandria: Amchan Publications, 1994.
Anderson, Judith Icke. *William Howard Taft, A Personal History.* New York: W. W.
  Norton, 1981.
Ashby, Leroy. *The Speerless Leader: Senator Borah and the Progressive Movement in the
  1920s.* Urbana: University of Illinois Press, 1972.
Bailey, Thomas A. *Wilson and the Peacemakers.* New York: Macmillan, 1947.

Barton, Albert O. *La Follette's Winning of Wisconsin, 1894–1904*. Des Moines: Homestead, 1922.

Bates, J. Leonard. *The Origins of the Teapot Dome: Progressives, Parties and Petroleum, 1909–1921*. Urbana: University of Illinois Press, 1963.

Beider, Robert. *Native American Communities in Wisconsin, 1600–1960*. Madison: University of Wisconsin Press, 1995.

Biel, Steven. *Down with the Old Canoe: A Cultural History of the Titanic Disaster*. New York: W. W. Norton, 1996.

Bennett, Ira E., ed. *Editorials from the Washington Post*. Washington, D.C.: Washington Post, 1921.

Blum, John Morton. *The Republican Roosevelt*. Cambridge: Harvard University Press, 1954.

Bogue, Allan, and Robert Taylor. *The University of Wisconsin: One Hundred and Twenty-Five Years*. Madison: University of Wisconsin Press, 1975.

Boller, Paul F., Jr., ed. *Presidential Anecdotes*. New York: Oxford University Press, 1982.

Bourne, Randolph. *The Letters of Randolph Bourne*. Edited by Eric Sandeen. New York: Whitston, 1981.

Brandeis, Louis D. *Letters of Louis D. Brandeis*. Edited by Melvin I. Urofsky and David M. Devy. New York: State University of New York Press, 1978.

Brands, H. W. *TR: The Last Romantic*. New York: Basic, 1997.

Breaman, John. *Albert J. Beveridge, American Nationalist*. Chicago: University of Chicago Press, 1971.

Broderick, Francis L. *Progressives at Risk: Electing a President in 1912*. New York: Greenwood, 1989.

Brye, David. *Wisconsin Voting Patterns in the Twentieth Century*. New York: Garland, 1979.

Buenker, John D. *The Progressive Era, 1893–1914*. Vol. 4 of *The History of Wisconsin*. Madison: State Historical Society of Wisconsin, 1998.

———. *Urban Liberalism and Progressive Reform*. New York: Scribner, 1973.

Buenker, John D., and Nicholas C. Burckel. *Progressive Reform: A Guide to Information Sources*. Detroit: Gale Research, 1980.

Buenker, John D., and Robert M. Crunden. *Progressivism*. Cambridge, Mass.: Schenkman, 1977.

Buenker, John D., and Edward Kantowicz. *Historical Dictionary of the Progressive Era*. New York: Greenwood, 1988.

Burrow, James. *Organized Medicine in the Progressive Era*. Baltimore: Johns Hopkins University Press, 1977.

Burgchardt, Carl R. *Robert M. La Follette Sr.: Voice of Conscience*. New York: Greenwood, 1992.

Burton, David. *Theodore Roosevelt*. New York: Twayne, 1972.

Butt, Archie. *Taft and Roosevelt: The Intimate Letters of Archie Butt*. 2 vols. New York: Doubleday, 1930.

Byrd, Robert. *The Senate, 1789–1989*. 4 vols. Washington, D.C.: U.S. Government Printing Office, 1988–1994.

Caine, Stanley P. *The Myth of Progressive Reform: Railroad Regulation in Wisconsin 1903–1910*. Madison: State Historical Society of Wisconsin, 1970.

Casdorph, Paul. *Republicans, Negroes, and Progressives in the South, 1912–1916*. Alabama: University of Alabama Press, 1981.

Case, Victoria, and Robert Osmund Case. *We Called It Culture: The Story of Chautauqua*. New York: Doubleday, 1948.

Cashman, Sean Dennis. *America in the Age of the Titans*. New York: New York University Press, 1988.

Chambers, John Whiteclay, II. *To Raise an Army: The Draft Comes to Modern America*. New York: Free Press, 1987.

Cherny, Robert W. *American Politics in the Gilded Age, 1868–1900*. The American History Series. Wheeling, Ill.: Harlan Davidson, 1997.

———. *A Righteous Cause: The Life of William Jennings Bryan*. Boston: Little, Brown, 1985.

Chessman, G. Wallace. *Theodore Roosevelt and the Politics of Power*. Boston: Little, Brown, 1969.

Cole, Wayne S. *An Interpretive History of American Foreign Relations*. Illinois: Dorsey, 1974.

Coletta, Paolo E. *The Presidency of William Howard Taft*. Wichita: University of Kansas Press, 1973.

Cooper, John Milton, Jr. *Pivotal Decades*. New York: W. W. Norton, 1990.

———. *The Warrior and the Priest*. Cambridge: Belknap, 1983.

———, ed. *Causes and Consequences of World War I*. New York: Quadrangle, 1972.

Cremin, Lawrence. *The Transformation of the School*. New York: Knopf, 1961.

Cott, Nancy F. *The Bonds of Womanhood: "Woman's Sphere" in New England, 1780–1835*. New Haven: Yale University Press, 1977.

Crunden, Robert. *Ministers of Reform*. New York: Basic, 1982.

Current, Richard N. *The Civil War Era, 1848–1873*. Vol. 2 of *The History of Wisconsin*. Madison: State Historical Society of Wisconsin, 1976.

———. *Pine Logs and Politics: A Life of Philetus Sawyer*. Madison: State Historical Society of Wisconsin, 1950.

———. *Wisconsin: A Bicentennial History*. New York: W. W. Norton, 1977.

Curti, Merle, and Vernon Carstensen. *The University of Wisconsin: A History*. Madison: University of Wisconsin, 1949.

Danbom, David. *The World of Hope*. Philadelphia: Temple University Press, 1987.

Davis, Allen. *Spearhead for Reform*. New York: Oxford University Press, 1967.

Degregorio, William A. *The Complete Book of U.S. Presidents*. New York: Wing, 1993.

Deverell, William, and Tom Sitton. *California Progressivism Revisited*. Berkeley: University of California Press, 1994.

DeWitt, John. *William Allen White: Maverick on Main Street*. Westport, Conn.: Greenwood, 1975.

Dillon, Dennis G. *Argyle, Wisconsin; Boyhood Home of Bob La Follette*. Argyle: D. G. Dillon, 1992.

Diner, Steven J. *A Very Different Age: Americans of the Progressive Era*. New York: Hill and Wang, 1998.

Doan, Edward N. *The La Follettes and the Wisconsin Idea*. New York: Rinehart, 1947.

Ebner, Michael H., and Eugene M. Tobin, eds. *The Age of Urban Reform*. New York: National University Publications, 1977.

Edwards, Rebecca. *Angels in the Machinery: Gender in Party Politics from the Civil War to the Progressive Era*. New York: Oxford University Press, 1997.

Eisenach, Eldon. *The Lost Promise of Progressivism*. Kansas: University Press of Kansas, 1994.

Ekirch, Arthur A. *Progressivism in America: A Study of the Era from Theodore Roosevelt to Woodrow Wilson*. New York: New Viewpoints, 1974.

Esposito, David. *The Legacy of Woodrow Wilson: American War Aims in World War I*. Westport, Conn.: Praeger, 1996.

Feinman, Ronald. *Twilight of Progressivism*. Baltimore: Johns Hopkins University Press, 1981.

Filler, Louis. *Appointment at Armageddon*. Westport, Conn.: Greenwood, 1976.

———. *Progressivism and Muckraking*. New York: R. R. Bowker, 1976.

Fink, Leon, ed. *Major Problems in the Gilded Age and the Progressive Era*. Lexington, Mass.: D. C. Heath, 1993.

Fitzpatrick, Ellen. *Endless Crusade*. New York: Oxford University Press, 1990.

Freeman, Lucy, Sherry La Follette, and George A. Zabriskie. *Belle: A Biography of Belle Case La Follette*. New York: Beaufort, 1986.

Frost, Elizabeth, ed. *The Bully Pulpit*. New York: New England Publishing Associated, 1988.

Gable, John. *The Bull Moose Years*. New York: Kennikat, 1978.

Gara, Larry. *A Short History of Wisconsin*. Madison: State Historical Society of Wisconsin, 1962.

Gardner, Joseph L. *Departing Glory: Theodore Roosevelt as Ex-President*. New York: Charles Scribner's Sons, 1973.

Gatewood, Willard B. *Theodore Roosevelt and the Art of Controversy*. Baton Rouge: Louisiana State University Press, 1970.

George, Alexander, and Juliette George. *Woodrow Wilson and Colonel House: A Personality Study*. New York: Dover, 1964.

Giffin, Frederick. *Six Who Protested: Radical Opposition to the First World War*. New York: Kennikat, 1977.

Gilbert, Clinton. *"You Takes Your Choice."* New York: G. P. Putnam's Sons, 1924.

Gillespie, J. David. *Politics at the Periphery: Third Parties in Two-Party America*. Columbia: University of South Carolina Press, 1993.

Glad, Paul. *War, a New Era, and Depression, 1914–1940*. Vol. 5 of *History of Wisconsin*. Madison: State Historical Society of Wisconsin, 1990.

Goodwyn, Lawrence. *The Populist Moment*. Oxford: University Press, 1978.

Gould, Lewis, ed. *The Progressive Era*. New York: Syracuse University Press, 1974.

Graham, Otis. *An Encore for Reform: The Old Progressives and the New Deal*. London: Oxford University Press, 1967.

———. *The Great Campaigns*. New Jersey: Prentice-Hall, 1971.

Grantham, Dewey W. *Southern Progressivism*. Knoxville: University of Tennessee Press, 1983.

———, ed. *Theodore Roosevelt*. New Jersey: Prentice-Hall, 1971.

Greabner, Norman A., Gilbert Fite, and Philip White. *History of the American People*. New York: McGraw-Hill, 1975.

Greenbaum, Fred. *Robert Marion La Follette*. Boston: Twayne, 1975.

Griffith, Sally Foreman. *Home Town News*. New York: Oxford University Press, 1989.

Gunther, John. *Roosevelt in Retrospect: A Profile in History*. New York: Harper and Brothers, 1950.

Harbaugh, William Henry. *The Life and Times of Theodore Roosevelt*. Rev. ed. London: Oxford University Press, 1978.

———. *The Writing of Theodore Roosevelt*. New York: Bobbs-Merrill, 1967.

Heckscher, August. *Woodrow Wilson*. New York: Charles Scribner's Sons, 1991.

Himmelberg, Robert F., ed. *Growth of the Regulatory State, 1900–1917*. New York: Garland, 1994.

Hofstadter, Richard. *The Age of Reform*. New York: Vintage, 1955.

———. *The American Political Tradition and the Men Who Made It*. New York: Alfred A. Knopf, 1982.

———. *The Progressive Movement*. New Jersey: Prentice-Hall, 1963.

Holt, James. *Congressional Insurgents and the Party System, 1909–1916*. Cambridge: Harvard University Press, 1967.

Jernigan, E. Jay. *William Allen White*. Boston: Twayne, 1983.

Johnson, Robert. *The Peace Progressives and American Foreign Policy*. Cambridge: Harvard University Press, 1995.

Johnson, Roger T. *Robert M. La Follette, Jr., and the Decline of the Progressive Party in Wisconsin*. Hamden, Conn.: Archon, 1970.

Joyner, Conrad. *The Republican Dilemma*. Tucson: University of Arizona Press, 1963.

Kanowitz, Leo. *Women and the Law: The Unfinished Revolution*. Albuquerque: University of New Mexico Press, 1969.

Kaplan, Justin. *Lincoln Steffens: A Biography*. New York: Simon and Schuster, 1974.

Keller, Morton. *Regulating a New Society*. Cambridge: Harvard University Press, 1994.

———, ed. *Theodore Roosevelt: A Profile*. New York: Hill and Wang, 1967.

Kellogg, Louise. *The French Regime in Wisconsin and the Northwest*. New York: Cooper Square, 1968.

Kennedy, David M. *Over Here: The First World War and American Society*. New York: Oxford University Press, 1980.

———, ed. *Progressivism: The Critical Issues*. Boston: Little, Brown, 1971.

Kloppenberg, James. *Uncertain Victory*. New York: Oxford University Press, 1986.

Koepplin, Leslie. *A Relationship of Reform*. New York: Garland, 1990.

Kohut, Heinz. *The Analysis of the Self*. New York: International Universities Press, 1971.

Kolko, Gabriel. *The Triumph of Conservatism: A Reinterpretation of American History, 1900–1916*. New York: Free Press of Glencoe, 1963.

Kuhlman, Erika. *Petticoats and White Feathers: Gender Conformity, Race, the Progressive Peace Movement, and the Debate Over War, 1895–1919*. Westport, Conn.: Greenwood, 1997.

La Follette, Belle Case, and Fola La Follette. *Robert M. La Follette*. 2 vols. New York: Macmillan, 1953.

La Follette, Philip. *Adventures in Politics: The Memoir of Philip La Follette*. Edited by Donald Young. New York: Holt, Rinehart and Winston, 1970.

La Follette, Robert M. *La Follette's Autobiography*. Madison: Robert M. La Follette Company 1911, 1913; reprint, Madison: University of Wisconsin Press, 1960.

Lasswell, Harold D. *Psychopathology and Politics*. Chicago: University of Chicago Press, 1930, 1977.

Lear, Linda. *Harold Ickes: The Aggressive Progressive*. New York: Garland, 1981.

Leavitt, Judith. *The Healthiest City*. Princeton: Princeton University Press, 1982.

Lewis, David Levering. *W. E. B. Du Bois: Biography of a Race, 1868–1919*. New York: Henry Holt, 1993.

Link, Arthur S. *The Higher Realism of Woodrow Wilson*. Nashville: Vanderbilt University Press, 1971.

———. *The Paradox of Southern Progressivism, 1880–1930*. Chapel Hill: University of North Carolina Press, 1992.

———. *Wilson: The Road to the White House*. Princeton: Princeton University Press.

———. *Woodrow Wilson and the Progressive Era*. New York: Harper & Row, 1954.

———. *Woodrow Wilson: Revolution, War and Peace*. Arlington Heights, Ill.: AHM Publishing, 1979.

Link, Arthur S., and William Leary. *The Progressive Era and the Great War, 1896–1920*. New York: Appleton-Century-Crofts, 1969.

Link, Arthur S., and Richard McCormick. *Progressivism*. Arlington Heights, Ill.: Harlan Davidson, 1983.

Lodge, Henry Cabot. *The Senate of the United States*. New York: Charles Scribners Sons, 1921.

Lovejoy, Allen Frasier. *La Follette and the Establishment of the Direct Primary in Wisconsin, 1890–1904*. New Haven: Yale University Press, 1941.

Lowitt, Richard. *George W. Norris: The Making of a Progressive, 1861–1912*. New York: Syracuse University Press, 1963.

———. *George W. Norris: The Persistence of a Progressive, 1913–1933*. Urbana: University of Illinois Press, 1971.

Macartney, Clarence Edward Noble. *Men Who Missed It: Great Americans Who Missed the White House*. Philadelphia: Dorrence, 1940.

McBride, Genevieve G. *On Wisconsin Women*. Madison: University of Wisconsin Press, 1993.

McCormick, Richard L. *The Party Period and Public Policy*. New York: Oxford University Press, 1986.

McFarland, Gerald. *Mugwumps, Morals and Politics, 1884–1920*. Amherst: University of Massachusetts Press, 1975.

MacKay, Kenneth C. *The Progressive Movement of 1924*. New York: Columbia University Press, 1947.

Maney, Patrick J. *"Young Bob" La Follette: A Biography of Robert M. La Follette Jr., 1895–1953*. Columbia: University of Missouri Press, 1978.

Mann, Arthur. *The Progressive Era: Liberal Renaissance or Liberal Failure?* New York: Holt, Rinehart and Winston, 1963.

Manners, William. *T.R. and Will: The Friendship That Split the Republican Party.* New York: Harcourt, Brace and World, 1969.

Margulies, Herbert F. *The Decline of the Progressive Movement in Wisconsin, 1890–1920.* Madison: State Historical Society in Wisconsin, 1968.

———. *Senator Lenroot of Wisconsin.* Columbia: University of Missouri Press, 1977.

Maxwell, Robert S. *Emanuel L. Philipp: Wisconsin Stalwart.* Madison: State Historical Society of Wisconsin, 1959.

———. *La Follette: Great Lives Observed.* New York: Prentice and Hall, 1969.

———. *La Follette and the Rise of the Progressives in Wisconsin.* Madison: State Historical Society of Wisconsin, 1956.

May, Martha. *The "Problem of Duty."* Madison: Institute for Legal Studies, 1986.

Meier, August. *Negro Thought in America, 1880–1915: Racial Ideologies in the Age of Booker T. Washington.* Ann Arbor: University of Michigan Press, 1963.

Meyer, Stephen. *"Stalin Over Wisconsin."* New Brunswick: Rutgers University Press, 1992.

Michaud, L'Abbé Adolphe. *Généalogie des Familles de la Rivière Quelle.* Quebec: Imp. H. Chasse, 1908.

Middleton, George. *These Things Are Mine.* New York: Macmillan, 1947.

Miller, Alice. *The Drama of the Gifted Child.* Translated from the German by Ruth Ward. New York: Basic, 1981.

Miller, John E. *Governor Philip F. La Follette, the Wisconsin Progressives, and the New Deal.* Columbia: University of Missouri Press, 1982.

Money, John. *Destroying Angel: Sex, Fitness and Food in the Legacy of Degeneracy Theory, Graham Crackers, Kellogg's Corn Flakes and American Health History.* New York: Prometheus, 1985.

Morris, Edmund. *The Rise of Theodore Roosevelt.* New York: Ballantine, 1979.

Mowry, George E. *The California Progressives.* Chicago: Quadrangle, 1951.

———. *The Era of Theodore Roosevelt and the Birth of Modern America, 1900–1912.* New York: Harper & Row, 1958.

———. *Theodore Roosevelt and the Progressive Movement.* Madison: University of Wisconsin Press, 1946.

Mulder, John. *Woodrow Wilson: The Years of Preparation.* Princeton: Princeton University Press, 1978.

Mulder, Ronald. *The Insurgent Progressives in the United States Senate and the New Deal.* New York: Garland, 1979.

Nesbit, Robert C. *Urbanization and Industrialization 1873–1893.* Vol. 3 of *The History of Wisconsin.* Madison: State Historical Society of Wisconsin, 1985.

———. *Wisconsin: A History.* Wisconsin: University of Wisconsin Press, 1973.

Noggle, Burl. *Teapot Dome: Oil and Politics in the 1920's.* Baton Rouge: Louisiana State University Press, 1962.

Norris, George W. *Fighting Liberal: The Autobiography of George W. Norris.* New York: Macmillan, 1945.

Nye, Russel B. *Midwestern Progressive Politics: A Historical Study of Its Origins and Developments, 1870–1958.* Michigan: State University Press, 1959.

O'Connor, Richard. *The German-Americans*. Boston: Little, Brown, 1968.

Olin, Spencer. *California's Prodigal Sons*. Berkeley: University of California Press, 1968.

Olson, Keith W. *Biography of a Progressive: Franklin K. Lane*. Westport, Conn.: Greenwood, 1979.

Painter, Nell Irvin. *Standing at Armageddon: The United States, 1877–1919*. New York: W. W. Norton, 1987.

Palermo, Patrick. *Lincoln Steffens*. Boston: Twayne, 1978.

Pells, Richard H. *Radical Visions and American Dreams*. New York: Harper & Row, 1973.

Peterson, H. C., and Gilbert C. Fite. *Opponents of War, 1917–1918*. Seattle: University of Washington Press, 1957.

Phillips, David Graham. *The Treason of the Senate*. Chicago: Quadrangle, 1964.

Pickering, George. *Creative Malady: Illness in the Lives and Minds of Charles Darwin, Florence Nightingale, Mary Baker Eddy, Sigmund Freud, Marcel Proust, and Elizabeth Barrett Browning*. New York: Oxford University Press, 1974.

Pinchot, Amos. *History of the Progressive Party*. New York: New York University Press, 1958.

Piott, Steven L. *Holy Joe: Joseph W. Folk and the Missouri Idea*. Columbia: University of Missouri Press, 1998.

Pringle, Henry F. *The Life and Times of William Howard Taft*. New York: Farrar and Rinehart, 1939.

———. *Theodore Roosevelt: A Biography*. New York: Harcourt Brace, 1931.

Rippley, La Vern. *The Immigrant Experience in Wisconsin*. Boston: Twayne, 1985.

Robertson, James. *No Third Choice: Progressives in Republican Politics, 1916–1921*. New York: Garland, 1983.

Rochester, Stuart I. *American Liberal Disillusionment in the Wake of World War I*. University Park: Pennsylvania State University Press, 1977.

Rodgers, Daniel T. *Atlantic Crossings: Social Politics in a Progressive Age*. Cambridge: Harvard University Press, 1998.

Roosevelt, Theodore. *An Autobiography*. New York: Charles Scribner's Sons, 1924.

———. *Fear God and Take Your Own Part*. New York: George H. Doran, 1916.

———. *The Letters of Theodore Roosevelt*. Edited by Elting E. Morison. 8 vols. Cambridge: Harvard University Press, 1951–1954.

———. *Presidential Addresses and State Papers: European Addresses*. 8 vols. New York: Review of Reviews, 1910.

———. *The Works of Theodore Roosevelt*. 16 vols. New York: P. F. Collier, 1897.

Roosevelt, Theodore, and Henry Cabot Lodge. *Selections from the Correspondence of Theodore Roosevelt and Henry Cabot Lodge 1844–1918*. Edited by Henry Cabot Lodge and Charles F. Redmond. 2 vols. New York: Charles Scribners Sons, 1925.

Rose-Ackerman, Susan. *Rethinking the Progressive Agenda*. New York: Free Press, 1992.

Roseboom, Eugene. *A History of Presidential Elections*. New York: Macmillan, 1964.

Rosenstone, Steven J., Roy Behr, and Edward Lazarus. *Third Parties in America: Citizen Response to Majority Party Failure*. Princeton: Princeton University Press, 1984.

Rovere, Richard H. *Senator Joe McCarthy*. New York: Harper & Row, 1959.

Runyan, William McKinley. *Life Histories and Psychobiography*. New York: Oxford University Press, 1982.

————, ed. *Psychology and Historical Interpretation*. New York: Oxford University Press, 1988.

Ryan, Mary P. *Womanhood in America*. New York: New Viewpoints, 1975.

Ryley, Thomas. *A Little Group of Willful Men*. New York: National University Publications, 1975.

Sarasohn, David. *The Party of Reform*. Jackson: University Press of Mississippi, 1989.

Schlesinger, Arthur M., Jr. *The Politics of Upheaval*. Boston: Houghton Mifflin, 1960.

Schneider, Dorothy, and Carl J. Schneider. *American Women in the Progressive Era, 1900–1920*. New York: Facts on File, 1993.

Sellery, G. C. *Some Ferments at Wisconsin, 1901–1947: Memories and Reflections*. Madison: University of Wisconsin Press, 1960.

Shannon, David. *Progressivism and Postwar Disillusionment, 1898–1928*. New York: McGraw-Hill, 1966.

Silby, Joel H., Allan G. Bogue, and William H. Flanigan. *The History of American Electoral Behavior*. Stanford, Calif.: Center for Advanced Study in the Behavioral Sciences, 1978.

Sitton, Tom. *John Randolph Haynes, California Progressive*. Stanford: Stanford University Press, 1992.

Sklar, Kathryn Kish. *Catherine Beecher: A Study in American Domesticity*. New Haven: Yale University Press, 1973.

————. *Florence Kelley and the Nation's Work: The Rise of Women's Political Culture, 1830–1900*. New Haven: Yale University Press, 1995.

Sklar, Martin. *The Corporate Reconstruction of American Capitalism, 1890–1916*. Cambridge: Cambridge University Press, 1988.

Smith, Alice. *From Exploration to Statehood*. Vol. 1 of *The History of Wisconsin*. Madison: State Historical Society of Wisconsin, 1973.

Smith, Daniel. *American Intervention, 1917: Sentiment, Self-Interest, or Ideals*. Boston: Houghton Mifflin, 1966.

Smith, Page. *America Enters the World: A People's History of the Progressive Era and World War I*. New York: McGraw-Hill, 1985.

Soltow, Lee. *Patterns of Wealthholding in Wisconsin since 1850*. Madison: University of Wisconsin Press, 1971.

Somers, Gerald George. *Labor, Management, and Social Policy*. Madison: University of Wisconsin Press, 1963.

Spignesi, Stephen J. *The Complete Titanic*. Secaucus, N.J.: Carol Publishing Group, 1998.

Stave, Bruce M., and Sondra Astor Stave, ed. *Urban Bosses, Machines, and Progressive Reformers*. 2d rev. ed. Malabar, Fla.: R. E. Krieger, 1984.

Steffens, Joseph. *The World of Lincoln Steffens*. New York: Hill and Wang, 1962.

Steffens, Lincoln. *The Autobiography of Lincoln Steffens*. New York: Harcourt, Brace and World, 1931.

———. *Letters of Lincoln Steffens*. Edited by Ella Winter and Granville Hicks. 2 vols. New York: Harcourt, Brace, 1938.

———. *The Shame of Our Cities*. New York: Hill and Wang, 1957.

Steinschneider, Janice. *The Improved Woman: The Wisconsin Federation of Women's Clubs, 1895–1920*. New York: Carlson, 1994.

Stid, Daniel. *The President as Statesman: Woodrow Wilson and the Constitution*. Lawrence: University of Kansas Press, 1998.

Stinson, Robert. *Lincoln Steffens*. New York: F. Unger, 1979.

Stirn, Ernest. *An Annotated Bibliography of Robert M. La Follette*. Chicago: University of Chicago Press, 1937.

Stock, Catherine. *Rural Radicals*. Ithaca: Cornell University Press, 1996.

Stout, Ralph, ed. *Roosevelt in the Kansas City Star*. New York: Houghton Mifflin, 1921.

Thelen, David Paul. *The Early Life of Robert M. La Follette, 1855–1884*. Chicago: Loyola University Press, 1966.

———. *The New Citizenship: Origins of Progressivism in Wisconsin, 1885–1900*. Missouri: University of Missouri Press, 1972.

———. *Robert M. La Follette and the Insurgent Spirit*. Boston: Little, Brown, 1976.

Thompson, John A. *Reformers and War*. Cambridge: Cambridge University Press, 1987.

Thompson, Kenneth W., ed. *Lessons from Defeated Presidential Candidates*. Maryland: University Press of America, 1994.

Thompson, William. *Continuity and Change, 1940–1965*. Vol. 6 of *History of Wisconsin*. Madison: State Historical Society of Wisconsin, 1988.

Timberlake, James. *Prohibition and the Progressive Movement*. Cambridge: Harvard University Press, 1966.

Tobin, Eugene. *To Organize or Perish*. New York: Greenwood, 1986.

Tomasky, Michael. *Left for Dead*. New York: Free Press, 1996.

Torelle, Ellen, ed. *The Political Philosophy of Robert M. La Follette*. Madison: Robert M. La Follette Co., 1920.

Tsuang, Ming, Mauricio Tohen, and Gwendolyn Zahner. *Textbook in Psychiatric Epidemiology*. New York: Wiley Liss, 1995.

Unger, Irwin, and Debi Unger. *The Vulnerable Years: The United States, 1896–1917*. New York: New York University Press, 1978.

Warren, Sidney. *The Battle for the Presidency*. New York: J. B. Lippincott, 1968.

Waterhouse, David. *The Progressive Movement of 1924 and the Development of Interest Group Liberalism*. New York: Garland, 1991.

Weinstein, James. *The Corporate Ideal in the Liberal State, 1900–1918*. Westport, Conn.: Greenwood, 1968.

Weisberg, D. Kelly, ed. *Women and the Law: A Social Historical Perspective*. Cambridge: Schenkman, 1992.

Weisberger, Bernard A. *The La Follettes of Wisconsin: Love and Politics in Progressive America*. Madison: University of Wisconsin Press, 1994.

Wiebe, Robert H. *The Search for Order*. New York: Hill and Wang, 1967.

———. *Self-Rule*. Chicago: University of Chicago Press, 1995.

Wilson, Woodrow. *Woodrow Wilson Papers*. Edited by Arthur S. Link. 69 vols. Princeton: Princeton University Press, 1966.

Woodward, C. Vann. *Origins of the New South, 1877–1913*. Baton Rouge: Louisiana State University Press, 1951.

*Articles*

Acrea, Kenneth. "The Wisconsin Reform Coalition, 1892–1900: La Follette's Rise to Power." *Wisconsin Magazine of History* 52, no. 2 (1968–69): 132–57.

Altmeyer, Arthur. "The Wisconsin Idea and Social Security." *Wisconsin Magazine of History* 42 (Autumn 1958): 19–25.

Auerbach, Jerold S. "The La Follette Committee: Labor and Civil Liberties in the New Deal." *Journal of American History* 51, no. 3 (1964): 435–59.

Bach, George R. "Father-Fantasies and Father-Typing in Father-Separated Children." *Child Development* 17 (1946): 63–80.

Blythe, Samuel G. "The Future of Radicalism." *Saturday Evening Post* (10 Jan. 1925): 12–13, 174–78.

Brownlee, W. Elliot, Jr. "Income Taxation and the Political Economy of Wisconsin." *Wisconsin Magazine of History* 59, no. 4 (1976): 299–324.

Buenker, John. "Robert La Follette's Progressive Odyssey." *Wisconsin Magazine of History* 82, no. 1 (1998): 2–31.

Carstensen, Vernon. "The Origin and Development of the Wisconsin Idea." *Wisconsin Magazine of History* 39, no. 2 (Spring 1956): 181–88.

———. "Wisconsin Regents: Academic Freedom and Innovation, 1900–1925." *Wisconsin Magazine of History* 48, no. 2 (1965): 101–10.

"The Case of Senator La Follette." *Current Opinion* 63 (Nov. 1917): 289–92.

Cavallo, Dom. "Social Reform and the Movement to Organize Children's Play during the Progressive Era." *History of Childhood Quarterly* 3 (Spring 1976): 509–21.

Cooper, John Milton, Jr. "Robert M. La Follette: Political Prophet." *Wisconsin Magazine of History* 69, no. 2 (1985–86): 91–105.

Dalton, Kathleen, "Why America Loved Theodore Roosevelt." *Psychohistory Review* 8 (Winter 1976): 16–26.

Dubbert, Joe L. "Progressivism and the Masculinity Crisis." *Psychoanalytic Review* 61 (1974): 443.

Feinman, Ronald L. Review of *Governor Philip F. La Follette* by John E. Miller. *Reviews in American History* 11, no. 3 (Sept. 1983): 409–13.

Filene, Peter. "An Obituary for 'The Progressive Movement.'" *American Quarterly* 22 (Spring 1970): 30.

Garraty, John A. "La Follette: The Promise Unfulfilled." *American Heritage* 13 (April 1962): 76–88.

George, Alexander L. "Power as a Compensatory Value for Political Leaders." *Journal of Social Issues* 24 (1968): 29–49.

Gores, Stan. "The Attempted Assassination of Teddy Roosevelt." *Wisconsin Magazine of History* 53, no. 4 (Summer 1970): 269–77.

Griffith, Robert. "Old Progressives and the Cold War." *Journal of American History* 66 (Sept. 1979): 334–47.

————. "Prelude to Insurgency: Irvine L. Lenroot and the Republican Primary of 1908." *Wisconsin Magazine of History* 49, no. 1 (1965): 16–23.

Hagensick, A. Clarke. "Purging History in Wisconsin: Promises and Pitfalls." *Wisconsin Magazine of History* 67, no. 4 (1984): 278–92.

Hale, William Baynard, "La Follette, Pioneer Progressive." *World's Work* 22 (July 1911): 14591–600.

Haney, Richard C. "The Rise of Wisconsin's New Democrats: A Political Realignment in the Mid-Twentieth Century." *Wisconsin Magazine of History* 58, no. 2 (1974–75): 90–106.

Hantke, Richard. "Elisha W. Keyes, The Bismarck of Western Politics." *Wisconsin Magazine of History* 31 (Sept. 1947): 29–41.

————. "Elisha Keyes and the Radical Republicans." *Wisconsin Magazine of History* 35 (Spring 1952): 203–8.

Hass, Paul H. "The Suppression of John F. Deitz: An Episode of the Progressive Era in Wisconsin." *Wisconsin Magazine of History* 57, no. 4 (Summer 1974): 254–309.

Havig, Alan. "A Disputed Legacy: Roosevelt Progressives and the La Follette Campaign of 1924." *Mid-America* 1971 53 (1): 44–64.

Haynes, F. E. "La Follette and La Follettism." *Atlantic Monthly* 134 (October 1924): 536–44.

————. "The Sign of the Latest Third Party Movement." *Mississippi Valley Historical Review* 12 (Sept. 1924): 177–86.

Helgeson, Arlan. "The Wisconsin Treasury Cases." *Wisconsin Magazine of History* 35 (Winter 1951): 129–36.

Hicks, J. D. "The Third Party Tradition in American Politics." *Mississippi Valley Historical Review* 20 (June 1933): 3–28.

Hilgard, Josephine, Martha Newman, and Fern Fisk. "Strength of Adult Ego Following Childhood Bereavement." *American Journal of Orthopsychiatry* 30 (Oct. 1960): 788–98.

Hoeveler, J. David. "The University and the Social Gospel: The Intellectual Origins of the 'Wisconsin Idea.'" *Wisconsin Magazine of History* 59, no. 4 (1976): 282–98.

Holter, Darryl. "Labor Spies and Union Busting in Wisconsin, 1890–1940." *Wisconsin Magazine of History* 68, no. 4 (1985): 243–65.

"Immortals for the United States Senate." *Life* 42 (6 May 1957): 73–74.

Johnston, Scott D. "Robert La Follette and the Socialists: Aspects of the 1924 Presidential Campaign Re-examined." *Social Science* 50, no. 2 (1975): 67–77.

Jones, Richard Lloyd. "Among La Follette's People." *Collier's* 45 (3 Sept. 1910): 17–18.

Kades, Michael. "Incumbent without a Party." *Wisconsin Magazine of History* 80, no. 1 (Fall 1996): 2–35.

Kedro, Milan James. "Autobiography as a Key to Identity in the Progressive Era." *History of Childhood Quarterly* 2 (Winter 1975): 391–407.

Kennedy, Padraic Colum. "La Follette and the Russians." *Mid-America* 53, no. 3 (1971): 190–208.

————."La Follette's Foreign Policy: From Imperialism to Anti-Imperialism." *Wisconsin Magazine of History* 46, no. 4 (Summer 1963): 287–93.

————. "La Follette's Imperialist Flirtation." *Pacific Historical Review* 29 (1960): 131–43.

————. "Lenroot, La Follette, and the Campaign of 1906." *Wisconsin Magazine of History* 42 (Spring 1959): 163–74.

Knoll, E. "Spry Octogenarian." *The Progressive* 53 (Feb. 1989): 4.

————. "La Follette's Folly." *The Progressive* 58 (May 1994): 6.

"La Follette as Boss Ventriloquist." *Current of Opinion* 77 (Aug. 1924): 143–44.

Lawson, Steven F. "Progressives and the Supreme Court: A Case for Judicial Reform in the 1920s." *Historian* 42, no. 3 (1980): 419–36.

Lerner, Gerda. "The Lady and the Mill Girl: Changes in the Status of Women in the Age of Jackson." *Mid-Continental American Studies Journal* 10 (Spring 1969): 5–15.

Libecap, Gary. "What Really Happened at Teapot Dome." In *Second Thoughts: Myths and Morals in U.S. Economic History*, ed. Donald N. McCloskey, 157–62. New York: Oxford University Press, 1993.

Lorence, James. "'Dynamite for the Brain': The Growth and Decline of Socialism in Central and Lakeshore Wisconsin, 1910–1920." *Wisconsin Magazine of History* 66, no. 4 (1983): 250–73.

Lowitt, Richard. "Robert M. La Follette and the Waning Insurgent Spirit." *Reviews in American History* (June 1976): 244–50.

McCurdy, John W. "The Emancipated, Aggravated, Indispensable American Seaman." *U.S. Naval Institute Proceedings* 95, no. 5 (1969): 58–62.

"March of Events." *World's Work* 49 (Dec. 1924): 117–20.

Margulies, Herbert. "The Background of the La Follette–McGovern Schism." *Wisconsin Magazine of History* 40 (Autumn 1956): 21–29.

————. "The Decline of Wisconsin Progressivism, 1911–1914." *Mid-America* 39 (July 1957): 131–72.

————. "The Election of 1920 in Wisconsin: The Return of 'Normalcy' Reappraised." *Wisconsin Magazine of History* 42 (Autumn 1958): 19–25.

————. "The La Follette–Philipp Alliance of 1918." *Wisconsin Magazine of History* 38 (Summer 1955): 248–49.

————."La Follette, Roosevelt, and the Republican Presidential Nomination of 1912." *Mid-America* 58 (Jan. 1976): 54–76.

————. "Robert M. La Follette Goes to the Senate, 1905." *Wisconsin Magazine of History* 59, no. 3 (1976): 214–25.

————. "Robert M. La Follette as Presidential Aspirant: The First Campaign, 1908." *Wisconsin Magazine of History* 80, no. 4 (1997): 258–79.

Martinson, David. "Coverage of La Follette Offers Insights for 1972 Campaign." *Journalism Quarterly* 52, no. 3 (1975): 539–42.

Maxwell, Robert. "La Follette and the Election of 1900." *Wisconsin Magazine of History* 35 (Autumn 1959): 23–29.

Morris, Edmund. "Theodore Roosevelt, President." *American Heritage* 32 (June/July 1981): 4–14.

Nagera, Humberta. "Children's Reaction to the Death of Important Objects." *Psychoanalytic Study of the Child* 25: 360–400.

An Onlooker. "Twenty Years of La Follette." *American Review of Reviews* 66 (Oct. 1922): 398–400.

Raushenbush, Paul A. "Starting Unemployment Compensation in Wisconsin." *Unemployment Compensation Review* (Apr.–May 1967): 17–34.

Reisner, Edward. "First Woman Graduate: Belle Case La Follette or Elsie Buck." *Gargoyle* (University of Wisconsin Law School Forum) 22, no. 3 (Winter 1991–92): 10–11.

"Robert Marion La Follette: A Swashbuckling Dumas Hero Caught and Civilized." *Current Opinion* 77 (Sept. 1924): 298–99.

Rodgers, Daniel T. "In Search of Progressivism." *Reviews in American History* 10 (1982): 113–32.

Roe, Gwyneth King, and Max C. Otto. "Two Views of the La Follettes." *Wisconsin Magazine of History* 42–43 (Winter 1958–59): 102–14.

Rogin, Michael. "Progressivism and the Electorate." *Journal of American History* 55 no. 2 (1968): 297–314.

Rosenof, Theodore. "'Young Bob' La Follette on American Capitalism." *Wisconsin Magazine of History* 55, no. 2 (1971–72): 130–39.

Ross, Irwin. "The Man Who Freed the Sailors." *American History Illustrated* 4, no. 5 (1969): 45–47.

Sargent, Noel. "The La Follette Veto." *The Forum* 68 (Sept. 1922): 775–83.

Sayre, W. S. "Robert M. La Follette, Jr." In *The American Politician*, ed. John Thomas Salter, 138–49. Chapel Hill: University of North Carolina Press, 1938.

"Senator La Follette, The German-American Alliance and the American Buzz-Saw." *Current Opinion* 64 (Apr. 1918): 231–32.

Shannon, David A. "Was McCarthy a Political Heir of La Follette?" *Wisconsin Magazine of History* 45 (Autumn 1961): 3–9.

Shover, John L. "The California Progressives and the 1924 Campaign." *California Historical Quarterly* 51, no. 1 (1972): 59–74.

Smith, Daniel Scott. "Family Limitation, Sexual Control, and Domestic Feminism in Victorian American." In *Clio's Consciousness Raised*, ed. Mary Hartman and Lois Banner, 119–36. New York: Harper & Row, 1974.

Smith, Page. "Anxiety and Despair in American History." *William and Mary Quarterly* 26 (July 1969): 416–24.

Smith-Rosenberg, Carroll. "The Female World of Love and Ritual." *Signs* 1 (Autumn 1975): 1–29.

Stave, Bruce. "The 'La Follette Revolution' and the Pittsburgh Vote, 1932." *Mid-America* 49, no. 4 (1967): 244–51.

Steffens, Lincoln. "Roosevelt–Taft–La Follette on What the Matter Is in America and What to Do about It." *Everybody's Magazine* 18 (June 1908): 723–36.

Strother, French. "The Death of the 'Wisconsin Idea.'" *World's Work* 50 (Oct. 1925): 620–24.

Sullivan, M. "Looking Back on La Follette." *World's Work* 49 (Jan. 1925): 324–31.

Sutton, Walter A. "Bryan, La Follette, Norris: Three Mid-Western Politicians." *Journal of the West* 8, no. 4 (1969): 613–30.

Thelen, David P. "The Boss and the Upstart: Keyes and La Follette, 1880–1884." *Wisconsin Magazine of History* 47, no. 2 (Winter 1963–64): 103–15.

———. "La Follette and the Temperance Crusade." *Wisconsin Magazine of History* 47, no. 4 (Summer 1964): 291–300.

———. "Patterns of Consumer Consciousness in the Progressive Movement: Robert M. La Follette, the Antitrust Persuasion, and Labor Legislation." In *Quest for Social Justice*, ed. Ralph Aderman, 19–47. Madison: University of Wisconsin Press, 1983.

———. "Robert M. La Follette, Public Prosecutor." *Wisconsin Magazine of History* 47, no. 3 (Spring 1964): 214–23.

———. "Robert La Follette's Leadership, 1891–1906: The Old and New Politics and the Dilemma of the Progressive Politician." *Pacific Northwest Quarterly* 62, no. 3 (1971): 97–109.

Tobin, Eugene M. "The Political Economy of George L. Record: A Progressive Alternative to Socialism." *Historian* 39, no. 4 (1977): 702–16.

Unger, Nancy C. "The Burden of a Great Name: Robert M. La Follette, Jr." *Psychohistory Review* 23, no. 2 (Winter 1995): 167–91.

———. "The 'Political Suicide' of Robert M. La Follette: Public Disaster, Private Catharsis." *Psychohistory Review* 21, no. 2 (Winter 1993): 187–220.

———. Review of *The La Follettes of Wisconsin* by Bernard Weisberger. *History: Reviews of New Books* 23 (Spring 1995): 110.

———. "Robert M. La Follette." In *Biographical Dictionary of Literary Influences: The Nineteenth Century*. New York: Greenwood, 2000.

———. "Robert M. La Follette," and "Robert M. La Follette, Jr." In *Historic World Leaders*, edited by Anne Commire, 4:445–48. Detroit: Gale Research, 1994. Full text of both entries reproduced in *Biography Resource Center*. Farmington Hills, Mich.: Gale Group, Aug. 1999. (http://www.galenet.com/servlet/BioRC)

———. "The Two Worlds of Belle La Follette." *Wisconsin Magazine of History* 83, no. 2 (Winter 1999–2000): 82–110.

Ward, Geoffrey. "Importance of Being Bob." *American Heritage* 45 (Nov. 1994): 14.

Warren, Louis A. "The Lincoln and La Follette Families in Pioneer Drama." *Wisconsin Magazine of History* 12 (June 1929): 359–76.

Weibull, Jorgen. "The Wisconsin Progressives, 1900–1914." *Mid-America* 47 (July 1965): 191–221.

Weisberger, Bernard A. "Changes and Choices: Two and a Half Generations of La Follette Women." *Wisconsin Magazine of History* 76, no. 4 (1993): 248–70.

Welter, Barbara. "The Cult of True Womanhood, 1829–1860." *American Quarterly* 18 (Summer 1966): 151–75.

Wilbur, Henry W. "A Coming Man." *Gunton's Magazine* 23 (Sept. 1902): 250–53.

Wolf, T. Phillip. "Bronson Cutting and Franklin Roosevelt: Factors in Presidential Endorsement." *New Mexico Historical Review* 52, no. 4 (1977): 317–34.

*Dissertations and Theses*

Blount, William G. "Robert M. La Follette in the Senate, 1906–1912." M.A. thesis, Clark University, 1948.

Chandler, Madelynne K. "Robert M. La Follette in American Foreign Policy." M.A. thesis, Butler University, 1966.

Cos, Grant C. "Robert M. La Follette and the Campaign for Railroad Legislation." M.A. thesis, Emerson College, 1990.

Fahey, Marie. "La Follette's Senatorial Background as a Presidential Candidate in 1924." M.A. thesis, Stanford University, 1956.

Fitzpatrick, John James, III. "Senator Hiram W. Johnson: A Life History, 1866–1945." Ph.D. diss., University of California Berkeley, 1975.

Flehinger, Brett. "'Public Interest': Robert M. La Follette and the Economics of Democratic Progressivism." Ph.D. diss., Harvard University, 1997.

Gisselman, Gary. "A Point in the Continuum: Robert M. La Follette, Progressivism, and the 1922 Election in Wisconsin." M.A. thesis, University of Wisconsin, 1970.

Hartman, Maryann. "The Chautauqua Speaking of Robert La Follette." Ph.D. diss., Bowling State University, 1969.

Kelley, Peggy A. "La Follette's Legacy." M.A. thesis, Michigan State University, 1994.

Kent, Alan. "Portrait in Isolationism: The La Follettes and Foreign Policy." Ph.D. diss., University of Michigan, 1957.

Lahman, Carroll Pollock. "Robert M. La Follette as Public Speaker and Political Leader, 1855–1905." Ph.D. diss., University of Washington, 1939.

Manning, Eugene A. "Old Bob La Follette: Champion of the People." Ph.D. diss., University of Wisconsin, 1966.

Mohler, Samuel. "Robert M. La Follette in the World War I Period." M.A. thesis, University of Washington, 1936.

Montgomery, Dee Ann. "An Intellectual Profile of Belle La Follette: Progressive Editor, Political Strategist, and Feminist." Ph.D. diss., Indiana University, 1975.

Peterson, Robert R. "The La Follette Vote in 1924 and Its Effect on the Third Party Movement." M.A. thesis, University of Washington, 1969.

Sayre, Wallace S. "Robert M. La Follette: A Study of Political Methods." Ph.D. diss., New York University, 1930.

Unger, Nancy. "The Righteous Reformer: A Life History of Robert M. La Follette, 1855–1925." Ph.D. diss., University of Southern California, 1985.

Wagner, Selma. "Theodore Roosevelt and Robert M. La Follette." M.A. thesis, Arizona State University, 1966.

Williams, John R. "La Follette's Foreign Policy." M.A. thesis, Johns Hopkins University, 1947.

*Multimedia*

Payson, Parker. *Great American Speeches: Eighty Years of Political Oratory* (videotape). 2 vols. New York: Pieri & Spring Productions, 1997.

Riley, Jocelyn. *Belle Case La Follette, 1859–1931* (videotape and brochure). Madison: Her Own Words, 1987. Available from Her Own Words, P.O. 5264, Madison, WI 53705.

———. *Votes for Women?!* (videotape and resource guide). Madison: Her Own Words, 1990.

# INDEX

Bipolar disorder (manic depression), 80

*Birth of a Nation* (D. W. Griffith), 228

Blaine, John J. (gubernatorial candidate, Wisc.), 163, 234

Blatch, Harriet Stanton (feminist), 291

"Bleeding Kansas," 7

*Bloomington (Ind.) Daily Bulletin*, 45, 136

Bolshevism, 268–69, 285

Booth, Edwin (actor), 45

Borah, William E. (senator, Idaho), 1–2, 271

Bourne, Jonathan (senator, Ore.), 185, 189

Brandeis, Alice, 256

Brandeis, Louis D. (Justice, U.S. Supreme Court), 190, 191, 231, 232, 256, 261, 276, 335 (n. 19)

Bray, William (state representative, Wisc.), 150–51

Breweries, 48–49

Bristow, Joseph (senator, Kans.), 186, 188, 189, 217, 335 (n. 22)

*Brooklyn Daily Eagle*, 136

Brown, Edgar G. (African American leader), 88

Bruley, Judge, 72

Bryan, William Jennings (U.S. secretary of state), 134, 184, 223, 305; 1896 presidential campaign program, 108; and seamen's bill, 227; World War I policy, 241–42, 243, 254, 255

Bryant, George E., 29, 146; as La Follette's "political godfather," 78–79, 84, 323 (n. 15)

Bryce, James (historian), 73

Buchanan, Alexander (mother's first husband), 9

Buchanan, Ellen (half-sister). *See* Eastman, Ellen Buchanan

Bull Moose Party, 218, 219, 292

Burgchardt, Carl R. (biographer), 38

Bushnell, Allen R. (representative, Wisc.), 96

Business. *See* Big Business

Calhoun, John (senator, S.C.), 309

California, 80, 170, 171, 193, 216, 250, 266, 276

Campaign financing: as La Follette issue, 1, 122, 135, 184, 278; as La Follette political debt to Stephenson, 150; as Doug La Follette issue, 178; T. Roosevelt reform proposal, 191; analysis of third-party spending, 299

Canadian reciprocity, 214

Carlisle, John (representative, Ky.), 94

Case, Anson (father-in-law), 49, 191

Case, Belle. *See* La Follette, Belle Case

Case, Lucetta Moore (wife's grandmother), 48

Case, Mary Nesbit (mother-in-law), 49

Catt, Carrie Chapman (suffragist), 88

*A Century of Dishonor* (Helen Hunt Jackson), 91

Chautauqua circuit, 42, 130, 135, 200, 282

Cherny, Robert (historian), 73

Chicago Conference for Progressive Political Action, 173

Child labor, 122, 228, 264, 291, 307; Child Labor Tax Law, 290

*Cincinnati Times Star*, 247

Civil Liberties Committee (Senate), 175, 177

Civil rights: as Bob La Follette cause, 1, 87, 88–91, 120–21, 228; Civil Rights bill, 23; as Belle La Follette cause, 54, 55–56, 228; protection of seamen's, 226–27; wartime curbs on, 252–53, 256, 263–64. *See also* African Americans

Civil Service (U.S.): and racial segregation, 55–56, 228; reforms, 56, 120, 135, 137; postal employee unionization, 224

Civil War, 18, 20, 22–23; veterans, 24–25

Clapp, Moses (senator, Minn.), 186, 188, 342 (n. 19)

Clay, Henry (senator, Ky.), 175, 309

Clayton bill, 230–31

Labor force: La Follette reform agenda for, 1, 22, 29, 122, 240, 289; limitation of railroad workers' hours, 1, 147, 238; seamen's rights, 1, 226–27; women's issues, 54; immigrant conditions, 86–87; problems in early 1900s, 139–40; problems in mid-1920s, 288

Labor Party, 274

Labor unions, 176, 288, 297, 299; antitrust exemptions for, 1, 230–31; antitrust actions against, 96; coal strikes, 139–42; postal employee, 224; seamen's rights, 226–27; Supreme Court decisions regarding, 290

La Fayette, Marquis de, 8

La Follet, Jesse (paternal grandfather), 9, 46

La Follet, Usual (paternal great–uncle), 9

La Follette, Belle Case (wife, 1859–1931), 32, 46, 47–68, 191

—early life and education of: family background, 47, 49; formative influences, 48–49; as University of Wisconsin student, 34–35, 37, 49–50; first woman graduate of University of Wisconsin Law School, 53–55, 318 (n. 13)

—personal traits and history of: conflict over woman's proper role, 47, 48, 62–67, 317–18 (n. 3); death, eulogy, and obituary of, 47, 66, 68, 174; conscientiousness of, 49; shyness of, 49, 58–59, 86; personal appearance of, 50–53; personality of, 66, 86, intelligence and legal talent of, 54; advocacy of physical fitness, 55; seriousness and inflexibility of, 56, 62, 319 (n. 19); behavior resembling Bob's, 56, 230; idealism of, 62; moral rectitude of, 66; travel and vacations, 94, 170, 282–83; health problems of, 271, 274–75, 301

—political activism of: support of pacifism, 2, 36, 54–55, 162; involvement in social and political causes, 49, 54–56; African American civil rights advocacy, 54, 55–56, 228, 322 (n. 9); equal rights advocacy, 63–64, 88–90; as a progressive, 189; position on world federation, 270; opinions on Soviet system, 283

—professional talents and career of: publicly acclaimed speeches given during college years, 49–50; teaching career, 51; author of "I Married a Lawyer" short story, 53, 59, 61, 69, 155; editor of *La Follette's Weekly Magazine* departments, 55, 56, 65, 185, 189; writing talent, 55; public speaking talent, 56, 58; public speaking tours, 230, 231, 232

—role as mother: close relationship with son Bobbie, 47, 173–74, 266, 267, 333 (n. 38); birth of daughter Fola, 53–54; births of three other children, 106; emotional manipulativeness of, 153; home schooling of children, 154; attempts to control adult children, 154–55, 319 (n. 18); emphasis on family solidarity, 156, 159; objections to daughters' decisions to marry, 157–58; indulgence of Bobbie, 166–67, 169, 170–71

—role as political wife: refusal of Bob's Senate seat, 47, 66; influence on Bob, 47, 193; dislike of Washington social scene, 59–61, 82, 85–86; time spent in Washington, 59–61, 82, 85–86, 93–94, 180, 267–68; and personal conflicts, 63–68; refusal to campaign directly for Bob, 64, 349 (n. 28); assessment of Bob's litigation skill, 74, 76; and Bob's House career, 84, 323 (n. 13); on Bob's maiden congressional speech, 88, 322 (n. 6); and congressional campaigns, 91–93; and T. Roosevelt, 95, 241; reaction to Bob's congressional defeat, 98; and Bob's political stances, 101; on Bob's antitrust campaign, 103; on Bob's refusal of Currency Comptroller post, 109; and Bob's gubernatorial terms, 124, 127, 130, 138; and Bob's appointment to Senate, 134; on Bob's Senate speeches, 144, 145; and Bob's career in Senate, 148, 187, 188; on Bob's speeches and speaking tours, 152, 190, 356; and Bob's presidential campaigns, 202, 214, 215, 294; at White House dinner, 229; and Bob's antiwar filibuster, 246, 251; and Bob's opposition to World War I, 257, 259, 262, 263

—role as wife: and resemblance to Bob's sister, 14; on mother-in-law's personality, 15, 16, 53; courtship and marriage, 50–53; Bob's high valuation of her judgment, 54, 56–57, 65; as influence on Bob's career, 56–57, 64–65; egalitarian marital relationship, 57–58; marital disagreements, 58; objections to Bob's political career, 58–60, 69; as Bob's alter ego, 60, 323 (n. 13); and Bob's emotional dependence, 60, 62–63, 82; concern about family financial strains, 60–64, 69, 94, 98, 106, 146–47, 184–85, 186, 192, 263, 267, 271, 321 (n. 18); role as Bob's health guardian, 62–63, 82–83, 125, 135–36, 151, 227, 268; assessment of marital dynamics, 66; lengthy separations from Bob, 82, 230, 231, 267, 268, 271; and Bob's personality, 93; on Bob's reaction to death of mother, 105–6; and Maple Bluff Farm, 135; opposition to magazine venture, 184–85; criticism of Bob, 186–87; on Bob's emotional "breakdown," 202–3, 207, 208–9; loving farewell tribute to Bob, 303

—and women's issues: and founding of Women's International League for Peace and Freedom, 54; wide-ranging support of women's issues, 54–55, 63–64; personal conflict over proper role of women, 47, 48, 62–66, 68; voting rights advocacy, 63, 64, 214, 268

La Follette, Bronson (grandson), 175, 178

La Follette, Charles (cousin), 112

La Follette, Doug (first cousin twice removed; 1940–), 178–79, 309

La Follette, Fola [Flora Dodge] (daughter, 1883–1970), 163, 271; birth of, 53–54; as coauthor of father's biography, 58, 161, 203, 205, 214, 251, 255; and father's illnesses, 82, 232; as child, 85, 93; father's efforts to control, 155; stage career of, 155, 161, 194; marriage of, 157–58, 161, 331 (n. 12); career and activism of, 161; on father's death, 303

La Follette, Harvey (uncle), 12, 324–25 (n. 21)

La Follette, Isabel [Isen] (daughter-in-law), 160

La Follette, Joseph (grandson), 175

La Follette, Josephine (sister). See Siebecker, Josephine La Follette

La Follette, Josiah (father, 1817–1856), 9–12, 13, 50, 103; Bob's idealization of, 15–16, 17, 18, 22, 26, 27, 100; disinterment and reburial of, 16–17, 106; similarities of Bascom to, 35; similarities of Bryant to, 78–79

La Follette, Marion (brother), 9, 11, 12, 16–17

La Follette, Mary [later Sucher] (daughter, 1899–1988), 58, 106, 157, 163, 170, 191; and family solidarity, 153–54, 155–56; mother's opposition to marriage of, 158–59; adult life of, 161–62; tubercular gland surgery of, 202, 203, 205; response to vilification of father, 259; birth of first child, 297, 301

—emotional life of: as limiting political effectiveness, 2–4, 219–20; effects of father's early death on, 17–19; identification with Hamlet, 28; illnesses as somaticizations of, 80–82, 84, 98, 99, 151–52; periods of depression, 81, 125; homesickness and loneliness as freshman senator, 145–46; rumored nervous breakdowns, 206, 208–9, 230; refusal to face painful feelings, 213–14

—opposition to World War I: 36, 191, 235–36, 239–62, 278; vilification for, 2, 36, 169–70, 247, 249–50, 255–59; speech expressing, 249–50, 341 (n. 10); praise for, 250, 251, 255–56, 257, 261, 342–43 (n. 26); confidence in moral superiority of, 251; and St. Paul speech, 254–56, 257; postwar rehabilitation, 260–61, 276, 278; official vindication, 262, 275–76; and bitterness over past hurts, 263

—personality traits of: paranoia, 2, 183, 189, 312 (n. 5), 337 (n. 16); inability to compromise, 2–3, 42, 148–49, 220, 309; political costs of, 2–4, 219–20; strengths and weaknesses of, 3, 4; sense of moral superiority, 3, 107, 123, 124, 125, 142, 149, 151, 175, 189, 201, 286; youthful prankishness, 17, 26, 28, 29, 38; importance of physical appearance to, 18–19; loathing of secrecy, 21–22; approval seeking by, 28, 220, 227; self-righteousness of, 32, 70–71, 77, 80, 85, 90–91, 96, 99, 107, 126, 149, 175, 212, 215, 225–26, 246, 251, 253, 255, 262, 271, 295–96, 324 (n. 7), 330 (n. 22); exaggerations and fabrications of, 34, 73, 78, 182; dramatic flair, 40–41, 44–45, 73, 99; propensity to overwork, 63, 99, 186–87, 200–201, 281, 282; perfectionism, 74, 76, 128, 267; illnesses as permission to recuperate

from overwork, 80–81; illnesses as emotional necessity, 80–82, 98, 99; need for attention, 82; eagerness to please, 85; reputation for humorlessness, 93; self-deprecating wit, 93; sanctimoniousness, 123, 124; unwillingness to delegate authority, 130–31, 181, 220; forcefulness of, 149–50; aggressiveness, 151; agendas for sons, 152; self-image as lone altruistic crusader, 215, 338 (n. 34); righteous indignation, 222; self-absorption, 222–23; black-and-white worldview of, 225–26; inability to work as member of team, 235; complaints about critics, 263; fascination with death, 302–3, 350 (n. 44); self-destructive behaviors, 309

—personal life of: devotion to sister, 14; lifelong closeness with women, 14; disinterment and reburial of father and brother, 16–17; penchant for hairdressing, 18, 19, 30, 128; personal appearance and grooming, 19, 30, 45, 85, 190, 294, 330 (n. 22); religious beliefs of, 22, 26, 315–16 (n. 14); financial investments, 40, 128, 228–29; consideration of theatrical career, 45–46; gender views of, 50–51; marriage to Belle Case, 51; financial problems, 60–62, 63, 94, 98, 106, 108, 125, 128, 135, 146–47, 185, 186, 213, 227, 232–33, 271–72; travel rationales and vacations, 80–81, 106, 126, 152, 301; friendship with Philip Fox, 83; ethics of, 87, 91, 100; Washington rental residences, 93–94, 227, 271–72, 285; Dakota ranch, 94, 98; death of mother, 105–6; Maple Bluff Farm, 135; friendship with Louis Brandeis, 190, 191

—physical health of: youthful feigned illnesses, 29, 84; Belle as "health guardian," 62–63, 82–83, 125, 135–36, 151, 227, 268; health problems

of, 79, 109, 190, 227, 230, 231; gall
bladder surgeries, 79–80, 192–93,
273, 346 (n. 23); illness as retreat
from pressure, 79–80; patterns of
health problems, 80, 106–7, 281–
82, 320 (n. 32); personal gains from
illness, 80–81; recuperative trips,
80–81, 82–83, 106, 126; illness as
emotional necessity, 80–82, 84, 98,
99, 151–52; congressional years as
free from illness, 97; following death
of mother, 106; amid gubernatorial
pressures, 125–26, 136; during first
weeks of senatorship, 142–43; during first Senate term, 151–52; in last
years, 172, 286; during 1908 presidential nomination campaign, 182,
183; as excuse for poor campaign
showing, 182; during Senate filibuster, 183; as excuse for not meeting with T. Roosevelt, 195; during
1912 presidential nomination campaign, 201–2; and Philadelphia
speech, 203; probable stroke, 231–
32; during European tour, 283; heart
condition, 283, 285–86, 295, 321–
22 (n. 25), 347 (nn. 9–10); effects
of final presidential campaign, 301;
heart attacks, 302, 303; death and
eulogies to, 303, 305–6, 321 (n. 21);
smoking and drinking habits of,
321 (n. 16)
—political career of: achievements, 1;
assessments of, 1, 2–3, 4–5; as radical, 2, 123–24, 278, 280, 281; emotional limitations, 2–4, 219–20; contradictory and inconsistent positions,
4; loyalty of followers, 4, 136, 137;
wife's influence on, 47, 193; wife's
discomfort with, 58–59, 64, 78–79;
prohibition stance, 77–78, 253, 321
(n. 16); denial of ambitions, 78; illnesses as rationalization for election
losses, 81; letters to supporters, 83–
84; personal popularity, 85; civil
rights activism, 87, 88–90, 120–21,

239; political philosophy, 87, 121–
22; "demagogue" label, 93; personalized constituent relations, 93, 96;
conflict with Sawyer as turning point
in, 100–104, 105, 324 (n. 6); hostility toward opponents and critics,
101, 263, 323 (n. 5); as antitrust
champion, 102–3; as self-styled crusader, 103; friendship with McKinley,
104; persuasive abilities, 105; fur-
thered by oratorical skills, 109, 110–
11; reliance on patronage, 120;
brand of progressivism, 121–22;
messianic conception of leadership,
122; core supporters, 129–30; growing national reputation, 130; image
as people's only true representative,
131; and emphasis on personal over
party beliefs, 147; resentment of
T. Roosevelt, 149, 180, 191, 195,
213, 218, 222–23, 229; reputation
as fearless fighter, 150; as progressive movement leader, 192; national
reputation, 193; loss of respect after
1912 campaign, 219; relationship
with Wilson, 223–30 passim, 264,
265, 268, 273, 276; costs of repeated
presidential bids, 235; rehabilitation
of reputation, 263, 278, 280; isolationism, 269–70; European tour,
281, 282–85; legacies, 306–9. See
also La Follette, Belle Case: role as
political wife; and specific offices and
presidential campaigns
—presidential campaign of 1924: reform platform, 2, 289–90, 307; overall campaign, 64, 173, 281, 282, 286,
288–302, 349 (nn. 26, 33, 36); optimism about winning, 296–97
—presidential nomination campaign of
1896: 106, 107–8
—presidential nomination campaign
of 1908: 180–84
—presidential nomination campaign
of 1912: overall campaign, 57, 196–
99, 200–220, 222–25, 251; ap-

186, 230, 231, 232–33; on presidential campaign of 1912, 209, 218, 224, 297; as La Follette's permanent record of vindication, 233, 351 (n. 6); foreign affairs positions, 236; antiwar articles, 239; and Espionage Act, 253; as source of family dissent, 263; on presidential campaign of 1924, 297, 300

La Jolla, Calif., 80, 170, 171

Land policy, 190, 214, 266–67; Native American sales of land, 25, 148; coal reserve bill, 145, 148–49, 150, 266–67; naval oil reserves, 272, 276–78, 289

Lane, Harry (senator, Ore.), 245, 250, 342 (n. 19)

Lea, Luke (senator, Tenn.), 245, 246

League of Nations, 265, 269, 271, 274

Le Follet, Jean (paternal great-great grandfather), 8

Le Follet, Joseph (paternal great-grandfather), 8, 9

Lehman, Herbert (senator, N.Y.), 178

Lenin, V. I., 269

Lenroot, Irving (senator, Wisc.), 135, 146, 258, 259, 274, 278, 286

Leupp, F. E. (commissioner of Indian Affairs), 150

Lewis Prize, 50

Lincoln, Abraham, 1, 9, 20, 22, 306, 350 (n. 1)

Link, Arthur S. (historian), 225

Lippmann, Walter (journalist), 290

*Little House in the Big Woods* (Wilder), 9

Lodge, Henry Cabot (senator, Mass.), 262, 270, 271

Lumber industry, 25, 97, 110, 145, 272

*Lusitania* (British liner), sinking of, 241, 249, 254, 255

Lyon, W. P. (jurist), 54

McAdoo, William G. (U.S. secretary of treasury), 55, 288

*McCall's* (magazine), 233

McCarthy, Joseph R. (senator, Wisc.), 177, 178

*McClure's* (magazine), 27, 131

McCormick, Mendill, 229

McCullough, John (actor), 45, 317 (n. 29)

McDonald, Ramsey, 292

McGovern, Francis (governor, Wisc.), 185, 224; effectiveness as progressive, 138, 192; and 1912 Republican nominating convention, 217, 218, 219; strained relations with La Follette, 228–29, 234, 274; senatorial nomination, 233, 234

Machine politics: La Follette's contradictory position on, 4, 120, 137; and Keyes's influence, 23, 24, 73–74; La Follette's first encounter with, 73–74; La Follette's speeches against, 109, 111–12; La Follette's involvement with, 150. *See also* Patronage

MacKay, Kenneth C. (historian), 2

McKinley, William (representative, Ohio; U.S. president), 95, 104, 106, 109; offers La Follette office of Comptroller of Currency, 109–10; assassination of, 128, 218

McKinley Tariff, 95, 97, 104

McMurray, Howard (senatorial candidate, Wisc.), 177

Madison, Wisc., 31, 33, 305, 328 (n. 23)

*Madison Capital Times*, 169, 309

Madison Club, 258

*Madison Democrat*, 42, 258, 261

Mammoth Oil Company, 277

Maney, Patrick (historian), 271

Manic depression (bipolar disorder), 80

Manly, Basil (progressive), 282, 307

Manly, Molly (progressive), 282

Mann-Elkins Act, 189

Maple Bluff Farm, 60, 135, 177, 192, 274, 297

Marbury, Charles (physician), 168

Margulies, Herbert (historian), 120

Watson, James (senator, Ind.), 301, 307
Ways and Means Committee (House),
94, 95, 104
Weaver, James (Populist presidential
candidate, 1892), 104
Webster, Daniel (senator, Mass.), 309
Weeks, John (senator, Mass.), 252
Weyerhaeuser, Frederick (lumber tycoon), 25
"What It Means to Be an Insurgent
Senator's Wife" (Belle La Follette),
59
Wheeler, Burton K. (senator, Mont.),
290–91, 307
White, William Allen (journalist), 5,
147, 189, 195, 309
Wickersham, George (U.S. attorney
general), 186, 188
Wilder, Laura Ingalls (author), 9
Williams, John Sharp (senator, Miss.),
249–50, 262, 336 (n. 1)
Wilson, Margaret (daughter of W. Wilson), 56
Wilson, Woodrow (governor, N.J.; U.S.
president), 56, 190, 203, 205, 212–
13, 219, 317 (n. 18); racial attitudes,
56, 228; initially warm relations with
La Follette, 223–24, 225, 229–30;
New Freedom, 223–24, 231, 238,
276; political philosophy, 223–24,
227–28, 230, 231, 264–65; election
to presidency, 225; similarities to
La Follette, 225, 271; ideological distancing from La Follette, 227–28,
230; presidency of, 227; and antitrust campaign, 231; foreign policy,
236; steps toward entry into World
War I, 239, 240, 242, 243–44, 247–
48, 254; and German submarine
warfare, 241; denunciation of peace
senators, 246–47, 342 (n. 18); and
La Follette's antiwar statements,
258; and Wisconsin senatorial contest, 258–59; postwar program, 261,
264–71; La Follette's criticisms of,
264, 265, 268, 273, 276; campaign

for League of Nations, 273; stroke,
273
Wisconsin: La Follette core political
supporters in, 4, 129–30; geography
of, 7, 9–10; history of, 7–8; La Follette family move to, 9; pioneer experience in, 9–10; multiethnic populace, 10, 24; Civil War years, 20;
Republican Party in, 20, 23, 24–25,
31, 73–74, 124, 185, 233, 234;
wheat production, 21; post–Civil
War, 23–26, 29; population (1870),
24; dairy industry, 25, 90; lumber
industry, 25, 272; Reform Party, 31–
33; La Follette gubernatorial terms,
36, 81, 120–38; breweries, 48–49;
temperance movement, 48–49, 54;
woman suffrage convention, 48;
Keyes machine, 73–74; Democratic
election sweep of 1890, 97; Englishonly educational instruction mandate, 97, 105; Populism, 104; grassroots reform movements, 105, 110;
La Follette gubernatorial ambition,
107–8, 110–12; political and economic problems, 121; direct primary approval, 133–34; McGovern
reforms, 138; progressive reform
movement, 138, 185, 192, 234; effects of direct primary, 146; gubernatorial contests, 146, 219, 224, 273,
274; La Follette political influence
in, 146; Philip Follette's gubernatorial terms, 160; Progressive Party,
175; senatorial contests, 177, 233–
34, 258–59, 278, 280, 307–9; La
Follette family name recognition,
178–79; La Follette political legacy
in, 178–79; presidential primary
(1912), 214, 216; state income tax,
226; La Follette critics, 234, 258;
La Follette longtime supporters,
238; and La Follette antiwar position, 257–58; as first state ratifying
woman suffrage amendment, 268,
345 (n. 12); mourners for La Fol-

All of these efforts, along with his uncompromising nature, earned him the nickname, not always
affectionately used, of "Fighting Bob."

Based on La Follette family letters, diaries, and
other papers, this biography includes startling
details of La Follette's early childhood and the
true story behind the "nervous breakdown"
during his campaign for the Republican presidential nomination in 1912. Unger also covers La
Follette's spirited opposition to American entry
into World War I and his third-party bid for the
presidency in 1924. She also explores his relationship with his remarkable wife, feminist Belle Case
La Follette, and with his sons, both of whom
succeeded him in politics. The La Follette who
emerges from this retelling is an imperfect yet
appealing man who deserves to be remembered
as one of the United States' most important
politicians.

NANCY C. UNGER is assistant professor of
history at Santa Clara University.

The University of North Carolina Press
Post Office Box 2288, Chapel Hill, NC 27515-2288
www.uncpress.unc.edu